International Debt Statistics 2021

International Debt Statistics 2021

Table of Contents

Foreword

The COVID-19 pandemic is a crisis like no other. It has taken lives and disrupted livelihoods in every corner of the globe. It has knocked more economies into simultaneous recession than at any time since 1870. It has ended a two-decade streak of steady global progress in poverty reduction, pushing up to 150 million people into extreme poverty by 2021.

For the poorest countries, however, the crisis arrived at a moment of particular peril. In 2019, as this report shows, almost half of all low-income countries were either already in debt distress or at a high risk of it. Unsustainable debt burdens have the potential to siphon off resources these countries need immediately to fund the health crisis and accelerate economic recovery efforts—an issue the World Bank and the International Monetary Fund have sought to address by calling for the Debt Service Suspension Initiative (DSSI). The overhang of debt may slow investment and growth for years to come—a burden on the poor that now needs to be addressed by creditors across the world taking prompt steps to permanently reduce unsustainable debt stocks for the poorest countries.

International Debt Statistics 2021 (IDS) affirms that achieving long-term debt sustainability will depend on a large-scale shift in the world's approach to debt transparency. The report provides more detailed and more disaggregated data on external debt than ever before in its nearly 70-year history, taking important strides in filling existing data gaps for low- and middle-income countries where the risks are greatest.

The data include breakdowns of what each borrowing country owes to official and private creditors by creditor country and the expected month-by-month debt-service payments owed to them through 2021. Increased debt transparency will help many low- and middle-income countries assess and manage their external debt through the current crisis and work with policy makers toward sustainable debt levels and terms.

IDS provides a unique data set to shape the solutions that will be needed in the coming years. It shows a creditor landscape that is changing quickly—with developing countries borrowing from new sources of bilateral and commercial financing and increasingly complex debt instruments. These trends compound the difficulty of managing COVID-19-related debt crises, adding to the value of more granular debt data.

We are also engaged in a continual review and refinement of the data. For example, we are working to ensure that more debt instruments, including central bank deposits and currency swaps, are captured in the data set. We are also working to gather additional debt information such as the status of loan guarantees and collateral.

In addition, we are conducting data reconciliation with creditors. In this regard, I want to thank the creditor countries that have compared the new data with their own records to clarify gaps. This latest step in transparency will help improve our estimates of debt sustainability and—for some of the poorest countries—highlights the need for debt-stock reduction to start the recovery process.

According to the latest data, total external debt stocks of low-income countries eligible for the DSSI rose 9 percent in 2019 to $744 billion, equivalent on average to one-third of their combined gross national income. Lending from private creditors was the fastest-growing component of the external debt of DSSI-eligible borrowers, up fivefold since 2010. Obligations to private creditors totaled $102 billion at the end of 2019.

The debt stock of DSSI-eligible countries to official bilateral creditors, composed mostly of Group of Twenty (G-20) countries, reached $178 billion in 2019 and accounted for 27 percent of the long-term debt stock of low-income countries. Within the G-20 creditor group, there have been some important shifts characterized by a marked increase in lending by G-20 member countries that are themselves middle-income countries. For example, China, by far the largest creditor, has seen its share of the combined debt owed to G-20 countries rise from 45 percent in 2013 to 63 percent at end-2019. Over the same period the share for Japan, the second-largest G-20 creditor, has remained broadly the same at 15 percent.

These trends suggest that future sovereign debt restructurings will be more complex for many of the poorest countries. For most International Development Association borrowers, private creditors account for a relatively small share of the countries' external public debt. However, they account for a significant share in several countries: for example, Côte d'Ivoire (60 percent), Ghana (58 percent), and Chad, St. Lucia, and Zambia (all 50 percent). Private sector participation in achieving a sustainable debt trajectory will be critical.

The risk is that too many poor countries will emerge from the COVID-19 crisis with a large debt overhang that could take years to manage. To build durable economic recoveries, countries will need to achieve long-term debt sustainability. They will need to achieve a much greater level of productive investment and financing—for infrastructure, health, education, and employment.

Reliable data and accountability will be critical for borrowers and creditors alike, providing the cornerstone for robust new investment and good development outcomes. The World Bank is committed to working with governments and partners to achieve that outcome—by continually improving data coverage, quality, timelessness, and transparency.

David Malpass
President
The World Bank Group

Acknowledgments

This volume was prepared by the Debt Statistics Team of the Development Data Group (DECDG) at the World Bank, led by Evis Rucaj and comprising Parul Agarwal, Arzu Aytekin Balibek, Daniella Kathyuska Bolanos-Misas, Allen Charles Church Jr., Wendy Ven-dee Huang, Malvina Pollock, Rubena Sukaj, and Rasiel Vellos. The overview of current developments was prepared by the Debt Statistics Team; country economists reviewed the data tables. The team was assisted by Nancy Kebe. The work was carried out under the management of Nada Hamadeh, Program Manager, and the direction of Haishan Fu, Director, DECDG.

Valuable guidance and input was provided by Carmen M. Reinhart, Vice President and Chief Economist, Development Economics (DEC).

International Debt Statistics electronic products were prepared by a team led by Anna Maria Kojzar and Sebastian Ariel Dolber and comprising Ramgopal Erabelly, Rahul Abhinav Polabiona, Fatih Dogan, Rajesh Kumar Danda, and Ugendran Machakkalai. The cover was designed by Jomo Tariku. Jewel McFadden from DEC Knowledge and Strategy and Michael Harrup and Orlando Mota from Global Corporate Solutions, Design and Publications, coordinated the publication and dissemination of the book.

PART I
Overview

Executive Summary

Developments in the external debt of low- and middle-income countries in 2019 took place against the backdrop of a synchronized downturn in the global economy with deceleration in global gross domestic product (GDP) growth to about 2.4 percent, the lowest rate of expansion since the 2008 financial crisis. A combination of factors affected the global economy in 2019, including rising trade barriers, ongoing trade disputes, and increased geopolitical tensions. Growth prospects were also dampened by country-specific outcomes in several of the largest emerging market economies and by structural factors in advanced economies, such as low productivity growth and aging demographics. Heightened policy uncertainty weighed on international trade and investor confidence, and the subdued outlook led to a decline in most commodity prices. GDP growth in low- and middle-income countries, many of which are commodity exporters, contracted to about 3.5 percent in 2019 from 4.3 percent in 2018, reflecting a structural slowdown in China and a markedly slower pace of growth in several large emerging markets.

Aggregate financial inflows to low- and middle-income countries (debt and equity) fell 14 percent in 2019, relative to the 2018 level, the second consecutive year of decline, driven by lower flows to China. Even though China dominated the volume and trajectory of 2019 aggregate financial flows to low- and middle-income countries, its share fell to 39 percent from almost 49 percent of comparable flows in 2018. Aggregate financial flows to China fell 39 percent in 2019, driven down by a 29 percent reduction in net equity inflows and a 48 percent fall in net debt flows. This was in marked contrast to aggregate net financial flows to other low- and middle-income countries, which rose on average 9 percent in 2019, with a 24 percent rise in net equity inflows offsetting a 7 percent fall in net debt inflows.

Prior to the onset of the COVID-19 pandemic, rising public debt levels and heightened debt vulnerabilities were already a cause for concern, particularly in many of the world's poorest countries. Debt-related risks reflect higher public and private debt levels and a changing creditor landscape with new sources of bilateral and commercial financing and increasing complexity of debt instruments with nonstandard terms and clauses, including nondisclosure clauses. This evolution of external financing patterns compounds the task of managing COVID-19-related debt crises and gives rise to new demands for more granular debt data transparency regarding the volume and terms of amounts borrowed and lent.

The World Bank has long played a lead role in the compilation and dissemination of external debt statistics and the enhancement and expansion of debt data coverage to meet institutional needs, the needs of policy makers and analysts, and those of the international community. *International Debt Statistics,* the World Bank's flagship publication on external debt data instituted in response to the first global oil crisis of 1973 and now in its 57th consecutive year of publication, is frequently refined to provide more timely and disaggregated data series. This edition provides, for the first time, disaggregated information on public and publicly guaranteed debt stocks and flows by creditor country, including official bilateral creditors and multilateral institution entities. This data set will assist policy makers and analysts in assessing the potential impact of debt service suspension from the Debt Service Suspension Initiative (DSSI) launched by the Group of 20 (G-20) in April 2020 and implemented with the assistance of the World Bank and the International Monetary Fund (IMF) and sets a standard for greater debt data transparency by member countries of the World Bank and the IMF, as borrowers and as lenders.

International Debt Statistics 2021 presents comprehensive stock and flow data for 120 low- and middle-income countries and a summary overview of the key elements driving outcomes in 2019 debt stocks and financial flows. The headline numbers may mask divergent trends because of the dominance of the largest economies. This is especially true in regard to China, where the volumes of financial flows and external debt stock are not large relative to the size of the domestic economy (external debt as a share of gross national income [GNI] was 15 percent at end-2019), but are significant in relation to those of other low- and middle-income countries. To assist in the interpretation of the data, the overview takes a look behind the headline numbers and analyzes recent developments and trends at the regional and country level as well as for the subgroup of DSSI-eligible countries.

Key messages from the 2019 data are as follows:

- Net financial (debt and equity) flows to low- and middle-income countries totaled $0.9 trillion in 2019, 14 percent below the 2018 level and registering the second consecutive year of decline. Net debt inflows fell 28 percent to $383 billion from $532 billion in 2018 in contrast to stable foreign direct investment (FDI) inflows of $479 billion, little changed from 2018, and rising portfolio equity inflows, up 23 percent to $48 billion.

- Net financial flows to countries eligible for the DSSI rose 16 percent in 2019 to $103 billion, a record high for the decade and much faster than those to other low- and middle-income countries. The increase in net financial flows was the outcome of a 10 percent rise in net debt inflows to $66 billion from $60 billion in 2018 and a 36 percent rise in FDI.

- External debt stocks at end-2019 passed the $8 trillion mark with the overall pace of accumulation (5.4 percent) unchanged from 2018. Long-term external debt was the fastest-growing component; it rose 7 percent to $6 trillion, equivalent to 73 percent of total external debt stock. Short-term external debt stocks rose marginally (1.5 percent) to $2.2 trillion at end-2019.

- Net debt inflows were $383 billion in 2019, 28 percent below the 2018 level and less than half the comparable inflows in 2017. Short-term debt inflows contracted 86 percent to $30 billion from $219 billion in 2018, following an outflow of short-term debt from China (–$14 billion) in 2019, compared to an inflow of $188 billion in 2018. On average, net short-term debt inflows to low- and middle-income countries, excluding China, rose 43 percent in 2019 to $43 billion.

- Net long-term inflows rose by 13 percent to $353 billion in 2019 with a 4 percent rise in inflows to public and publicly guaranteed borrowers and a 32 percent increase in inflows to nonguaranteed private sector borrowers. China's long-term debt inflows rose 81 percent, equivalent to 45 percent of the combined 2019 long-term debt inflows to low- and middle-income countries. Long-term debt inflows to other low- and middle-income countries, excluding China, followed a different trajectory. They fell, on average, by 14 percent in 2019 to $195 billion: inflows to public and publicly guaranteed borrowers rose 9 percent and inflows to nonguaranteed private sector borrowers dropped precipitously by 57 percent.

- Bondholders accounted for the largest share of net long-term debt inflows to low- and middle-income countries in 2019. Net inflows from bondholders were $234 billion, 30 percent higher than the comparable 2018 figure, and equivalent to two-thirds of 2019 long-term net debt inflows. Bondholders accounted for two-thirds of long-term debt inflows to China and for 55 percent of comparable inflows to other low- and middle-income countries, on average.

- The World Bank was the mainstay of inflows from official creditors. Net inflows from the World Bank (International Bank for Reconstruction and Development [IBRD] and International Development Association [IDA]) rose 31 percent in 2019 to $19 billion, equivalent to just over half of inflows from multilateral creditors, excluding the IMF. Net inflows from bilateral creditors fell 50 percent to $9 billion, equivalent to just 3 percent of 2019 long-term debt inflows from official and private creditors, excluding the IMF, on account of a sharp contraction in China's inflows resulting from the combined effect of a 28 percent fall in new disbursements and a 46 percent rise in principal payments.

- New bond issuance by the 120 low- and middle-income countries reporting to the Debtor Reporting System (DRS) totaled $376 billion in 2019, 16 percent higher than in 2018. Issuance in 2019 was characterized by a surge in bond issues by private sector entities, which rose 37 percent to $129 billion. China was the dominant player and accounted for 35 percent of bonds issued in 2019.

Aggregate Financial Flows to Low- and Middle-Income Countries

Financial flows to low- and middle-income countries fell for the second consecutive year in 2019. Aggregate net financial flows, debt and equity combined, totaled $0.9 trillion in 2019, 14 percent lower than the comparable figure for 2018. Measured relative to borrower countries' GNI, aggregate financial flows were equivalent to 2.9 percent, a marked decrease from 3.5 percent in 2018 and well short of the 6.9 percent recorded in 2010. The decline in net financial flows was the outcome of a 28 percent drop in net debt inflows (gross disbursements of new financing minus principal payments), which fell to $383 billion from $532 billion in 2018. The contraction in net debt inflows contrasted with equity inflows, which remained stable. FDI inflows, long considered the most resilient and least volatile component of financial flows, totaled $479 billion, down marginally from the 2018 level, whereas portfolio equity inflows rose 23 percent to $48 billion.

The headline number masks sharp divergence in the volume and trend of financial flows to China and other low- and middle-income countries in 2019. As in prior years, China dominated both

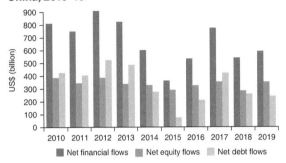

Figure O.1 **Aggregate Net Financial Flows to Low- and Middle-Income Countries, excluding China, 2010–19**

Sources: World Bank Debtor Reporting System; International Monetary Fund; and Bank for International Settlements.

the volume and direction of aggregate financial flows to low- and middle-income countries, but in 2019, its share of these flows dropped sharply to 35 percent from almost 50 percent of comparable flows in 2018. Aggregate financial flows to China fell 39 percent in 2019, driven down by a 29 percent reduction in net equity inflows and a steeper reduction in net debt flows, which fell by 48 percent (box O.1). This was in marked contrast to aggregate net financial flows to other low- and middle-income countries: they rose 9 percent in 2019 with a 24 percent rise in net equity inflows offsetting a 7 percent fall in net debt inflows.

Table O.1 **Aggregate Net Financial Flows to Low- and Middle-Income Countries, 2010–19**
US$ (billion)

	2010	2011	2012	2013	2014	2015	2016	2017	2018	2019
Net financial flows, debt and equity	1,359.0	1,318.6	1,224.0	1,448.9	1,125.2	196.7	729.9	1,261.0	1,060.9	909.7
Percent of GNI (%)	6.9	5.7	4.9	5.5	4.1	0.8	2.8	4.4	3.5	2.9
Net Debt Inflows	716.4	718.5	594.2	813.9	535.7	−319.2	218.7	732.6	531.9	382.8
Long-term	288.5	411.9	471.4	448.8	392.2	160.6	254.7	405.9	313.4	353.1
Official creditors	63.9	32.6	34.6	32.8	53.1	51.8	61.5	57.7	82.0	68.0
World Bank (IBRD and IDA)	22.6	5.6	11.9	13.2	14.7	16.7	13.8	12.4	14.7	19.3
IMF	7.8	−0.7	−6.4	−11.6	−1.3	6.5	5.1	3.6	30.9	21.6
Private creditors	224.6	379.3	436.8	416.0	339.1	108.8	193.2	348.2	231.4	285.1
Bonds	108.3	155.7	220.2	165.7	168.1	60.5	126.6	281.4	180.1	233.7
Banks and other private	116.3	223.5	216.6	250.3	171.0	48.3	66.5	66.9	51.3	51.4
Short-term	427.9	306.6	122.8	365.2	143.5	−479.7	−36.0	326.7	218.5	29.8
Net equity flows	642.6	600.1	629.8	635.0	589.5	515.9	511.3	528.3	529.0	526.9
Net foreign direct investment inflows	524.3	602.3	537.0	567.4	505.0	496.0	462.4	462.9	490.4	479.4
Net portfolio equity inflows	118.4	−2.2	92.9	67.6	84.5	19.9	48.9	65.4	38.6	47.5
Change in reserves (− = increase)	−689.8	−454.8	−285.5	−514.9	91.2	603.9	278.8	−308.3	84.6	−183.3
Memorandum item										
Workers remittances	299.3	337.2	363.0	380.8	410.4	424.0	411.7	442.9	478.6	494.8

Sources: World Bank Debtor Reporting System, International Monetary Fund, and Bank for International Settlements.

Box O.1 As China Implements Further Capital Market Liberalization Its Debt Portfolio Diversifies

China is by far the largest recipient of financial inflows, not only in the East Asia and Pacific region, but also among low- and middle-income countries. Over the last decade, China recorded almost $4 trillion in net financial inflows, which accounted for 37 percent of all inflows to low- and middle-income countries. In 2019, China recorded inflows of $330 billion with debt accounting for 45 percent and equity the remaining 55 percent, primarily from FDI.

China's external debt stock at the end of 2019 was $2.1 trillion, 8 percent higher than the comparable debt stock at the end of 2018, with short-term external debt accounting for 57 percent of the total, of which 30 percent was trade credit. Most of the increase in debt stocks in 2019 is attributable to long-term external debt. By the end of 2019, China recorded close to $909 billion, an increase of 22 percent from the end of 2018. A major contributor was the $132 billion issuance of bonds, primarily private sector bonds, which increased

the debt stock by 42 percent. Bonds issued by the public sector made up about 46 percent. The share of domestic currency renminbi debt owed to non-residents has increased because of China's efforts to liberalize their financial account. The new State Administration of Foreign Exchange regulation,[a] which opened foreign investors' access to China's domestic securities market, established the inclusion of the renminbi bonds in the Bloomberg Barclays Global Aggregate Index and China-A shares in the FTSE Russell emerging markets index and automated links between the Shanghai, London, and Hong Kong SAR, China, markets. These measures have supported domestic currency bond issuance and helped diversify China's debt securities portfolio and attracted portfolio equity flows. Equity inflows slowed by 29 percent in 2019 from the previous year, but China remained the largest recipient among all low- and middle-income recipients of foreign direct investment and portfolio equity inflows, respectively, $131 billion and $45 billion.

Figure BO.1.1 Aggregate Net Financial Flows to China, 2010–19

Sources: World Bank Debtor Reporting System; International Monetary Fund; and Bank for International Settlements.

a. State Administration of Foreign Exchange regulation on Foreign Exchange Administration for Domestic Securities Investments by Qualified Foreign Institutional Investors (June 2018).

External Debt Stocks in 2019

External debt stocks topped $8 trillion at end-2019, with the pace of debt accumulation much the same as in 2018. The total external debt of the 120 low- and middle-income countries for which data are presented in *International Debt Statistics 2021* rose by 5.4 percent in 2019 to $8.1 trillion, a rate of accumulation almost identical to that

in 2018, but close to half the 10.5 percent rise in external debt stock recorded in 2017. The increase in external debt stocks in 2019 was the outcome of net debt inflows of $383 billion and valuation changes in year-on-year exchange rates in relation to the US dollar (about half the external debt of low- and middle-income countries is denominated in currencies other than the US dollar). Long-term external debt was the fastest-growing component, rising 7 percent to $6 trillion, equivalent to 73 percent of total external debt stock. Short-term debt stocks rose marginally (1.5 percent) to $2.2 trillion at end-2019.

China accounted for 26 percent of the 2019 external debt stock of low- and middle-income countries and heavily influenced outcomes. China's external debt stock rose 8 percent in 2019, propelled by a surge in long-term borrowing by both public and private sector entities. Long-term external debt stock rose 22 percent to $909 billion at the end of 2019, with a near parallel rate of increase in the obligations of the government and public sector entities and those of private borrowers without any government guarantee. Short-term debt stock fell $14 billion (a little more than 1 percent), reflecting the slowdown in trade volumes, but remained by far the most significant component of total external debt stock at 57 percent, down from 62 percent at the end of 2018.

Excluding China, external debt stocks in other low- and middle-income countries rose 4.6 percent on average in 2019 but with wide divergence in the pace of debt accumulation at the country level. The external debt stock of the top 10 borrowers,[1] excluding China, rose on average 4.1 percent in 2019 to $3.6 trillion, with parallel rates of accumulation in long-term and short-term debt. The combined end-2019 debt stock of these countries accounted for almost 60 percent of the external debt stocks of low- and middle-income countries excluding China. Outcomes for individual countries in the group ranged from an increase in debt stock of 9 percent in South Africa to a decline of 1.5 percent for Argentina, as the latter grappled with a challenging macroeconomic situation, an unwieldy stock of dollar-denominated debt, and double-digit inflation. In low- and middle-income countries (excluding China and other top 10 borrowers) external debt stock rose slightly faster, on average by 5.5 percent in 2019, with short-term debt stock rising at the same rate as long-term debt by 6.7 percent.

Outcomes at the regional and country levels were divergent. Countries in Sub-Saharan Africa

<hr>

[1] The top 10 borrowers, defined as those with the largest end-2019 external debt stock, are Argentina, Brazil, China, India, Indonesia, Mexico, the Russian Federation, Thailand, Turkey, and South Africa.

Figure O.2 External Debt Stocks of Low- and Middle-Income Countries, 2010–19

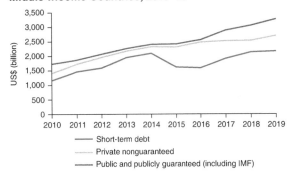

Sources: World Bank Debtor Reporting System; and Bank for International Settlements.

recorded the fastest accumulation of external debt stock in 2019, on average 9.4 percent, propelled by a comparable rise in the debt stock of the major regional economies, including Nigeria and South Africa and other borrowers across the region. India drove the 6 percent rise in debt stocks in the South Asia region, but the increase was mirrored in the 9.5 percent rise in the external debt stock of Bangladesh, reflecting the implementation of large infrastructure projects, and the 7.8 percent increase in Pakistan, driven by higher inflows of budgetary support from multilateral creditors, including the first disbursement under the IMF Extended Fund Facility in July 2019. External debt stock rose 6.4 percent in East Asia and the Pacific, excluding China, with the major borrowers (Indonesia, the Philippines, and Thailand) all recording an increase of 5–6 percent and Vietnam recording an increase of 10.9 percent, driven by

Figure O.3 Top 10 Low- and Middle-Income Borrowers, excluding China, 2018–19

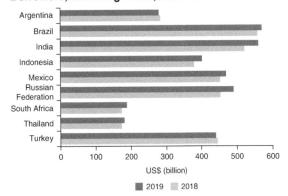

Sources: World Bank Debtor Reporting System; and Bank for International Settlements.

Figure O.4 **External Debt Stocks: Regional Distribution and Trends, 2017–19**

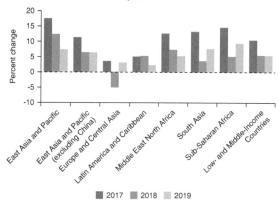

Sources: World Bank Debtor Reporting System; and Bank for International Settlements.

a 24.6 percent increase in short-term debt. Debt stocks rose on average 5.3 percent in the Middle East and North Africa region, propelled by a 14.9 percent rise in external debt stocks in the region's largest borrower, the Arab Republic of Egypt, following an $8 billion eurobond issuance and the disbursement of the last tranche ($4 billion) from the IMF 2016 Extended Fund Facility. External debt stocks rebounded in the Europe and Central Asia region, rising 3.1 percent in 2019 (after a 5 percent contraction in 2018), largely in response to an 8.1 percent increase in the obligations of the Russian Federation. Countries in Latin America

and the Caribbean recorded the smallest increase in external debt stocks in 2019, 2.3 percent, reflecting a general slowdown in economic activity across the Latin American region, with moderate debt accumulation by Brazil and Mexico (on average, 3 percent), but offset by a 1.5 percent contraction in Argentina's external debt stock.

The maturity structure and borrower composition of external debt stocks is characterized by a stark difference between China and other low- and middle-income countries. For most low- and middle-income countries, external debt obligations are predominantly long term, and the largest share is owed by governments and other public sector entities. The composition of China's external debt stock is atypical for low- and middle-income countries: more than half (57 percent) of the end-2019 external debt stock was short term, and only 15 percent of long-term obligations were accounted for by public sector borrowers. The combined end-2019 external debt stocks of low- and middle-income countries, including China, comprised public and publicly guarantee debt (40 percent), whereas the obligations of private sector entities without a government guarantee accounted for 33 percent, and short-term debt for 27 percent. Excluding China significantly alters the picture: the share of short-term debt falls to 16 percent, and the share of long-term debt owed by public and publicly guaranteed borrowers rises to 49 percent.

Figure O.5 **External Debt Stocks of Low- and Middle-Income Countries, excluding China, Maturity Structure and Borrower Type, 2010–19**

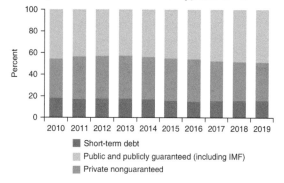

Sources: World Bank Debtor Reporting System; and Bank for International Settlements.

Figure O.6 **External Debt Stocks of China, Maturity Structure and Borrower Type, 2010–19**

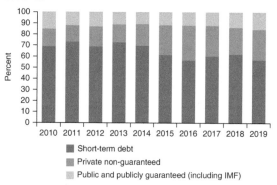

Sources: World Bank Debtor Reporting System; and Bank for International Settlements.

External Debt Flows in 2019

The synchronized global slowdown and ongoing trade disputes weighed heavily on external debt flows in 2019. Net debt inflows to low- and middle-income countries continued their downward trajectory in 2019, falling to $383 billion, 28 percent below the 2018 level and well below half the comparable inflows in 2017. The decline was primarily the outcome of a severe contraction in short-term debt inflows, which fell 86 percent to $30 billion from $219 billion in 2018. Much of the decline can be attributed to a precipitous drop in short-term debt flows to China, which turned negative (–$14 billion) in 2019, a marked contrast to inflows of $188 billion recorded in 2018. Short-term debt inflows to Argentina also collapsed and those to Mexico fell 82 percent pulling short-term inflows to countries in Latin America and the Caribbean down 70 percent to $13 billion from $43 billion in 2018. In contrast, short-term inflows rebounded in Russia and Turkey to $9.4 billion and $6.6 billion, respectively, from outflows of $2.7 billion and $3.4 billion in 2018. Inflows to other regions held up and on average net short-term debt inflows to low- and middle-income countries, excluding China, rose 43 percent in 2019 to $43 billion.

Long-term debt inflows to China and those to other low- and middle-income countries were on a very different trajectory in 2019. Net long-term inflows rose 13 percent in 2019 to $353 billion from $313 billion in 2018, with a 4 percent increase in inflows to public and publicly guaranteed borrowers followed by a 32 percent increase

in inflows to private sector borrowers without a government guarantee. China absorbed 45 percent of long-term debt inflows to low- and middle-income countries in 2019, up from one-third of comparable flows in 2018. It registered an 81 percent rise in net long-term inflows in 2019 driven by a threefold increase in inflows to nonguaranteed private sector borrowers (box O.1). It was a very different story for other low- and middle-income countries: long-term debt inflows fell to $195 billion, 14 percent below the comparable inflow in 2018, on account of a 9 percent expansion in inflows to public and publicly guaranteed borrowers and a precipitous 57 percent drop in those to nonguaranteed private sector borrowers.

Net long-term debt inflows in 2019 were sustained by inflows from bondholders. Inflows from bondholders rose 30 percent in 2019 to $234 billion, offsetting a 17 percent downturn in inflows from official creditors. Almost half of the 2019 inflows from bondholders went to China. The increase in overall bond issuance in 2019 was accompanied by a shift in borrower composition, with a 5 percent drop in new issues by sovereigns and public sector borrowers more than offset by a 42 percent rise in issuance by private sector entities (box O.2). Bondholders accounted for two-thirds of long-term debt inflows to China in 2019 and, on average, for 55 percent of comparable inflows to other low- and middle-income countries.

The World Bank (IBRD and IDA) was the mainstay of inflows from official creditors. Inflows from official creditors fell 17 percent in 2019 to $68 billion from $82 billion in 2018, of which multilateral institutions accounted for

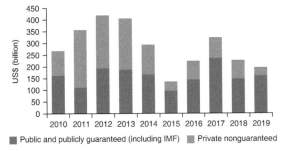

Figure O.7 **Net Long-Term External Debt Flows, excluding China, Borrower Composition, 2010–19**

Source: World Bank Debtor Reporting System.

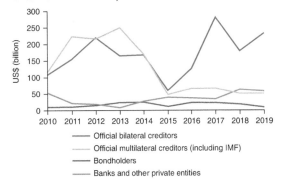

Figure O.8 **Creditor Composition of Net Long-Term External Debt Flows, 2010–19**

Source: World Bank Debtor Reporting System.

Figure O.9 Net Long-Term Inflows from Official Creditors, excluding IMF, 2010–19

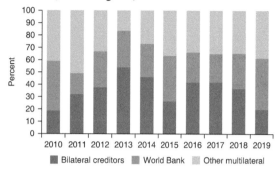

Source: World Bank Debtor Reporting System.

Figure O.10 Long-Term Debt Inflows to Public and Publicly Guaranteed Borrowers, Regional Distribution, 2019

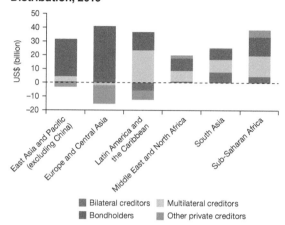

Source: World Bank Debtor Reporting System.

86 percent. Inflows from multilateral institutions declined 7 percent to $59 billion, dragged down by the 30 percent drop in IMF inflows: $22 billion in 2019 from $30 billion in 2018, in large measure because of the substantially lower flows to Argentina ($16.2 billion in 2019 versus $28.6 billion in 2018). Excluding the IMF, inflows from other multilateral institutions totaled $37 billion, a 14.6 percent increase over the 2018 level, and were kept stable by inflows from the World Bank (IBRD and IDA). These inflows rose 31 percent in 2019 to $19 billion, equivalent to just over half of inflows from multilateral creditors in 2019. Bilateral creditors saw the sharpest contraction in flows, down 50 percent to $9 billion, equivalent to just 3 percent of 2019 long-term debt inflows from official and private creditors, driven by the sharp contraction in inflows from China to $3.8 billion in 2019 from $16.2 billion in 2018, resulting from the combined effect of a 28 percent fall in disbursements and a 46 percent increase in principal repayments.

The composition of 2019 net long-term debt inflows to public and publicly guaranteed borrowers differed markedly at the regional level. Net long-term debt inflows to public and

publicly guaranteed borrowers, excluding China, totaled $162 billion in 2019, of which bondholders accounted for 67 percent; multilateral creditors, including the IMF, 36 percent; and bilateral creditors 7 percent. Flows from commercial banks and other private sector entities were negative (10 percent). Countries in Sub-Saharan Africa accounted for the largest share of net long-term inflows at 24 percent, followed by the East Asia and Pacific region, excluding China, at 18 percent. Inflows from bilateral creditors were directed primarily at Sub-Saharan Africa (41 percent) and Europe and Central Asia (26 percent), while those from multilateral creditors were concentrated in Latin America and the Caribbean (41 percent), reflecting the large IMF inflow to Argentina, and in Sub-Saharan African (26 percent). Inflows from bondholders were the dominant component of net inflows to countries in Europe and Central Asia but were also an important share of net inflows to all regions. Net inflows from bonds ranged from 35 percent of net inflows from all creditors to Europe and Central Asia, to 8 percent of comparable inflows to both South Asia and the Middle East and North Africa.

Box O.2 International Bond Issuance in 2019

Global slowdown, market turbulence, and credit downgrades did not deter bond issuance by low- and middle-income countries in 2019. Ultra-low interest rates in advanced economies fueled a search for higher yields elsewhere. New bond issuance by the 120 low- and middle-income countries reporting to the World Bank Debtor Reporting System totaled $376 billion in 2019, 16 percent higher than the comparable figure for 2018 but below the 2017 record high of $401 billion. Issuance in 2019 was characterized by a surge in bond issues by private sector entities; up 37 percent over the prior-year level to $129 billion. New issuance by sovereigns and other public sector entities increased at a more moderate pace, rising 7 percent to $247 billion.

China was the dominant player among low- and middle-income countries. It issued $132 billion in international bonds in 2019, 16 percent higher than the prior year, and equivalent to 35 percent of the combined issuance by low- and middle-income countries, the same percentage share as 2018. Bond issuance by private sector entities in China rose 42 percent in 2019 to $72 billion, in contrast to those by public sector entities, which fell 5 percent to $61 billion. Bond issues by other low- and middle-income countries rose, on average, 5 percent in 2019 to $73 billion and were also characterized by a sharp jump in issuance by private entities, up 65 percent, and a contraction in issues by sovereigns and public sector entities, down 23 percent.

The volume and composition of bond issuance at the regional level was mixed. Countries in the South Asia region issued $20 billion, a near threefold increase over the comparable figure for 2018. This increase was led by a surge in issuance by private sector entities in India, particularly in the energy and financial sector, and sovereign bond issues of $4.4 billion by Sri Lanka. In Europe and Central Asia, issuance rose 85 percent in 2019 to $66 billion; in contrast to other regions, the majority, about 75 percent, was by public sector borrowers. The Russian Federation and Turkey accounted for two-thirds of these issues and the same share of those by private sector entities in the region. Countries in Sub-Saharan Africa issued $20 billion, relatively unchanged from 2018 but with divergent push-pull factors: South Africa's $5 billion sovereign issue, its largest ever eurobond, was offset by a 25 percent fall in issuance by other countries in the region after an $18 billion record high in 2018. Sovereign issues in 2019 from Sub-Saharan borrowers, for example, Angola, Ghana, and Kenya, were characterized by longer maturities and included 30-year tranches. Latin America and the Caribbean was the only region with lower bond issuance, down 13 percent from the prior year. This decline was driven by a 20 percent contraction in issuance by public sector entities, mostly in Argentina, and only partially offset by a 10 percent increase in issues by private sector entities, primarily those in Mexico.

Table BO.2.1 Bond Issuance by Low- and Middle-Income Countries, 2018–19
US$ (billion)

	Public issuers		Corporate issuers		All issuers	
	2018	2019	2018	2019	2018	2019
East Asia and Pacific	93.0	94.3	60.1	80.9	153.1	175.2
of which: China	63.7	60.7	50.4	71.6	114.1	132.3
Europe and Central Asia	25.3	50.2	10.4	15.7	35.6	65.8
Latin America and the Caribbean	73.7	59.0	20.9	22.9	94.6	82.0
Middle East and North Africa	12.7	13.3	0.3	0.0	13.0	13.3
South Asia	5.4	12.9	0.9	7.3	6.3	20.3
Sub-Saharan Africa	19.1	16.9	1.7	2.5	20.8	19.4
Low- and middle-income countries	**229.1**	**246.7**	**94.4**	**129.3**	**323.4**	**376.0**

Source: World Bank Debtor Reporting System.

Supporting Debt Data Transparency

The COVID-19 pandemic and its devastating effect on the global economy has highlighted once again the need for timely, accurate, and transparent external debt data, a recurrent theme in earlier economic crises. National governments and their creditors rely on these data to reduce the risk of debt crises and to take remedial action should they occur. The World Bank and its sister institution, the IMF, have long been at the forefront of efforts to promote enhanced public debt transparency by member countries, as borrowers or as creditors. *World Debt Tables*, the forerunner of *International Debt Statistics,* represented the first public dissemination by the World Bank of external debt data for individual low- and middle-income countries. It was launched in 1973 in response to the economic fallout from the first global oil crisis. The initiatives taken in *International Debt Statistics 2021* are just one part of the World Bank's much broader agenda to promote the comprehensive disclosure of public debt by borrowing countries and the institution's extensive program of advisory and technical support to assist borrowers in comprehensively recording and reporting public debt.

The World Bank is taking the lead in disseminating data that provide the creditor composition of low- and middle-income countries' external debt. *International Debt Statistics 2020* provided users with new data on the borrower composition of the external debt obligations of low- and middle-income countries, with information on borrowing disaggregated by public corporations and guarantees provided by governments. This year, *International Debt Statistics 2021* presents, for the first time, an expanded data set that provides detailed information on the lending by creditor countries to low- and middle-income countries in addition to the disaggregation of countries' external debt by type of creditor, which has been a long-standing element of the external debt data disseminated by the World Bank. Calls for greater debt transparency and the need for granular data have made these data set changes key tools with which to assess countries' need for debt-service relief during the unfolding COVID-19 pandemic.

Information on the borrower-creditor matrix of external debt enhances transparency and analyses. The new series builds on the disaggregated data set released early this year for IDA borrowers and other countries eligible for the DSSI. It sets a standard for greater debt transparency to assist policy makers and analysts in evaluating the support the world's poorest countries may need during the pandemic and the effort required from creditors. This new data set disaggregates public and publicly guaranteed debt external stocks and flows (disbursements and principal and interest payments) by creditor type and creditor country. The data are drawn from the World Bank DRS to which World Bank borrowers (IBRD and IDA) report annually, loan by loan, on stocks and flows for long-term external debt owed by public agencies or private agencies with public guarantees and in aggregate on long-term external debt owed by the private sector with no public guarantee, and quarterly, loan by loan, on the terms and conditions of new public and publicly guaranteed loan commitments.

External creditors are defined by residency and by lender, not by guarantor. From its origins, the DRS was set up to allow for the assessment of the volume and lending terms of individual creditors and creditor groups and to facilitate loan-level validation of debtor and creditor records. Creditor classification follows the definitions used in *System of National Accounts* (SNA 2008) and the Sixth Edition of the IMF's *Balance of Payments and International Investment Position Manual* (BPM6) and is based on the criteria of *residency,* not *nationality.* For example, a loan from Citibank (London) is recorded as a loan from the United Kingdom, not the United States, where Citibank is headquartered. The definition of external debt also does not include contingent liabilities. This does not mean that debt guaranteed, on the side of the creditor, is excluded from the measure of the borrowers' obligations but that it is attributed to the *creditor,* specified as the lender of record in the loan contract, and not the *guarantor* unless and until the guarantee is called. Thus, in the creditor type classification, a loan from a private sector entity with support (guarantee) from an official bilateral export credit agency or a multilateral institution will be classified as private creditor in category (3) or (4) described in the next paragraph.

There are limitations on identifying the creditor for some types of lending. Creditors are grouped into five creditor types: (1) bilateral creditors, (2) multilateral creditors, (3) suppliers' credits, (4) commercial banks and other private entities, and (5) bonds. Bilateral and multilateral creditors are combined as Official Creditors and the other three creditor types are combined as Private Creditors. DRS reporting countries provide the creditor country and the name of the creditor extending the loan for public and publicly guaranteed loan commitments, except for bonds (where the multiplicity of individual holders renders this intractable) and syndicated commercial bank loans where multiple banks may be involved.

The new data set enriches the ways in which external debt data can support analyses and policy making. Figure O.11, which disaggregates the composition of low- and middle-income countries' bilateral obligations, is just one example. It separates these obligations between those owed to bilateral creditors from high-income countries and those owed to bilateral creditors from countries classified as low and middle income, and the major creditor in each of these categories is Japan and China. It confirms the rising importance of low- and middle-income countries lending to each other and the increasing importance of China in this process. Over the past decade low-and middle-income countries' share of their combined obligations to bilateral creditors has more than doubled to 45 percent from 20 percent in 2010, with China's share rising more than threefold. The data set that underpins the figure can now also be analyzed for each creditor-debtor pair, for regions, or for select subgroups.

Ongoing efforts to bring greater debt transparency to external debt data have also raised questions about how data in *International Debt Statistics* are defined and what they include. Data presented in

International Debt Statistics draw on information the World Bank collects and maintains on the external debt of its member countries through the DRS. Established in 1952, the DRS is the single most important source of verifiable information on the external indebtedness of low- and middle-income countries. The DRS defines external debt by *residency* and *maturity* as any debt obligation of a resident to a nonresident with an original maturity of more than one year. Debt includes (1) special drawing rights (SDR) allocations and currency and deposits (including unallocated gold accounts); (2) debt securities; (3) insurance, pension, and standardized guarantee schemes; and (4) trade credit and advances and other accounts payable. All debt that falls within these parameters and is reported by debtor countries is captured in the DRS and included in the data presented in *International Debt Statistics*. Data on short-term obligations are drawn from information provided, on a voluntary basis, by national authorities in DRS reporting countries or from the short-term debt statistics compiled by the Bank for International Settlements.

A specific question is how accurately the deposits of foreign official entities at the central bank and currency swap arrangements that represent loans from other central banks are reflected in external debt stocks of low- and middle-income countries. Deposits from one central bank to another are commonplace and often occur in low- and middle-income countries. How they are captured in the DRS depends on the original maturity structure of the deposit. Most deposits are of a short-term duration and thus outside the parameters of the DRS reporting requirement. They will, however, be captured in central bank statistics in their measure of short-term obligations. Conversely, term deposits, for example, those extended by the Saudi Arabian Monetary Fund to Egypt and others, with fixed interest rates and average maturities beyond the one-year mark, fall within the definition of long-term debt, and are reported to the DRS and included in *International Debt Statistics*. The DRS also considers one-year deposits that are consistently rolled over (de facto) to be long-term debt. Currency swap arrangements have two aspects, the length of time the arrangement is in effect and the length of time the swap operation may be active (box O.3). Most currency swap arrangements have been of short-term duration.

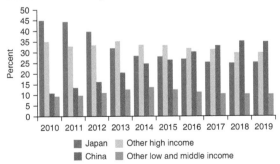

Figure O.11 Creditor Composition of Debt Owed to Bilateral Creditors, 2010–19

Source: World Bank Debtor Reporting System.

Box O.3 Currency Swap Arrangements

Currency swaps between central banks are not new. The US Federal Reserve (the Fed) initiated them in the early 1960s, but they came to the forefront during the 2008 financial crisis when such swaps by the Fed became one of the most important cross-border policy responses for helping to alleviate potentially devastating dollar funding problems for non-US banks. As part of the US response to the COVID-19 pandemic, the Fed has once again taken steps to ensure that foreign central banks have uninterrupted access to US dollars, and extended its currency swap arrangements to a broader group of countries.

Since the early 2000s and especially since 2008, many central banks, including those of low- and middle-income countries, have put in place currency swap arrangements. The core rationale for establishing a currency swap line is to promote orderly currency exchange markets. Currency swap arrangements are typically initially established for periods of one to three years and renewed when the term expires. Currency swap lines are a precautionary measure and a facility that central banks can activate quickly, should the need arise. In this sense they are akin to an overdraft facility on a checking account. New swap line arrangements between the Fed and the central banks of Canada and Mexico, for example, were put in place in 1994 under the North American Framework Agreement. They have a one-year duration, renewed annually. Canada has not drawn on its line, and Mexico drew in the mid-1990s on its currency swap line, which was increased to $9 billion in 2018.

Activation, that is, a draw on a currency swap line, involves two transactions, which will be illustrated using the example of a draw on a currency swap line with the Fed.[a] The first transaction is when central bank X draws on its swap line with the Fed; it sells a specified amount of its domestic currency to the Fed in exchange for US dollars at the prevailing market exchange rate.

The Fed holds the domestic currency it receives in its account at central bank X. The US dollars the Fed provides are deposited in the account that central bank X maintains with the Federal Reserve Bank of New York. Simultaneously, the Fed and central bank X enter into a binding agreement that specifies the date for the second swap transaction when central bank X is obligated to buy back its domestic currency at the same exchange rate. This second transaction effectively unwinds the swap. At the conclusion of the second transaction, central bank X also pays related interest charges, calculated at an agreed market-based rate. Maturities on currency swap line draws with the Fed have ranged historically from overnight to a maximum of twelve months. At present, the maximum is set at three months.

An important development of the past decade has been the renminbi currency swap program put in place by the People's Bank of China (PBC). The PBC signed its first currency swap arrangement with the Central Bank of Korea in 2008 and since then has concluded about 35 renminbi swap arrangements estimated to total the equivalent of $500 billion. Information on central bank websites and press reports suggest that about 20 of these arrangements are with low- and middle-income countries. The PBC arrangements typically have a one- to three-year term and are subsequently renewed. PBC currency swap arrangements have been in place with the central banks of Argentina and Indonesia since 2009, and with the European Central Bank and the Bank of England since 2013. There is no currency swap arrangement between the Fed and the PBC. Some countries, including Argentina, Mongolia, Pakistan, and the Russian Federation, have activated their PBC currency swap lines in recent years to meet short-term liquidity needs where some renminbi received were exchanged for US dollars. Other swap lines include the Association of Southeast Asian Nations (ASEAN) Swap Arrangement and the Chiang Mai Initiative.

a. Draws on currency swap lines of other central banks operate in much the same manner.

Table O.2 Aggregate Net Financial Flows to DSSI-Eligible Countries, 2010–19
US$ (billion)

	2010	2011	2012	2013	2014	2015	2016	2017	2018	2019
Net financial flows, debt and equity	73.3	88.0	84.7	96.6	90.2	83.4	75.3	89.3	88.7	102.8
Percent of GNI (%)	5.3	5.5	4.9	5.1	4.3	4.1	3.8	4.3	4.1	4.6
Net Debt Inflows	34.6	39.1	43.7	62.6	50.9	44.8	40.1	51.2	59.8	65.6
Long-term	27.1	38.2	38.4	53.0	53.1	40.9	42.2	44.7	62.8	57.2
Official creditors	16.0	17.1	17.2	20.1	25.7	24.7	33.3	29.8	33.6	36.5
World Bank (IBRD and IDA)	4.0	3.9	4.4	5.4	6.8	7.7	6.6	8.0	9.4	12.3
IMF	3.0	1.2	-1.1	-2.1	-0.1	1.7	1.0	0.4	1.0	1.9
Private creditors	11.1	21.1	21.1	32.8	27.4	16.2	8.9	14.9	29.3	20.7
Bonds	-1.3	1.6	4.5	4.9	13.5	7.5	3.0	12.8	16.4	6.6
Banks and other private	12.4	19.5	16.7	27.9	13.9	8.8	5.9	2.1	12.9	14.1
Short-term	7.6	0.9	5.3	9.6	-2.2	3.9	-2.0	6.5	-3.1	8.4
Net equity flows	38.7	48.9	41.0	34.0	39.3	38.6	35.2	38.1	28.9	37.1
Net foreign direct investment inflows	35.2	46.0	34.1	27.9	36.0	38.6	34.9	35.4	28.5	38.7
Net portfolio equity inflows	3.5	2.9	6.9	6.1	3.3	0.0	0.3	2.6	0.4	-1.6
Change in reserves (- = increase)	-8.0	-12.8	-24.8	-17.1	11.2	3.6	5.8	-19.0	7.2	5.5

Sources: World Bank Debtor Reporting System; International Monetary Fund; and Bank for International Settlements.

IDA Borrowers Eligible for the DSSI: External Debt Stocks and Flows

Aggregate financial flows to countries eligible for the DSSI[2] rose 16 percent in 2019, far faster than to other low- and middle-income countries. Aggregate net financial flows, debt and equity combined, totaled $103 billion in 2019, and measured relative to DSSI-eligible countries' GNI were equivalent to 5 percent. The increase in net financial flows was the outcome of a 10 percent rise in net debt inflows (gross disbursements of new financing minus principal payments), which rose to $66 billion from $60 billion in 2018 and a 28 percent rise in equity inflows. FDI inflows totaled $39 billion from $29 billion in 2018 and more than offset negative portfolio equity flows.

The external debt stock of DSSI-eligible countries accumulated at nearly twice the rate of

that in other low- and middle-income countries in 2019. The combined external debt stock of DSSI-eligible countries rose 9 percent in 2019 to $744 billion, equivalent on average to 33 percent of their combined GNI (measured in nominal terms). The pace of debt accumulation in 2019 was comparable to that of China and almost twice the rate of increase registered by other low- and middle-income countries. Long-term debt stocks rose by 9 percent and short-term debt rose by 16 percent, bringing external debt stocks at end-2019 to double the level at end-2010. The 11 percent rise in the long-term nonguaranteed external debt obligations of private sector entities in 2019 outpaced the 8 percent increase in the long-term external debt stock of public and publicly guaranteed borrowers. However, in relation to total long-term debt, the share of private sector entities stayed about the same from 2018 to 2019, roughly 25 percent.

The rise in public and publicly guaranteed external debt of DSSI-eligible countries over the past decade was coupled with an increase in market-based financing. The combined long-term external debt stock of public and publicly guaranteed borrowers was $523 billion at the end of 2019, double the comparable figure at the end of 2010. Official creditors, including the IMF,

---

[2] Eligibility for the Debt Service Suspension Initiative is reserved for countries eligible to borrow from IDA at the time the initiative was endorsed in April 2020 and for countries on the United Nations list of Least Developed Countries that are in current standing in regard to their debt service with the World Bank and the International Monetary Fund as of FY2020. The following IDA borrowers are not eligible for the DSSI: Eritrea, Sudan, the Syrian Arab Republic, and Zimbabwe.

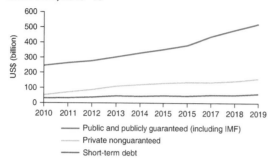

Figure O.12 External Debt Stock of DSSI-Eligible Countries, 2010–19

Sources: World Bank Debtor Reporting System; and Bank for International Settlements.

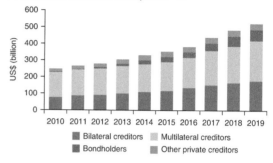

Figure O.13 DSSI-Eligible Countries' Creditor Composition of Long-Term Public and Publicly Guaranteed External Debt, 2010–19

Source: World Bank Debtor Reporting System.

accounted for the largest share of DSSI-eligible countries' external public and publicly guaranteed debt stock at the end of 2019 (81 percent), but financing from private creditors was the fastest-growing component. Obligations to private creditors totaled $102 billion at the end of 2019, a near fivefold increase over the comparable figure at the start of the decade, and raised their share of the combined debt owed to all creditors to 19 percent (from 8 percent in 2010). Multilateral creditors, including the IMF, were DSSI-eligible countries' most important creditors, with a total outstanding of $243 billion at end-2019, which is equivalent to 46 percent of total public and publicly guaranteed debt.

Financing from official creditors has been characterized by changes in the creditor composition of bilateral creditors. DSSI-eligible

countries' obligations to bilateral creditors have risen 77 percent since 2013 to $178 billion at end-2019, equivalent to 41 percent of debt owed to official creditors, up from 28 percent in 2013. Over this same period the creditor composition of obligations to bilateral creditors has undergone a significant change. G-20 countries account for most of the bilateral debt of DSSI-eligible countries, 91 percent of end-2019 obligations, up slightly from 85 percent at end-2013. However, within the G-20 creditor group there have been some important shifts characterized by a marked increase in lending by G-20 member countries that are themselves low- and middle-income countries (for example, China, India, and Russia). China, by far the largest creditor, has seen its share of the combined debt owed to G-20 countries rise from 45

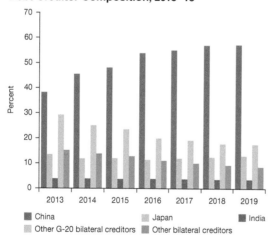

Figure O.14 DSSI-Eligible Countries' Bilateral Debt-Creditor Composition, 2013–19

Source: World Bank Debtor Reporting System.

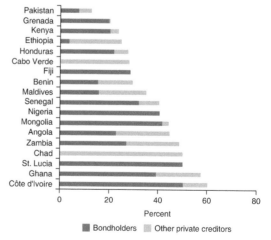

Figure O.15 DSSI-Eligible Countries' Share of Public and Publicly Guaranteed Debt Owed to Private Creditors at end-2019

Source: World Bank Debtor Reporting System.

percent in 2013 to 63 percent at end-2019. Over the same period the share for Japan, the second largest G-20 creditor, has remained broadly the same at 15 percent.

Obligations to private creditors are owed mostly to bondholders. Public and publicly guaranteed debt owed to private creditors totaled $102 billion at end-2019, equivalent to 16 percent of DSSI-eligible countries' combined long-term external public debt stock. Most of this debt, 65 percent, was owed to bondholders, with the remaining 35 percent of obligations owed to commercial banks and other private entities, including commodity trading companies. Governments have used funds raised from bond issues for budgetary support, infrastructure projects, and refinancing of prior bond issues to take advantage of longer maturities and lower interest rates. Debt owed to other private creditors includes company and commercial bank loans with official support (guarantees) from bilateral export credit agencies or multilateral institutions. Most of this debt has been used to finance large-scale infrastructure projects, with some collateralized against future export receipts for oil or other commodities.

Obligations to private creditors were concentrated in a few countries. Eighteen DSSI-eligible countries accounted for 90 percent of debt owed to all private creditors by DSSI countries at end-2019, and 92 percent of that was owed to bondholders. In these 18 countries, private creditors' share in end-2019 public and publicly guaranteed debt stock averaged 33 percent and ranged from 60 percent in Côte d'Ivoire to 13 percent

in Pakistan, the largest debtor among DSSI-countries. Except for Cabo Verde and Chad, all DSSI- eligible countries with a significant share of debt owed to private creditors have issued eurobonds and half of the 18 countries are blend IBRD/IDA or IBRD borrowers assessed as creditworthy for market-based financing.

Debt Indicators, 2010–2019

Debt indicators indicate that debt burdens may be key contributors to economic vulnerabilities in low- and middle-income countries. The external debt burden of low- and middle-income countries combined remains moderate. The ratio of external debt to GNI averaged 26 percent at end-2019, only marginally higher than the 2018 average of 25 percent, and the ratio of external debt to export earnings deteriorated slightly, rising to an average of 107 percent from 101 percent in 2018. China's low level of external debt relative to GNI, 15 percent, and to exports, 73 percent, at end-2019 weighs heavily on the averages. For low- and middle-income countries, excluding China, the ratio of external debt to GNI averaged 35 percent and the external debt-to-exports ratio averaged 127 percent at end-2019.

The ratio of external debt stocks to GNI for borrower countries has risen over the past decade in many low- and middle-income countries. Country-specific indicators vary widely but

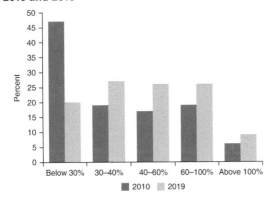

Figure O.16 **External Debt-to-GNI Ratio, Low- and Middle-Income Country Distribution, 2010 and 2019**

Sources: World Bank Debtor Reporting System; and International Monetary Fund.

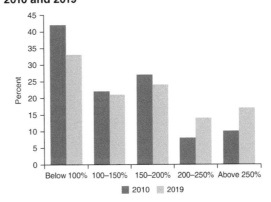

Figure O.17 **External Debt-to-Export Ratio, Low- and Middle-Income Country Distribution, 2010 and 2019**

Sources: World Bank Debtor Reporting System; and International Monetary Fund.

Box O.4 Debt-to-GDP versus Debt-to-GNI Ratios

Gross domestic product (GDP) and gross national income (GNI) both measure a country's income, but GDP counts only income received from domestic sources, whereas GNI includes net income received from abroad. The World Bank favors the use of GNI for operational purposes. Member countries' relative poverty is measured in relation to GNI per capita, and this measure underpins the annual income classification published by the World Bank and the IDA operational cut-off ($1,185 per capita for FY21) and the IBRD and IDA lending terms (interest rate and maturity) for specified borrowers. *International Debt Statistics* follows this convention and provides users with GNI data for each reporting country and the relevant external ratios of debt stock and debt service to GNI ratios.

The IMF uses the concept of GDP in Article IV consultation reports and IMF programs to measure macroeconomic outcomes. The practice is carried forward to the joint Bank-Fund Debt

Sustainability Analysis, with debt stocks and debt service measured in relation to GDP. Conceptually GDP may be regarded as a more accurate measure of a national government's capacity to raise domestic resources from which debt-related obligations must be serviced.

For most countries the difference between GDP and GNI is minimal. For example, the World Bank calculates US GNI to be only 1.2 percent higher than GDP in 2019. GNI may be lower than GDP if nonresidents control a sizable proportion of a country's production or higher than GDP if, for example, a country receives a large amount of foreign aid. For most low- and middle-income countries, the difference between end-2019 GDP and GNI was small but there were some outliers; aid-dependent Pacific islands such as Kiribati and Tuvalu had a GNI significantly higher than their GDP. Conversely, in countries such as Liberia and Sierra Leone, GDP surpassed GNI by 13 percent and 7 percent, respectively.

---

the number of low- and middle-income countries that have seen a marked increase in the ratio of external debt stocks to GNI suggest that mounting concerns over unsustainable debt burdens and heightened risk of debt crises in some countries are not unfounded. The percentage of low- and middle-income countries with a debt-to-GNI ratio below 30 percent fell from 45 percent in 2010 to 22 percent at end-2019. Thirty-two percent of low- and middle-income countries had external debt-to-GNI ratios above 60 percent at end-2019, compared with 23 percent in 2010, and in 9 percent of countries the ratio surpassed 100 percent, one-third more than the share of countries with a comparable ratio in 2010.

The number of low- and middle-income countries registering increases in the ratio of external debt stock to exports of goods and services also increased sharply. At end-2019, 55 percent of low- and middle-income countries had external debt-to-export ratios of over 150 percent, as compared to 45 percent in 2010. In 17 percent of the countries the ratio exceeded 250 percent at end-2019, a sharp increase from 2010 when only 10 percent of countries had ratios in excess of 250 percent.

Equity Flows in 2019

Equity flows are a significant element of financial flows to low- and middle-income countries. Over the past decade they averaged $570 billion per year and typically accounted for more than half of annual aggregate flows (debt and equity combined) and a much higher share when debt flows fell sharply or, as in 2015, were negative. Most equity inflows consisted of FDI, on average 90 percent per year since 2010, with only a handful of low- and middle-income countries being the beneficiaries of portfolio equity flows to any significant degree.

FDI inflows to low- and middle-income countries fell marginally in 2019 but were characterized by a marked change in destination for some of the largest recipients. FDI inflows to low- and middle-income countries totaled $479 billion in 2019, a marginal (2 percent) drop from the prior year. Inflows to China, the second-largest FDI recipient globally after the United States, contracted 29 percent to $131 billion, a sharp reversal from the 32 percent rise recorded in 2018. China's share of FDI inflows to low- and middle-income countries fell to 27 percent from 38 percent in 2018. The combined FDI inflows to other major recipients, Brazil, India and Russia, rose 31 percent in 2019 to $140 billion, propelled by the threefold rise in inflows to Russia. For low- and middle-income countries other than the four largest recipients, FDI inflows rose, on average, 5 percent in 2019 to $208 billion from $198 billion in 2018, equivalent to 43 percent of 2019 FDI inflows, up from 40 percent in 2018.

There was significant divergence in 2019 inflows among regional groups. Four regions, Europe and Central Asia, Latin America and the Caribbean, South Asia, and Sub-Saharan Africa reported increases in FDI inflows in 2019 ranging from 11 percent in South Asia to 50 percent in Europe and Central Asia. FDI inflows to countries in East Asia and Pacific fell 24 percent, or a more moderate 5 percent when China is excluded. In the Middle East and North Africa FDI inflows in 2019 were down 13 percent from the prior year's level.

European and Central Asian countries saw the biggest increase in FDI inflows, up 50 percent in 2019 to $66 billion, propelled by a rebound in inflows to Russia. They rose four-fold to $29 billion from $10 billion in 2018 with reinvested earnings topping $20 billion and new investment turning positive, after a large-scale disinvestment in 2018. Other countries in the region saw FDI inflows rise 9 percent, with a resurgence in inflows to Ukraine of 21 percent and a near threefold increase in FDI inflows to Uzbekistan, in response to economic liberalization. These increases offset the 16 percent contraction in inflows to Turkey, triggered by greater economic uncertainty and weaker economic growth.

Countries in *Sub-Saharan Africa* recorded a 26 percent increase in FDI inflows in 2019 to $23 billion. Much of this increase is attributable to a slowdown in net divestment from Angola caused by repatriation in the oil sector. FDI flows remained negative in 2019 (–$4.7 billion) but less so than in 2018 (–$7.1 billion). FDI inflows to Nigeria jumped 81 percent to $3.3 billion, accompanied by some diversification from the oil sector, and rose 71 percent in Côte d'Ivoire, to $1 billion, in tandem with the country's sustained economic growth. Net FDI inflows to Ethiopia, the largest FDI recipient in Eastern Africa, fell 25 percent to $2.5 billion partly because of instability in some regions, but with broad-based investment across manufacturing and services. FDI inflows to Ghana followed a similar trajectory, down 22 percent to $2.3 billion, but investments remained largely focused on oil and gas facilities.

FDI inflows to countries in *Latin America and the Caribbean* rose 14 percent in 2019 to $138 billion, with higher inflows to all major economies in the region except Argentina. FDI inflows to Brazil increased 19 percent to $68 billion, equivalent to almost half of 2019 inflows to the region, in response to improved economic conditions and the launch of a wide-ranging privatization program that raised more than $20 billion. FDI inflows to Colombia were up 22 percent to $12 billion, of which a third went to the oil and mining sector, and rose 42 percent in Peru to $9 billion boosted by inflows to the mining and energy sector. FDI inflows to Mexico rose 20 percent to $31 billion despite lingering uncertainties related to the ratification of the new regional trade agreement with the United States

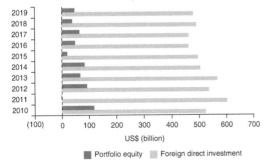

Figure O.18 Net Equity Inflows to Low- and Middle-Income Countries, 2010–19

Sources: International Monetary Fund; and United Nations Conference on Trade and Development (UNCTAD).

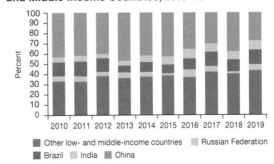

Figure O.19 FDI to China and Other Select Low- and Middle-Income Countries, 2010–19

Sources: International Monetary Fund; and United Nations Conference on Trade and Development (UNCTAD).

Figure O.20 **Foreign Direct Investment Inflows: Regional Distribution, 2017–19**

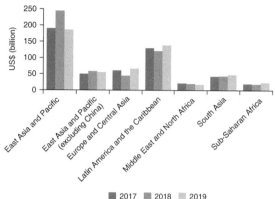

Sources: International Monetary Fund; and United Nations Conference on Trade and Development (UNCTAD).

and Canada. Half of 2019 inflows went to the automotive industry. The deepening economic crisis in Argentina deterred investors and FDI inflows fell 38 percent from the 2018 level to $6.5 billion.

The 11 percent rise in FDI inflows to countries in *South Asia* was driven by India where additional relaxation of investment barriers in mid-2019, including in retail and insurance, boosted FDI by 10 percent in 2019 to $43 billion, directed largely at the technology and communication industry. FDI inflows to Bangladesh also rose 10 percent to $1.4 billion, mostly into the garment industry, and inflows to Pakistan rebounded to $2 billion, up one-third compared with 2018 FDI inflows. The increase was driven by equity investment in energy, the financial sector, and textiles and led by British and Chinese investors.

FDI inflows to the *Middle East and North Africa* region fell 13 percent, reflecting a marked slowdown in investment across the region. FDI inflows to Morocco decreased by half to $1.4 billion, dropped 18 percent in Tunisia to $817 million in tandem with slower economic growth, and fell 16 percent in Lebanon to $2.2 billion with investors deterred by the ongoing macroeconomic crisis. In contrast, Egypt was a bright spot. FDI inflows rose 11 percent to $9 billion in response to economic reforms that improved macroeconomic stability and bolstered investor confidence. A significant share of these flows went into the oil and

gas sector, but telecommunications and consumer goods also attracted investment.

Countries in the *East Asia and Pacific* region had the largest decline in FDI inflows in 2019. They fell 24 percent to $186 billion on account of the steep drop in FDI inflows to China, which fell 29 percent to $131 billion, equivalent to 71 percent of inflows to the region. The decline was driven in part by trade tensions but also by a shift toward intercompany lending, reflected in the 2019 increase in net debt inflows to private sector entities. FDI inflows to Indonesia were up 24 percent to a record $25 billion, with strong investment in manufacturing, mining, and financial services. Among the small economies, Cambodia received record high FDI inflows of $3.7 billion in 2019, led by increases in manufacturing and services by predominantly Asian investors. FDI in Thailand fell 50 percent to $6.8 billion and 14 percent in Vietnam to $12 billion, pulling 2019 FDI to countries in the region other than China down 5 percent to $55 billion.

Portfolio equity flows are small in comparison with FDI and are directed at only a small number of low- and middle-income countries. Portfolio equity inflows are by far the most concentrated element of financial flows to low and middle-income countries, and the number of low- and middle-income countries that have benefited to any significant degree from these flows over the past decade is limited. Cumulative portfolio equity inflows from 2010 to 2019 totaled $581 billion, of which 91 percent went to three countries: China, $331 billion (57 percent); Brazil, $94 billion (16 percent); and India, $101 billion (17 percent).

Portfolio equity flows to low- and middle-income countries centered on China and India in 2019. The volatility that marks portfolio equity flows to emerging markets was again evident in 2019. Portfolio equity inflows to low- and middle-income countries rose 23 percent in 2019 to $47 billion from $39 billion in 2018, with investors favoring China and India and again retreating from most other emerging markets in 2019 over concerns that centered on both domestic and global economic conditions and because of attractive options in alternative markets,

Figure O.21 Portfolio Equity Flows to Low- and Middle-Income Countries, 2017–19

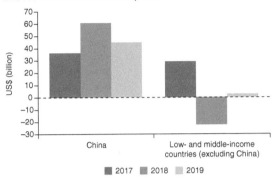

Source: International Monetary Fund.

Figure O.22 Portfolio Equity Flows to Major Recipients, 2017–19

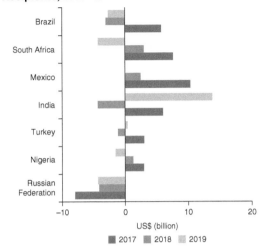

Source: International Monetary Fund.

particularly the United States. Net inflows to China fell 26 percent to $45 billion from $61 billion in 2018 despite further measures in 2019 by the Chinese government to liberalize the financial market. These measures included implementation of automated access between the Shanghai and London markets, following the link to the Hong Kong SAR, China, market in 2018, and FTSE Russell inclusion of Chinese A-shares in its emerging market index. Investor concerns

centered on slower economic growth, weakening of the renminbi, tight controls on outbound capital, and ongoing trade tensions with the United States. In contrast to China, net portfolio inflows to India rebounded to $14 billion after registering an outflow of $4 billion in 2018 driven by attractive valuations and improvements in market access. Excluding China and India, portfolio equity flows to low- and middle-income countries saw an $11 billion outflow in 2019.

PART II
Aggregate and Country Tables

ALL LOW- AND MIDDLE-INCOME COUNTRIES

(US$ billion, unless otherwise indicated)

	2009	2015	2016	2017	2018	2019
Summary external debt data by debtor type						
Total external debt stocks	**3,618**	**6,340**	**6,623**	**7,317**	**7,719**	**8,139**
Use of IMF credit	131	110	112	122	150	170
Long-term external debt	2,751	4,613	4,924	5,281	5,433	5,801
Public and publicly guaranteed sector	1,465	2,305	2,448	2,760	2,904	3,100
Public sector	1,459	2,300	2,444	2,757	2,901	3,098
of which: General government	1,090	1,644	1,760	1,999	2,099	2,280
Private sector guaranteed by public sector	6	5	4	3	3	3
Private sector not guaranteed	1,286	2,309	2,476	2,521	2,530	2,701
Short-term external debt	736	1,617	1,588	1,914	2,136	2,168
Disbursements (long-term)	**488**	**773**	**950**	**1,105**	**1,052**	**1,191**
Public and publicly guaranteed sector	204	306	338	472	436	453
Public sector	202	306	338	471	436	453
of which: General government	139	210	228	308	278	317
Private sector guaranteed by public sector	2	0	0	0	0	0
Private sector not guaranteed	284	467	612	633	616	738
Principal repayments (long-term)	**385**	**619**	**700**	**703**	**769**	**860**
Public and publicly guaranteed sector	119	221	194	204	254	254
Public sector	118	220	193	203	253	254
of which: General government	71	113	100	108	133	125
Private sector guaranteed by public sector	0	1	1	1	1	0
Private sector not guaranteed	267	399	507	499	515	606
Interest payments (long-term)	**107**	**169**	**170**	**185**	**205**	**222**
Public and publicly guaranteed sector	50	79	83	97	105	119
Public sector	50	79	83	97	105	119
of which: General government	40	60	63	74	78	83
Private sector guaranteed by public sector	0	0	0	0	0	0
Private sector not guaranteed	57	91	87	89	100	103
Summary external debt stock by creditor type						
Long-term external debt stocks	**2,751**	**4,613**	**4,924**	**5,281**	**5,433**	**5,801**
Public and publicly guaranteed debt from:	1,465	2,305	2,448	2,760	2,904	3,100
Official creditors	762	909	967	1,052	1,089	1,130
Multilateral	429	558	583	635	657	691
of which: World Bank	221	278	287	311	320	338
Bilateral	334	351	384	417	433	439
Private creditors	703	1,396	1,481	1,709	1,814	1,970
Bondholders	444	948	1,048	1,262	1,376	1,527
Commercial banks and others	259	447	433	446	438	443
Private nonguaranteed debt from:	1,286	2,309	2,476	2,521	2,530	2,701
Bondholders	180	365	396	475	484	564
Commercial banks and others	1,106	1,943	2,080	2,046	2,046	2,137
Use of IMF credit	131	110	112	122	150	170
Net financial inflows						
Net debt inflows						
Use of IMF credit	17	7	5	4	31	22
Long-term	103	154	250	402	282	331
Official creditors	52	45	56	54	51	46
Multilateral	43	33	33	31	32	37
of which: World Bank	17	17	14	12	15	19
Bilateral	9	12	24	23	19	9
Private creditors	50	109	193	348	231	285
Bondholders	47	61	127	281	180	234
Banks and others	3	48	67	67	51	51
Short-term	41	-480	-36	327	219	30
Net equity inflows						
Foreign direct investment	358	496	462	463	490	479
Portfolio equity	124	20	49	65	39	47
Debt ratios						
External debt stocks to exports (%)	85	99	108	105	101	107
External debt stocks to GNI (%)	22	24	25	25	25	26
Debt service to exports (%)	12	13	15	14	14	15
Short-term to external debt stocks (%)	20	26	24	26	28	27
Multilateral to external debt stocks (%)	12	9	9	9	9	8
Reserves to external debt stocks (%)	125	91	83	79	74	72
Gross national income (GNI)	16,159	26,092	26,205	28,810	30,561	31,423

EAST ASIA AND PACIFIC

(US$ billion, unless otherwise indicated)

	2009	2015	2016	2017	2018	2019
Summary external debt data by debtor type						
Total external debt stocks	**829**	**2,004**	**2,112**	**2,482**	**2,789**	**2,995**
Use of IMF credit	19	16	16	17	17	17
Long-term external debt	501	1,042	1,166	1,277	1,400	1,619
Public and publicly guaranteed sector	297	442	476	546	641	729
Public sector	296	442	475	546	641	728
of which: General government	220	343	365	404	448	511
Private sector guaranteed by public sector	0	0	0	0	0	0
Private sector not guaranteed	205	599	691	731	759	890
Short-term external debt	309	945	930	1,188	1,372	1,359
Disbursements (long-term)	**88**	**224**	**277**	**362**	**407**	**510**
Public and publicly guaranteed sector	39	69	60	98	131	130
Public sector	39	69	60	98	131	130
of which: General government	28	46	45	49	65	82
Private sector guaranteed by public sector	0	0	0	0	0	0
Private sector not guaranteed	49	155	217	264	276	380
Principal repayments (long-term)	**73**	**160**	**216**	**231**	**252**	**309**
Public and publicly guaranteed sector	19	48	35	34	34	43
Public sector	19	48	35	34	34	43
of which: General government	13	14	22	15	18	19
Private sector guaranteed by public sector	0	0	0	0	0	0
Private sector not guaranteed	53	112	182	197	218	266
Interest payments (long-term)	**13**	**33**	**29**	**35**	**47**	**57**
Public and publicly guaranteed sector	9	12	12	14	18	22
Public sector	9	12	12	14	18	22
of which: General government	7	8	9	10	13	14
Private sector guaranteed by public sector	0	0	0	0	0	0
Private sector not guaranteed	4	21	17	21	29	35
Summary external debt stock by creditor type						
Long-term external debt stocks	**501**	**1,042**	**1,166**	**1,277**	**1,400**	**1,619**
Public and publicly guaranteed debt from:	297	442	476	546	641	729
Official creditors	207	192	203	208	211	215
Multilateral	81	98	101	106	110	115
of which: World Bank	44	54	55	59	60	62
Bilateral	126	94	102	101	101	100
Private creditors	90	251	273	338	430	513
Bondholders	61	205	223	284	371	449
Commercial banks and others	29	46	50	54	59	64
Private nonguaranteed debt from:	205	599	691	731	759	890
Bondholders	21	115	132	183	216	275
Commercial banks and others	184	485	559	548	543	615
Use of IMF credit	19	16	16	17	17	17
Net financial inflows						
Net debt inflows						
Use of IMF credit	0	0	0	0	0	0
Long-term	16	63	60	131	155	201
Official creditors	6	2	0	0	4	4
Multilateral	6	6	4	4	5	5
of which: World Bank	2	3	2	2	2	2
Bilateral	0	-3	-4	-3	-1	-1
Private creditors	10	61	60	130	151	197
Bondholders	13	25	40	111	124	137
Banks and others	-3	36	20	19	27	60
Short-term	68	-431	-16	259	184	-13
Net equity inflows						
Foreign direct investment	151	259	193	190	244	186
Portfolio equity	40	4	24	35	49	46
Debt ratios						
External debt stocks to exports (%)	46	60	66	69	72	77
External debt stocks to GNI (%)	13	16	16	17	17	18
Debt service to exports (%)	5	7	8	9	9	11
Short-term to external debt stocks (%)	37	47	44	48	49	45
Multilateral to external debt stocks (%)	10	5	5	4	4	4
Reserves to external debt stocks (%)	324	186	163	146	128	122
Gross national income (GNI)	6,250	12,896	13,175	14,438	16,109	16,738

26

EUROPE AND CENTRAL ASIA

(US$ billion, unless otherwise indicated)

	2009	2015	2016	2017	2018	2019
Summary external debt data by debtor type						
Total external debt stocks	1,076	1,356	1,443	1,495	1,420	1,464
Use of IMF credit	43	28	29	30	29	27
Long-term external debt	864	1,121	1,209	1,231	1,163	1,189
Public and publicly guaranteed sector	302	436	447	501	466	493
Public sector	302	435	446	500	466	492
of which: General government	160	231	247	283	277	314
Private sector guaranteed by public sector	0	1	1	1	0	0
Private sector not guaranteed	562	685	762	730	696	696
Short-term external debt	169	206	206	234	228	249
Disbursements (long-term)	163	134	238	246	173	219
Public and publicly guaranteed sector	45	51	53	89	50	86
Public sector	45	51	53	89	50	86
of which: General government	26	39	31	46	32	57
Private sector guaranteed by public sector	0	0	0	0	0	0
Private sector not guaranteed	118	83	185	157	123	133
Principal repayments (long-term)	175	202	164	188	222	207
Public and publicly guaranteed sector	31	68	42	45	79	58
Public sector	31	68	42	45	79	58
of which: General government	11	35	13	19	34	20
Private sector guaranteed by public sector	0	0	0	0	0	0
Private sector not guaranteed	144	134	122	143	143	149
Interest payments (long-term)	40	43	44	44	43	43
Public and publicly guaranteed sector	9	12	15	17	19	19
Public sector	9	12	15	17	19	19
of which: General government	7	10	9	10	12	12
Private sector guaranteed by public sector	0	0	0	0	0	0
Private sector not guaranteed	30	31	29	27	24	24
Summary external debt stock by creditor type						
Long-term external debt stocks	864	1,121	1,209	1,231	1,163	1,189
Public and publicly guaranteed debt from:	302	436	447	501	466	493
Official creditors	83	112	117	131	132	134
Multilateral	53	77	81	90	90	88
of which: World Bank	30	37	37	40	40	40
Bilateral	30	35	37	41	42	45
Private creditors	220	324	329	370	335	359
Bondholders	73	147	164	196	194	232
Commercial banks and others	146	177	165	174	141	127
Private nonguaranteed debt from:	562	685	762	730	696	696
Bondholders	36	56	67	78	77	84
Commercial banks and others	525	629	696	652	619	613
Use of IMF credit	43	28	29	30	29	27
Net financial inflows						
Net debt inflows						
Use of IMF credit	11	5	1	0	-1	-2
Long-term	-12	-68	74	57	-50	11
Official creditors	12	7	7	7	4	3
Multilateral	10	5	5	4	2	0
of which: World Bank	2	1	1	1	1	0
Bilateral	2	2	2	3	2	3
Private creditors	-24	-76	67	51	-54	9
Bondholders	-12	-8	25	35	0	44
Banks and others	-13	-68	42	16	-54	-36
Short-term	-26	-61	-2	27	-6	20
Net equity inflows						
Foreign direct investment	58	49	77	60	44	66
Portfolio equity	7	-8	-1	-5	-7	-4
Debt ratios						
External debt stocks to exports (%)	140	147	171	149	121	126
External debt stocks to GNI (%)	46	48	53	49	46	47
Debt service to exports (%)	29	27	25	24	24	22
Short-term to external debt stocks (%)	16	15	14	16	16	17
Multilateral to external debt stocks (%)	5	6	6	6	6	6
Reserves to external debt stocks (%)	55	38	36	38	41	44
Gross national income (GNI)	2,362	2,847	2,703	3,032	3,106	3,146

LATIN AMERICA AND THE CARIBBEAN

(US$ billion, unless otherwise indicated)

	2009	2015	2016	2017	2018	2019
Summary external debt data by debtor type						
Total external debt stocks	**899**	**1,667**	**1,703**	**1,789**	**1,883**	**1,927**
Use of IMF credit	23	20	20	21	48	65
Long-term external debt	747	1,386	1,447	1,521	1,544	1,557
Public and publicly guaranteed sector	434	758	814	878	912	919
Public sector	430	756	812	876	911	917
of which: General government	336	517	559	605	631	641
Private sector guaranteed by public sector	4	3	2	2	2	2
Private sector not guaranteed	313	628	632	644	632	638
Short-term external debt	129	261	236	247	291	304
Disbursements (long-term)	**156**	**241**	**276**	**272**	**260**	**243**
Public and publicly guaranteed sector	72	92	126	137	128	101
Public sector	70	91	126	137	128	101
of which: General government	47	52	80	87	84	65
Private sector guaranteed by public sector	2	0	0	0	0	0
Private sector not guaranteed	84	150	150	135	132	142
Principal repayments (long-term)	**93**	**163**	**196**	**182**	**171**	**228**
Public and publicly guaranteed sector	41	55	63	76	74	94
Public sector	40	54	62	75	74	94
of which: General government	29	29	30	43	30	44
Private sector guaranteed by public sector	0	1	1	1	1	0
Private sector not guaranteed	53	108	134	106	96	134
Interest payments (long-term)	**39**	**65**	**67**	**74**	**71**	**76**
Public and publicly guaranteed sector	22	40	39	48	43	50
Public sector	22	40	39	48	43	50
of which: General government	18	31	32	38	34	35
Private sector guaranteed by public sector	0	0	0	0	0	0
Private sector not guaranteed	17	25	27	26	28	27
Summary external debt stock by creditor type						
Long-term external debt stocks	**747**	**1,386**	**1,447**	**1,521**	**1,544**	**1,557**
Public and publicly guaranteed debt from:	434	758	814	878	912	919
Official creditors	142	198	202	211	217	217
Multilateral	110	151	156	158	167	173
of which: World Bank	40	56	57	57	58	61
Bilateral	32	47	46	53	50	44
Private creditors	292	561	613	667	695	702
Bondholders	253	425	480	535	555	558
Commercial banks and others	39	135	133	131	140	144
Private nonguaranteed debt from:	313	628	632	644	632	638
Bondholders	97	170	170	182	158	167
Commercial banks and others	217	458	462	462	474	470
Use of IMF credit	23	20	20	21	48	65
Net financial inflows						
Net debt inflows						
Use of IMF credit	0	0	0	0	29	17
Long-term	63	79	80	90	89	15
Official creditors	17	7	5	8	6	1
Multilateral	13	8	6	3	8	6
of which: World Bank	6	2	2	-1	2	2
Bilateral	3	-1	0	6	-2	-6
Private creditors	47	72	74	82	83	14
Bondholders	42	27	55	70	43	16
Banks and others	5	45	19	12	39	-2
Short-term	-3	8	-30	13	43	13
Net equity inflows						
Foreign direct investment	61	105	104	130	121	138
Portfolio equity	41	14	21	20	-2	-4
Debt ratios						
External debt stocks to exports (%)	124	173	178	166	162	164
External debt stocks to GNI (%)	24	35	37	34	38	39
Debt service to exports (%)	19	24	28	24	22	27
Short-term to external debt stocks (%)	14	16	14	14	15	16
Multilateral to external debt stocks (%)	12	9	9	9	9	9
Reserves to external debt stocks (%)	56	43	43	43	41	39
Gross national income (GNI)	3,779	4,800	4,652	5,193	4,964	4,880

MIDDLE EAST AND NORTH AFRICA
(US$ billion, unless otherwise indicated)

	2009	2015	2016	2017	2018	2019
Summary external debt data by debtor type						
Total external debt stocks	183	240	267	301	323	340
Use of IMF credit	8	11	13	17	18	22
Long-term external debt	142	188	202	231	256	267
Public and publicly guaranteed sector	114	146	158	182	200	215
Public sector	113	145	157	182	199	215
of which: General government	89	110	117	135	148	162
Private sector guaranteed by public sector	1	0	0	0	0	0
Private sector not guaranteed	28	42	44	48	57	52
Short-term external debt	33	41	52	53	49	52
Disbursements (long-term)	21	39	40	44	49	37
Public and publicly guaranteed sector	12	27	28	31	32	29
Public sector	12	27	28	31	32	29
of which: General government	10	20	18	23	22	24
Private sector guaranteed by public sector	0	0	0	0	0	0
Private sector not guaranteed	9	13	12	13	17	8
Principal repayments (long-term)	19	20	24	23	22	25
Public and publicly guaranteed sector	11	11	15	13	12	13
Public sector	11	11	15	13	12	13
of which: General government	7	8	10	9	7	9
Private sector guaranteed by public sector	0	0	0	0	0	0
Private sector not guaranteed	8	10	10	10	11	12
Interest payments (long-term)	6	6	7	8	9	11
Public and publicly guaranteed sector	4	4	5	5	7	8
Public sector	4	4	5	5	7	8
of which: General government	3	3	4	4	5	6
Private sector guaranteed by public sector	0	0	0	0	0	0
Private sector not guaranteed	1	2	2	2	3	3
Summary external debt stock by creditor type						
Long-term external debt stocks	142	188	202	231	256	267
Public and publicly guaranteed debt from:	114	146	158	182	200	215
Official creditors	78	91	103	115	117	121
Multilateral	35	44	49	57	58	62
of which: World Bank	12	16	18	22	24	26
Bilateral	43	47	53	57	58	59
Private creditors	35	55	55	68	83	94
Bondholders	24	46	47	59	70	78
Commercial banks and others	11	9	8	8	13	16
Private nonguaranteed debt from:	28	42	44	48	57	52
Bondholders	1	1	1	0	1	1
Commercial banks and others	28	42	44	48	56	51
Use of IMF credit	8	11	13	17	18	22
Net financial inflows						
Net debt inflows						
Use of IMF credit	0	1	3	3	2	4
Long-term	2	19	15	21	27	12
Official creditors	3	8	13	7	4	5
Multilateral	3	3	7	5	2	4
of which: World Bank	1	2	2	2	2	3
Bilateral	-1	5	6	2	2	1
Private creditors	0	11	2	14	23	7
Bondholders	0	7	1	11	11	9
Banks and others	-1	5	1	3	12	-2
Short-term	3	1	11	1	-5	3
Net equity inflows						
Foreign direct investment	27	16	19	21	19	17
Portfolio equity	1	-1	1	-1	0	1
Debt ratios						
External debt stocks to exports (%)	58	82	97	101	98	117
External debt stocks to GNI (%)	18	20	22	26	27	27
Debt service to exports (%)	8	9	12	11	10	13
Short-term to external debt stocks (%)	18	17	19	18	15	15
Multilateral to external debt stocks (%)	19	18	18	19	18	18
Reserves to external debt stocks (%)	153	101	84	..	..	..
Gross national income (GNI)	1,012	1,204	1,232	1,170	1,188	1,239

SOUTH ASIA
(US$ billion, unless otherwise indicated)

	2009	2015	2016	2017	2018	2019
Summary external debt data by debtor type						
Total external debt stocks	366	635	624	707	733	789
Use of IMF credit	19	15	16	17	16	17
Long-term external debt	293	517	501	564	586	636
Public and publicly guaranteed sector	170	271	270	318	330	354
Public sector	170	271	270	318	330	353
of which: General government	151	222	224	273	279	297
Private sector guaranteed by public sector	0	0	0	0	0	0
Private sector not guaranteed	123	245	231	246	256	282
Short-term external debt	54	103	107	126	130	136
Disbursements (long-term)	36	80	59	104	84	103
Public and publicly guaranteed sector	18	35	26	61	43	50
Public sector	18	35	26	61	43	50
of which: General government	14	24	20	54	29	35
Private sector guaranteed by public sector	0	0	0	0	0	0
Private sector not guaranteed	18	45	33	43	41	53
Principal repayments (long-term)	15	45	72	48	58	52
Public and publicly guaranteed sector	9	17	25	20	29	26
Public sector	9	17	25	20	29	26
of which: General government	6	8	16	11	21	17
Private sector guaranteed by public sector	0	0	0	0	0	0
Private sector not guaranteed	7	28	47	28	29	27
Interest payments (long-term)	6	12	12	13	18	18
Public and publicly guaranteed sector	3	4	4	5	6	7
Public sector	3	4	4	5	6	7
of which: General government	2	2	3	4	5	5
Private sector guaranteed by public sector	0	0	0	0	0	0
Private sector not guaranteed	4	8	8	9	12	10
Summary external debt stock by creditor type						
Long-term external debt stocks	293	517	501	564	586	636
Public and publicly guaranteed debt from:	170	271	270	318	330	354
Official creditors	146	164	171	188	203	219
Multilateral	95	107	109	118	121	129
of which: World Bank	62	67	68	72	72	75
Bilateral	51	57	61	70	82	90
Private creditors	24	107	100	130	126	135
Bondholders	13	73	69	101	94	102
Commercial banks and others	11	34	31	29	33	33
Private nonguaranteed debt from:	123	245	231	246	256	282
Bondholders	16	8	10	15	14	19
Commercial banks and others	107	237	220	231	242	263
Use of IMF credit	19	15	16	17	16	17
Net financial inflows						
Net debt inflows						
Use of IMF credit	4	1	1	0	0	1
Long-term	20	35	-13	56	26	51
Official creditors	7	6	8	11	17	16
Multilateral	6	4	4	4	5	8
of which: World Bank	2	2	2	1	2	3
Bilateral	2	2	4	6	12	8
Private creditors	13	29	-22	45	9	35
Bondholders	2	13	-2	36	-7	14
Banks and others	11	17	-20	9	16	21
Short-term	4	0	4	19	4	5
Net equity inflows						
Foreign direct investment	37	45	48	42	43	48
Portfolio equity	24	2	2	6	-5	14
Debt ratios						
External debt stocks to exports (%)	111	119	116	117	110	117
External debt stocks to GNI (%)	22	24	21	21	21	22
Debt service to exports (%)	7	11	16	11	12	11
Short-term to external debt stocks (%)	15	16	17	18	18	17
Multilateral to external debt stocks (%)	26	17	18	17	17	16
Reserves to external debt stocks (%)	82	63	66	66	60	64
Gross national income (GNI)	1,687	2,700	2,905	3,343	3,444	3,597

SUB-SAHARAN AFRICA
(US$ billion, unless otherwise indicated)

	2009	2015	2016	2017	2018	2019
Summary external debt data by debtor type						
Total external debt stocks	266	439	474	543	571	625
Use of IMF credit	20	19	19	20	21	23
Long-term external debt	203	359	399	458	484	535
Public and publicly guaranteed sector	149	251	283	336	355	392
Public sector	148	251	283	336	354	392
of which: General government	134	221	248	299	317	356
Private sector guaranteed by public sector	1	0	0	0	0	0
Private sector not guaranteed	54	108	116	122	129	143
Short-term external debt	43	60	57	65	66	68
Disbursements (long-term)	25	55	61	77	79	79
Public and publicly guaranteed sector	18	33	45	55	52	57
Public sector	18	33	45	55	52	57
of which: General government	14	28	34	49	46	54
Private sector guaranteed by public sector	0	0	0	0	0	0
Private sector not guaranteed	7	22	16	22	27	22
Principal repayments (long-term)	11	29	27	30	44	38
Public and publicly guaranteed sector	8	22	14	15	26	20
Public sector	8	22	14	15	26	20
of which: General government	4	18	9	10	22	16
Private sector guaranteed by public sector	0	0	0	0	0	0
Private sector not guaranteed	2	7	13	15	18	18
Interest payments (long-term)	4	11	12	12	16	17
Public and publicly guaranteed sector	3	7	8	8	11	13
Public sector	3	7	8	8	11	13
of which: General government	3	6	7	7	10	11
Private sector guaranteed by public sector	0	0	0	0	0	0
Private sector not guaranteed	1	4	4	4	4	4
Summary external debt stock by creditor type						
Long-term external debt stocks	203	359	399	458	484	535
Public and publicly guaranteed debt from:	149	251	283	336	355	392
Official creditors	106	152	172	199	209	224
Multilateral	55	81	87	104	110	124
of which: World Bank	32	48	52	61	65	74
Bilateral	51	71	85	95	99	101
Private creditors	43	99	111	136	145	168
Bondholders	21	52	64	87	93	109
Commercial banks and others	23	46	47	50	52	59
Private nonguaranteed debt from:	54	108	116	122	129	143
Bondholders	8	16	16	17	17	18
Commercial banks and others	46	93	99	105	112	124
Use of IMF credit	20	19	19	20	21	23
Net financial inflows						
Net debt inflows						
Use of IMF credit	2	0	0	1	2	1
Long-term	14	26	34	47	35	41
Official creditors	8	16	23	21	15	18
Multilateral	5	9	8	12	10	14
of which: World Bank	3	6	5	6	6	9
Bilateral	3	7	15	9	5	5
Private creditors	6	11	11	26	20	23
Bondholders	2	-4	7	18	9	14
Banks and others	4	14	4	8	11	9
Short-term	-4	3	-4	8	-2	1
Net equity inflows						
Foreign direct investment	24	23	22	19	19	23
Portfolio equity	11	8	2	10	4	-6
Debt ratios						
External debt stocks to exports (%)	88	128	148	147	137	153
External debt stocks to GNI (%)	25	28	33	35	36	38
Debt service to exports (%)	5	12	13	12	15	14
Short-term to external debt stocks (%)	16	14	12	12	12	11
Multilateral to external debt stocks (%)	21	19	18	19	19	20
Reserves to external debt stocks (%)	58	36	30	29	28	..
Gross national income (GNI)	1,073	1,576	1,455	1,540	1,601	1,652

AFGHANISTAN
(US$ million, unless otherwise indicated)

	2009	2015	2016	2017	2018	2019
Summary external debt data by debtor type						
Total external debt stocks	**2,480**	**2,597**	**2,596**	**2,752**	**2,679**	**2,662**
Use of IMF credit	353	300	277	285	275	277
Long-term external debt	2,106	2,009	1,965	1,998	1,970	1,965
Public and publicly guaranteed sector	2,106	1,990	1,950	1,982	1,949	1,944
Public sector	2,106	1,990	1,950	1,982	1,949	1,944
of which: General government	2,106	1,990	1,950	1,982	1,949	1,944
Private sector guaranteed by public sector	..	..	..	..	..	..
Private sector not guaranteed	..	19	15	16	22	21
Short-term external debt	21	288	355	470	434	420
Disbursements (long-term)	**109**	**26**	**12**	**3**	**16**	**29**
Public and publicly guaranteed sector	109	26	12	3	16	29
Public sector	109	26	12	3	16	29
of which: General government	109	26	12	3	16	29
Private sector guaranteed by public sector	..	..	..	..	..	..
Private sector not guaranteed	..	..	..	..	..	..
Principal repayments (long-term)	**3**	**24**	**27**	**27**	**31**	**31**
Public and publicly guaranteed sector	3	19	23	23	25	25
Public sector	3	19	23	23	25	25
of which: General government	3	19	23	23	25	25
Private sector guaranteed by public sector	..	..	..	..	..	..
Private sector not guaranteed	..	5	4	4	6	6
Interest payments (long-term)	**7**	**10**	**8**	**9**	**9**	**9**
Public and publicly guaranteed sector	7	9	8	8	8	7
Public sector	7	9	8	8	8	7
of which: General government	7	9	8	8	8	7
Private sector guaranteed by public sector	..	..	..	..	..	..
Private sector not guaranteed	..	1	1	1	1	1
Summary external debt stock by creditor type						
Long-term external debt stocks	**2,106**	**2,009**	**1,965**	**1,998**	**1,970**	**1,965**
Public and publicly guaranteed debt from:	2,106	1,990	1,950	1,982	1,949	1,944
Official creditors	2,106	1,990	1,950	1,982	1,949	1,944
Multilateral	1,017	1,030	991	1,023	983	955
of which: World Bank	466	370	351	364	348	338
Bilateral	1,089	960	958	959	965	989
Private creditors	0	..	..	..	..	..
Bondholders	..	..	..	..	..	..
Commercial banks and others	0	..	..	..	..	..
Private nonguaranteed debt from:	..	19	15	16	22	21
Bondholders	..	..	..	..	..	..
Commercial banks and others	..	19	15	16	22	21
Use of IMF credit	353	300	277	285	275	277
Net financial inflows						
Net debt inflows						
Use of IMF credit	17	-20	-15	-8	-4	4
Long-term	106	2	-15	-24	-14	-2
Official creditors	106	7	-11	-19	-8	3
Multilateral	108	-8	-9	-19	-15	-20
of which: World Bank	27	-8	-8	-19	-15	-20
Bilateral	-2	16	-2	0	7	23
Private creditors	..	-5	-4	-4	-6	-6
Bondholders	..	..	..	..	..	..
Banks and others	..	-5	-4	-4	-6	-6
Short-term	..	88	26	80	-68	-44
Net equity inflows						
Foreign direct investment	56	169	94	52	119	23
Portfolio equity	0	0	0	0	0	0
Debt ratios						
External debt stocks to exports (%)	113	152	189	189	141	143
External debt stocks to GNI (%)	20	13	13	13	14	14
Debt service to exports (%)	0	3	4	4	3	3
Short-term to external debt stocks (%)	1	11	14	17	16	16
Multilateral to external debt stocks (%)	41	40	38	37	37	36
Reserves to external debt stocks (%)	141	240	249	261	273	279
Gross national income (GNI)	12,404	20,087	19,542	20,440	19,675	19,402

ALBANIA
(US$ million, unless otherwise indicated)

	2009	2015	2016	2017	2018	2019
Summary external debt data by debtor type						
Total external debt stocks	**4,605**	**8,447**	**8,516**	**9,801**	**9,868**	**9,626**
Use of IMF credit	144	244	387	489	470	448
Long-term external debt	3,780	6,617	6,482	7,421	7,494	7,367
Public and publicly guaranteed sector	2,874	3,844	3,761	4,335	4,559	4,442
Public sector	2,874	3,844	3,761	4,335	4,559	4,442
of which: General government	2,487	3,550	3,489	4,051	4,246	4,160
Private sector guaranteed by public sector	..	..	..	..	..	..
Private sector not guaranteed	906	2,773	2,722	3,085	2,935	2,924
Short-term external debt	681	1,586	1,647	1,892	1,904	1,812
Disbursements (long-term)	**725**	**1,322**	**450**	**776**	**1,269**	**457**
Public and publicly guaranteed sector	558	957	205	421	931	207
Public sector	558	957	205	421	931	207
of which: General government	496	953	189	420	792	202
Private sector guaranteed by public sector	..	..	..	..	..	..
Private sector not guaranteed	167	365	245	355	338	250
Principal repayments (long-term)	**122**	**1,073**	**488**	**407**	**922**	**498**
Public and publicly guaranteed sector	80	500	191	222	554	263
Public sector	80	500	191	222	554	263
of which: General government	57	479	161	198	456	234
Private sector guaranteed by public sector	..	..	..	..	..	..
Private sector not guaranteed	43	573	297	185	368	234
Interest payments (long-term)	**96**	**98**	**95**	**96**	**147**	**122**
Public and publicly guaranteed sector	71	90	84	83	120	105
Public sector	71	90	84	83	120	105
of which: General government	60	86	82	80	114	102
Private sector guaranteed by public sector	..	..	..	..	..	..
Private sector not guaranteed	24	9	11	12	28	17
Summary external debt stock by creditor type						
Long-term external debt stocks	**3,780**	**6,617**	**6,482**	**7,421**	**7,494**	**7,367**
Public and publicly guaranteed debt from:	2,874	3,844	3,761	4,335	4,559	4,442
Official creditors	2,134	2,586	2,532	2,984	3,037	3,004
Multilateral	1,467	1,946	1,890	2,279	2,362	2,338
of which: World Bank	874	1,020	991	1,300	1,301	1,330
Bilateral	666	641	642	705	675	666
Private creditors	740	1,258	1,229	1,351	1,522	1,438
Bondholders	82	631	611	696	942	925
Commercial banks and others	658	626	617	656	580	514
Private nonguaranteed debt from:	906	2,773	2,722	3,085	2,935	2,924
Bondholders	23	133	148	192	329	306
Commercial banks and others	884	2,640	2,573	2,894	2,606	2,618
Use of IMF credit	144	244	387	489	470	448
Net financial inflows						
Net debt inflows						
Use of IMF credit	-10	100	156	77	-7	-20
Long-term	603	249	-38	369	347	-40
Official creditors	177	13	3	243	137	-1
Multilateral	151	-19	-11	240	148	1
of which: World Bank	32	-3	2	226	40	44
Bilateral	26	33	14	3	-11	-2
Private creditors	426	236	-40	126	210	-39
Bondholders	-1	56	15	43	340	-20
Banks and others	426	180	-56	83	-130	-19
Short-term	-469	-162	61	245	12	-92
Net equity inflows						
Foreign direct investment	1,040	877	1,048	1,073	1,271	1,245
Portfolio equity	-4	9	-15	-12	-3	7
Debt ratios						
External debt stocks to exports (%)	134	240	219	213	188	182
External debt stocks to GNI (%)	39	73	71	75	65	64
Debt service to exports (%)	7	34	15	11	21	12
Short-term to external debt stocks (%)	15	19	19	19	19	19
Multilateral to external debt stocks (%)	32	23	22	23	24	24
Reserves to external debt stocks (%)	50	37	36	36	39	38
Gross national income (GNI)	11,852	11,521	12,054	13,054	15,130	15,122

33

ALGERIA

(US$ million, unless otherwise indicated)

	2009	2015	2016	2017	2018	2019
Summary external debt data by debtor type						
Total external debt stocks	7,414	4,671	5,463	5,707	5,710	5,492
Use of IMF credit	1,878	1,660	1,611	1,706	1,666	1,657
Long-term external debt	4,043	1,188	1,866	1,904	1,725	1,571
Public and publicly guaranteed sector	3,062	870	1,653	1,716	1,523	1,398
Public sector	2,884	867	1,650	1,713	1,521	1,397
of which: General government	956	350	1,247	1,366	1,268	1,205
Private sector guaranteed by public sector	178	3	3	3	2	1
Private sector not guaranteed	982	318	214	188	202	173
Short-term external debt	1,492	1,823	1,986	2,096	2,319	2,264
Disbursements (long-term)	226	47	1,032	11	44	33
Public and publicly guaranteed sector	102	0	984	1	0	0
Public sector	102	0	984	1	0	0
of which: General government	23	0	984	0	0	0
Private sector guaranteed by public sector	0	0	0	0	0	0
Private sector not guaranteed	123	47	49	11	44	33
Principal repayments (long-term)	910	582	302	176	151	118
Public and publicly guaranteed sector	388	167	149	140	122	93
Public sector	378	166	149	139	121	92
of which: General government	24	47	44	41	40	36
Private sector guaranteed by public sector	10	1	0	1	1	1
Private sector not guaranteed	522	415	153	36	29	25
Interest payments (long-term)	124	79	22	31	29	25
Public and publicly guaranteed sector	75	21	17	27	26	23
Public sector	74	21	17	27	26	23
of which: General government	10	8	6	20	21	20
Private sector guaranteed by public sector	1	0	0	0	0	0
Private sector not guaranteed	49	59	5	4	3	2
Summary external debt stock by creditor type						
Long-term external debt stocks	4,043	1,188	1,866	1,904	1,725	1,571
Public and publicly guaranteed debt from:	3,062	870	1,653	1,716	1,523	1,398
Official creditors	2,197	752	1,580	1,682	1,512	1,393
Multilateral	11	1	949	1,079	1,031	1,007
of which: World Bank	10	1	1	0	..	..
Bilateral	2,186	751	630	603	481	386
Private creditors	864	118	73	34	11	6
Bondholders	..	..	..	..	..	..
Commercial banks and others	864	118	73	34	11	6
Private nonguaranteed debt from:	982	318	214	188	202	173
Bondholders	..	..	..	..	..	..
Commercial banks and others	982	318	214	188	202	173
Use of IMF credit	1,878	1,660	1,611	1,706	1,666	1,657
Net financial inflows						
Net debt inflows						
Use of IMF credit	..	..	..	..	..	..
Long-term	-684	-535	731	-165	-107	-85
Official creditors	-54	-117	880	-97	-99	-88
Multilateral	-1	0	983	-1	0	0
of which: World Bank	-1	0	0	-1	..	..
Bilateral	-53	-117	-103	-96	-99	-88
Private creditors	-630	-418	-149	-68	-8	3
Bondholders	..	..	..	..	..	..
Banks and others	-630	-418	-149	-68	-8	3
Short-term	189	-152	163	110	223	-55
Net equity inflows						
Foreign direct investment	2,833	-396	1,650	1,202	1,466	1,382
Portfolio equity	0	..	..	..	..	..
Debt ratios						
External debt stocks to exports (%)	14	12	16	14	13	..
External debt stocks to GNI (%)	5	3	3	3	3	3
Debt service to exports (%)	2	2	1	1	1	..
Short-term to external debt stocks (%)	20	39	36	37	41	41
Multilateral to external debt stocks (%)	0	0	17	19	18	18
Reserves to external debt stocks (%)	2,010	3,097	2,094	1,711	1,405	1,152
Gross national income (GNI)	135,898	161,577	158,461	164,797	169,358	165,788

ANGOLA

(US$ million, unless otherwise indicated)

	2009	2015	2016	2017	2018	2019
Summary external debt data by debtor type						
Total external debt stocks	**20,168**	**56,269**	**56,815**	**50,910**	**51,912**	**52,460**
Use of IMF credit	787	532	396	389	1,374	1,861
Long-term external debt	16,789	47,571	52,040	46,827	48,227	47,776
Public and publicly guaranteed sector	13,630	27,301	34,463	33,892	35,557	35,031
Public sector	13,630	27,301	34,463	33,892	35,557	35,031
of which: General government	6,986	14,855	18,412	20,353	22,633	23,368
Private sector guaranteed by public sector	0	..	..	..	..	..
Private sector not guaranteed	3,158	20,270	17,577	12,934	12,669	12,745
Short-term external debt	2,593	8,166	4,379	3,694	2,311	2,822
Disbursements (long-term)	**6,701**	**5,380**	**13,189**	**4,985**	**7,722**	**7,236**
Public and publicly guaranteed sector	3,543	3,592	13,189	4,985	6,693	5,365
Public sector	3,543	3,592	13,189	4,985	6,693	5,365
of which: General government	1,726	3,592	5,189	3,725	4,893	4,365
Private sector guaranteed by public sector	0	..	..	..	..	..
Private sector not guaranteed	3,158	1,788	..	..	1,028	1,871
Principal repayments (long-term)	**3,531**	**6,017**	**8,015**	**9,249**	**6,257**	**7,184**
Public and publicly guaranteed sector	3,131	3,964	5,988	5,733	4,964	5,865
Public sector	3,130	3,964	5,988	5,733	4,964	5,865
of which: General government	802	1,176	1,594	1,954	2,551	3,604
Private sector guaranteed by public sector	1	..	..	..	..	..
Private sector not guaranteed	400	2,054	2,027	3,515	1,293	1,319
Interest payments (long-term)	**459**	**1,379**	**1,775**	**1,071**	**2,280**	**2,308**
Public and publicly guaranteed sector	392	1,078	1,413	751	1,838	1,885
Public sector	392	1,078	1,413	751	1,838	1,885
of which: General government	206	563	991	380	1,103	1,205
Private sector guaranteed by public sector	0	..	..	..	..	..
Private sector not guaranteed	67	301	362	320	442	423
Summary external debt stock by creditor type						
Long-term external debt stocks	**16,789**	**47,571**	**52,040**	**46,827**	**48,227**	**47,776**
Public and publicly guaranteed debt from:	13,630	27,301	34,463	33,892	35,557	35,031
Official creditors	4,661	11,909	21,333	22,567	21,451	19,388
Multilateral	448	1,602	2,018	2,239	2,268	2,847
of which: World Bank	385	929	940	1,025	1,042	1,636
Bilateral	4,213	10,307	19,314	20,328	19,183	16,541
Private creditors	8,969	15,392	13,131	11,325	14,106	15,643
Bondholders	..	2,500	2,500	2,500	6,000	8,000
Commercial banks and others	8,969	12,892	10,631	8,825	8,106	7,643
Private nonguaranteed debt from:	3,158	20,270	17,577	12,934	12,669	12,745
Bondholders	..	..	..	..	..	..
Commercial banks and others	3,158	20,270	17,577	12,934	12,669	12,745
Use of IMF credit	787	532	396	389	1,374	1,861
Net financial inflows						
Net debt inflows						
Use of IMF credit	353	-345	-124	-30	1,012	495
Long-term	3,170	-637	5,174	-4,264	1,465	51
Official creditors	788	-439	9,431	1,187	-1,104	-2,059
Multilateral	15	479	432	184	44	585
of which: World Bank	13	472	26	55	31	600
Bilateral	772	-918	8,999	1,002	-1,148	-2,645
Private creditors	2,383	-197	-4,256	-5,451	2,569	2,110
Bondholders	..	1,500	0	..	3,500	2,000
Banks and others	2,383	-1,697	-4,256	-5,451	-931	110
Short-term	187	514	-3,785	-660	-1,362	513
Net equity inflows						
Foreign direct investment	2,743	4,974	-122	-7,293	-7,104	-4,739
Portfolio equity	..	0	0	0	0	0
Debt ratios						
External debt stocks to exports (%)	49	163	198	142	124	146
External debt stocks to GNI (%)	32	51	59	44	56	60
Debt service to exports (%)	10	23	35	29	21	27
Short-term to external debt stocks (%)	13	15	8	7	4	5
Multilateral to external debt stocks (%)	2	3	4	4	4	5
Reserves to external debt stocks (%)	68	42	42	34	30	31
Gross national income (GNI)	63,484	110,286	95,850	114,618	93,524	87,199

ARGENTINA

(US$ million, unless otherwise indicated)

	2009	2015	2016	2017	2018	2019
Summary external debt data by debtor type						
Total external debt stocks	**133,695**	**177,185**	**189,332**	**236,963**	**283,624**	**279,306**
Use of IMF credit	3,167	2,799	2,716	2,877	30,923	46,924
Long-term external debt	111,243	114,951	145,599	178,626	185,119	165,120
Public and publicly guaranteed sector	75,797	72,821	105,908	127,552	134,909	116,662
Public sector	75,664	72,821	105,908	127,552	134,909	116,640
of which: General government	72,687	71,911	105,193	126,958	134,476	116,134
Private sector guaranteed by public sector	133	0	0	0	0	22
Private sector not guaranteed	35,446	42,130	39,691	51,074	50,210	48,458
Short-term external debt	19,286	59,434	41,017	55,461	67,583	67,262
Disbursements (long-term)	**7,547**	**16,520**	**54,737**	**58,921**	**58,211**	**17,839**
Public and publicly guaranteed sector	3,602	8,599	40,188	41,047	48,369	10,927
Public sector	3,602	8,599	40,188	41,047	48,369	10,905
of which: General government	3,165	8,272	40,090	41,047	48,369	10,719
Private sector guaranteed by public sector	..	0	..	..	..	22
Private sector not guaranteed	3,946	7,920	14,549	17,873	9,842	6,913
Principal repayments (long-term)	**11,306**	**10,821**	**11,677**	**24,169**	**20,855**	**27,428**
Public and publicly guaranteed sector	5,592	6,365	5,363	17,821	15,787	22,611
Public sector	5,565	6,364	5,363	17,821	15,787	22,611
of which: General government	5,342	5,977	5,106	17,723	15,698	22,524
Private sector guaranteed by public sector	27	1	..	..	..	..
Private sector not guaranteed	5,714	4,455	6,313	6,348	5,069	4,817
Interest payments (long-term)	**3,366**	**6,076**	**13,404**	**14,814**	**12,285**	**9,907**
Public and publicly guaranteed sector	2,031	5,146	12,304	12,427	10,989	9,060
Public sector	2,030	5,146	12,304	12,427	10,989	9,060
of which: General government	1,906	5,110	12,270	12,394	10,959	9,032
Private sector guaranteed by public sector	1	0	..	..	..	..
Private sector not guaranteed	1,335	931	1,100	2,387	1,296	847
Summary external debt stock by creditor type						
Long-term external debt stocks	**111,243**	**114,951**	**145,599**	**178,626**	**185,119**	**165,120**
Public and publicly guaranteed debt from:	75,797	72,821	105,908	127,552	134,909	116,662
Official creditors	22,295	27,156	26,697	28,236	29,040	29,101
Multilateral	16,267	19,778	20,237	21,342	23,005	23,873
of which: World Bank	5,305	5,852	6,048	6,327	6,879	7,128
Bilateral	6,028	7,379	6,460	6,894	6,034	5,228
Private creditors	53,502	45,664	79,212	99,316	105,869	87,561
Bondholders	51,276	42,709	76,838	97,400	104,593	86,588
Commercial banks and others	2,226	2,955	2,374	1,916	1,276	972
Private nonguaranteed debt from:	35,446	42,130	39,691	51,074	50,210	48,458
Bondholders	6,850	8,516	11,703	16,405	15,508	15,271
Commercial banks and others	28,595	33,614	27,988	34,669	34,702	33,187
Use of IMF credit	3,167	2,799	2,716	2,877	30,923	46,924
Net financial inflows						
Net debt inflows						
Use of IMF credit	..	..	..	..	28,623	16,166
Long-term	-3,759	5,699	43,061	34,752	37,356	-9,588
Official creditors	1,703	702	-465	1,358	892	88
Multilateral	1,420	-78	462	1,066	1,669	874
of which: World Bank	236	-142	198	239	557	249
Bilateral	283	780	-927	292	-778	-785
Private creditors	-5,462	4,997	43,526	33,394	36,464	-9,676
Bondholders	-1,185	3,123	39,003	27,275	31,366	-11,021
Banks and others	-4,276	1,873	4,523	6,120	5,098	1,345
Short-term	-904	25,341	-18,073	17,471	12,149	-986
Net equity inflows						
Foreign direct investment	5,027	9,377	7,992	9,095	10,449	6,496
Portfolio equity	-212	239	985	3,013	-508	65
Debt ratios						
External debt stocks to exports (%)	191	245	255	303	340	326
External debt stocks to GNI (%)	41	30	35	38	57	65
Debt service to exports (%)	21	25	35	51	41	47
Short-term to external debt stocks (%)	14	34	22	23	24	24
Multilateral to external debt stocks (%)	12	11	11	9	8	9
Reserves to external debt stocks (%)	34	13	19	22	23	15
Gross national income (GNI)	322,658	582,645	545,339	626,315	501,244	432,302

ARMENIA

(US$ million, unless otherwise indicated)

	2009	2015	2016	2017	2018	2019
Summary external debt data by debtor type						
Total external debt stocks	**4,935**	**8,831**	**9,856**	**10,228**	**10,726**	**11,887**
Use of IMF credit	725	536	528	530	451	375
Long-term external debt	3,681	7,631	8,256	8,810	9,141	9,918
Public and publicly guaranteed sector	2,379	3,998	4,472	5,228	5,371	5,655
Public sector	2,379	3,998	4,472	5,228	5,371	5,655
of which: General government	2,361	3,899	4,351	5,015	5,151	5,441
Private sector guaranteed by public sector	..	..	..	..	..	..
Private sector not guaranteed	1,302	3,633	3,784	3,583	3,770	4,262
Short-term external debt	529	664	1,072	889	1,134	1,595
Disbursements (long-term)	**1,247**	**1,967**	**1,855**	**1,501**	**1,678**	**2,380**
Public and publicly guaranteed sector	941	984	603	677	347	870
Public sector	941	984	603	677	347	870
of which: General government	934	911	575	588	321	856
Private sector guaranteed by public sector	..	..	..	..	..	..
Private sector not guaranteed	306	984	1,252	824	1,331	1,510
Principal repayments (long-term)	**300**	**1,308**	**1,173**	**1,117**	**1,282**	**1,586**
Public and publicly guaranteed sector	21	260	73	91	138	568
Public sector	21	260	73	91	138	568
of which: General government	21	257	69	85	125	550
Private sector guaranteed by public sector	..	..	..	..	..	..
Private sector not guaranteed	279	1,048	1,101	1,026	1,144	1,018
Interest payments (long-term)	**79**	**199**	**224**	**238**	**269**	**362**
Public and publicly guaranteed sector	23	100	123	140	162	189
Public sector	23	100	123	140	162	189
of which: General government	23	99	120	136	156	183
Private sector guaranteed by public sector	..	..	..	..	..	..
Private sector not guaranteed	56	99	101	98	107	174
Summary external debt stock by creditor type						
Long-term external debt stocks	**3,681**	**7,631**	**8,256**	**8,810**	**9,141**	**9,918**
Public and publicly guaranteed debt from:	2,379	3,998	4,472	5,228	5,371	5,655
Official creditors	2,375	2,955	3,423	4,163	4,310	4,499
Multilateral	1,427	2,466	2,824	3,237	3,278	3,352
of which: World Bank	1,214	1,652	1,742	1,810	1,798	1,824
Bilateral	948	489	599	927	1,032	1,147
Private creditors	4	1,043	1,049	1,064	1,061	1,156
Bondholders	..	1,000	1,000	1,000	1,000	1,098
Commercial banks and others	4	43	49	64	61	59
Private nonguaranteed debt from:	1,302	3,633	3,784	3,583	3,770	4,262
Bondholders	..	..	..	..	..	..
Commercial banks and others	1,302	3,633	3,784	3,583	3,770	4,262
Use of IMF credit	725	536	528	530	451	375
Net financial inflows						
Net debt inflows						
Use of IMF credit	442	-9	8	-29	-68	-73
Long-term	947	660	681	384	396	795
Official creditors	920	403	522	578	208	207
Multilateral	309	385	410	301	87	86
of which: World Bank	177	92	123	5	14	31
Bilateral	611	18	113	277	122	120
Private creditors	28	257	159	-193	188	588
Bondholders	..	300	0	0	0	98
Banks and others	28	-43	159	-193	188	490
Short-term	8	-245	408	-183	245	461
Net equity inflows						
Foreign direct investment	718	154	219	70	302	161
Portfolio equity	1	4	4	-3	0	-5
Debt ratios						
External debt stocks to exports (%)	203	220	223	188	184	181
External debt stocks to GNI (%)	55	80	91	86	85	86
Debt service to exports (%)	17	38	33	26	29	32
Short-term to external debt stocks (%)	11	8	11	9	11	13
Multilateral to external debt stocks (%)	29	28	29	32	31	28
Reserves to external debt stocks (%)	41	20	22	23	21	24
Gross national income (GNI)	9,007	10,982	10,791	11,935	12,619	13,901

AZERBAIJAN

(US$ million, unless otherwise indicated)

	2009	2015	2016	2017	2018	2019
Summary external debt data by debtor type						
Total external debt stocks	**4,549**	**13,319**	**14,590**	**15,301**	**16,211**	**15,840**
Use of IMF credit	303	213	206	219	214	212
Long-term external debt	3,651	11,558	12,988	14,407	15,428	15,011
Public and publicly guaranteed sector	3,337	8,712	10,624	12,470	13,956	13,976
Public sector	3,337	8,712	10,624	12,470	13,956	13,976
of which: General government	1,958	6,675	7,339	8,052	7,540	7,776
Private sector guaranteed by public sector	..	..	..	..	..	..
Private sector not guaranteed	314	2,847	2,363	1,937	1,471	1,035
Short-term external debt	595	1,548	1,396	675	570	617
Disbursements (long-term)	**857**	**3,499**	**2,813**	**2,886**	**3,269**	**1,270**
Public and publicly guaranteed sector	807	1,087	2,702	2,822	3,250	1,266
Public sector	807	1,087	2,702	2,822	3,250	1,266
of which: General government	372	737	1,178	1,104	902	767
Private sector guaranteed by public sector	..	..	..	..	..	..
Private sector not guaranteed	50	2,412	111	64	19	4
Principal repayments (long-term)	**265**	**1,584**	**1,329**	**1,771**	**2,122**	**1,647**
Public and publicly guaranteed sector	213	583	735	1,262	1,639	1,201
Public sector	213	583	735	1,262	1,639	1,201
of which: General government	99	387	488	510	1,384	523
Private sector guaranteed by public sector	..	..	..	..	..	..
Private sector not guaranteed	53	1,001	594	509	483	447
Interest payments (long-term)	**67**	**294**	**403**	**443**	**538**	**496**
Public and publicly guaranteed sector	55	208	259	326	446	429
Public sector	55	208	259	326	446	429
of which: General government	28	149	165	201	252	257
Private sector guaranteed by public sector	..	..	..	..	..	..
Private sector not guaranteed	12	86	144	117	91	66
Summary external debt stock by creditor type						
Long-term external debt stocks	**3,651**	**11,558**	**12,988**	**14,407**	**15,428**	**15,011**
Public and publicly guaranteed debt from:	3,337	8,712	10,624	12,470	13,956	13,976
Official creditors	2,287	4,796	5,644	6,662	6,885	7,318
Multilateral	1,459	3,722	4,587	5,569	5,789	6,084
of which: World Bank	939	2,096	2,203	2,665	2,538	2,395
Bilateral	829	1,073	1,057	1,093	1,096	1,234
Private creditors	1,050	3,916	4,981	5,809	7,071	6,658
Bondholders	..	2,250	3,250	3,750	3,750	3,750
Commercial banks and others	1,050	1,666	1,731	2,059	3,321	2,908
Private nonguaranteed debt from:	314	2,847	2,363	1,937	1,471	1,035
Bondholders	..	..	..	..	..	..
Commercial banks and others	314	2,847	2,363	1,937	1,471	1,035
Use of IMF credit	303	213	206	219	214	212
Net financial inflows						
Net debt inflows						
Use of IMF credit	-19	-2	..	..	..	..
Long-term	592	1,915	1,483	1,115	1,147	-377
Official creditors	334	339	865	901	246	433
Multilateral	319	385	891	914	245	302
of which: World Bank	158	200	122	435	-116	-140
Bilateral	15	-46	-26	-13	0	130
Private creditors	258	1,575	618	214	901	-810
Bondholders	..	..	1,000	500	..	0
Banks and others	258	1,575	-382	-286	901	-810
Short-term	-541	-473	-152	-721	-105	47
Net equity inflows						
Foreign direct investment	2,525	4,048	4,500	2,867	1,403	1,504
Portfolio equity	0	24	0	0	0	19
Debt ratios						
External debt stocks to exports (%)	20	63	79	72	60	63
External debt stocks to GNI (%)	11	26	41	39	36	34
Debt service to exports (%)	2	9	10	11	10	9
Short-term to external debt stocks (%)	13	12	10	4	4	4
Multilateral to external debt stocks (%)	32	28	31	36	36	38
Reserves to external debt stocks (%)	118	47	40	44	41	44
Gross national income (GNI)	40,772	51,047	35,395	39,106	44,653	45,987

BANGLADESH
(US$ million, unless otherwise indicated)

	2009	2015	2016	2017	2018	2019
Summary external debt data by debtor type						
Total external debt stocks	**25,372**	**35,960**	**38,474**	**46,812**	**52,132**	**57,088**
Use of IMF credit	1,475	1,613	1,546	1,625	1,536	1,414
Long-term external debt	21,964	27,716	29,093	34,422	41,566	45,937
Public and publicly guaranteed sector	21,179	24,370	26,000	31,027	36,328	41,037
Public sector	21,179	24,370	26,000	31,027	36,328	41,037
of which: General government	21,125	23,825	25,441	30,445	35,753	40,441
Private sector guaranteed by public sector	..	..	..	..	..	..
Private sector not guaranteed	785	3,346	3,093	3,395	5,238	4,901
Short-term external debt	1,933	6,631	7,835	10,765	9,029	9,737
Disbursements (long-term)	**1,931**	**2,774**	**3,259**	**5,521**	**9,690**	**9,181**
Public and publicly guaranteed sector	1,497	2,236	3,079	4,743	6,994	6,068
Public sector	1,497	2,236	3,079	4,743	6,994	6,068
of which: General government	1,497	2,211	3,048	4,720	6,949	6,005
Private sector guaranteed by public sector	..	..	..	..	..	..
Private sector not guaranteed	434	538	180	778	2,696	3,113
Principal repayments (long-term)	**770**	**1,266**	**1,325**	**1,468**	**2,033**	**4,688**
Public and publicly guaranteed sector	699	965	892	993	1,180	1,257
Public sector	699	965	892	993	1,180	1,257
of which: General government	695	965	892	974	1,142	1,220
Private sector guaranteed by public sector	..	..	..	..	..	..
Private sector not guaranteed	71	301	433	475	853	3,431
Interest payments (long-term)	**208**	**233**	**269**	**418**	**485**	**639**
Public and publicly guaranteed sector	197	208	228	359	372	487
Public sector	197	208	228	359	372	487
of which: General government	195	198	217	347	360	476
Private sector guaranteed by public sector	..	..	..	..	..	..
Private sector not guaranteed	11	25	40	59	113	152
Summary external debt stock by creditor type						
Long-term external debt stocks	**21,964**	**27,716**	**29,093**	**34,422**	**41,566**	**45,937**
Public and publicly guaranteed debt from:	21,179	24,370	26,000	31,027	36,328	41,037
Official creditors	21,136	24,338	25,973	30,999	36,305	41,018
Multilateral	18,378	19,987	20,819	23,492	24,944	27,158
of which: World Bank	10,746	11,534	11,890	13,621	14,501	15,788
Bilateral	2,758	4,351	5,155	7,507	11,361	13,860
Private creditors	43	32	27	28	23	19
Bondholders	..	..	..	..	..	..
Commercial banks and others	43	32	27	28	23	19
Private nonguaranteed debt from:	785	3,346	3,093	3,395	5,238	4,901
Bondholders	..	..	..	..	..	..
Commercial banks and others	785	3,346	3,093	3,395	5,238	4,901
Use of IMF credit	1,475	1,613	1,546	1,625	1,536	1,414
Net financial inflows						
Net debt inflows						
Use of IMF credit	-23	209	-19	-13	-52	-114
Long-term	1,161	1,508	1,934	4,053	7,656	4,493
Official creditors	809	1,274	2,191	3,753	5,818	4,814
Multilateral	952	1,022	1,390	1,580	1,954	2,350
of which: World Bank	63	599	716	1,020	1,219	1,387
Bilateral	-143	252	801	2,174	3,864	2,464
Private creditors	351	234	-257	299	1,839	-321
Bondholders	..	..	..	..	..	..
Banks and others	351	234	-257	299	1,839	-321
Short-term	40	2,480	1,204	2,930	-1,736	708
Net equity inflows						
Foreign direct investment	584	2,437	2,127	1,477	1,242	1,371
Portfolio equity	-104	-105	114	258	-33	-28
Debt ratios						
External debt stocks to exports (%)	149	102	102	119	117	127
External debt stocks to GNI (%)	23	17	16	18	18	18
Debt service to exports (%)	6	5	5	5	6	13
Short-term to external debt stocks (%)	8	18	20	23	17	17
Multilateral to external debt stocks (%)	72	56	54	50	48	48
Reserves to external debt stocks (%)	40	75	83	70	60	56
Gross national income (GNI)	110,603	207,743	234,168	260,441	286,536	316,907

BELARUS
(US$ million, unless otherwise indicated)

	2009	2015	2016	2017	2018	2019
Summary external debt data by debtor type						
Total external debt stocks	**22,079**	**38,258**	**37,516**	**39,584**	**38,768**	**40,730**
Use of IMF credit	3,449	511	496	525	513	510
Long-term external debt	9,553	26,273	26,398	29,335	28,729	30,026
Public and publicly guaranteed sector	6,242	15,837	18,142	20,988	19,988	19,511
Public sector	6,223	15,800	18,142	20,988	19,988	19,511
of which: General government	4,548	12,444	13,642	16,727	16,894	17,132
Private sector guaranteed by public sector	19	37	0	..	..	..
Private sector not guaranteed	3,311	10,436	8,257	8,346	8,741	10,514
Short-term external debt	9,076	11,474	10,622	9,725	9,526	10,194
Disbursements (long-term)	**1,985**	**3,778**	**2,615**	**5,811**	**3,743**	**4,106**
Public and publicly guaranteed sector	1,265	2,992	2,143	4,349	2,673	1,996
Public sector	1,265	2,992	2,143	4,349	2,673	1,996
of which: General government	1,242	2,173	1,935	4,039	2,367	1,656
Private sector guaranteed by public sector	..	0	0	..	..	..
Private sector not guaranteed	720	786	472	1,462	1,070	2,111
Principal repayments (long-term)	**1,283**	**3,710**	**5,014**	**3,030**	**4,130**	**2,900**
Public and publicly guaranteed sector	458	2,483	2,314	1,680	3,455	2,563
Public sector	458	2,478	2,277	1,680	3,455	2,563
of which: General government	119	1,926	893	1,029	1,998	1,512
Private sector guaranteed by public sector	..	5	37	..	..	..
Private sector not guaranteed	825	1,228	2,701	1,350	675	338
Interest payments (long-term)	**186**	**980**	**964**	**1,110**	**1,288**	**1,307**
Public and publicly guaranteed sector	115	781	745	868	1,022	1,015
Public sector	113	777	743	868	1,022	1,015
of which: General government	100	593	559	688	789	817
Private sector guaranteed by public sector	2	4	2	..	..	..
Private sector not guaranteed	71	199	219	241	265	292
Summary external debt stock by creditor type						
Long-term external debt stocks	**9,553**	**26,273**	**26,398**	**29,335**	**28,729**	**30,026**
Public and publicly guaranteed debt from:	6,242	15,837	18,142	20,988	19,988	19,511
Official creditors	4,694	13,005	14,071	15,974	16,495	16,595
Multilateral	261	2,838	3,360	3,942	3,810	3,480
of which: World Bank	256	642	725	822	905	948
Bilateral	4,433	10,167	10,710	12,032	12,685	13,115
Private creditors	1,548	2,832	4,071	5,014	3,493	2,916
Bondholders	19	800	800	2,200	2,000	2,162
Commercial banks and others	1,528	2,032	3,271	2,814	1,493	755
Private nonguaranteed debt from:	3,311	10,436	8,257	8,346	8,741	10,514
Bondholders	..	..	..	..	..	..
Commercial banks and others	3,311	10,436	8,257	8,346	8,741	10,514
Use of IMF credit	3,449	511	496	525	513	510
Net financial inflows						
Net debt inflows						
Use of IMF credit	2,825	-77	..	..	..	..
Long-term	702	67	-2,400	2,780	-388	1,206
Official creditors	1,155	1,350	914	1,812	727	15
Multilateral	211	-293	526	563	-124	-329
of which: World Bank	213	52	83	98	83	39
Bilateral	943	1,643	387	1,249	851	344
Private creditors	-453	-1,283	-3,313	968	-1,115	1,191
Bondholders	..	-1,000	0	1,400	-200	154
Banks and others	-453	-283	-3,313	-432	-915	1,036
Short-term	1,517	-1,353	-852	-897	-199	667
Net equity inflows						
Foreign direct investment	1,823	1,434	1,086	1,068	1,390	1,093
Portfolio equity	1	5	0	6	4	7
Debt ratios						
External debt stocks to exports (%)	89	115	123	106	89	95
External debt stocks to GNI (%)	44	71	82	75	67	67
Debt service to exports (%)	7	15	20	12	13	10
Short-term to external debt stocks (%)	41	30	28	25	25	25
Multilateral to external debt stocks (%)	1	7	9	10	10	9
Reserves to external debt stocks (%)	22	7	9	14	13	17
Gross national income (GNI)	50,065	53,957	45,508	52,645	57,886	61,171

BELIZE

(US$ million, unless otherwise indicated)

	2009	2015	2016	2017	2018	2019
Summary external debt data by debtor type						
Total external debt stocks	**1,291**	**1,280**	**1,290**	**1,339**	**1,349**	**1,378**
Use of IMF credit	35	25	24	25	25	25
Long-term external debt	1,246	1,248	1,262	1,309	1,320	1,349
Public and publicly guaranteed sector	1,037	1,153	1,177	1,231	1,260	1,286
Public sector	1,037	1,153	1,177	1,231	1,260	1,286
of which: General government	1,012	1,147	1,167	1,215	1,226	1,244
Private sector guaranteed by public sector	0	..	..	..	..	..
Private sector not guaranteed	209	94	85	78	61	63
Short-term external debt	10	7	4	5	4	4
Disbursements (long-term)	**79**	**95**	**69**	**107**	**77**	**79**
Public and publicly guaranteed sector	66	93	67	98	71	70
Public sector	66	93	67	98	71	70
of which: General government	66	89	63	91	53	60
Private sector guaranteed by public sector	0	..	..	..	..	..
Private sector not guaranteed	13	2	2	9	6	9
Principal repayments (long-term)	**69**	**52**	**54**	**57**	**65**	**50**
Public and publicly guaranteed sector	51	40	43	44	42	44
Public sector	51	40	43	44	42	44
of which: General government	44	39	42	44	41	41
Private sector guaranteed by public sector	0	..	..	..	..	..
Private sector not guaranteed	18	12	11	12	22	6
Interest payments (long-term)	**56**	**46**	**48**	**48**	**49**	**54**
Public and publicly guaranteed sector	45	37	42	42	43	50
Public sector	45	37	42	42	43	50
of which: General government	43	37	42	41	43	48
Private sector guaranteed by public sector	0	..	..	..	..	..
Private sector not guaranteed	11	9	7	6	6	4
Summary external debt stock by creditor type						
Long-term external debt stocks	**1,246**	**1,248**	**1,262**	**1,309**	**1,320**	**1,349**
Public and publicly guaranteed debt from:	1,037	1,153	1,177	1,231	1,260	1,286
Official creditors	432	627	650	679	706	734
Multilateral	251	307	317	336	348	368
of which: World Bank	17	14	17	16	19	19
Bilateral	182	320	334	344	358	366
Private creditors	604	527	527	552	554	552
Bondholders	21	527	527	527	527	527
Commercial banks and others	583	0	..	25	27	25
Private nonguaranteed debt from:	209	94	85	78	61	63
Bondholders	..	..	..	..	..	..
Commercial banks and others	209	94	85	78	61	63
Use of IMF credit	35	25	24	25	25	25
Net financial inflows						
Net debt inflows						
Use of IMF credit	7	..	..	..	..	..
Long-term	10	43	14	50	13	28
Official creditors	28	53	24	28	27	28
Multilateral	19	16	10	18	13	19
of which: World Bank	-5	1	3	0	2	0
Bilateral	9	37	13	10	14	8
Private creditors	-18	-11	-9	22	-14	0
Bondholders	-1	0	0	0	0	0
Banks and others	-17	-11	-9	22	-14	0
Short-term	0	0	0	0	0	0
Net equity inflows						
Foreign direct investment	102	59	33	32	122	103
Portfolio equity	0	..	..	0	0	0
Debt ratios						
External debt stocks to exports (%)	176	123	132	129	125	121
External debt stocks to GNI (%)	105	79	77	80	80	81
Debt service to exports (%)	17	9	10	10	11	9
Short-term to external debt stocks (%)	1	1	0	0	0	0
Multilateral to external debt stocks (%)	19	24	25	25	26	27
Reserves to external debt stocks (%)	17	34	29	23	22	20
Gross national income (GNI)	1,227	1,628	1,667	1,681	1,690	1,707

BENIN
(US$ million, unless otherwise indicated)

	2009	2015	2016	2017	2018	2019
Summary external debt data by debtor type						
Total external debt stocks	**1,327.6**	**2,191.2**	**2,277.9**	**2,817.0**	**3,607.5**	**3,898.9**
Use of IMF credit	131.6	202.3	187.0	226.4	244.6	266.7
Long-term external debt	983.9	1,913.9	2,029.0	2,519.2	3,307.5	3,611.1
Public and publicly guaranteed sector	983.9	1,913.9	2,029.0	2,519.2	3,307.5	3,611.1
Public sector	983.9	1,913.9	2,029.0	2,519.2	3,307.5	3,611.1
of which: General government	983.9	1,913.9	2,029.0	2,519.2	3,307.5	3,611.1
Private sector guaranteed by public sector	..	..	..	..	..	..
Private sector not guaranteed	..	..	..	..	..	..
Short-term external debt	212.0	74.9	61.9	71.4	55.4	21.0
Disbursements (long-term)	**140.9**	**285.4**	**240.2**	**386.1**	**1,061.1**	**760.8**
Public and publicly guaranteed sector	140.9	285.4	240.2	386.1	1,061.1	760.8
Public sector	140.9	285.4	240.2	386.1	1,061.1	760.8
of which: General government	140.9	285.4	240.2	386.1	1,061.1	760.8
Private sector guaranteed by public sector	..	..	..	..	..	..
Private sector not guaranteed	..	..	..	..	..	..
Principal repayments (long-term)	**31.6**	**45.2**	**60.6**	**54.1**	**169.6**	**415.6**
Public and publicly guaranteed sector	31.6	45.2	60.6	54.1	169.6	415.6
Public sector	31.6	45.2	60.6	54.1	169.6	415.6
of which: General government	31.6	45.2	60.6	54.1	169.6	415.6
Private sector guaranteed by public sector	..	..	..	..	..	..
Private sector not guaranteed	..	..	..	..	..	..
Interest payments (long-term)	**11.9**	**24.2**	**27.9**	**32.7**	**40.1**	**76.7**
Public and publicly guaranteed sector	11.9	24.2	27.9	32.7	40.1	76.7
Public sector	11.9	24.2	27.9	32.7	40.1	76.7
of which: General government	11.9	24.2	27.9	32.7	40.1	76.7
Private sector guaranteed by public sector	..	..	..	..	..	..
Private sector not guaranteed	..	..	..	..	..	..
Summary external debt stock by creditor type						
Long-term external debt stocks	**983.9**	**1,913.9**	**2,029.0**	**2,519.2**	**3,307.5**	**3,611.1**
Public and publicly guaranteed debt from:	983.9	1,913.9	2,029.0	2,519.2	3,307.5	3,611.1
Official creditors	983.9	1,913.9	2,029.0	2,478.1	2,492.0	2,546.8
Multilateral	820.7	1,557.1	1,675.9	2,058.2	2,040.5	2,107.7
of which: World Bank	309.2	680.5	764.5	914.2	983.9	1,081.8
Bilateral	163.2	356.8	353.0	419.9	451.6	439.1
Private creditors	..	0.0	0.0	41.1	815.5	1,064.3
Bondholders	..	..	..	..	..	556.6
Commercial banks and others	..	0.0	0.0	41.1	815.5	507.7
Private nonguaranteed debt from:	..	..	..	..	..	..
Bondholders	..	..	..	..	..	..
Commercial banks and others	..	..	..	..	..	..
Use of IMF credit	131.6	202.3	187.0	226.4	244.6	266.7
Net financial inflows						
Net debt inflows						
Use of IMF credit	15.7	-8.4	-9.7	27.6	23.9	23.5
Long-term	109.4	240.2	179.6	332.0	891.5	345.2
Official creditors	109.3	240.2	179.6	293.3	90.7	81.9
Multilateral	100.8	168.6	166.3	245.3	42.0	88.2
of which: World Bank	51.4	87.0	107.9	102.5	93.4	104.3
Bilateral	8.6	71.6	13.3	47.9	48.7	-6.2
Private creditors	..	..	..	38.7	800.8	263.3
Bondholders	..	..	..	..	..	554.7
Banks and others	..	..	..	38.7	800.8	-291.4
Short-term	96.3	-9.1	-7.4	8.7	-14.9	-1.0
Net equity inflows						
Foreign direct investment	-32.2	96.7	31.2	44.3	-13.8	230.2
Portfolio equity	9.0	77.1	9.4	17.5	-0.3	..
Debt ratios						
External debt stocks to exports (%)	88.8	77.3	69.0	82.1	91.2	..
External debt stocks to GNI (%)	13.7	19.4	19.4	22.4	25.6	27.4
Debt service to exports (%)	3.2	2.8	3.0	3.0	5.9	..
Short-term to external debt stocks (%)	16.0	3.4	2.7	2.5	1.5	0.5
Multilateral to external debt stocks (%)	61.8	71.1	73.6	73.1	56.6	54.1
Reserves to external debt stocks (%)	92.6	33.4	..	..	..	..
Gross national income (GNI)	9,666.6	11,295.6	11,718.3	12,561.4	14,106.0	14,247.2

BHUTAN

(US$ million, unless otherwise indicated)

	2009	2015	2016	2017	2018	2019
Summary external debt data by debtor type						
Total external debt stocks	**786.5**	**2,011.1**	**2,289.7**	**2,607.9**	**2,552.0**	**2,703.3**
Use of IMF credit	9.4	8.3	8.1	8.5	8.3	8.3
Long-term external debt	772.2	2,002.8	2,281.5	2,596.4	2,539.3	2,667.2
Public and publicly guaranteed sector	772.2	1,945.1	2,221.2	2,540.8	2,484.2	2,616.3
Public sector	772.2	1,945.1	2,221.2	2,540.8	2,484.2	2,616.3
of which: General government	707.9	1,839.5	2,118.2	2,431.3	2,383.9	2,505.1
Private sector guaranteed by public sector	..	..	..	..	..	..
Private sector not guaranteed	..	57.7	60.3	55.6	55.1	50.9
Short-term external debt	5.0	0.0	0.1	3.0	4.3	27.8
Disbursements (long-term)	**117.9**	**354.4**	**402.0**	**219.8**	**168.1**	**198.4**
Public and publicly guaranteed sector	117.9	297.0	365.0	219.8	168.1	197.7
Public sector	117.9	297.0	365.0	219.8	168.1	197.7
of which: General government	55.9	297.0	365.0	219.8	168.1	184.7
Private sector guaranteed by public sector	..	..	..	..	..	..
Private sector not guaranteed	..	57.3	36.9	..	..	0.7
Principal repayments (long-term)	**41.1**	**91.7**	**75.4**	**46.3**	**51.3**	**28.4**
Public and publicly guaranteed sector	41.1	90.3	41.6	41.6	50.8	23.6
Public sector	41.1	90.3	41.6	41.6	50.8	23.6
of which: General government	41.1	43.5	41.6	41.6	50.8	23.6
Private sector guaranteed by public sector	..	..	..	..	..	..
Private sector not guaranteed	..	1.4	33.8	4.7	0.5	4.9
Interest payments (long-term)	**34.4**	**37.2**	**35.2**	**36.1**	**35.8**	**32.2**
Public and publicly guaranteed sector	34.4	37.1	34.3	33.9	34.0	30.8
Public sector	34.4	37.1	34.3	33.9	34.0	30.8
of which: General government	34.4	31.2	29.1	28.6	28.9	23.4
Private sector guaranteed by public sector	..	..	..	..	..	..
Private sector not guaranteed	..	0.1	1.0	2.2	1.7	1.5
Summary external debt stock by creditor type						
Long-term external debt stocks	**772.2**	**2,002.8**	**2,281.5**	**2,596.4**	**2,539.3**	**2,667.2**
Public and publicly guaranteed debt from:	772.2	1,945.1	2,221.2	2,540.8	2,484.2	2,616.3
Official creditors	767.1	1,904.4	2,186.0	2,505.5	2,455.0	2,592.0
Multilateral	284.4	468.9	460.2	532.5	563.4	646.2
of which: World Bank	113.9	183.4	177.6	219.0	243.7	270.9
Bilateral	482.7	1,435.5	1,725.8	1,973.0	1,891.6	1,945.8
Private creditors	5.1	40.6	35.2	35.3	29.2	24.3
Bondholders	..	..	..	..	..	..
Commercial banks and others	5.1	40.6	35.2	35.3	29.2	24.3
Private nonguaranteed debt from:	..	57.7	60.3	55.6	55.1	50.9
Bondholders	..	..	..	..	..	..
Commercial banks and others	..	57.7	60.3	55.6	55.1	50.9
Use of IMF credit	9.4	8.3	8.1	8.5	8.3	8.3
Net financial inflows						
Net debt inflows						
Use of IMF credit	..	..	..	..	..	..
Long-term	76.8	262.7	326.6	173.5	116.8	170.0
Official creditors	71.9	211.1	327.8	182.6	122.0	178.5
Multilateral	45.6	14.9	1.3	48.1	41.4	85.3
of which: World Bank	18.7	20.7	-0.4	29.7	30.5	28.8
Bilateral	26.3	196.2	326.4	134.5	80.5	93.2
Private creditors	4.9	51.5	-1.2	-9.1	-5.2	-8.6
Bondholders	..	..	..	..	..	..
Banks and others	4.9	51.5	-1.2	-9.1	-5.2	-8.6
Short-term	-3.0	-3.4	0.1	2.9	1.3	23.5
Net equity inflows						
Foreign direct investment	6.2	5.7	11.5	-0.7	3.3	12.6
Portfolio equity	..	0.0	0.0	0.0	0.0	0.0
Debt ratios						
External debt stocks to exports (%)	132.1	268.8	343.4	349.4	313.5	329.9
External debt stocks to GNI (%)	66.5	108.1	116.0	116.6	114.6	..
Debt service to exports (%)	12.7	17.2	16.6	11.1	10.7	7.5
Short-term to external debt stocks (%)	0.6	0.0	0.0	0.1	0.2	1.0
Multilateral to external debt stocks (%)	36.2	23.3	20.1	20.4	22.1	23.9
Reserves to external debt stocks (%)	113.3	54.9	49.2	46.3	38.7	45.4
Gross national income (GNI)	1,183.4	1,860.8	1,973.5	2,237.5	2,226.5	..

BOLIVIA, PLURINATIONAL STATE OF

(US$ million, unless otherwise indicated)

	2009	2015	2016	2017	2018	2019
Summary external debt data by debtor type						
Total external debt stocks	**5,780**	**9,895**	**10,994**	**12,990**	**13,248**	**14,344**
Use of IMF credit	257	227	221	234	228	227
Long-term external debt	5,219	9,242	10,299	12,486	12,317	13,435
Public and publicly guaranteed sector	2,572	6,335	7,010	9,151	9,905	10,951
Public sector	2,572	6,335	7,010	9,151	9,905	10,951
of which: General government	2,364	6,304	6,984	9,126	9,884	10,933
Private sector guaranteed by public sector	..	0	0	..	..	..
Private sector not guaranteed	2,647	2,906	3,289	3,336	2,412	2,484
Short-term external debt	304	426	475	270	703	683
Disbursements (long-term)	**523**	**1,408**	**1,432**	**2,661**	**1,373**	**1,698**
Public and publicly guaranteed sector	426	1,016	1,002	2,390	1,198	1,472
Public sector	426	1,016	1,002	2,390	1,198	1,472
of which: General government	369	1,016	1,002	2,390	1,198	1,472
Private sector guaranteed by public sector	..	0	..	..	..	..
Private sector not guaranteed	97	392	430	271	176	227
Principal repayments (long-term)	**455**	**811**	**550**	**688**	**640**	**658**
Public and publicly guaranteed sector	197	374	280	331	360	412
Public sector	197	373	280	331	360	412
of which: General government	192	246	276	328	356	409
Private sector guaranteed by public sector	..	0	0	..	..	..
Private sector not guaranteed	257	438	270	357	280	246
Interest payments (long-term)	**119**	**170**	**211**	**283**	**346**	**399**
Public and publicly guaranteed sector	71	153	185	250	316	371
Public sector	71	153	185	250	316	371
of which: General government	70	150	184	250	316	370
Private sector guaranteed by public sector	..	0	0	..	..	..
Private sector not guaranteed	48	17	26	33	30	28
Summary external debt stock by creditor type						
Long-term external debt stocks	**5,219**	**9,242**	**10,299**	**12,486**	**12,317**	**13,435**
Public and publicly guaranteed debt from:	2,572	6,335	7,010	9,151	9,905	10,951
Official creditors	2,480	5,323	5,999	7,141	7,897	8,910
Multilateral	1,989	4,648	5,282	6,156	6,710	7,418
of which: World Bank	316	735	770	830	847	927
Bilateral	491	674	717	985	1,187	1,492
Private creditors	92	1,013	1,011	2,010	2,008	2,041
Bondholders	0	1,000	1,000	2,000	2,000	2,000
Commercial banks and others	92	13	11	10	8	41
Private nonguaranteed debt from:	2,647	2,906	3,289	3,336	2,412	2,484
Bondholders	..	..	..	..	..	..
Commercial banks and others	2,647	2,906	3,289	3,336	2,412	2,484
Use of IMF credit	257	227	221	234	228	227
Net financial inflows						
Net debt inflows						
Use of IMF credit	..	..	..	..	..	..
Long-term	68	596	882	1,973	733	1,040
Official creditors	234	644	724	1,060	840	1,027
Multilateral	172	786	661	826	613	713
of which: World Bank	32	259	57	19	37	84
Bilateral	62	-142	63	235	227	314
Private creditors	-166	-48	159	913	-106	13
Bondholders	-10	0	0	1,000	0	0
Banks and others	-156	-48	159	-87	-106	13
Short-term	34	137	49	-205	433	-20
Net equity inflows						
Foreign direct investment	505	371	193	706	220	-186
Portfolio equity	0	19	21	30	24	13
Debt ratios						
External debt stocks to exports (%)	102	99	131	132	126	138
External debt stocks to GNI (%)	35	31	33	36	34	36
Debt service to exports (%)	10	10	9	10	10	10
Short-term to external debt stocks (%)	5	4	4	2	5	5
Multilateral to external debt stocks (%)	34	47	48	47	51	52
Reserves to external debt stocks (%)	131	117	77	65	54	30
Gross national income (GNI)	16,666	31,873	33,320	36,448	39,316	40,101

BOSNIA AND HERZEGOVINA

(US$ million, unless otherwise indicated)

	2009	2015	2016	2017	2018	2019
Summary external debt data by debtor type						
Total external debt stocks	**14,006**	**13,824**	**14,323**	**15,236**	**15,980**	**16,600**
Use of IMF credit	539	800	770	592	466	398
Long-term external debt	12,010	12,377	12,905	14,359	14,748	15,843
Public and publicly guaranteed sector	3,570	4,390	4,401	4,841	4,929	4,880
Public sector	3,570	4,390	4,401	4,841	4,929	4,880
of which: General government	3,562	4,064	4,035	4,430	4,523	4,532
Private sector guaranteed by public sector	..	..	..	..	..	..
Private sector not guaranteed	8,440	7,987	8,504	9,517	9,819	10,964
Short-term external debt	1,457	647	647	286	766	359
Disbursements (long-term)	**474**	**1,247**	**1,407**	**1,468**	**1,053**	**1,699**
Public and publicly guaranteed sector	321	362	401	308	607	410
Public sector	321	362	401	308	607	410
of which: General government	321	235	330	293	556	392
Private sector guaranteed by public sector	..	..	..	..	..	..
Private sector not guaranteed	153	885	1,007	1,160	446	1,290
Principal repayments (long-term)	**230**	**510**	**757**	**451**	**485**	**536**
Public and publicly guaranteed sector	110	342	267	304	342	391
Public sector	110	342	267	304	342	391
of which: General government	109	333	250	286	302	321
Private sector guaranteed by public sector	..	..	..	..	..	..
Private sector not guaranteed	120	168	490	147	143	145
Interest payments (long-term)	**217**	**240**	**261**	**283**	**303**	**332**
Public and publicly guaranteed sector	63	56	65	63	77	80
Public sector	63	56	65	63	77	80
of which: General government	63	53	62	61	75	77
Private sector guaranteed by public sector	..	..	..	..	..	..
Private sector not guaranteed	153	184	196	219	226	253
Summary external debt stock by creditor type						
Long-term external debt stocks	**12,010**	**12,377**	**12,905**	**14,359**	**14,748**	**15,843**
Public and publicly guaranteed debt from:	3,570	4,390	4,401	4,841	4,929	4,880
Official creditors	3,029	4,136	4,203	4,672	4,606	4,594
Multilateral	2,198	3,319	3,397	3,769	3,734	3,739
of which: World Bank	1,520	1,551	1,514	1,572	1,610	1,584
Bilateral	831	817	806	903	872	855
Private creditors	540	254	198	169	322	286
Bondholders	322	121	98	89	256	231
Commercial banks and others	219	132	100	80	66	55
Private nonguaranteed debt from:	8,440	7,987	8,504	9,517	9,819	10,964
Bondholders	..	..	..	..	..	..
Commercial banks and others	8,440	7,987	8,504	9,517	9,819	10,964
Use of IMF credit	539	800	770	592	466	398
Net financial inflows						
Net debt inflows						
Use of IMF credit	282	-54	-6	-218	-114	-66
Long-term	245	737	650	1,018	568	1,164
Official creditors	208	55	183	58	100	49
Multilateral	187	91	175	27	102	56
of which: World Bank	-7	57	0	-36	81	-12
Bilateral	22	-36	8	30	-3	-6
Private creditors	36	682	467	960	468	1,114
Bondholders	..	-21	-21	-21	176	-21
Banks and others	36	703	487	981	291	1,135
Short-term	295	-134	1	-362	481	-407
Net equity inflows						
Foreign direct investment	-202	264	281	433	560	429
Portfolio equity	0	2	3	5	-2	1
Debt ratios						
External debt stocks to exports (%)	263	220	215	191	176	192
External debt stocks to GNI (%)	77	85	85	85	79	83
Debt service to exports (%)	9	13	17	12	11	11
Short-term to external debt stocks (%)	10	5	5	2	5	2
Multilateral to external debt stocks (%)	16	24	24	25	23	23
Reserves to external debt stocks (%)	32	34	35	42	42	43
Gross national income (GNI)	18,292	16,321	16,936	18,015	20,125	20,016

BOTSWANA

(US$ million, unless otherwise indicated)

	2009	2015	2016	2017	2018	2019
Summary external debt data by debtor type						
Total external debt stocks	**1,643**	**2,237**	**2,126**	**1,741**	**1,782**	**1,565**
Use of IMF credit	90	80	77	82	80	79
Long-term external debt	1,395	1,772	1,670	1,552	1,451	1,346
Public and publicly guaranteed sector	1,395	1,772	1,670	1,552	1,451	1,334
Public sector	1,395	1,772	1,670	1,552	1,451	1,334
of which: General government	1,382	1,741	1,648	1,538	1,447	1,334
Private sector guaranteed by public sector	..	..	..	..	..	..
Private sector not guaranteed	..	0	..	..	0	12
Short-term external debt	158	385	379	108	251	139
Disbursements (long-term)	**1,007**	**13**	**44**	**12**	**47**	**48**
Public and publicly guaranteed sector	1,007	13	44	12	47	26
Public sector	1,007	13	44	12	47	26
of which: General government	1,007	13	44	12	47	26
Private sector guaranteed by public sector	..	..	..	..	..	..
Private sector not guaranteed	..	..	..	..	..	22
Principal repayments (long-term)	**36**	**220**	**141**	**144**	**144**	**152**
Public and publicly guaranteed sector	36	141	141	144	144	141
Public sector	36	141	141	144	144	141
of which: General government	32	132	133	135	135	137
Private sector guaranteed by public sector	..	..	..	..	..	..
Private sector not guaranteed	..	80	..	..	..	10
Interest payments (long-term)	**9**	**20**	**18**	**29**	**31**	**40**
Public and publicly guaranteed sector	9	16	18	29	31	40
Public sector	9	16	18	29	31	40
of which: General government	9	16	18	29	31	40
Private sector guaranteed by public sector	..	..	..	..	..	..
Private sector not guaranteed	..	5	..	..	..	1
Summary external debt stock by creditor type						
Long-term external debt stocks	**1,395**	**1,772**	**1,670**	**1,552**	**1,451**	**1,346**
Public and publicly guaranteed debt from:	1,395	1,772	1,670	1,552	1,451	1,334
Official creditors	1,394	1,741	1,648	1,538	1,447	1,334
Multilateral	1,251	1,667	1,583	1,476	1,389	1,287
of which: World Bank	5	131	159	151	174	172
Bilateral	143	75	65	63	58	47
Private creditors	2	31	22	13	4	0
Bondholders	..	..	..	..	..	..
Commercial banks and others	2	31	22	13	4	0
Private nonguaranteed debt from:	..	0	..	..	0	12
Bondholders	..	0	..	..	..	..
Commercial banks and others	..	..	..	..	0	12
Use of IMF credit	90	80	77	82	80	79
Net financial inflows						
Net debt inflows						
Use of IMF credit	..	..	..	..	..	..
Long-term	971	-208	-97	-132	-97	-104
Official creditors	972	-119	-88	-123	-88	-111
Multilateral	976	-108	-81	-118	-84	-100
of which: World Bank	0	-1	27	-7	22	-2
Bilateral	-4	-11	-7	-5	-4	-11
Private creditors	-1	-89	-9	-9	-9	8
Bondholders	..	-80	..	..	..	..
Banks and others	-1	-9	-9	-9	-9	8
Short-term	113	-35	-6	-271	143	-112
Net equity inflows						
Foreign direct investment	213	311	47	160	174	195
Portfolio equity	18	-104	-123	-47	-137	-45
Debt ratios						
External debt stocks to exports (%)	37	30	25	24	23	25
External debt stocks to GNI (%)	16	16	15	11	10	9
Debt service to exports (%)	1	3	2	2	2	3
Short-term to external debt stocks (%)	10	17	18	6	14	9
Multilateral to external debt stocks (%)	76	75	74	85	78	82
Reserves to external debt stocks (%)	530	337	338	430	374	394
Gross national income (GNI)	10,029	13,967	14,376	16,122	17,248	16,961

BRAZIL

(US$ million, unless otherwise indicated)

	2009	2015	2016	2017	2018	2019
Summary external debt data by debtor type						
Total external debt stocks	**281,651**	**543,397**	**543,257**	**543,000**	**557,741**	**569,398**
Use of IMF credit	4,526	4,001	3,881	4,112	4,015	3,992
Long-term external debt	237,339	487,055	482,174	486,480	486,882	485,471
Public and publicly guaranteed sector	87,513	172,887	174,683	181,161	190,192	193,734
Public sector	84,931	170,432	172,853	179,675	189,132	192,745
of which: General government	66,846	68,703	71,178	70,026	70,449	74,583
Private sector guaranteed by public sector	2,582	2,455	1,830	1,485	1,060	988
Private sector not guaranteed	149,826	314,168	307,492	305,320	296,690	291,737
Short-term external debt	39,786	52,341	57,202	52,408	66,844	79,935
Disbursements (long-term)	**57,675**	**93,786**	**106,247**	**96,730**	**105,057**	**114,547**
Public and publicly guaranteed sector	13,732	20,051	19,729	30,315	28,808	23,867
Public sector	12,217	19,814	19,608	30,188	28,675	23,682
of which: General government	6,603	3,032	5,732	7,094	4,655	8,921
Private sector guaranteed by public sector	1,515	238	121	128	134	185
Private sector not guaranteed	43,943	73,735	86,518	66,415	76,249	90,680
Principal repayments (long-term)	**30,473**	**71,342**	**94,709**	**75,668**	**74,509**	**123,447**
Public and publicly guaranteed sector	7,788	22,929	18,983	23,218	28,432	30,489
Public sector	7,649	22,031	18,238	22,718	27,874	30,236
of which: General government	6,025	5,141	3,809	8,450	3,645	4,659
Private sector guaranteed by public sector	138	898	745	500	558	252
Private sector not guaranteed	22,685	48,413	75,726	52,450	46,077	92,958
Interest payments (long-term)	**13,554**	**17,724**	**21,605**	**18,467**	**18,681**	**25,696**
Public and publicly guaranteed sector	5,656	5,895	5,537	6,696	5,679	11,379
Public sector	5,585	5,811	5,460	6,639	5,630	11,339
of which: General government	4,891	3,330	3,163	3,348	3,186	3,543
Private sector guaranteed by public sector	72	85	78	57	49	40
Private sector not guaranteed	7,898	11,828	16,068	11,771	13,002	14,317
Summary external debt stock by creditor type						
Long-term external debt stocks	**237,339**	**487,055**	**482,174**	**486,480**	**486,882**	**485,471**
Public and publicly guaranteed debt from:	87,513	172,887	174,683	181,161	190,192	193,734
Official creditors	32,702	42,083	41,064	48,327	47,860	43,167
Multilateral	25,013	31,657	32,071	32,678	33,386	33,262
of which: World Bank	10,065	15,753	16,255	16,390	16,213	16,253
Bilateral	7,689	10,426	8,993	15,650	14,474	9,905
Private creditors	54,811	130,805	133,619	132,833	142,332	150,567
Bondholders	47,350	46,628	46,843	44,874	41,979	43,507
Commercial banks and others	7,461	84,176	86,776	87,959	100,354	107,060
Private nonguaranteed debt from:	149,826	314,168	307,492	305,320	296,690	291,737
Bondholders	53,342	51,276	46,930	48,026	32,686	37,553
Commercial banks and others	96,483	262,891	260,562	257,294	264,004	254,184
Use of IMF credit	4,526	4,001	3,881	4,112	4,015	3,992
Net financial inflows						
Net debt inflows						
Use of IMF credit	..	..	..	..	..	..
Long-term	27,202	22,444	11,538	21,062	30,548	-8,900
Official creditors	3,387	-239	-1,012	7,140	-358	-4,689
Multilateral	405	507	427	633	787	-105
of which: World Bank	-598	474	516	159	-114	43
Bilateral	2,982	-746	-1,439	6,506	-1,144	-4,584
Private creditors	23,815	22,682	12,550	13,922	30,906	-4,211
Bondholders	17,770	-5,443	-7,710	-643	1,287	-521
Banks and others	6,045	28,125	20,260	14,565	29,619	-3,689
Short-term	3,142	-5,818	4,860	-4,798	14,440	13,092
Net equity inflows						
Foreign direct investment	19,906	41,888	48,854	63,999	57,322	67,961
Portfolio equity	37,071	9,787	11,040	5,674	-3,062	-2,689
Debt ratios						
External debt stocks to exports (%)	149	240	236	197	194	199
External debt stocks to GNI (%)	17	31	31	27	30	32
Debt service to exports (%)	23	40	51	35	33	53
Short-term to external debt stocks (%)	14	10	11	10	12	14
Multilateral to external debt stocks (%)	9	6	6	6	6	6
Reserves to external debt stocks (%)	84	65	67	68	67	62
Gross national income (GNI)	1,630,133	1,768,302	1,757,604	2,024,254	1,832,171	1,790,969

47

BULGARIA
(US$ million, unless otherwise indicated)

	2009	2015	2016	2017	2018	2019
Summary external debt data by debtor type						
Total external debt stocks	**55,683**	**40,379**	**39,994**	**40,989**	**40,103**	**40,501**
Use of IMF credit	958	847	821	870	850	845
Long-term external debt	36,928	30,759	30,563	30,583	29,708	29,762
Public and publicly guaranteed sector	5,080	8,781	11,050	11,630	11,506	11,186
Public sector	5,080	8,781	11,050	11,630	11,506	11,186
of which: General government	4,287	8,495	10,171	10,424	10,419	10,195
Private sector guaranteed by public sector	..	..	..	..	..	..
Private sector not guaranteed	31,848	21,978	19,513	18,953	18,202	18,576
Short-term external debt	17,797	8,773	8,609	9,536	9,546	9,895
Disbursements (long-term)	**8,635**	**7,236**	**7,090**	**5,445**	**5,052**	**4,554**
Public and publicly guaranteed sector	530	3,752	2,875	312	917	150
Public sector	530	3,752	2,875	312	917	150
of which: General government	500	3,712	2,216	46	892	150
Private sector guaranteed by public sector	..	..	..	..	..	..
Private sector not guaranteed	8,105	3,484	4,215	5,132	4,135	4,405
Principal repayments (long-term)	**3,990**	**7,175**	**5,795**	**6,844**	**5,055**	**4,286**
Public and publicly guaranteed sector	404	230	274	1,355	300	256
Public sector	404	230	274	1,355	300	256
of which: General government	316	174	220	1,294	203	179
Private sector guaranteed by public sector	..	..	..	..	..	..
Private sector not guaranteed	3,585	6,945	5,521	5,489	4,754	4,029
Interest payments (long-term)	**800**	**2,106**	**2,170**	**1,713**	**1,388**	**1,179**
Public and publicly guaranteed sector	208	169	247	304	269	276
Public sector	208	169	247	304	269	276
of which: General government	181	162	237	290	253	261
Private sector guaranteed by public sector	..	..	..	..	..	..
Private sector not guaranteed	592	1,936	1,923	1,408	1,118	903
Summary external debt stock by creditor type						
Long-term external debt stocks	**36,928**	**30,759**	**30,563**	**30,583**	**29,708**	**29,762**
Public and publicly guaranteed debt from:	5,080	8,781	11,050	11,630	11,506	11,186
Official creditors	3,331	2,685	3,046	3,664	3,214	3,050
Multilateral	2,516	2,376	2,786	3,339	2,966	2,839
of which: World Bank	1,509	786	920	1,148	831	727
Bilateral	815	309	261	325	247	211
Private creditors	1,749	6,096	8,004	7,967	8,292	8,136
Bondholders	1,725	6,089	7,997	7,960	8,286	8,130
Commercial banks and others	24	7	6	7	6	6
Private nonguaranteed debt from:	31,848	21,978	19,513	18,953	18,202	18,576
Bondholders	146	1,497	1,549	1,686	1,405	1,489
Commercial banks and others	31,702	20,481	17,964	17,267	16,797	17,086
Use of IMF credit	958	847	821	870	850	845
Net financial inflows						
Net debt inflows						
Use of IMF credit	..	..	..	..	..	..
Long-term	4,646	61	1,295	-1,399	-2	268
Official creditors	263	27	434	31	-91	-107
Multilateral	268	81	492	-14	-15	-70
of which: World Bank	285	-87	150	-80	-60	-87
Bilateral	-5	-54	-58	45	-76	-36
Private creditors	4,383	34	861	-1,430	89	375
Bondholders	-495	3,548	2,220	-941	560	86
Banks and others	4,878	-3,514	-1,359	-488	-471	289
Short-term	-537	-2,331	-159	897	-113	260
Net equity inflows						
Foreign direct investment	2,249	2,791	1,498	983	1,404	490
Portfolio equity	8	-9	-20	155	109	-52
Debt ratios						
External debt stocks to exports (%)	228	121	112	99	89	91
External debt stocks to GNI (%)	111	82	77	71	60	61
Debt service to exports (%)	20	28	23	21	15	13
Short-term to external debt stocks (%)	32	22	22	23	24	24
Multilateral to external debt stocks (%)	5	6	7	8	7	7
Reserves to external debt stocks (%)	31	51	59	65	67	64
Gross national income (GNI)	50,333	49,050	52,132	57,542	66,815	66,046

48

BURKINA FASO
(US$ million, unless otherwise indicated)

	2009	2015	2016	2017	2018	2019
Summary external debt data by debtor type						
Total external debt stocks	1,918	2,632	2,825	3,129	3,286	3,662
Use of IMF credit	201	283	286	284	269	310
Long-term external debt	1,718	2,349	2,539	2,845	3,017	3,353
Public and publicly guaranteed sector	1,716	2,339	2,532	2,835	3,006	3,342
Public sector	1,716	2,339	2,532	2,835	3,006	3,342
of which: General government	1,716	2,339	2,532	2,835	3,006	3,342
Private sector guaranteed by public sector	..	..	..	..	..	..
Private sector not guaranteed	2	10	7	10	11	10
Short-term external debt	0	0	0	0	0	0
Disbursements (long-term)	218	274	264	184	340	462
Public and publicly guaranteed sector	217	271	262	183	338	462
Public sector	217	271	262	183	338	462
of which: General government	217	271	262	183	338	462
Private sector guaranteed by public sector	..	..	..	..	..	..
Private sector not guaranteed	1	3	2	1	2	..
Principal repayments (long-term)	28	71	71	78	78	92
Public and publicly guaranteed sector	28	70	70	77	77	91
Public sector	28	70	70	77	77	91
of which: General government	28	70	70	77	77	91
Private sector guaranteed by public sector	..	..	..	..	..	..
Private sector not guaranteed	0	1	1	1	1	1
Interest payments (long-term)	15	23	31	33	32	32
Public and publicly guaranteed sector	15	22	31	32	31	31
Public sector	15	22	31	32	31	31
of which: General government	15	22	31	32	31	31
Private sector guaranteed by public sector	..	..	..	..	..	..
Private sector not guaranteed	0	0	0	0	1	0
Summary external debt stock by creditor type						
Long-term external debt stocks	1,718	2,349	2,539	2,845	3,017	3,353
Public and publicly guaranteed debt from:	1,716	2,339	2,532	2,835	3,006	3,342
Official creditors	1,694	2,336	2,531	2,835	3,006	3,342
Multilateral	1,403	2,039	2,195	2,506	2,664	3,003
of which: World Bank	721	1,038	1,171	1,334	1,458	1,673
Bilateral	292	298	336	329	342	340
Private creditors	22	3	1	0	..	0
Bondholders	..	..	..	..	..	..
Commercial banks and others	22	3	1	0	..	0
Private nonguaranteed debt from:	2	10	7	10	11	10
Bondholders	..	..	..	..	..	..
Commercial banks and others	2	10	7	10	11	10
Use of IMF credit	201	283	286	284	269	310
Net financial inflows						
Net debt inflows						
Use of IMF credit	54	12	12	-18	-9	42
Long-term	190	203	193	106	262	370
Official creditors	190	204	194	107	261	371
Multilateral	183	163	199	129	241	370
of which: World Bank	90	130	166	78	166	228
Bilateral	7	41	-5	-23	20	1
Private creditors	0	-1	0	-1	1	-1
Bondholders	..	..	..	..	..	..
Banks and others	0	-1	0	-1	1	-1
Short-term	-8	0	0	0	0	0
Net equity inflows						
Foreign direct investment	9	108	166	93	242	208
Portfolio equity	0	4	35	28	31	..
Debt ratios						
External debt stocks to exports (%)	168	90	82	80	69	..
External debt stocks to GNI (%)	..	23	24	23	21	24
Debt service to exports (%)	4	4	4	3	3	..
Short-term to external debt stocks (%)	0	0	0	0	0	0
Multilateral to external debt stocks (%)	73	77	78	80	81	82
Reserves to external debt stocks (%)	68	10	..	..	..	..
Gross national income (GNI)	..	11,321	11,997	13,640	15,719	15,326

BURUNDI

(US$ million, unless otherwise indicated)

	2009	2015	2016	2017	2018	2019
Summary external debt data by debtor type						
Total external debt stocks	607.2	626.0	602.8	614.0	589.3	578.4
Use of IMF credit	206.7	217.6	193.6	188.1	166.4	149.1
Long-term external debt	393.5	408.1	408.9	425.6	422.7	428.9
Public and publicly guaranteed sector	393.5	408.1	408.9	425.6	422.7	428.9
Public sector	393.5	408.1	408.9	425.6	422.7	428.9
of which: General government	392.2	408.1	397.6	414.4	411.5	413.3
Private sector guaranteed by public sector	..	..	..	..	..	..
Private sector not guaranteed	..	..	..	..	..	..
Short-term external debt	7.0	0.3	0.3	0.3	0.3	0.3
Disbursements (long-term)	39.3	21.0	19.0	20.1	10.7	27.6
Public and publicly guaranteed sector	39.3	21.0	19.0	20.1	10.7	27.6
Public sector	39.3	21.0	19.0	20.1	10.7	27.6
of which: General government	39.3	21.0	7.8	20.1	10.7	22.9
Private sector guaranteed by public sector	..	..	..	..	..	..
Private sector not guaranteed	..	..	..	..	..	..
Principal repayments (long-term)	8.5	5.7	11.5	15.7	8.4	20.6
Public and publicly guaranteed sector	8.5	5.7	11.5	15.7	8.4	20.6
Public sector	8.5	5.7	11.5	15.7	8.4	20.6
of which: General government	7.8	5.7	11.5	15.7	8.4	20.3
Private sector guaranteed by public sector	..	..	..	..	..	..
Private sector not guaranteed	..	..	..	..	..	..
Interest payments (long-term)	3.6	3.7	3.7	2.7	3.1	2.5
Public and publicly guaranteed sector	3.6	3.7	3.7	2.7	3.1	2.5
Public sector	3.6	3.7	3.7	2.7	3.1	2.5
of which: General government	3.6	3.7	3.7	2.7	3.0	2.5
Private sector guaranteed by public sector	..	..	..	..	..	..
Private sector not guaranteed	..	..	..	..	..	..
Summary external debt stock by creditor type						
Long-term external debt stocks	393.5	408.1	408.9	425.6	422.7	428.9
Public and publicly guaranteed debt from:	393.5	408.1	408.9	425.6	422.7	428.9
Official creditors	393.5	408.1	408.9	425.6	422.7	428.9
Multilateral	303.4	307.2	310.6	318.4	314.5	318.5
of which: World Bank	147.2	150.6	143.0	148.2	141.5	137.5
Bilateral	90.1	100.9	98.3	107.2	108.3	110.4
Private creditors	..	..	..	..	..	..
Bondholders	..	..	..	..	..	..
Commercial banks and others	..	..	..	..	..	..
Private nonguaranteed debt from:	..	..	..	..	..	..
Bondholders	..	..	..	..	..	..
Commercial banks and others	..	..	..	..	..	..
Use of IMF credit	206.7	217.6	193.6	188.1	166.4	149.1
Net financial inflows						
Net debt inflows						
Use of IMF credit	13.4	-10.5	-18.0	-16.6	-17.6	-16.2
Long-term	30.8	15.3	7.5	4.4	2.3	7.0
Official creditors	30.8	15.3	7.5	4.4	2.3	7.0
Multilateral	25.8	2.9	9.0	-3.4	0.4	4.9
of which: World Bank	8.6	-3.2	-3.2	-3.2	-3.3	-3.2
Bilateral	5.0	12.4	-1.5	7.7	1.9	2.1
Private creditors	..	..	..	..	..	..
Bondholders	..	..	..	..	..	..
Banks and others	..	..	..	..	..	..
Short-term	-7.0	-48.0	0.0	0.0	0.0	0.0
Net equity inflows						
Foreign direct investment	0.3	49.6	0.1	0.3	1.0	1.0
Portfolio equity	..	..	..	..	..	..
Debt ratios						
External debt stocks to exports (%)	507.2	323.5	289.1	216.1	195.2	..
External debt stocks to GNI (%)	34.4	20.2	20.4	19.4	19.4	19.2
Debt service to exports (%)	16.6	13.9	16.0	12.3	9.7	..
Short-term to external debt stocks (%)	1.2	0.0	0.0	0.0	0.0	0.0
Multilateral to external debt stocks (%)	50.0	49.1	51.5	51.9	53.4	55.1
Reserves to external debt stocks (%)	53.0	21.6	15.6	15.7	11.3	19.0
Gross national income (GNI)	1,764.5	3,102.7	2,958.8	3,167.5	3,043.0	3,019.5

50

CABO VERDE
(US$ million, unless otherwise indicated)

	2009	2015	2016	2017	2018	2019
Summary external debt data by debtor type						
Total external debt stocks	**724.6**	**1,550.2**	**1,551.7**	**1,790.0**	**1,767.5**	**1,821.2**
Use of IMF credit	25.4	12.7	12.3	13.1	12.8	12.7
Long-term external debt	697.7	1,537.5	1,539.4	1,776.9	1,754.7	1,808.5
Public and publicly guaranteed sector	697.7	1,537.5	1,539.4	1,776.9	1,754.7	1,808.5
Public sector	697.7	1,534.3	1,536.3	1,774.0	1,752.1	1,806.5
of which: General government	697.7	1,534.3	1,536.3	1,774.0	1,752.1	1,806.5
Private sector guaranteed by public sector	..	3.2	3.1	2.9	2.6	2.0
Private sector not guaranteed	..	..	..	..	..	..
Short-term external debt	1.5	0.0	0.0	0.0	0.0	0.1
Disbursements (long-term)	**102.3**	**141.2**	**69.5**	**111.8**	**75.2**	**118.4**
Public and publicly guaranteed sector	102.3	141.2	69.5	111.8	75.2	118.4
Public sector	102.3	141.2	69.5	111.8	75.2	118.4
of which: General government	102.3	141.2	69.5	111.8	75.2	118.4
Private sector guaranteed by public sector	..	..	..	..	..	..
Private sector not guaranteed	..	..	..	..	..	..
Principal repayments (long-term)	**24.5**	**23.7**	**25.6**	**32.6**	**36.7**	**42.1**
Public and publicly guaranteed sector	24.5	23.7	25.6	32.6	36.7	42.1
Public sector	24.5	23.7	25.6	32.2	36.5	41.5
of which: General government	24.5	23.7	25.6	32.2	36.5	41.5
Private sector guaranteed by public sector	..	..	..	0.4	0.2	0.6
Private sector not guaranteed	..	..	..	..	..	..
Interest payments (long-term)	**6.8**	**17.8**	**18.1**	**18.1**	**19.2**	**19.2**
Public and publicly guaranteed sector	6.8	17.8	18.1	18.1	19.2	19.2
Public sector	6.8	17.8	18.1	18.1	19.2	19.1
of which: General government	6.8	17.8	18.1	18.1	19.2	19.1
Private sector guaranteed by public sector	..	..	..	..	..	0.1
Private sector not guaranteed	..	..	..	..	..	..
Summary external debt stock by creditor type						
Long-term external debt stocks	**697.7**	**1,537.5**	**1,539.4**	**1,776.9**	**1,754.7**	**1,808.5**
Public and publicly guaranteed debt from:	697.7	1,537.5	1,539.4	1,776.9	1,754.7	1,808.5
Official creditors	691.2	1,076.7	1,077.7	1,238.3	1,240.5	1,301.5
Multilateral	533.9	735.2	737.2	811.6	816.9	882.5
of which: World Bank	286.4	357.4	344.7	361.7	351.4	406.1
Bilateral	157.3	341.5	340.5	426.7	423.6	419.0
Private creditors	6.5	460.7	461.7	538.6	514.2	507.0
Bondholders	..	..	..	..	..	..
Commercial banks and others	6.5	460.7	461.7	538.6	514.2	507.0
Private nonguaranteed debt from:	..	..	..	..	..	..
Bondholders	..	..	..	..	..	..
Commercial banks and others	..	..	..	..	..	..
Use of IMF credit	25.4	12.7	12.3	13.1	12.8	12.7
Net financial inflows						
Net debt inflows						
Use of IMF credit	-1.5	-0.3	..	..	..	..
Long-term	77.8	117.5	43.9	79.2	38.5	76.3
Official creditors	81.4	88.9	27.5	66.7	38.5	73.9
Multilateral	45.8	57.7	20.7	17.0	28.4	74.1
of which: World Bank	0.5	17.4	-2.0	-6.3	-1.0	57.0
Bilateral	35.6	31.2	6.8	49.7	10.1	-0.2
Private creditors	-3.6	28.6	16.4	12.5	0.0	2.5
Bondholders	..	..	..	..	..	..
Banks and others	-3.6	28.6	16.4	12.5	0.0	2.5
Short-term	..	..	..	..	..	..
Net equity inflows						
Foreign direct investment	122.8	99.9	125.5	120.0	107.8	100.0
Portfolio equity	1.9	0.0	0.0	0.0	0.0	0.0
Debt ratios						
External debt stocks to exports (%)	123.8	230.6	209.7	216.8	177.1	175.2
External debt stocks to GNI (%)	43.4	100.8	96.8	104.8	92.0	93.9
Debt service to exports (%)	5.6	6.2	5.9	6.1	5.6	5.9
Short-term to external debt stocks (%)	0.2	0.0	0.0	0.0	0.0	0.0
Multilateral to external debt stocks (%)	73.7	47.4	47.5	45.3	46.2	48.5
Reserves to external debt stocks (%)	54.9	31.9	36.9	34.5	34.3	40.5
Gross national income (GNI)	1,668.5	1,537.7	1,603.7	1,708.7	1,920.6	1,939.5

CAMBODIA

(US$ million, unless otherwise indicated)

	2009	2015	2016	2017	2018	2019
Summary external debt data by debtor type						
Total external debt stocks	3,295	9,424	10,049	11,414	13,522	15,329
Use of IMF credit	132	116	113	120	117	116
Long-term external debt	2,933	7,988	8,209	9,516	11,039	11,801
Public and publicly guaranteed sector	2,739	5,626	5,820	6,566	6,984	7,562
Public sector	2,739	5,626	5,820	6,566	6,984	7,562
of which: General government	2,739	5,626	5,820	6,566	6,984	7,562
Private sector guaranteed by public sector	..	..	..	..	..	..
Private sector not guaranteed	194	2,362	2,388	2,951	4,056	4,239
Short-term external debt	230	1,320	1,727	1,778	2,366	3,413
Disbursements (long-term)	404	1,654	1,075	1,967	2,749	2,049
Public and publicly guaranteed sector	209	619	520	658	716	824
Public sector	209	619	520	658	716	824
of which: General government	209	619	520	658	716	824
Private sector guaranteed by public sector	..	..	..	..	..	..
Private sector not guaranteed	194	1,036	555	1,310	2,033	1,226
Principal repayments (long-term)	26	610	642	887	1,109	1,260
Public and publicly guaranteed sector	26	80	113	139	180	218
Public sector	26	80	113	139	180	218
of which: General government	26	80	113	139	180	218
Private sector guaranteed by public sector	..	..	..	..	..	..
Private sector not guaranteed	..	530	529	747	928	1,042
Interest payments (long-term)	21	63	83	87	103	139
Public and publicly guaranteed sector	21	57	72	72	85	93
Public sector	21	57	72	72	85	93
of which: General government	21	57	72	72	85	93
Private sector guaranteed by public sector	..	..	..	..	..	..
Private sector not guaranteed	1	7	11	15	17	47
Summary external debt stock by creditor type						
Long-term external debt stocks	2,933	7,988	8,209	9,516	11,039	11,801
Public and publicly guaranteed debt from:	2,739	5,626	5,820	6,566	6,984	7,562
Official creditors	2,739	5,626	5,820	6,566	6,984	7,562
Multilateral	1,501	1,681	1,735	1,938	1,957	2,102
of which: World Bank	566	541	518	550	544	585
Bilateral	1,237	3,945	4,086	4,628	5,026	5,459
Private creditors	..	..	..	..	..	..
Bondholders	..	..	..	..	..	..
Commercial banks and others	..	..	..	..	..	..
Private nonguaranteed debt from:	194	2,362	2,388	2,951	4,056	4,239
Bondholders	..	..	..	..	300	300
Commercial banks and others	194	2,362	2,388	2,951	3,756	3,939
Use of IMF credit	132	116	113	120	117	116
Net financial inflows						
Net debt inflows						
Use of IMF credit	..	..	..	..	..	..
Long-term	377	1,044	433	1,081	1,641	790
Official creditors	183	539	407	518	536	606
Multilateral	68	64	106	98	65	157
of which: World Bank	16	-11	-7	1	7	44
Bilateral	115	475	301	420	470	450
Private creditors	194	505	26	562	1,105	183
Bondholders	..	..	..	..	300	..
Banks and others	194	505	26	562	805	183
Short-term	149	233	407	51	588	1,046
Net equity inflows						
Foreign direct investment	928	1,823	2,476	2,788	3,213	3,663
Portfolio equity	0	0	0	0	0	0
Debt ratios						
External debt stocks to exports (%)	66	69	68	70	71	70
External debt stocks to GNI (%)	33	56	53	55	59	62
Debt service to exports (%)	1	5	5	6	7	7
Short-term to external debt stocks (%)	7	14	17	16	17	22
Multilateral to external debt stocks (%)	46	18	17	17	14	14
Reserves to external debt stocks (%)	87	73	84	99	99	111
Gross national income (GNI)	9,951	16,945	18,788	20,800	22,915	24,752

CAMEROON

(US$ million, unless otherwise indicated)

	2009	2015	2016	2017	2018	2019
Summary external debt data by debtor type						
Total external debt stocks	**3,237**	**7,305**	**7,827**	**10,010**	**10,864**	**12,815**
Use of IMF credit	453	358	318	602	714	760
Long-term external debt	2,782	6,648	7,246	8,880	9,717	11,678
Public and publicly guaranteed sector	2,167	5,731	6,234	7,954	9,014	10,275
Public sector	2,167	5,731	6,234	7,954	9,014	10,275
of which: General government	2,157	5,729	6,233	7,953	9,013	10,274
Private sector guaranteed by public sector	..	..	..	..	..	..
Private sector not guaranteed	615	918	1,012	925	703	1,403
Short-term external debt	3	299	262	528	433	377
Disbursements (long-term)	**356**	**1,703**	**1,458**	**1,648**	**1,692**	**2,644**
Public and publicly guaranteed sector	147	1,646	1,209	1,588	1,638	1,807
Public sector	147	1,646	1,209	1,588	1,638	1,807
of which: General government	147	1,646	1,209	1,588	1,638	1,807
Private sector guaranteed by public sector	..	..	..	..	..	..
Private sector not guaranteed	209	57	249	61	53	837
Principal repayments (long-term)	**344**	**317**	**614**	**413**	**621**	**788**
Public and publicly guaranteed sector	115	270	341	175	371	463
Public sector	115	270	341	175	371	463
of which: General government	110	270	340	175	370	462
Private sector guaranteed by public sector	..	..	..	..	..	..
Private sector not guaranteed	229	47	273	238	250	325
Interest payments (long-term)	**57**	**157**	**280**	**272**	**405**	**349**
Public and publicly guaranteed sector	26	115	168	240	237	237
Public sector	26	115	168	240	237	237
of which: General government	26	115	168	240	237	237
Private sector guaranteed by public sector	..	..	..	..	..	..
Private sector not guaranteed	31	42	112	32	168	112
Summary external debt stock by creditor type						
Long-term external debt stocks	**2,782**	**6,648**	**7,246**	**8,880**	**9,717**	**11,678**
Public and publicly guaranteed debt from:	2,167	5,731	6,234	7,954	9,014	10,275
Official creditors	2,156	4,746	5,283	6,880	7,800	8,954
Multilateral	687	1,619	1,886	2,448	3,208	3,768
of which: World Bank	303	798	897	1,306	1,432	1,733
Bilateral	1,469	3,127	3,396	4,431	4,592	5,186
Private creditors	11	984	951	1,075	1,214	1,321
Bondholders	..	750	687	687	687	687
Commercial banks and others	11	234	265	388	527	635
Private nonguaranteed debt from:	615	918	1,012	925	703	1,403
Bondholders	..	..	..	..	..	..
Commercial banks and others	615	918	1,012	925	703	1,403
Use of IMF credit	**453**	**358**	**318**	**602**	**714**	**760**
Net financial inflows						
Net debt inflows						
Use of IMF credit	147	-31	-30	258	128	50
Long-term	12	1,386	845	1,235	1,071	1,856
Official creditors	24	547	896	1,318	1,112	1,230
Multilateral	71	209	247	480	857	599
of which: World Bank	41	90	127	353	165	312
Bilateral	-47	339	649	837	255	630
Private creditors	-12	839	-51	-82	-41	626
Bondholders	..	750	-63	..	..	..
Banks and others	-12	89	12	-82	-41	626
Short-term	0	123	-36	262	-95	-62
Net equity inflows						
Foreign direct investment	817	65	48	219	476	782
Portfolio equity	0	-21	0	0	0	..
Debt ratios						
External debt stocks to exports (%)	59	106	121	148	145	..
External debt stocks to GNI (%)	12	24	24	29	29	34
Debt service to exports (%)	7	7	14	11	14	..
Short-term to external debt stocks (%)	0	4	3	5	4	3
Multilateral to external debt stocks (%)	21	22	24	24	30	29
Reserves to external debt stocks (%)	114	48	28	32	32	..
Gross national income (GNI)	25,904	30,492	32,085	34,348	37,875	38,004

CENTRAL AFRICAN REPUBLIC

(US$ million, unless otherwise indicated)

	2009	2015	2016	2017	2018	2019
Summary external debt data by debtor type						
Total external debt stocks	**550.6**	**730.7**	**735.3**	**762.5**	**819.5**	**880.2**
Use of IMF credit	162.1	174.9	184.6	235.4	279.1	296.5
Long-term external debt	303.1	465.5	461.9	438.2	452.0	451.8
Public and publicly guaranteed sector	303.1	465.5	461.9	438.2	452.0	451.8
Public sector	303.1	465.5	461.9	438.2	452.0	451.8
of which: General government	282.2	450.6	447.5	435.2	449.4	450.1
Private sector guaranteed by public sector	..	..	..	..	..	..
Private sector not guaranteed	..	..	..	..	..	..
Short-term external debt	85.5	90.3	88.7	88.9	88.4	131.9
Disbursements (long-term)	**22.6**	**88.1**	**11.0**	**14.6**	**61.1**	**27.5**
Public and publicly guaranteed sector	22.6	88.1	11.0	14.6	61.1	27.5
Public sector	22.6	88.1	11.0	14.6	61.1	27.5
of which: General government	22.6	88.1	11.0	14.6	61.1	27.5
Private sector guaranteed by public sector	..	..	..	..	..	..
Private sector not guaranteed	..	..	..	..	..	..
Principal repayments (long-term)	**8.4**	**0.9**	**4.3**	**15.3**	**9.9**	**14.2**
Public and publicly guaranteed sector	8.4	0.9	4.3	15.3	9.9	14.2
Public sector	8.4	0.9	4.3	15.3	9.9	14.2
of which: General government	8.3	0.8	4.3	2.7	9.6	13.4
Private sector guaranteed by public sector	..	..	..	..	..	..
Private sector not guaranteed	..	..	..	..	..	..
Interest payments (long-term)	**3.0**	**2.6**	**1.5**	**3.2**	**2.0**	**2.2**
Public and publicly guaranteed sector	3.0	2.6	1.5	3.2	2.0	2.2
Public sector	3.0	2.6	1.5	3.2	2.0	2.2
of which: General government	3.0	2.6	1.5	1.3	2.0	2.2
Private sector guaranteed by public sector	..	..	..	..	..	..
Private sector not guaranteed	..	..	..	..	..	..
Summary external debt stock by creditor type						
Long-term external debt stocks	**303.1**	**465.5**	**461.9**	**438.2**	**452.0**	**451.8**
Public and publicly guaranteed debt from:	303.1	465.5	461.9	438.2	452.0	451.8
Official creditors	266.7	419.7	416.2	392.2	406.1	407.2
Multilateral	49.8	75.6	78.5	95.9	151.8	149.9
of which: World Bank	9.0	58.6	59.9	64.2	98.5	107.0
Bilateral	217.0	344.1	337.7	296.3	254.3	257.3
Private creditors	36.3	45.8	45.7	46.0	45.9	44.6
Bondholders	..	..	..	..	..	..
Commercial banks and others	36.3	45.8	45.7	46.0	45.9	44.6
Private nonguaranteed debt from:	..	..	..	..	..	..
Bondholders	..	..	..	..	..	..
Commercial banks and others	..	..	..	..	..	..
Use of IMF credit	162.1	174.9	184.6	235.4	279.1	296.5
Net financial inflows						
Net debt inflows						
Use of IMF credit	20.3	5.4	15.5	38.8	50.1	19.0
Long-term	14.2	87.2	6.7	-0.6	51.2	13.2
Official creditors	12.4	67.2	6.7	-0.6	51.2	13.2
Multilateral	-2.2	8.7	4.5	13.4	59.7	2.2
of which: World Bank	2.1	7.9	3.1	1.1	37.1	9.0
Bilateral	14.6	58.5	2.2	-14.0	-8.5	11.0
Private creditors	1.8	20.0	0.0	0.0	0.0	0.0
Bondholders	..	..	..	..	..	..
Banks and others	1.8	20.0	0.0	0.0	0.0	0.0
Short-term	-8.0	-0.8	-2.7	0.6	-0.2	10.3
Net equity inflows						
Foreign direct investment	42.3	3.0	7.3	6.9	18.0	25.6
Portfolio equity	..	..	..	..	..	..
Debt ratios						
External debt stocks to exports (%)	..	..	..	..	..	..
External debt stocks to GNI (%)	26.8	42.6	39.8	35.0	34.3	36.9
Debt service to exports (%)	..	..	..	..	..	..
Short-term to external debt stocks (%)	15.5	12.4	12.1	11.7	10.8	15.0
Multilateral to external debt stocks (%)	9.0	10.3	10.7	12.6	18.5	17.0
Reserves to external debt stocks (%)	38.2	29.3	32.6	47.6	44.1	..
Gross national income (GNI)	2,053.3	1,716.9	1,847.8	2,177.9	2,386.7	2,386.0

CHAD
(US$ million, unless otherwise indicated)

	2009	2015	2016	2017	2018	2019
Summary external debt data by debtor type						
Total external debt stocks	1,874	2,894	3,034	3,405	3,523	3,571
Use of IMF credit	113	137	193	254	395	470
Long-term external debt	1,750	2,756	2,824	3,123	3,098	3,075
Public and publicly guaranteed sector	1,750	2,756	2,824	3,123	3,098	3,075
Public sector	1,750	2,756	2,824	3,123	3,098	3,075
of which: General government	1,715	2,756	2,824	3,123	3,098	3,075
Private sector guaranteed by public sector	..	..	..	..	..	..
Private sector not guaranteed	..	..	..	..	..	..
Short-term external debt	12	0	17	28	31	26
Disbursements (long-term)	34	51	151	242	52	20
Public and publicly guaranteed sector	34	51	151	242	52	20
Public sector	34	51	151	242	52	20
of which: General government	34	51	151	242	52	20
Private sector guaranteed by public sector	..	..	..	..	..	..
Private sector not guaranteed	..	..	..	..	..	..
Principal repayments (long-term)	42	34	19	14	43	30
Public and publicly guaranteed sector	42	34	19	14	43	30
Public sector	42	34	19	14	43	30
of which: General government	41	34	19	14	43	30
Private sector guaranteed by public sector	..	..	..	..	..	..
Private sector not guaranteed	..	..	..	..	..	..
Interest payments (long-term)	23	56	105	111	134	127
Public and publicly guaranteed sector	23	56	105	111	134	127
Public sector	23	56	105	111	134	127
of which: General government	23	56	105	111	134	127
Private sector guaranteed by public sector	..	..	..	..	..	..
Private sector not guaranteed	..	..	..	..	..	..
Summary external debt stock by creditor type						
Long-term external debt stocks	1,750	2,756	2,824	3,123	3,098	3,075
Public and publicly guaranteed debt from:	1,750	2,756	2,824	3,123	3,098	3,075
Official creditors	1,731	1,218	1,286	1,584	1,559	1,537
Multilateral	1,522	549	562	687	660	652
of which: World Bank	896	187	180	189	181	176
Bilateral	210	668	724	897	898	884
Private creditors	19	1,539	1,539	1,539	1,539	1,539
Bondholders	..	..	..	..	..	..
Commercial banks and others	19	1,539	1,539	1,539	1,539	1,539
Private nonguaranteed debt from:	..	..	..	..	..	..
Bondholders	..	..	..	..	..	..
Commercial banks and others	..	..	..	..	..	..
Use of IMF credit	113	137	193	254	395	470
Net financial inflows						
Net debt inflows						
Use of IMF credit	-13	44	62	49	149	77
Long-term	-8	17	132	228	10	-10
Official creditors	-7	17	132	228	10	-10
Multilateral	-2	10	57	84	-9	-2
of which: World Bank	-15	-10	-2	-1	-4	-4
Bilateral	-5	7	75	143	18	-8
Private creditors	-1	..	0	0	0	0
Bondholders	..	..	..	..	..	..
Banks and others	-1	..	0	0	0	0
Short-term	8	0	0	0	0	0
Net equity inflows						
Foreign direct investment	375	560	245	363	461	567
Portfolio equity	..	..	..	..	..	..
Debt ratios						
External debt stocks to exports (%)	..	..	..	..	..	..
External debt stocks to GNI (%)	21	27	31	34	32	32
Debt service to exports (%)	..	..	..	..	..	..
Short-term to external debt stocks (%)	1	0	1	1	1	1
Multilateral to external debt stocks (%)	81	19	19	20	19	18
Reserves to external debt stocks (%)	33	13	0	0	4	..
Gross national income (GNI)	8,868	10,618	9,912	9,870	11,075	11,141

CHINA
(US$ million, unless otherwise indicated)

	2009	2015	2016	2017	2018	2019
Summary external debt data by debtor type						
Total external debt stocks	454,515	1,333,777	1,413,804	1,704,516	1,961,528	2,114,163
Use of IMF credit	10,958	9,686	9,396	9,954	9,721	9,665
Long-term external debt	203,049	501,847	603,012	663,929	732,906	899,185
Public and publicly guaranteed sector	100,892	146,070	160,192	196,294	259,689	318,065
Public sector	100,749	146,009	160,144	196,260	259,669	318,058
of which: General government	55,343	98,751	99,109	101,853	126,558	161,780
Private sector guaranteed by public sector	143	61	48	34	20	7
Private sector not guaranteed	102,157	355,777	442,820	467,635	473,217	581,120
Short-term external debt	240,509	822,244	801,396	1,030,633	1,218,901	1,205,312
Disbursements (long-term)	24,317	108,771	162,013	227,029	247,602	338,243
Public and publicly guaranteed sector	7,150	26,681	20,639	51,019	79,731	79,493
Public sector	7,150	26,681	20,639	51,019	79,731	79,493
of which: General government	3,314	13,873	10,264	6,482	29,611	38,598
Private sector guaranteed by public sector	0	0	0	0	0	0
Private sector not guaranteed	17,167	82,090	141,374	176,010	167,870	258,750
Principal repayments (long-term)	33,468	84,115	131,319	144,688	160,496	180,605
Public and publicly guaranteed sector	6,492	32,254	16,476	15,447	15,293	20,634
Public sector	6,477	32,240	16,462	15,433	15,279	20,620
of which: General government	3,034	3,678	9,951	3,775	4,779	3,376
Private sector guaranteed by public sector	15	14	14	14	14	14
Private sector not guaranteed	26,976	51,862	114,844	129,241	145,203	159,972
Interest payments (long-term)	3,206	9,414	11,211	16,565	27,184	35,730
Public and publicly guaranteed sector	2,191	2,370	2,035	3,350	6,135	8,670
Public sector	2,188	2,370	2,034	3,349	6,134	8,670
of which: General government	1,334	665	754	1,479	2,825	3,387
Private sector guaranteed by public sector	3	1	1	1	1	1
Private sector not guaranteed	1,015	7,044	9,175	13,215	21,049	27,059
Summary external debt stock by creditor type						
Long-term external debt stocks	203,049	501,847	603,012	663,929	732,906	899,185
Public and publicly guaranteed debt from:	100,892	146,070	160,192	196,294	259,689	318,065
Official creditors	75,211	53,659	59,894	56,215	54,502	53,840
Multilateral	33,493	33,568	33,430	34,191	34,439	35,427
of which: World Bank	22,461	17,048	16,215	16,356	16,095	16,271
Bilateral	41,718	20,091	26,464	22,025	20,062	18,413
Private creditors	25,681	92,410	100,298	140,079	205,188	264,225
Bondholders	11,626	66,945	69,469	101,554	163,960	214,523
Commercial banks and others	14,055	25,466	30,829	38,524	41,228	49,701
Private nonguaranteed debt from:	102,157	355,777	442,820	467,635	473,217	581,120
Bondholders	7,020	84,370	101,999	152,191	179,902	234,623
Commercial banks and others	95,137	271,408	340,821	315,443	293,314	346,497
Use of IMF credit	10,958	9,686	9,396	9,954	9,721	9,665
Net financial inflows						
Net debt inflows						
Use of IMF credit	..	..	..	..	..	..
Long-term	-9,151	24,655	30,694	82,340	87,106	157,638
Official creditors	1,366	-3,893	-3,814	-3,653	-1,702	-698
Multilateral	1,120	-226	31	399	382	1,063
of which: World Bank	-38	-623	-727	-15	-205	205
Bilateral	246	-3,667	-3,844	-4,052	-2,083	-1,761
Private creditors	-10,516	28,548	34,508	85,993	88,808	158,336
Bondholders	-39	8,776	22,273	82,189	94,185	105,319
Banks and others	-10,477	19,773	12,234	3,805	-5,377	53,017
Short-term	53,321	-417,208	-20,848	229,237	188,268	-13,589
Net equity inflows						
Foreign direct investment	126,956	211,785	164,930	140,569	185,911	131,251
Portfolio equity	29,117	14,964	23,416	36,209	60,668	44,906
Debt ratios						
External debt stocks to exports (%)	33	52	58	63	68	73
External debt stocks to GNI (%)	9	12	13	14	14	15
Debt service to exports (%)	3	5	7	8	8	10
Short-term to external debt stocks (%)	53	62	57	60	62	57
Multilateral to external debt stocks (%)	7	3	2	2	2	2
Reserves to external debt stocks (%)	532	251	214	185	158	148
Gross national income (GNI)	5,093,171	11,019,762	11,188,326	12,300,722	13,843,520	14,308,060

COLOMBIA

(US$ million, unless otherwise indicated)

	2009	2015	2016	2017	2018	2019
Summary external debt data by debtor type						
Total external debt stocks	53,678	113,363	120,504	125,546	132,742	138,695
Use of IMF credit	1,157	1,023	993	1,051	1,027	1,021
Long-term external debt	48,508	100,405	108,231	111,466	116,798	121,746
Public and publicly guaranteed sector	35,547	69,100	73,026	73,968	74,384	74,587
Public sector	35,020	68,844	72,780	73,731	74,161	74,377
of which: General government	29,950	45,479	47,784	50,856	54,100	54,522
Private sector guaranteed by public sector	527	256	246	237	224	210
Private sector not guaranteed	12,961	31,306	35,205	37,498	42,414	47,159
Short-term external debt	4,013	11,935	11,280	13,029	14,918	15,928
Disbursements (long-term)	13,136	19,254	18,508	17,291	22,912	15,786
Public and publicly guaranteed sector	8,095	10,414	6,857	7,074	6,887	5,036
Public sector	8,044	10,414	6,857	7,074	6,887	5,036
of which: General government	5,618	6,854	4,611	5,454	5,712	3,779
Private sector guaranteed by public sector	51	0	..	0	0	0
Private sector not guaranteed	5,041	8,840	11,651	10,217	16,025	10,750
Principal repayments (long-term)	5,929	9,120	10,494	16,280	17,863	12,065
Public and publicly guaranteed sector	1,803	1,754	2,742	6,651	6,754	4,658
Public sector	1,803	1,745	2,733	6,642	6,741	4,644
of which: General government	1,454	1,374	2,058	2,887	2,143	3,248
Private sector guaranteed by public sector	0	10	10	10	13	13
Private sector not guaranteed	4,126	7,365	7,752	9,628	11,109	7,408
Interest payments (long-term)	2,708	4,555	4,820	5,480	5,875	6,401
Public and publicly guaranteed sector	1,981	3,103	3,117	3,528	3,581	3,802
Public sector	1,966	3,100	3,111	3,522	3,574	3,794
of which: General government	1,751	2,041	2,005	2,278	2,257	2,498
Private sector guaranteed by public sector	15	3	5	5	7	7
Private sector not guaranteed	727	1,452	1,703	1,952	2,293	2,600
Summary external debt stock by creditor type						
Long-term external debt stocks	48,508	100,405	108,231	111,466	116,798	121,746
Public and publicly guaranteed debt from:	35,547	69,100	73,026	73,968	74,384	74,587
Official creditors	15,328	23,120	24,970	25,351	27,522	27,552
Multilateral	14,793	18,090	19,764	20,325	21,795	22,468
of which: World Bank	6,571	8,610	9,516	9,520	10,233	10,582
Bilateral	535	5,030	5,206	5,026	5,727	5,083
Private creditors	20,219	45,980	48,056	48,617	46,862	47,035
Bondholders	17,438	38,508	39,601	42,576	40,852	41,581
Commercial banks and others	2,781	7,472	8,456	6,041	6,011	5,454
Private nonguaranteed debt from:	12,961	31,306	35,205	37,498	42,414	47,159
Bondholders	2,709	8,650	9,146	10,206	9,521	10,481
Commercial banks and others	10,252	22,656	26,058	27,292	32,892	36,677
Use of IMF credit	1,157	1,023	993	1,051	1,027	1,021
Net financial inflows						
Net debt inflows						
Use of IMF credit	..	..	..	..	..	..
Long-term	7,207	10,134	8,014	1,011	5,049	3,721
Official creditors	1,467	1,286	2,039	152	2,501	180
Multilateral	1,579	1,003	1,861	344	1,683	795
of which: World Bank	1,115	357	945	-279	908	410
Bilateral	-112	283	178	-192	818	-615
Private creditors	5,740	8,848	5,976	859	2,547	3,541
Bondholders	6,759	5,409	1,606	3,820	-2,284	1,715
Banks and others	-1,018	3,439	4,369	-2,961	4,831	1,826
Short-term	-1,620	-286	-655	1,749	1,889	1,011
Net equity inflows						
Foreign direct investment	7,303	9,718	9,176	12,043	9,931	12,162
Portfolio equity	67	640	-363	472	-823	-1,232
Debt ratios						
External debt stocks to exports (%)	134	225	257	234	220	233
External debt stocks to GNI (%)	24	39	43	41	41	44
Debt service to exports (%)	22	28	34	42	41	32
Short-term to external debt stocks (%)	7	11	9	10	11	11
Multilateral to external debt stocks (%)	28	16	16	16	16	16
Reserves to external debt stocks (%)	46	41	38	37	36	37
Gross national income (GNI)	225,258	289,331	279,763	306,185	325,127	313,494

57

COMOROS

(US$ million, unless otherwise indicated)

	2009	2015	2016	2017	2018	2019
Summary external debt data by debtor type						
Total external debt stocks	**286.8**	**130.6**	**190.6**	**197.2**	**255.6**	**275.6**
Use of IMF credit	23.4	29.2	26.6	26.1	22.3	30.7
Long-term external debt	258.6	99.9	162.5	170.1	232.0	243.3
Public and publicly guaranteed sector	258.6	99.9	162.5	170.1	232.0	243.3
Public sector	258.6	99.9	162.5	170.1	232.0	243.3
of which: General government	258.6	99.9	132.8	140.0	152.8	165.6
Private sector guaranteed by public sector	..	..	..	..	..	..
Private sector not guaranteed	..	..	..	..	..	..
Short-term external debt	4.7	1.5	1.5	1.1	1.2	1.6
Disbursements (long-term)	**0.3**	**..**	**69.4**	**5.5**	**68.2**	**14.5**
Public and publicly guaranteed sector	0.3	..	69.4	5.5	68.2	14.5
Public sector	0.3	..	69.4	5.5	68.2	14.5
of which: General government	0.3	..	37.0	5.5	14.1	14.5
Private sector guaranteed by public sector	..	..	..	..	..	..
Private sector not guaranteed	..	..	..	..	..	..
Principal repayments (long-term)	**7.2**	**6.9**	**4.4**	**1.9**	**2.0**	**0.7**
Public and publicly guaranteed sector	7.2	6.9	4.4	1.9	2.0	0.7
Public sector	7.2	6.9	4.4	1.9	2.0	0.7
of which: General government	7.2	6.9	3.1	0.3	0.4	0.7
Private sector guaranteed by public sector	..	..	..	..	..	..
Private sector not guaranteed	..	..	..	..	..	..
Interest payments (long-term)	**2.9**	**0.2**	**0.2**	**0.1**	**1.0**	**0.1**
Public and publicly guaranteed sector	2.9	0.2	0.2	0.1	1.0	0.1
Public sector	2.9	0.2	0.2	0.1	1.0	0.1
of which: General government	2.9	0.2	0.2	0.1	0.7	0.1
Private sector guaranteed by public sector	..	..	..	..	..	..
Private sector not guaranteed	..	..	..	..	..	..
Summary external debt stock by creditor type						
Long-term external debt stocks	**258.6**	**99.9**	**162.5**	**170.1**	**232.0**	**243.3**
Public and publicly guaranteed debt from:	258.6	99.9	162.5	170.1	232.0	243.3
Official creditors	258.6	99.9	162.5	170.1	232.0	243.3
Multilateral	213.0	56.9	53.2	54.2	54.0	68.0
of which: World Bank	120.4	13.5	12.9	13.3	12.7	12.3
Bilateral	45.6	43.0	109.3	115.8	178.0	175.3
Private creditors	..	..	..	..	..	..
Bondholders	..	..	..	..	..	..
Commercial banks and others	..	..	..	..	..	..
Private nonguaranteed debt from:	..	..	..	..	..	..
Bondholders	..	..	..	..	..	..
Commercial banks and others	..	..	..	..	..	..
Use of IMF credit	23.4	29.2	26.6	26.1	22.3	30.7
Net financial inflows						
Net debt inflows						
Use of IMF credit	4.8	-0.4	-1.8	-2.0	-3.2	8.5
Long-term	-6.9	-6.9	64.9	3.6	66.2	13.9
Official creditors	-6.9	-6.9	64.9	3.6	66.2	13.9
Multilateral	-6.9	-2.0	-3.1	-0.3	0.3	14.1
of which: World Bank	-2.7	-0.3	-0.3	-0.3	-0.3	-0.3
Bilateral	..	-4.9	68.0	3.9	65.9	-0.3
Private creditors	..	..	..	..	..	..
Bondholders	..	..	..	..	..	..
Banks and others	..	..	..	..	..	..
Short-term	0.0	0.0	0.0	0.0	0.0	0.0
Net equity inflows						
Foreign direct investment	13.8	4.9	3.6	3.9	6.9	7.9
Portfolio equity	0.0	..	..	..	..	..
Debt ratios						
External debt stocks to exports (%)	353.1	126.6	164.6	145.0	158.9	181.7
External debt stocks to GNI (%)	31.8	13.5	18.7	18.2	21.6	23.2
Debt service to exports (%)	14.6	7.2	5.5	3.0	3.8	3.1
Short-term to external debt stocks (%)	1.7	1.1	0.8	0.6	0.5	0.6
Multilateral to external debt stocks (%)	74.3	43.6	27.9	27.5	21.1	24.7
Reserves to external debt stocks (%)	52.4	153.1	83.3	105.0	77.7	73.0
Gross national income (GNI)	900.5	969.9	1,018.2	1,083.4	1,185.4	1,190.5

CONGO, DEMOCRATIC REPUBLIC OF

(US$ million, unless otherwise indicated)

	2009	2015	2016	2017	2018	2019
Summary external debt data by debtor type						
Total external debt stocks	**13,093**	**5,328**	**5,022**	**5,084**	**4,956**	**5,438**
Use of IMF credit	1,601	1,098	989	954	839	1,130
Long-term external debt	10,873	4,065	3,817	4,004	4,023	4,099
Public and publicly guaranteed sector	10,873	4,065	3,817	4,004	4,023	4,099
Public sector	10,873	4,065	3,817	4,004	4,023	4,099
of which: General government	10,381	4,065	3,817	4,004	4,023	4,099
Private sector guaranteed by public sector	..	..	..	..	..	..
Private sector not guaranteed	..	..	..	..	..	..
Short-term external debt	619	165	215	126	94	209
Disbursements (long-term)	**131**	**282**	**65**	**348**	**233**	**480**
Public and publicly guaranteed sector	131	282	65	348	233	480
Public sector	131	282	65	348	233	480
of which: General government	131	282	65	348	233	480
Private sector guaranteed by public sector	..	..	..	..	..	..
Private sector not guaranteed	..	..	..	..	..	..
Principal repayments (long-term)	**225**	**222**	**271**	**182**	**180**	**366**
Public and publicly guaranteed sector	225	222	271	182	180	366
Public sector	225	222	271	182	180	366
of which: General government	198	222	271	182	180	366
Private sector guaranteed by public sector	..	..	..	..	..	..
Private sector not guaranteed	..	..	..	..	..	..
Interest payments (long-term)	**241**	**134**	**132**	**119**	**98**	**824**
Public and publicly guaranteed sector	241	134	132	119	98	824
Public sector	241	134	132	119	98	824
of which: General government	235	134	132	119	98	824
Private sector guaranteed by public sector	..	..	..	..	..	..
Private sector not guaranteed	..	..	..	..	..	..
Summary external debt stock by creditor type						
Long-term external debt stocks	**10,873**	**4,065**	**3,817**	**4,004**	**4,023**	**4,099**
Public and publicly guaranteed debt from:	10,873	4,065	3,817	4,004	4,023	4,099
Official creditors	10,525	4,055	3,816	4,003	3,993	3,997
Multilateral	4,186	1,872	1,724	1,995	2,037	2,122
of which: World Bank	2,497	841	827	942	1,098	1,288
Bilateral	6,339	2,182	2,091	2,008	1,956	1,875
Private creditors	349	11	2	1	30	102
Bondholders	..	..	..	..	..	..
Commercial banks and others	349	11	2	1	30	102
Private nonguaranteed debt from:	..	..	..	..	..	..
Bondholders	..	..	..	..	..	..
Commercial banks and others	..	..	..	..	..	..
Use of IMF credit	1,601	1,098	989	954	839	1,130
Net financial inflows						
Net debt inflows						
Use of IMF credit	132	-38	-78	-92	-94	295
Long-term	-94	60	-206	166	53	114
Official creditors	-73	58	-197	166	37	41
Multilateral	53	-31	-126	182	73	93
of which: World Bank	78	-8	11	65	180	195
Bilateral	-126	89	-71	-16	-36	-52
Private creditors	-21	2	-9	-1	16	72
Bondholders	..	..	..	..	..	..
Banks and others	-21	2	-9	-1	16	72
Short-term	-57	-17	15	9	-33	116
Net equity inflows						
Foreign direct investment	-243	1,674	1,205	1,340	1,617	1,478
Portfolio equity	..	-94	0	-10	-7	-30
Debt ratios						
External debt stocks to exports (%)	259	50	42	44	31	36
External debt stocks to GNI (%)	73	15	14	14	11	12
Debt service to exports (%)	12	4	4	3	2	8
Short-term to external debt stocks (%)	5	3	4	2	2	4
Multilateral to external debt stocks (%)	32	35	34	39	41	39
Reserves to external debt stocks (%)	8	23	14	14	13	..
Gross national income (GNI)	17,863	35,127	36,345	36,946	45,550	45,879

CONGO, REPUBLIC OF

(US$ million, unless otherwise indicated)

	2009	2015	2016	2017	2018	2019
Summary external debt data by debtor type						
Total external debt stocks	**5,046**	**4,219**	**3,998**	**4,361**	**4,314**	**5,181**
Use of IMF credit	168	123	116	120	115	157
Long-term external debt	4,623	3,648	3,696	3,969	3,933	4,801
Public and publicly guaranteed sector	4,623	3,648	3,696	3,969	3,933	4,801
Public sector	4,623	3,648	3,696	3,969	3,933	4,801
of which: General government	4,620	3,648	3,696	3,969	3,933	4,801
Private sector guaranteed by public sector	..	..	..	..	..	..
Private sector not guaranteed	..	..	..	..	..	..
Short-term external debt	256	448	187	272	266	223
Disbursements (long-term)	**12**	**122**	**348**	**957**	**478**	**2,449**
Public and publicly guaranteed sector	12	122	348	957	478	2,449
Public sector	12	122	348	957	478	2,449
of which: General government	12	122	348	957	478	2,449
Private sector guaranteed by public sector	..	..	..	..	..	..
Private sector not guaranteed	..	..	..	..	..	..
Principal repayments (long-term)	**114**	**338**	**259**	**289**	**301**	**405**
Public and publicly guaranteed sector	114	338	259	289	301	405
Public sector	114	338	259	289	301	405
of which: General government	114	338	259	289	301	405
Private sector guaranteed by public sector	..	..	..	..	..	..
Private sector not guaranteed	..	..	..	..	..	..
Interest payments (long-term)	**63**	**34**	**33**	**34**	**79**	**84**
Public and publicly guaranteed sector	63	34	33	34	79	84
Public sector	63	34	33	34	79	84
of which: General government	63	34	33	34	79	84
Private sector guaranteed by public sector	..	..	..	..	..	..
Private sector not guaranteed	..	..	..	..	..	..
Summary external debt stock by creditor type						
Long-term external debt stocks	**4,623**	**3,648**	**3,696**	**3,969**	**3,933**	**4,801**
Public and publicly guaranteed debt from:	4,623	3,648	3,696	3,969	3,933	4,801
Official creditors	3,626	2,827	2,970	3,401	3,462	4,429
Multilateral	446	224	259	687	675	894
of which: World Bank	298	110	122	153	192	243
Bilateral	3,181	2,604	2,711	2,713	2,787	3,535
Private creditors	996	821	726	569	471	372
Bondholders	454	399	377	350	322	295
Commercial banks and others	542	421	349	219	148	77
Private nonguaranteed debt from:	..	..	..	..	..	..
Bondholders	..	..	..	..	..	..
Commercial banks and others	..	..	..	..	..	..
Use of IMF credit	168	123	116	120	115	157
Net financial inflows						
Net debt inflows						
Use of IMF credit	4	-5	-4	-2	-2	43
Long-term	-103	-215	88	668	177	2,044
Official creditors	-44	-118	181	766	275	2,142
Multilateral	-6	11	51	407	-2	223
of which: World Bank	1	10	16	23	43	53
Bilateral	-38	-130	130	360	277	1,919
Private creditors	-58	-97	-93	-99	-97	-98
Bondholders	..	-18	-23	-27	-27	-27
Banks and others	-58	-79	-70	-72	-70	-71
Short-term	121	240	-266	135	-63	-47
Net equity inflows						
Foreign direct investment	555	-261	-232	4,417	4,315	3,366
Portfolio equity	1	..	..	..	..	..
Debt ratios						
External debt stocks to exports (%)	80	82	87	..	..	..
External debt stocks to GNI (%)	72	50	48	53	42	54
Debt service to exports (%)	3	7	6	..	..	..
Short-term to external debt stocks (%)	5	11	5	6	6	4
Multilateral to external debt stocks (%)	9	5	6	16	16	17
Reserves to external debt stocks (%)	75	53	18	9	10	..
Gross national income (GNI)	6,979	8,469	8,384	8,191	10,318	9,640

COSTA RICA
(US$ million, unless otherwise indicated)

	2009	2015	2016	2017	2018	2019
Summary external debt data by debtor type						
Total external debt stocks	**7,760**	**23,589**	**25,563**	**25,616**	**28,369**	**29,823**
Use of IMF credit	245	217	210	223	218	216
Long-term external debt	5,271	20,768	22,797	22,855	24,782	26,851
Public and publicly guaranteed sector	3,208	10,147	11,054	11,037	11,940	13,414
Public sector	3,208	10,147	11,054	11,037	11,940	13,414
of which: General government	2,315	5,845	6,142	6,264	6,581	8,457
Private sector guaranteed by public sector	..	..	..	..	..	..
Private sector not guaranteed	2,063	10,621	11,744	11,817	12,841	13,437
Short-term external debt	2,243	2,604	2,555	2,538	3,370	2,755
Disbursements (long-term)	**1,329**	**4,810**	**3,991**	**1,985**	**4,418**	**3,591**
Public and publicly guaranteed sector	559	1,649	1,351	599	1,701	2,508
Public sector	559	1,649	1,351	599	1,701	2,508
of which: General government	257	1,229	434	248	449	2,006
Private sector guaranteed by public sector	..	..	..	..	..	..
Private sector not guaranteed	770	3,161	2,640	1,386	2,716	1,083
Principal repayments (long-term)	**849**	**1,687**	**1,721**	**1,797**	**2,024**	**1,959**
Public and publicly guaranteed sector	573	318	444	485	897	1,073
Public sector	573	318	444	485	897	1,073
of which: General government	420	135	134	135	127	131
Private sector guaranteed by public sector	..	..	..	..	..	..
Private sector not guaranteed	276	1,369	1,277	1,312	1,127	886
Interest payments (long-term)	**342**	**1,028**	**1,055**	**1,109**	**1,261**	**1,123**
Public and publicly guaranteed sector	218	823	601	638	687	674
Public sector	218	823	601	638	687	674
of which: General government	173	470	356	364	368	375
Private sector guaranteed by public sector	..	..	..	..	..	..
Private sector not guaranteed	124	205	454	471	574	448
Summary external debt stock by creditor type						
Long-term external debt stocks	**5,271**	**20,768**	**22,797**	**22,855**	**24,782**	**26,851**
Public and publicly guaranteed debt from:	3,208	10,147	11,054	11,037	11,940	13,414
Official creditors	1,578	2,658	3,176	3,230	4,662	4,910
Multilateral	1,180	2,337	2,751	2,777	4,199	4,443
of which: World Bank	58	602	736	788	903	955
Bilateral	398	321	426	453	464	466
Private creditors	1,630	7,489	7,877	7,807	7,278	8,504
Bondholders	1,310	5,750	6,251	6,250	6,250	7,600
Commercial banks and others	320	1,739	1,626	1,557	1,028	904
Private nonguaranteed debt from:	2,063	10,621	11,744	11,817	12,841	13,437
Bondholders	..	1,350	1,850	2,150	2,100	2,100
Commercial banks and others	2,063	9,271	9,894	9,667	10,741	11,337
Use of IMF credit	245	217	210	223	218	216
Net financial inflows						
Net debt inflows						
Use of IMF credit	..	..	..	..	..	..
Long-term	480	3,123	2,270	188	2,394	1,632
Official creditors	168	322	519	184	1,333	209
Multilateral	94	278	414	171	1,321	208
of which: World Bank	17	2	135	52	115	52
Bilateral	75	45	105	13	12	1
Private creditors	312	2,800	1,751	3	1,061	1,423
Bondholders	-300	1,000	1,001	299	-50	1,350
Banks and others	612	1,800	750	-296	1,111	73
Short-term	-1,745	257	-49	-16	831	-614
Net equity inflows						
Foreign direct investment	1,661	2,291	1,468	2,410	1,970	1,931
Portfolio equity	8	1	42	43	44	55
Debt ratios						
External debt stocks to exports (%)	70	135	134	129	134	137
External debt stocks to GNI (%)	26	45	47	46	50	51
Debt service to exports (%)	11	16	15	15	16	14
Short-term to external debt stocks (%)	29	11	10	10	12	9
Multilateral to external debt stocks (%)	15	10	11	11	15	15
Reserves to external debt stocks (%)	52	33	30	28	26	30
Gross national income (GNI)	29,548	52,361	54,676	55,570	57,266	58,186

CÔTE D'IVOIRE
(US$ million, unless otherwise indicated)

	2009	2015	2016	2017	2018	2019
Summary external debt data by debtor type						
Total external debt stocks	**14,896**	**11,388**	**11,457**	**13,449**	**15,653**	**19,182**
Use of IMF credit	839	1,508	1,495	1,738	1,814	1,915
Long-term external debt	13,574	9,879	9,693	11,683	13,702	16,378
Public and publicly guaranteed sector	12,726	8,510	8,369	10,445	12,690	15,099
Public sector	12,726	8,510	8,369	10,445	12,690	15,099
of which: General government	12,724	8,510	8,369	10,445	12,673	15,069
Private sector guaranteed by public sector	..	..	..	..	..	..
Private sector not guaranteed	848	1,370	1,324	1,238	1,011	1,279
Short-term external debt	482	0	269	28	138	890
Disbursements (long-term)	**405**	**2,661**	**1,237**	**3,232**	**3,318**	**4,968**
Public and publicly guaranteed sector	85	2,660	897	3,091	3,198	4,396
Public sector	85	2,660	897	3,091	3,198	4,396
of which: General government	85	2,660	897	3,091	3,181	4,383
Private sector guaranteed by public sector	..	..	..	..	..	..
Private sector not guaranteed	320	1	341	141	120	572
Principal repayments (long-term)	**698**	**458**	**1,096**	**1,730**	**1,035**	**2,247**
Public and publicly guaranteed sector	533	134	726	1,418	701	1,946
Public sector	533	134	726	1,418	701	1,946
of which: General government	533	134	726	1,418	701	1,946
Private sector guaranteed by public sector	..	..	..	..	..	..
Private sector not guaranteed	165	324	370	312	334	302
Interest payments (long-term)	**289**	**289**	**402**	**399**	**453**	**556**
Public and publicly guaranteed sector	241	264	315	329	407	518
Public sector	241	264	315	329	407	518
of which: General government	241	264	315	329	406	517
Private sector guaranteed by public sector	..	..	..	..	..	..
Private sector not guaranteed	48	26	87	70	47	38
Summary external debt stock by creditor type						
Long-term external debt stocks	**13,574**	**9,879**	**9,693**	**11,683**	**13,702**	**16,378**
Public and publicly guaranteed debt from:	12,726	8,510	8,369	10,445	12,690	15,099
Official creditors	10,660	4,377	4,108	5,007	5,187	6,002
Multilateral	2,419	895	1,021	1,582	2,011	2,592
of which: World Bank	1,823	394	522	781	883	1,204
Bilateral	8,241	3,481	3,087	3,425	3,176	3,410
Private creditors	2,066	4,133	4,261	5,438	7,503	9,097
Bondholders	1,931	4,082	4,219	5,398	7,230	7,589
Commercial banks and others	135	51	43	40	273	1,508
Private nonguaranteed debt from:	848	1,370	1,324	1,238	1,011	1,279
Bondholders	..	..	..	..	..	..
Commercial banks and others	848	1,370	1,324	1,238	1,011	1,279
Use of IMF credit	839	1,508	1,495	1,738	1,814	1,915
Net financial inflows						
Net debt inflows						
Use of IMF credit	158	82	33	150	119	111
Long-term	-293	2,202	142	1,502	2,283	2,720
Official creditors	-448	1,534	43	540	328	811
Multilateral	-441	191	152	450	328	513
of which: World Bank	-101	165	140	205	497	236
Bilateral	-7	1,342	-109	90	132	298
Private creditors	155	668	99	962	-169	1,909
Bondholders	..	1,000	136	1,136	1,955	404
Banks and others	155	-332	-38	-173	1,928	1,506
Short-term	384	0	269	-241	27	752
Net equity inflows					110	
Foreign direct investment	401	378	531	644	590	1,009
Portfolio equity	2	0	8	24	15	..
Debt ratios						
External debt stocks to exports (%)	118	89	95	102	117	..
External debt stocks to GNI (%)	64	25	24	27	28	34
Debt service to exports (%)	9	6	13	17	12	..
Short-term to external debt stocks (%)	3	0	2	0	1	5
Multilateral to external debt stocks (%)	16	8	9	12	13	14
Reserves to external debt stocks (%)	22	41	..	..	..	..
Gross national income (GNI)	23,343	44,807	46,888	50,052	55,809	56,976

DJIBOUTI
(US$ million, unless otherwise indicated)

	2009	2015	2016	2017	2018	2019
Summary external debt data by debtor type						
Total external debt stocks	**898.1**	**1,226.5**	**1,701.1**	**2,266.8**	**2,321.2**	**2,552.4**
Use of IMF credit	39.5	49.1	45.8	44.0	36.7	31.6
Long-term external debt	738.3	1,173.4	1,601.7	1,944.7	2,044.8	2,145.3
Public and publicly guaranteed sector	738.3	1,173.4	1,601.7	1,944.7	2,044.8	2,145.3
Public sector	738.3	1,173.4	1,601.7	1,944.7	2,044.8	2,145.3
of which: General government	622.4	500.7	712.5	914.1	963.4	1,035.8
Private sector guaranteed by public sector	..	..	..	..	..	..
Private sector not guaranteed	..	..	..	..	..	..
Short-term external debt	120.3	4.0	53.7	278.1	239.6	375.4
Disbursements (long-term)	**67.4**	**415.2**	**472.9**	**337.1**	**140.6**	**136.3**
Public and publicly guaranteed sector	67.4	415.2	472.9	337.1	140.6	136.3
Public sector	67.4	415.2	472.9	337.1	140.6	136.3
of which: General government	60.8	28.4	243.8	195.7	75.6	94.1
Private sector guaranteed by public sector	..	..	..	..	..	..
Private sector not guaranteed	..	..	..	..	..	..
Principal repayments (long-term)	**22.6**	**27.5**	**31.0**	**25.1**	**27.2**	**34.7**
Public and publicly guaranteed sector	22.6	27.5	31.0	25.1	27.2	34.7
Public sector	22.6	27.5	31.0	25.1	27.2	34.7
of which: General government	10.8	19.2	23.4	18.3	17.4	21.8
Private sector guaranteed by public sector	..	..	..	..	..	..
Private sector not guaranteed	..	..	..	..	..	..
Interest payments (long-term)	**8.2**	**15.1**	**25.2**	**35.7**	**406.4**	**29.1**
Public and publicly guaranteed sector	8.2	15.1	25.2	35.7	406.4	29.1
Public sector	8.2	15.1	25.2	35.7	406.4	29.1
of which: General government	5.3	6.7	6.1	11.9	13.2	16.7
Private sector guaranteed by public sector	..	..	..	..	..	..
Private sector not guaranteed	..	..	..	..	..	..
Summary external debt stock by creditor type						
Long-term external debt stocks	**738.3**	**1,173.4**	**1,601.7**	**1,944.7**	**2,044.8**	**2,145.3**
Public and publicly guaranteed debt from:	738.3	1,173.4	1,601.7	1,944.7	2,044.8	2,145.3
Official creditors	714.1	1,168.5	1,597.5	1,940.7	2,040.9	2,141.7
Multilateral	399.5	456.5	492.4	535.4	572.5	633.7
of which: World Bank	158.4	129.9	127.9	143.6	152.2	161.3
Bilateral	314.6	712.0	1,105.1	1,405.3	1,468.4	1,508.0
Private creditors	24.2	4.9	4.2	4.0	3.9	3.6
Bondholders	..	..	..	..	..	..
Commercial banks and others	24.2	4.9	4.2	4.0	3.9	3.6
Private nonguaranteed debt from:	..	..	..	..	..	..
Bondholders	..	..	..	..	..	..
Commercial banks and others	..	..	..	..	..	..
Use of IMF credit	39.5	49.1	45.8	44.0	36.7	31.6
Net financial inflows						
Net debt inflows						
Use of IMF credit	-1.9	-1.5	-1.9	-4.4	-6.3	-4.9
Long-term	44.8	387.7	441.9	312.0	113.4	101.5
Official creditors	49.9	390.3	442.6	312.2	113.6	101.8
Multilateral	35.0	41.1	43.0	24.7	43.8	62.3
of which: World Bank	5.5	-0.7	2.0	7.8	12.1	10.0
Bilateral	14.9	349.2	399.5	287.5	69.8	39.5
Private creditors	-5.1	-2.7	-0.7	-0.2	-0.1	-0.3
Bondholders	..	..	..	..	..	..
Banks and others	-5.1	-2.7	-0.7	-0.2	-0.1	-0.3
Short-term	-28.0	-74.0	49.1	220.4	-56.0	108.6
Net equity inflows						
Foreign direct investment	96.9	143.8	160.0	164.9	170.0	181.9
Portfolio equity	..	..	..	..	..	..
Debt ratios						
External debt stocks to exports (%)	205.8	34.4	62.0	54.1	50.2	48.8
External debt stocks to GNI (%)	83.9	47.6	62.0	78.9	74.5	74.0
Debt service to exports (%)	8.3	1.2	2.1	1.7	9.7	1.5
Short-term to external debt stocks (%)	13.4	0.3	3.2	12.3	10.3	14.7
Multilateral to external debt stocks (%)	44.5	37.2	28.9	23.6	24.7	24.8
Reserves to external debt stocks (%)	26.9	29.7	23.9	24.5	19.6	19.7
Gross national income (GNI)	1,070.8	2,574.6	2,745.4	2,874.2	3,113.7	3,451.5

DOMINICA

(US$ million, unless otherwise indicated)

	2009	2015	2016	2017	2018	2019
Summary external debt data by debtor type						
Total external debt stocks	**272**	**317**	**300**	**300**	**283**	**283**
Use of IMF credit	32	27	24	24	22	21
Long-term external debt	218	285	267	264	248	251
Public and publicly guaranteed sector	218	285	267	264	248	251
Public sector	218	285	267	264	248	251
of which: General government	191	260	243	243	229	231
Private sector guaranteed by public sector	..	..	..	..	..	..
Private sector not guaranteed	..	..	..	..	..	..
Short-term external debt	22	6	9	11	13	12
Disbursements (long-term)	**9**	**24**	**4**	**11**	**5**	**22**
Public and publicly guaranteed sector	9	24	4	11	5	22
Public sector	9	24	4	11	5	22
of which: General government	8	15	2	10	4	19
Private sector guaranteed by public sector	..	..	..	..	..	..
Private sector not guaranteed	..	..	..	..	..	..
Principal repayments (long-term)	**15**	**14**	**18**	**20**	**18**	**19**
Public and publicly guaranteed sector	15	14	18	20	18	19
Public sector	15	14	18	20	18	19
of which: General government	11	12	15	15	15	16
Private sector guaranteed by public sector	..	..	..	..	..	..
Private sector not guaranteed	..	..	..	..	..	..
Interest payments (long-term)	**6**	**7**	**7**	**8**	**9**	**7**
Public and publicly guaranteed sector	6	7	7	8	9	7
Public sector	6	7	7	8	9	7
of which: General government	5	6	7	7	8	6
Private sector guaranteed by public sector	..	..	..	..	..	..
Private sector not guaranteed	..	..	..	..	..	..
Summary external debt stock by creditor type						
Long-term external debt stocks	**218**	**285**	**267**	**264**	**248**	**251**
Public and publicly guaranteed debt from:	218	285	267	264	248	251
Official creditors	144	225	209	207	193	183
Multilateral	118	133	127	129	124	122
of which: World Bank	29	26	24	33	34	36
Bilateral	26	92	81	78	69	61
Private creditors	74	61	58	57	55	68
Bondholders	57	29	29	30	30	45
Commercial banks and others	17	32	30	28	26	23
Private nonguaranteed debt from:	..	..	..	..	..	..
Bondholders	..	..	..	..	..	..
Commercial banks and others	..	..	..	..	..	..
Use of IMF credit	32	27	24	24	22	21
Net financial inflows						
Net debt inflows						
Use of IMF credit	4	7	-2	-1	-2	-1
Long-term	-6	10	-14	-9	-13	4
Official creditors	-4	9	-12	-8	-11	-9
Multilateral	-1	5	-5	0	-4	-2
of which: World Bank	0	0	-1	7	2	2
Bilateral	-3	4	-7	-8	-7	-7
Private creditors	-2	1	-2	-1	-2	13
Bondholders	-2	3	0	1	..	15
Banks and others	0	-2	-2	-2	-2	-3
Short-term	-2	0	0	2	2	-2
Net equity inflows						
Foreign direct investment	26	18	42	25	14	33
Portfolio equity	..	0	0	0	0	..
Debt ratios						
External debt stocks to exports (%)	176	118	111	134	164	..
External debt stocks to GNI (%)	57	61	54	59	51	48
Debt service to exports (%)	14	9	10	13	17	..
Short-term to external debt stocks (%)	8	2	3	4	5	4
Multilateral to external debt stocks (%)	43	42	42	43	44	43
Reserves to external debt stocks (%)	28	40	74	71	68	59
Gross national income (GNI)	475	519	561	508	552	587

DOMINICAN REPUBLIC

(US$ million, unless otherwise indicated)

	2009	2015	2016	2017	2018	2019
Summary external debt data by debtor type						
Total external debt stocks	**11,854**	**26,727**	**28,291**	**31,168**	**33,974**	**35,919**
Use of IMF credit	1,094	403	281	297	290	289
Long-term external debt	9,005	23,145	24,958	28,869	31,496	33,115
Public and publicly guaranteed sector	8,162	15,815	17,186	20,226	23,485	27,584
Public sector	8,158	15,813	17,185	20,225	23,484	27,584
of which: General government	7,287	15,579	17,044	20,136	23,436	27,547
Private sector guaranteed by public sector	4	1	1	1	1	0
Private sector not guaranteed	843	7,330	7,772	8,643	8,011	5,531
Short-term external debt	1,755	3,179	3,053	2,001	2,187	2,515
Disbursements (long-term)	**1,483**	**6,096**	**3,724**	**5,055**	**5,073**	**4,963**
Public and publicly guaranteed sector	1,483	5,020	2,259	3,780	4,104	4,963
Public sector	1,483	5,020	2,259	3,780	4,104	4,963
of which: General government	1,456	5,020	2,259	3,780	4,104	4,962
Private sector guaranteed by public sector	0	0	..	0	0	0
Private sector not guaranteed	..	1,076	1,465	1,275	969	..
Principal repayments (long-term)	**896**	**3,782**	**2,075**	**1,961**	**1,478**	**3,280**
Public and publicly guaranteed sector	896	2,757	861	808	808	800
Public sector	895	2,756	861	807	808	799
of which: General government	729	2,688	770	748	769	788
Private sector guaranteed by public sector	1	0	0	0	0	0
Private sector not guaranteed	0	1,026	1,214	1,154	670	2,480
Interest payments (long-term)	**433**	**1,022**	**1,205**	**1,012**	**1,559**	**1,855**
Public and publicly guaranteed sector	325	775	922	716	1,087	1,435
Public sector	324	775	922	716	1,087	1,435
of which: General government	283	767	917	713	1,085	1,435
Private sector guaranteed by public sector	0	0	0	0	0	0
Private sector not guaranteed	108	247	282	296	472	419
Summary external debt stock by creditor type						
Long-term external debt stocks	**9,005**	**23,145**	**24,958**	**28,869**	**31,496**	**33,115**
Public and publicly guaranteed debt from:	8,162	15,815	17,186	20,226	23,485	27,584
Official creditors	5,479	5,678	5,818	5,710	5,986	6,608
Multilateral	2,614	4,150	4,439	4,454	4,704	5,093
of which: World Bank	756	932	933	923	923	939
Bilateral	2,865	1,528	1,379	1,256	1,281	1,515
Private creditors	2,683	10,137	11,368	14,516	17,499	20,976
Bondholders	490	8,312	9,812	13,212	16,308	18,755
Commercial banks and others	2,194	1,825	1,556	1,304	1,192	2,221
Private nonguaranteed debt from:	843	7,330	7,772	8,643	8,011	5,531
Bondholders	843	1,575	1,945	1,945	1,945	1,395
Commercial banks and others	0	5,755	5,827	6,698	6,066	4,136
Use of IMF credit	**1,094**	**403**	**281**	**297**	**290**	**289**
Net financial inflows						
Net debt inflows						
Use of IMF credit	261	-368	-114	..	..	..
Long-term	587	2,313	1,650	3,094	3,595	1,684
Official creditors	1,042	-1,252	157	-124	282	625
Multilateral	712	561	291	10	253	390
of which: World Bank	298	44	1	-10	0	16
Bilateral	331	-1,813	-134	-134	29	235
Private creditors	-455	3,565	1,493	3,218	3,313	1,059
Bondholders	-125	3,700	1,870	3,400	3,108	1,937
Banks and others	-330	-135	-377	-182	205	-878
Short-term	-182	693	-127	-1,051	186	328
Net equity inflows						
Foreign direct investment	1,070	2,187	2,340	3,733	2,677	2,887
Portfolio equity	0	0	0	0	0	0
Debt ratios						
External debt stocks to exports (%)	140	152	152	160	164	171
External debt stocks to GNI (%)	25	39	39	41	42	42
Debt service to exports (%)	17	30	19	16	15	25
Short-term to external debt stocks (%)	15	12	11	6	6	7
Multilateral to external debt stocks (%)	22	16	16	14	14	14
Reserves to external debt stocks (%)	30	20	22	22	23	25
Gross national income (GNI)	46,539	68,228	72,452	76,204	81,710	84,775

ECUADOR

(US$ million, unless otherwise indicated)

	2009	2015	2016	2017	2018	2019
Summary external debt data by debtor type						
Total external debt stocks	**13,366**	**28,402**	**35,377**	**41,152**	**44,935**	**51,725**
Use of IMF credit	452	400	739	783	765	2,114
Long-term external debt	11,568	26,940	33,766	39,276	43,094	48,757
Public and publicly guaranteed sector	7,102	20,153	25,572	31,629	35,481	38,396
Public sector	7,076	20,126	25,547	31,606	35,461	38,379
of which: General government	6,592	18,806	23,770	29,208	33,620	37,174
Private sector guaranteed by public sector	26	27	25	23	20	18
Private sector not guaranteed	4,466	6,787	8,195	7,647	7,613	10,360
Short-term external debt	1,346	1,062	871	1,093	1,076	854
Disbursements (long-term)	**1,180**	**7,370**	**9,991**	**10,228**	**10,360**	**9,625**
Public and publicly guaranteed sector	384	4,762	7,326	8,895	7,153	6,877
Public sector	375	4,762	7,326	8,895	7,153	6,877
of which: General government	374	4,742	6,481	7,849	6,941	6,748
Private sector guaranteed by public sector	9	0	..	0	0	0
Private sector not guaranteed	796	2,609	2,666	1,334	3,207	2,748
Principal repayments (long-term)	**7,277**	**3,807**	**3,861**	**4,559**	**6,443**	**6,508**
Public and publicly guaranteed sector	6,618	2,116	1,859	2,906	3,202	3,919
Public sector	6,618	2,114	1,857	2,904	3,200	3,917
of which: General government	6,570	1,841	1,469	2,476	2,431	3,152
Private sector guaranteed by public sector	0	2	2	2	2	2
Private sector not guaranteed	659	1,691	2,002	1,653	3,241	2,588
Interest payments (long-term)	**592**	**1,278**	**1,507**	**2,032**	**2,663**	**2,792**
Public and publicly guaranteed sector	400	1,057	1,200	1,753	2,238	2,385
Public sector	399	1,056	1,199	1,752	2,237	2,384
of which: General government	384	984	1,094	1,633	2,099	2,292
Private sector guaranteed by public sector	1	1	1	1	1	1
Private sector not guaranteed	191	221	306	279	425	407
Summary external debt stock by creditor type						
Long-term external debt stocks	**11,568**	**26,940**	**33,766**	**39,276**	**43,094**	**48,757**
Public and publicly guaranteed debt from:	7,102	20,153	25,572	31,629	35,481	38,396
Official creditors	5,806	14,149	16,742	16,785	16,901	17,832
Multilateral	4,386	7,555	8,202	8,707	9,495	10,794
of which: World Bank	542	257	246	399	617	1,251
Bilateral	1,420	6,594	8,540	8,078	7,405	7,038
Private creditors	1,297	6,004	8,830	14,844	18,580	20,564
Bondholders	1,098	3,397	6,114	12,565	15,250	18,307
Commercial banks and others	198	2,607	2,716	2,278	3,330	2,257
Private nonguaranteed debt from:	4,466	6,787	8,195	7,647	7,613	10,360
Bondholders	..	..	..	..	..	..
Commercial banks and others	4,466	6,787	8,195	7,647	7,613	10,360
Use of IMF credit	452	400	739	783	765	2,114
Net financial inflows						
Net debt inflows						
Use of IMF credit	..	..	364	0	0	1,353
Long-term	-6,096	3,563	6,130	5,669	3,917	3,117
Official creditors	-101	2,005	2,637	-11	180	956
Multilateral	54	1,617	649	519	813	1,306
of which: World Bank	-82	73	-11	153	218	634
Bilateral	-155	388	1,988	-530	-632	-350
Private creditors	-5,995	1,558	3,493	5,680	3,737	2,161
Bondholders	-6,090	376	2,717	6,451	2,685	3,057
Banks and others	95	1,182	776	-772	1,052	-896
Short-term	-306	36	-206	206	-33	-235
Net equity inflows						
Foreign direct investment	534	1,272	879	682	702	600
Portfolio equity	2	2	6	4	6	2
Debt ratios						
External debt stocks to exports (%)	84	132	175	181	175	197
External debt stocks to GNI (%)	22	29	36	40	43	50
Debt service to exports (%)	50	24	27	29	36	36
Short-term to external debt stocks (%)	10	4	2	3	2	2
Multilateral to external debt stocks (%)	33	27	23	21	21	21
Reserves to external debt stocks (%)	21	7	11	4	4	4
Gross national income (GNI)	61,249	97,562	98,125	101,978	104,733	104,330

66

EGYPT, ARAB REPUBLIC OF

(US$ million, unless otherwise indicated)

	2009	2015	2016	2017	2018	2019
Summary external debt data by debtor type						
Total external debt stocks	35,398	49,846	69,164	84,722	100,186	115,080
Use of IMF credit	1,408	1,245	3,856	7,401	9,220	13,130
Long-term external debt	31,428	44,177	53,362	66,193	80,625	90,665
Public and publicly guaranteed sector	31,354	44,154	53,206	65,787	80,179	90,305
Public sector	30,880	44,045	53,129	65,729	80,153	90,305
of which: General government	27,144	30,073	32,200	42,283	51,239	60,963
Private sector guaranteed by public sector	474	110	77	58	26	0
Private sector not guaranteed	74	23	157	406	446	360
Short-term external debt	2,561	4,424	11,945	11,128	10,341	11,284
Disbursements (long-term)	2,127	10,962	14,675	15,850	20,287	15,322
Public and publicly guaranteed sector	2,118	10,933	14,515	15,552	20,161	15,251
Public sector	2,118	10,933	14,515	15,552	20,161	15,251
of which: General government	1,601	7,849	6,280	11,927	11,302	12,329
Private sector guaranteed by public sector	0	0	..	..	..	..
Private sector not guaranteed	9	29	160	298	126	71
Principal repayments (long-term)	2,054	2,887	5,106	4,622	5,119	4,633
Public and publicly guaranteed sector	2,035	2,859	5,102	4,575	5,032	4,477
Public sector	1,928	2,849	5,071	4,547	5,002	4,451
of which: General government	1,540	2,286	3,987	2,704	1,994	2,115
Private sector guaranteed by public sector	106	10	31	27	30	26
Private sector not guaranteed	20	28	3	48	87	156
Interest payments (long-term)	809	715	1,027	1,579	2,220	3,389
Public and publicly guaranteed sector	807	714	1,026	1,565	2,204	3,370
Public sector	788	713	1,024	1,564	2,203	3,369
of which: General government	692	604	785	1,105	1,616	2,209
Private sector guaranteed by public sector	19	1	1	1	1	1
Private sector not guaranteed	2	0	2	14	16	19
Summary external debt stock by creditor type						
Long-term external debt stocks	31,428	44,177	53,362	66,193	80,625	90,665
Public and publicly guaranteed debt from:	31,354	44,154	53,206	65,787	80,179	90,305
Official creditors	28,467	37,854	47,544	52,767	55,970	57,636
Multilateral	8,723	11,716	15,846	18,876	20,119	21,508
of which: World Bank	3,250	5,597	7,114	8,435	9,930	11,250
Bilateral	19,743	26,138	31,698	33,891	35,851	36,128
Private creditors	2,887	6,300	5,662	13,020	24,209	32,669
Bondholders	2,175	4,850	3,600	10,000	15,800	23,273
Commercial banks and others	712	1,450	2,062	3,020	8,409	9,396
Private nonguaranteed debt from:	74	23	157	406	446	360
Bondholders	..	..	..	..	..	..
Commercial banks and others	74	23	157	406	446	360
Use of IMF credit	1,408	1,245	3,856	7,401	9,220	13,130
Net financial inflows						
Net debt inflows						
Use of IMF credit	..	..	2,738	3,229	2,029	3,959
Long-term	73	8,075	9,570	11,227	15,168	10,689
Official creditors	134	5,673	10,020	3,772	3,790	1,866
Multilateral	909	1,185	4,304	2,562	1,426	1,454
of which: World Bank	545	723	1,545	1,289	1,507	1,321
Bilateral	-776	4,488	5,716	1,210	2,364	411
Private creditors	-61	2,402	-450	7,455	11,379	8,823
Bondholders	..	1,500	-1,250	6,400	5,868	7,887
Banks and others	-61	902	800	1,055	5,511	937
Short-term	-281	1,103	7,521	-817	-787	943
Net equity inflows						
Foreign direct investment	6,712	6,925	8,107	7,409	8,141	9,010
Portfolio equity	393	14	610	224	220	-12
Debt ratios						
External debt stocks to exports (%)	78	132	203	194	191	211
External debt stocks to GNI (%)	19	15	21	37	41	39
Debt service to exports (%)	7	10	20	15	15	16
Short-term to external debt stocks (%)	7	9	17	13	10	10
Multilateral to external debt stocks (%)	25	24	23	22	20	19
Reserves to external debt stocks (%)	91	27	30	39	39	35
Gross national income (GNI)	189,136	326,961	328,426	230,777	244,596	292,150

67

EL SALVADOR

(US$ million, unless otherwise indicated)

	2009	2015	2016	2017	2018	2019
Summary external debt data by debtor type						
Total external debt stocks	**10,406**	**15,570**	**16,567**	**17,179**	**17,392**	**18,061**
Use of IMF credit	257	227	220	233	228	227
Long-term external debt	9,286	13,326	13,814	14,903	15,093	15,621
Public and publicly guaranteed sector	6,147	8,604	8,710	9,489	9,505	9,856
Public sector	6,144	8,603	8,710	9,489	9,505	9,856
of which: General government	5,525	7,969	7,965	8,655	8,727	9,063
Private sector guaranteed by public sector	3	1	0	0	0	..
Private sector not guaranteed	3,139	4,722	5,103	5,414	5,588	5,765
Short-term external debt	863	2,018	2,533	2,043	2,070	2,214
Disbursements (long-term)	**1,216**	**1,259**	**1,029**	**3,513**	**2,945**	**4,960**
Public and publicly guaranteed sector	910	394	410	978	588	1,419
Public sector	910	394	410	978	588	1,419
of which: General government	570	220	130	748	496	1,266
Private sector guaranteed by public sector	..	..	..	..	..	..
Private sector not guaranteed	306	865	619	2,535	2,357	3,541
Principal repayments (long-term)	**687**	**635**	**693**	**2,995**	**2,620**	**4,522**
Public and publicly guaranteed sector	560	406	455	434	437	1,179
Public sector	560	405	455	434	437	1,179
of which: General government	254	241	284	292	290	1,039
Private sector guaranteed by public sector	0	0	0	0	0	..
Private sector not guaranteed	127	229	238	2,561	2,183	3,343
Interest payments (long-term)	**476**	**643**	**660**	**768**	**889**	**1,029**
Public and publicly guaranteed sector	374	494	514	547	589	684
Public sector	374	494	514	547	589	684
of which: General government	341	469	483	511	539	632
Private sector guaranteed by public sector	0	0	0	0	0	..
Private sector not guaranteed	102	149	145	221	300	345
Summary external debt stock by creditor type						
Long-term external debt stocks	**9,286**	**13,326**	**13,814**	**14,903**	**15,093**	**15,621**
Public and publicly guaranteed debt from:	6,147	8,604	8,710	9,489	9,505	9,856
Official creditors	3,871	4,276	4,229	4,224	4,367	4,396
Multilateral	3,195	3,847	3,804	3,804	3,996	4,049
of which: World Bank	578	921	912	906	876	831
Bilateral	676	429	425	420	371	346
Private creditors	2,276	4,328	4,481	5,265	5,138	5,460
Bondholders	2,174	4,283	4,438	5,238	5,109	5,423
Commercial banks and others	103	45	43	27	29	37
Private nonguaranteed debt from:	3,139	4,722	5,103	5,414	5,588	5,765
Bondholders	..	38	38	38	38	12
Commercial banks and others	3,139	4,684	5,065	5,376	5,550	5,753
Use of IMF credit	257	227	220	233	228	227
Net financial inflows						
Net debt inflows						
Use of IMF credit	..	..	..	..	..	..
Long-term	529	624	336	518	325	438
Official creditors	354	-7	-44	-26	148	30
Multilateral	395	-7	-37	-2	194	54
of which: World Bank	168	-27	-9	0	-31	-45
Bilateral	-40	0	-7	-25	-46	-24
Private creditors	174	631	380	544	177	408
Bondholders	0	0	0	589	0	196
Banks and others	174	631	380	-44	177	212
Short-term	-679	0	515	-490	27	143
Net equity inflows						
Foreign direct investment	241	320	415	844	129	582
Portfolio equity	0	0	0	0	0	0
Debt ratios						
External debt stocks to exports (%)	242	221	237	233	225	220
External debt stocks to GNI (%)	61	70	72	73	71	70
Debt service to exports (%)	27	19	20	52	46	68
Short-term to external debt stocks (%)	8	13	15	12	12	12
Multilateral to external debt stocks (%)	31	25	23	22	23	22
Reserves to external debt stocks (%)	28	18	19	20	20	24
Gross national income (GNI)	17,046	22,346	22,945	23,592	24,647	25,716

ERITREA

(US$ million, unless otherwise indicated)

	2009	2015	2016	2017	2018	2019
Summary external debt data by debtor type						
Total external debt stocks	**1,050.7**	**873.3**	**797.3**	**820.8**	**791.2**	**771.7**
Use of IMF credit	23.8	21.0	20.4	21.6	21.1	21.0
Long-term external debt	1,013.0	782.4	750.3	772.0	736.1	718.1
Public and publicly guaranteed sector	1,013.0	782.4	750.3	772.0	736.1	718.1
Public sector	1,013.0	782.4	750.3	772.0	736.1	718.1
of which: General government	1,013.0	782.4	750.3	772.0	736.1	718.1
Private sector guaranteed by public sector	..	..	..	..	..	..
Private sector not guaranteed	..	..	..	..	..	..
Short-term external debt	13.9	69.9	26.6	27.1	34.0	32.7
Disbursements (long-term)	**57.6**	**14.7**	**9.5**	**6.9**	**4.2**	**4.2**
Public and publicly guaranteed sector	57.6	14.7	9.5	6.9	4.2	4.2
Public sector	57.6	14.7	9.5	6.9	4.2	4.2
of which: General government	57.6	14.7	9.5	6.9	4.2	4.2
Private sector guaranteed by public sector	..	..	..	..	..	..
Private sector not guaranteed	..	..	..	..	..	..
Principal repayments (long-term)	**11.3**	**28.8**	**23.4**	**23.7**	**24.9**	**18.4**
Public and publicly guaranteed sector	11.3	28.8	23.4	23.7	24.9	18.4
Public sector	11.3	28.8	23.4	23.7	24.9	18.4
of which: General government	11.3	28.8	23.4	23.7	24.9	18.4
Private sector guaranteed by public sector	..	..	..	..	..	..
Private sector not guaranteed	..	..	..	..	..	..
Interest payments (long-term)	**10.3**	**3.8**	**3.5**	**3.2**	**3.1**	**2.6**
Public and publicly guaranteed sector	10.3	3.8	3.5	3.2	3.1	2.6
Public sector	10.3	3.8	3.5	3.2	3.1	2.6
of which: General government	10.3	3.8	3.5	3.2	3.1	2.6
Private sector guaranteed by public sector	..	..	..	..	..	..
Private sector not guaranteed	..	..	..	..	..	..
Summary external debt stock by creditor type						
Long-term external debt stocks	**1,013.0**	**782.4**	**750.3**	**772.0**	**736.1**	**718.1**
Public and publicly guaranteed debt from:	1,013.0	782.4	750.3	772.0	736.1	718.1
Official creditors	972.1	751.5	720.3	738.0	703.6	686.2
Multilateral	657.5	572.5	557.5	587.3	571.6	567.1
of which: World Bank	476.8	432.9	420.0	444.9	434.5	432.0
Bilateral	314.6	179.0	162.8	150.7	132.0	119.0
Private creditors	40.9	30.9	29.9	34.1	32.5	31.9
Bondholders	..	..	..	..	..	..
Commercial banks and others	40.9	30.9	29.9	34.1	32.5	31.9
Private nonguaranteed debt from:	..	..	..	..	..	..
Bondholders	..	..	..	..	..	..
Commercial banks and others	..	..	..	..	..	..
Use of IMF credit	23.8	21.0	20.4	21.6	21.1	21.0
Net financial inflows						
Net debt inflows						
Use of IMF credit	..	..	..	..	..	..
Long-term	46.3	-14.1	-13.8	-16.8	-20.6	-14.2
Official creditors	46.3	-14.1	-13.8	-16.8	-20.6	-14.2
Multilateral	4.8	-0.4	-1.0	-1.6	-3.8	-1.7
of which: World Bank	0.8	0.0	0.0	0.0	0.0	..
Bilateral	41.6	-13.7	-12.8	-15.2	-16.8	-12.5
Private creditors	..	..	0.0	..	..	..
Bondholders	..	..	..	..	..	..
Banks and others	..	..	0.0	..	..	..
Short-term	-5.0	11.7	-45.7	-4.0	4.4	-4.4
Net equity inflows						
Foreign direct investment	91.0	49.3	52.3	55.5	61.0	67.1
Portfolio equity	..	..	..	..	..	..
Debt ratios						
External debt stocks to exports (%)	..	..	..	..	..	..
External debt stocks to GNI (%)	57.1	..	..	..	..	..
Debt service to exports (%)	..	..	..	..	..	..
Short-term to external debt stocks (%)	1.3	8.0	3.3	3.3	4.3	4.2
Multilateral to external debt stocks (%)	62.6	65.6	69.9	71.6	72.2	73.5
Reserves to external debt stocks (%)	8.6	16.6	18.2	17.5	20.6	24.8
Gross national income (GNI)	1,840.5	..	..	..	..	..

ESWATINI
(US$ million, unless otherwise indicated)

	2009	2015	2016	2017	2018	2019
Summary external debt data by debtor type						
Total external debt stocks	**524.2**	**367.5**	**487.6**	**652.2**	**515.4**	**631.3**
Use of IMF credit	75.7	66.9	64.9	68.8	67.2	66.8
Long-term external debt	428.0	286.0	359.7	397.7	424.4	533.0
Public and publicly guaranteed sector	428.0	286.0	359.7	397.7	424.4	533.0
Public sector	428.0	286.0	359.7	397.7	424.4	533.0
of which: General government	416.6	281.2	348.9	386.8	413.6	522.2
Private sector guaranteed by public sector	..	..	..	..	..	..
Private sector not guaranteed	..	..	..	..	..	..
Short-term external debt	20.5	14.6	63.0	185.8	23.9	31.5
Disbursements (long-term)	**14.7**	**38.9**	**99.8**	**55.7**	**69.5**	**142.5**
Public and publicly guaranteed sector	14.7	38.9	99.8	55.7	69.5	142.5
Public sector	14.7	38.9	99.8	55.7	69.5	142.5
of which: General government	14.7	38.9	93.8	55.7	69.5	142.5
Private sector guaranteed by public sector	..	..	..	..	..	..
Private sector not guaranteed	..	..	..	..	..	..
Principal repayments (long-term)	**35.0**	**24.4**	**31.0**	**31.5**	**32.6**	**35.4**
Public and publicly guaranteed sector	35.0	24.4	31.0	31.5	32.6	35.4
Public sector	35.0	24.4	31.0	31.5	32.6	35.4
of which: General government	32.0	24.4	31.0	31.5	32.6	35.4
Private sector guaranteed by public sector	..	..	..	..	..	..
Private sector not guaranteed	..	..	..	..	..	..
Interest payments (long-term)	**19.5**	**9.7**	**8.8**	**11.2**	**13.2**	**24.0**
Public and publicly guaranteed sector	19.5	9.7	8.8	11.2	13.2	24.0
Public sector	19.5	9.7	8.8	11.2	13.2	24.0
of which: General government	18.5	9.7	8.8	11.2	13.2	24.0
Private sector guaranteed by public sector	..	..	..	..	..	..
Private sector not guaranteed	..	..	..	..	..	..
Summary external debt stock by creditor type						
Long-term external debt stocks	**428.0**	**286.0**	**359.7**	**397.7**	**424.4**	**533.0**
Public and publicly guaranteed debt from:	428.0	286.0	359.7	397.7	424.4	533.0
Official creditors	389.7	272.2	344.9	381.9	412.0	520.3
Multilateral	261.1	156.2	177.4	208.3	219.4	234.8
of which: World Bank	10.0	21.8	27.6	38.8	39.8	36.4
Bilateral	128.6	116.0	167.6	173.6	192.6	285.6
Private creditors	38.3	13.7	14.7	15.7	12.4	12.7
Bondholders	..	..	..	..	..	..
Commercial banks and others	38.3	13.7	14.7	15.7	12.4	12.7
Private nonguaranteed debt from:	..	..	..	..	..	..
Bondholders	..	..	..	..	..	..
Commercial banks and others	..	..	..	..	..	..
Use of IMF credit	75.7	66.9	64.9	68.8	67.2	66.8
Net financial inflows						
Net debt inflows						
Use of IMF credit	..	..	..	..	..	..
Long-term	-20.3	14.5	68.8	24.1	36.8	107.1
Official creditors	-18.9	15.4	69.6	24.7	38.0	107.1
Multilateral	-11.5	-3.3	19.4	22.8	18.1	14.4
of which: World Bank	-6.9	7.7	5.8	11.2	1.0	-3.4
Bilateral	-7.4	18.7	50.2	1.9	20.0	92.7
Private creditors	-1.4	-0.9	-0.8	-0.6	-1.2	0.0
Bondholders	..	..	..	..	..	..
Banks and others	-1.4	-0.9	-0.8	-0.6	-1.2	0.0
Short-term	-31.0	-17.6	46.7	128.3	-168.5	6.8
Net equity inflows						
Foreign direct investment	53.1	34.2	2.3	45.4	-14.1	112.1
Portfolio equity	-6.6	..	..	..	..	..
Debt ratios						
External debt stocks to exports (%)	25.4	18.4	26.7	31.1	25.2	28.8
External debt stocks to GNI (%)	15.0	8.9	13.4	15.6	11.9	16.3
Debt service to exports (%)	2.7	1.7	2.2	2.2	2.3	2.8
Short-term to external debt stocks (%)	3.9	4.0	12.9	28.5	4.6	5.0
Multilateral to external debt stocks (%)	49.8	42.5	36.4	31.9	42.6	37.2
Reserves to external debt stocks (%)	182.9	149.1	115.7	86.3	85.5	69.8
Gross national income (GNI)	3,504.9	4,113.1	3,635.5	4,185.3	4,314.6	3,867.3

ETHIOPIA
(US$ million, unless otherwise indicated)

	2009	2015	2016	2017	2018	2019
Summary external debt data by debtor type						
Total external debt stocks	5,360	20,519	23,474	26,233	27,793	28,288
Use of IMF credit	368	397	335	301	242	318
Long-term external debt	4,763	19,573	22,211	25,298	26,802	27,490
Public and publicly guaranteed sector	4,763	19,573	22,211	25,298	26,802	27,490
Public sector	4,763	19,573	22,211	25,298	26,802	27,490
of which: General government	3,252	10,635	12,236	14,343	15,367	16,633
Private sector guaranteed by public sector	..	..	..	..	..	..
Private sector not guaranteed	..	..	..	..	..	..
Short-term external debt	229	550	927	634	749	480
Disbursements (long-term)	2,148	4,412	3,694	3,520	3,462	2,319
Public and publicly guaranteed sector	2,148	4,412	3,694	3,520	3,462	2,319
Public sector	2,148	4,412	3,694	3,520	3,462	2,319
of which: General government	851	1,375	1,971	1,754	1,974	1,561
Private sector guaranteed by public sector	..	..	..	..	..	..
Private sector not guaranteed	..	..	..	..	..	..
Principal repayments (long-term)	58	703	779	997	1,146	1,495
Public and publicly guaranteed sector	58	703	779	997	1,146	1,495
Public sector	58	703	779	997	1,146	1,495
of which: General government	31	95	110	146	169	215
Private sector guaranteed by public sector	..	..	..	..	..	..
Private sector not guaranteed	..	..	..	..	..	..
Interest payments (long-term)	37	303	398	433	433	665
Public and publicly guaranteed sector	37	303	398	433	433	665
Public sector	37	303	398	433	433	665
of which: General government	23	158	168	166	201	207
Private sector guaranteed by public sector	..	..	..	..	..	..
Private sector not guaranteed	..	..	..	..	..	..
Summary external debt stock by creditor type						
Long-term external debt stocks	4,763	19,573	22,211	25,298	26,802	27,490
Public and publicly guaranteed debt from:	4,763	19,573	22,211	25,298	26,802	27,490
Official creditors	3,500	13,268	15,862	18,547	19,616	20,668
Multilateral	2,313	6,775	8,155	10,103	11,063	12,180
of which: World Bank	1,422	4,753	5,746	7,040	8,338	9,354
Bilateral	1,187	6,493	7,707	8,444	8,554	8,488
Private creditors	1,263	6,304	6,349	6,751	7,186	6,821
Bondholders	..	1,000	1,000	1,000	1,000	1,000
Commercial banks and others	1,263	5,304	5,349	5,751	6,186	5,821
Private nonguaranteed debt from:	..	..	..	..	..	..
Bondholders	..	..	..	..	..	..
Commercial banks and others	..	..	..	..	..	..
Use of IMF credit	368	397	335	301	242	318
Net financial inflows						
Net debt inflows						
Use of IMF credit	165	-36	-52	-52	-53	78
Long-term	2,090	3,709	2,915	2,523	2,317	824
Official creditors	1,067	2,360	2,866	2,159	1,860	1,137
Multilateral	728	1,058	1,613	1,500	1,706	1,180
of which: World Bank	549	685	1,177	933	1,494	1,075
Bilateral	339	1,302	1,252	659	154	-43
Private creditors	1,023	1,349	49	364	456	-313
Bondholders	..	..	..	..	0	0
Banks and others	1,023	1,349	49	364	456	-313
Short-term	171	258	378	-293	115	-270
Net equity inflows						
Foreign direct investment	221	2,627	4,143	4,017	3,360	2,516
Portfolio equity	0	..	..	..	..	..
Debt ratios						
External debt stocks to exports (%)	156	341	397	394	361	368
External debt stocks to GNI (%)	17	32	32	32	33	30
Debt service to exports (%)	3	17	21	22	22	29
Short-term to external debt stocks (%)	4	3	4	2	3	2
Multilateral to external debt stocks (%)	43	33	35	39	40	43
Reserves to external debt stocks (%)	33	19	13	12	14	11
Gross national income (GNI)	32,396	64,327	74,054	81,285	83,892	95,641

71

FIJI

(US$ million, unless otherwise indicated)

	2009	2015	2016	2017	2018	2019
Summary external debt data by debtor type						
Total external debt stocks	**691.4**	**888.8**	**939.7**	**1,007.5**	**979.5**	**1,020.0**
Use of IMF credit	105.2	93.0	90.2	95.6	93.3	92.8
Long-term external debt	530.1	714.4	752.3	848.3	841.6	874.3
Public and publicly guaranteed sector	319.5	616.9	661.6	716.9	713.6	700.9
Public sector	319.5	616.9	661.6	716.9	713.6	700.9
of which: General government	287.2	580.9	628.7	683.0	681.3	668.7
Private sector guaranteed by public sector	..	..	..	..	..	..
Private sector not guaranteed	210.6	97.5	90.6	131.4	128.0	173.3
Short-term external debt	56.1	81.5	97.3	63.6	44.6	53.0
Disbursements (long-term)	**107.8**	**227.9**	**96.5**	**137.6**	**36.8**	**69.4**
Public and publicly guaranteed sector	20.0	227.9	96.5	59.4	36.8	17.1
Public sector	20.0	227.9	96.5	59.4	36.8	17.1
of which: General government	15.0	226.0	95.4	58.5	36.0	17.1
Private sector guaranteed by public sector	..	..	..	..	..	..
Private sector not guaranteed	87.8	..	..	78.2	..	52.3
Principal repayments (long-term)	**25.7**	**297.4**	**42.6**	**58.0**	**31.7**	**32.8**
Public and publicly guaranteed sector	10.3	265.6	35.8	20.7	28.3	25.7
Public sector	10.3	265.6	35.8	20.7	28.3	25.7
of which: General government	10.3	259.5	31.6	20.7	25.8	25.7
Private sector guaranteed by public sector	..	..	..	..	..	..
Private sector not guaranteed	15.3	31.8	6.8	37.4	3.4	7.1
Interest payments (long-term)	**19.5**	**36.0**	**22.5**	**24.8**	**26.5**	**146.8**
Public and publicly guaranteed sector	15.5	35.7	21.3	22.6	24.7	145.5
Public sector	15.5	35.7	21.3	22.6	24.7	145.5
of which: General government	13.5	35.7	21.0	22.6	24.7	145.5
Private sector guaranteed by public sector	..	..	..	..	..	..
Private sector not guaranteed	3.9	0.3	1.2	2.3	1.8	1.3
Summary external debt stock by creditor type						
Long-term external debt stocks	**530.1**	**714.4**	**752.3**	**848.3**	**841.6**	**874.3**
Public and publicly guaranteed debt from:	319.5	616.9	661.6	716.9	713.6	700.9
Official creditors	169.5	410.1	461.6	516.9	513.6	500.9
Multilateral	102.7	130.1	172.8	224.3	253.4	263.0
of which: World Bank	0.0	..	50.2	53.6	73.1	76.2
Bilateral	66.8	280.0	288.8	292.6	260.1	238.0
Private creditors	150.0	206.9	200.0	200.0	200.0	200.0
Bondholders	150.0	206.9	200.0	200.0	200.0	200.0
Commercial banks and others	..	..	..	..	..	..
Private nonguaranteed debt from:	210.6	97.5	90.6	131.4	128.0	173.3
Bondholders	..	..	..	..	..	..
Commercial banks and others	210.6	97.5	90.6	131.4	128.0	173.3
Use of IMF credit	105.2	93.0	90.2	95.6	93.3	92.8
Net financial inflows						
Net debt inflows						
Use of IMF credit	..	..	..	..	..	..
Long-term	82.1	-69.6	54.0	79.5	5.1	36.7
Official creditors	9.7	5.4	67.6	38.7	8.5	-8.6
Multilateral	-1.7	-7.7	42.5	51.4	29.1	9.6
of which: World Bank	-1.4	..	50.2	3.4	19.5	3.1
Bilateral	11.4	13.1	25.1	-12.7	-20.6	-18.2
Private creditors	72.5	-75.0	-13.7	40.8	-3.4	45.3
Bondholders	..	-43.2	-6.9	0.0	0.0	0.0
Banks and others	72.5	-31.8	-6.8	40.8	-3.4	45.3
Short-term	39.0	13.6	15.8	-33.6	-19.1	8.4
Net equity inflows						
Foreign direct investment	284.8	208.9	379.2	418.3	434.7	397.4
Portfolio equity	-1.1	..	..	..	..	..
Debt ratios						
External debt stocks to exports (%)	46.7	37.8	39.5	39.6	35.8	37.7
External debt stocks to GNI (%)	24.2	19.9	19.9	20.0	19.0	20.1
Debt service to exports (%)	3.1	14.3	2.8	3.3	2.2	6.7
Short-term to external debt stocks (%)	8.1	9.2	10.4	6.3	4.5	5.2
Multilateral to external debt stocks (%)	14.8	14.6	18.4	22.3	25.9	25.8
Reserves to external debt stocks (%)	82.3	103.3	96.6	110.7	96.6	102.1
Gross national income (GNI)	2,859.2	4,477.2	4,721.0	5,027.1	5,161.0	5,087.1

GABON

(US$ million, unless otherwise indicated)

	2009	2015	2016	2017	2018	2019
Summary external debt data by debtor type						
Total external debt stocks	2,725	5,119	5,336	6,499	6,766	7,193
Use of IMF credit	230	203	197	412	601	722
Long-term external debt	2,392	4,706	4,898	5,880	5,978	6,112
Public and publicly guaranteed sector	2,392	4,706	4,898	5,880	5,978	6,112
Public sector	2,392	4,706	4,898	5,880	5,978	6,112
of which: General government	2,390	4,699	4,884	5,830	5,922	6,054
Private sector guaranteed by public sector	..	..	..	..	..	..
Private sector not guaranteed	..	..	..	..	..	..
Short-term external debt	104	210	241	207	187	360
Disbursements (long-term)	318	834	433	1,173	718	594
Public and publicly guaranteed sector	318	834	433	1,173	718	594
Public sector	318	834	433	1,173	718	594
of which: General government	318	831	425	1,152	691	589
Private sector guaranteed by public sector	..	..	..	..	..	..
Private sector not guaranteed	..	..	..	..	..	..
Principal repayments (long-term)	275	274	172	450	474	387
Public and publicly guaranteed sector	275	274	172	450	474	387
Public sector	275	274	172	450	474	387
of which: General government	274	273	171	449	472	385
Private sector guaranteed by public sector	..	..	..	..	..	..
Private sector not guaranteed	..	..	..	..	..	..
Interest payments (long-term)	147	194	195	168	216	252
Public and publicly guaranteed sector	147	194	195	168	216	252
Public sector	147	194	195	168	216	252
of which: General government	147	194	195	167	215	250
Private sector guaranteed by public sector	..	..	..	..	..	..
Private sector not guaranteed	..	..	..	..	..	..
Summary external debt stock by creditor type						
Long-term external debt stocks	2,392	4,706	4,898	5,880	5,978	6,112
Public and publicly guaranteed debt from:	2,392	4,706	4,898	5,880	5,978	6,112
Official creditors	1,133	1,646	1,672	2,672	3,043	3,397
Multilateral	460	569	563	1,450	1,697	1,920
of which: World Bank	18	46	67	336	369	581
Bilateral	673	1,077	1,108	1,222	1,346	1,477
Private creditors	1,259	3,060	3,226	3,207	2,935	2,715
Bondholders	901	2,218	2,218	2,200	2,186	2,186
Commercial banks and others	358	842	1,008	1,007	749	529
Private nonguaranteed debt from:	..	..	..	..	..	..
Bondholders	..	..	..	..	..	..
Commercial banks and others	..	..	..	..	..	..
Use of IMF credit	230	203	197	412	601	722
Net financial inflows						
Net debt inflows						
Use of IMF credit	..	..	..	198	202	123
Long-term	44	561	262	722	244	207
Official creditors	-35	148	66	850	486	400
Multilateral	44	23	8	786	331	257
of which: World Bank	-2	17	21	249	64	220
Bilateral	-79	124	58	64	155	143
Private creditors	79	413	196	-128	-241	-193
Bondholders	..	500	..	-18	-14	..
Banks and others	79	-87	196	-110	-227	-193
Short-term	-7	135	21	-37	-11	178
Net equity inflows						
Foreign direct investment	608	-125	1,244	1,314	1,379	1,553
Portfolio equity	0	4	..	..	..	..
Debt ratios						
External debt stocks to exports (%)	40	93	..	..	..	..
External debt stocks to GNI (%)	25	39	41	46	43	46
Debt service to exports (%)	6	9	..	..	..	..
Short-term to external debt stocks (%)	4	4	5	3	3	5
Multilateral to external debt stocks (%)	17	11	11	22	25	27
Reserves to external debt stocks (%)	73	36	15	15	20	..
Gross national income (GNI)	10,693	13,189	12,935	13,986	15,755	15,511

GAMBIA, THE
(US$ million, unless otherwise indicated)

	2009	2015	2016	2017	2018	2019
Summary external debt data by debtor type						
Total external debt stocks	**528.2**	**534.7**	**527.1**	**668.3**	**696.3**	**717.9**
Use of IMF credit	75.2	88.4	80.0	93.9	84.1	77.2
Long-term external debt	409.6	434.8	429.4	560.6	594.5	616.6
Public and publicly guaranteed sector	409.6	434.8	429.4	560.6	594.5	616.6
Public sector	409.6	434.8	429.4	560.6	594.5	616.6
of which: General government	394.2	422.4	420.2	554.0	591.2	615.0
Private sector guaranteed by public sector	..	..	..	..	..	..
Private sector not guaranteed	..	..	..	..	..	..
Short-term external debt	43.3	11.5	17.6	13.7	17.8	24.0
Disbursements (long-term)	**32.3**	**52.4**	**29.7**	**147.3**	**73.1**	**54.9**
Public and publicly guaranteed sector	32.3	52.4	29.7	147.3	73.1	54.9
Public sector	32.3	52.4	29.7	147.3	73.1	54.9
of which: General government	30.9	52.4	29.7	147.3	73.1	54.9
Private sector guaranteed by public sector	..	..	..	..	..	..
Private sector not guaranteed	..	..	..	..	..	..
Principal repayments (long-term)	**11.9**	**30.5**	**30.3**	**30.6**	**32.5**	**31.9**
Public and publicly guaranteed sector	11.9	30.5	30.3	30.6	32.5	31.9
Public sector	11.9	30.5	30.3	30.6	32.5	31.9
of which: General government	10.7	27.1	27.2	27.4	29.3	30.4
Private sector guaranteed by public sector	..	..	..	..	..	..
Private sector not guaranteed	..	..	..	..	..	..
Interest payments (long-term)	**7.1**	**5.2**	**6.0**	**6.5**	**6.7**	**8.6**
Public and publicly guaranteed sector	7.1	5.2	6.0	6.5	6.7	8.6
Public sector	7.1	5.2	6.0	6.5	6.7	8.6
of which: General government	6.6	4.8	5.9	6.3	6.6	8.6
Private sector guaranteed by public sector	..	..	..	..	..	..
Private sector not guaranteed	..	..	..	..	..	..
Summary external debt stock by creditor type						
Long-term external debt stocks	**409.6**	**434.8**	**429.4**	**560.6**	**594.5**	**616.6**
Public and publicly guaranteed debt from:	409.6	434.8	429.4	560.6	594.5	616.6
Official creditors	406.2	428.6	425.1	557.7	593.5	616.6
Multilateral	290.7	310.6	303.7	406.5	436.2	451.1
of which: World Bank	64.3	55.0	57.2	105.1	115.8	117.7
Bilateral	115.5	118.1	121.4	151.2	157.3	165.6
Private creditors	3.4	6.2	4.3	2.9	0.9	0.0
Bondholders	..	..	..	..	..	..
Commercial banks and others	3.4	6.2	4.3	2.9	0.9	0.0
Private nonguaranteed debt from:	..	..	..	..	..	..
Bondholders	..	..	..	..	..	..
Commercial banks and others	..	..	..	..	..	..
Use of IMF credit	75.2	88.4	80.0	93.9	84.1	77.2
Net financial inflows						
Net debt inflows						
Use of IMF credit	15.8	5.5	-5.9	8.9	-7.8	-6.3
Long-term	20.4	21.9	-0.6	116.7	40.6	22.9
Official creditors	19.7	23.7	1.2	118.6	42.5	23.8
Multilateral	20.7	11.0	-2.5	89.6	36.1	15.7
of which: World Bank	2.0	-0.2	4.0	43.9	13.3	2.5
Bilateral	-1.0	12.7	3.7	29.0	6.5	8.2
Private creditors	0.8	-1.8	-1.8	-1.8	-1.9	-0.9
Bondholders	..	..	..	..	..	..
Banks and others	0.8	-1.8	-1.8	-1.8	-1.9	-0.9
Short-term	27.0	-1.0	7.9	-3.9	3.7	7.5
Net equity inflows						
Foreign direct investment	39.4	7.9	7.9	12.3	33.0	32.3
Portfolio equity	..	..	..	..	..	..
Debt ratios						
External debt stocks to exports (%)	185.2	201.0	214.7	254.5	199.6	202.1
External debt stocks to GNI (%)	37.1	40.4	36.5	45.5	43.6	41.4
Debt service to exports (%)	6.8	15.5	17.3	16.9	13.6	13.4
Short-term to external debt stocks (%)	8.2	2.1	3.3	2.1	2.6	3.3
Multilateral to external debt stocks (%)	55.0	58.1	57.6	60.8	62.6	62.8
Reserves to external debt stocks (%)	42.4	20.8	16.6	25.4	27.5	..
Gross national income (GNI)	1,422.1	1,322.3	1,442.5	1,469.9	1,595.5	1,733.8

GEORGIA

(US$ million, unless otherwise indicated)

	2009	2015	2016	2017	2018	2019
Summary external debt data by debtor type						
Total external debt stocks	**8,673**	**14,875**	**16,320**	**16,424**	**17,326**	**17,312**
Use of IMF credit	1,012	330	307	397	416	448
Long-term external debt	6,736	12,501	13,659	13,584	14,593	14,588
Public and publicly guaranteed sector	3,529	5,721	6,224	6,615	6,749	6,993
Public sector	3,529	5,721	6,224	6,615	6,749	6,993
of which: General government	2,656	4,233	4,443	5,032	5,257	5,535
Private sector guaranteed by public sector	..	..	..	..	..	..
Private sector not guaranteed	3,207	6,781	7,435	6,969	7,844	7,595
Short-term external debt	925	2,043	2,354	2,443	2,318	2,276
Disbursements (long-term)	**1,147**	**2,545**	**2,780**	**2,003**	**2,468**	**2,369**
Public and publicly guaranteed sector	678	733	839	536	567	616
Public sector	678	733	839	536	567	616
of which: General government	427	464	424	524	555	605
Private sector guaranteed by public sector	..	..	..	..	..	..
Private sector not guaranteed	469	1,812	1,941	1,467	1,900	1,753
Principal repayments (long-term)	**474**	**1,387**	**1,634**	**1,974**	**1,681**	**1,669**
Public and publicly guaranteed sector	140	435	256	434	300	324
Public sector	140	435	256	434	300	324
of which: General government	71	118	132	165	227	280
Private sector guaranteed by public sector	..	..	..	..	..	..
Private sector not guaranteed	334	952	1,379	1,540	1,381	1,345
Interest payments (long-term)	**251**	**661**	**905**	**526**	**609**	**576**
Public and publicly guaranteed sector	77	166	153	175	167	185
Public sector	77	166	153	175	167	185
of which: General government	69	79	87	99	111	122
Private sector guaranteed by public sector	..	..	..	..	..	..
Private sector not guaranteed	174	495	752	351	442	391
Summary external debt stock by creditor type						
Long-term external debt stocks	**6,736**	**12,501**	**13,659**	**13,584**	**14,593**	**14,588**
Public and publicly guaranteed debt from:	3,529	5,721	6,224	6,615	6,749	6,993
Official creditors	2,153	3,707	3,882	4,416	4,580	4,880
Multilateral	1,535	2,962	3,154	3,664	3,794	3,934
of which: World Bank	1,253	1,849	1,830	2,026	1,960	1,879
Bilateral	617	745	728	752	786	946
Private creditors	1,377	2,014	2,341	2,199	2,169	2,113
Bondholders	500	1,250	1,500	1,250	1,250	1,250
Commercial banks and others	877	764	841	949	919	863
Private nonguaranteed debt from:	3,207	6,781	7,435	6,969	7,844	7,595
Bondholders	..	900	1,054	1,152	1,660	1,875
Commercial banks and others	3,207	5,881	6,381	5,817	6,184	5,720
Use of IMF credit	**1,012**	**330**	**307**	**397**	**416**	**448**
Net financial inflows						
Net debt inflows						
Use of IMF credit	313	-73	-14	70	28	35
Long-term	673	1,158	1,146	29	787	700
Official creditors	357	335	253	315	259	344
Multilateral	333	330	265	337	212	181
of which: World Bank	255	133	19	125	-31	-58
Bilateral	24	5	-12	-22	48	163
Private creditors	316	824	892	-287	528	356
Bondholders	0	-100	404	-454	236	709
Banks and others	316	924	488	167	291	-353
Short-term	-112	248	230	181	-262	-19
Net equity inflows						
Foreign direct investment	567	1,707	2,117	1,708	1,241	1,106
Portfolio equity	12	5	-4	-2	4	-6
Debt ratios						
External debt stocks to exports (%)	236	214	230	189	170	159
External debt stocks to GNI (%)	81	102	113	106	102	102
Debt service to exports (%)	21	31	37	30	24	22
Short-term to external debt stocks (%)	11	14	14	15	13	13
Multilateral to external debt stocks (%)	18	20	19	22	22	23
Reserves to external debt stocks (%)	24	17	17	19	19	20
Gross national income (GNI)	10,723	14,615	14,440	15,447	16,915	17,039

GHANA
(US$ million, unless otherwise indicated)

	2009	2015	2016	2017	2018	2019
Summary external debt data by debtor type						
Total external debt stocks	**6,603**	**20,111**	**21,147**	**22,321**	**23,326**	**26,953**
Use of IMF credit	826	1,242	1,366	1,465	1,508	1,576
Long-term external debt	4,266	15,565	16,993	17,533	18,185	20,739
Public and publicly guaranteed sector	4,266	15,311	16,739	17,280	17,932	20,486
Public sector	4,266	15,311	16,739	17,280	17,932	20,486
of which: General government	3,926	14,288	15,720	16,181	16,837	19,419
Private sector guaranteed by public sector	..	..	..	..	..	..
Private sector not guaranteed	0	253	253	253	253	253
Short-term external debt	1,511	3,304	2,789	3,323	3,634	4,638
Disbursements (long-term)	**1,005**	**2,852**	**2,510**	**1,166**	**2,662**	**3,630**
Public and publicly guaranteed sector	1,005	2,852	2,510	1,166	2,662	3,630
Public sector	1,005	2,852	2,510	1,166	2,662	3,630
of which: General government	796	2,705	2,473	1,141	2,626	3,630
Private sector guaranteed by public sector	..	..	..	..	..	..
Private sector not guaranteed	..	..	..	..	..	..
Principal repayments (long-term)	**145**	**553**	**875**	**1,100**	**1,809**	**1,017**
Public and publicly guaranteed sector	145	553	875	1,100	1,809	1,017
Public sector	145	553	875	1,100	1,809	1,017
of which: General government	127	540	862	1,089	1,796	997
Private sector guaranteed by public sector	..	..	..	..	..	..
Private sector not guaranteed	..	..	..	..	..	..
Interest payments (long-term)	**75**	**336**	**554**	**745**	**675**	**688**
Public and publicly guaranteed sector	75	330	548	739	669	682
Public sector	75	330	548	739	669	682
of which: General government	67	322	539	731	660	674
Private sector guaranteed by public sector	..	..	..	..	..	..
Private sector not guaranteed	..	6	6	6	6	6
Summary external debt stock by creditor type						
Long-term external debt stocks	**4,266**	**15,565**	**16,993**	**17,533**	**18,185**	**20,739**
Public and publicly guaranteed debt from:	4,266	15,311	16,739	17,280	17,932	20,486
Official creditors	3,320	8,686	8,676	9,178	8,866	8,701
Multilateral	2,331	4,579	4,728	5,383	5,375	5,482
of which: World Bank	1,581	3,285	3,415	3,945	3,926	3,989
Bilateral	989	4,106	3,947	3,795	3,491	3,219
Private creditors	946	6,626	8,064	8,102	9,066	11,785
Bondholders	..	3,000	3,750	3,750	5,048	8,048
Commercial banks and others	946	3,626	4,314	4,352	4,018	3,737
Private nonguaranteed debt from:	0	253	253	253	253	253
Bondholders	0	253	253	253	253	253
Commercial banks and others	..	..	..	..	..	..
Use of IMF credit	826	1,242	1,366	1,465	1,508	1,576
Net financial inflows						
Net debt inflows						
Use of IMF credit	104	172	166	18	78	76
Long-term	860	2,299	1,636	66	853	2,613
Official creditors	671	810	162	142	-153	-121
Multilateral	403	596	280	399	107	133
of which: World Bank	240	474	235	323	75	88
Bilateral	268	214	-117	-256	-260	-254
Private creditors	189	1,489	1,473	-76	1,006	2,733
Bondholders	..	1,000	750	..	1,298	3,000
Banks and others	189	489	723	-76	-292	-267
Short-term	374	230	-503	409	290	1,005
Net equity inflows						
Foreign direct investment	1,940	3,192	3,485	3,255	2,989	2,319
Portfolio equity	535	..	..	..	..	..
Debt ratios						
External debt stocks to exports (%)	85	119	119	108	101	103
External debt stocks to GNI (%)	26	42	39	39	36	41
Debt service to exports (%)	3	6	9	10	12	7
Short-term to external debt stocks (%)	23	16	13	15	16	17
Multilateral to external debt stocks (%)	35	23	22	24	23	20
Reserves to external debt stocks (%)	51	27	26	30	25	26
Gross national income (GNI)	25,884	47,921	53,962	57,432	64,270	65,527

GRENADA
(US$ million, unless otherwise indicated)

	2009	2015	2016	2017	2018	2019
Summary external debt data by debtor type						
Total external debt stocks	**556.6**	**601.2**	**602.4**	**543.3**	**549.9**	**550.2**
Use of IMF credit	40.5	44.8	43.9	44.5	38.6	35.6
Long-term external debt	477.8	537.4	531.7	476.8	494.5	500.8
Public and publicly guaranteed sector	477.8	537.4	531.7	476.8	494.5	500.8
Public sector	477.8	537.4	531.7	476.8	494.5	500.8
of which: General government	474.1	536.3	530.9	476.5	494.5	500.8
Private sector guaranteed by public sector	..	..	..	..	..	..
Private sector not guaranteed	..	..	..	..	..	..
Short-term external debt	38.3	19.0	26.8	22.0	16.7	13.8
Disbursements (long-term)	**25.7**	**54.1**	**23.6**	**14.3**	**51.9**	**40.0**
Public and publicly guaranteed sector	25.7	54.1	23.6	14.3	51.9	40.0
Public sector	25.7	54.1	23.6	14.3	51.9	40.0
of which: General government	25.3	54.1	23.6	14.3	51.9	40.0
Private sector guaranteed by public sector	..	..	..	..	..	..
Private sector not guaranteed	..	..	..	..	..	..
Principal repayments (long-term)	**9.3**	**16.4**	**24.7**	**30.5**	**31.7**	**32.6**
Public and publicly guaranteed sector	9.3	16.4	24.7	30.5	31.7	32.6
Public sector	9.3	16.4	24.7	30.5	31.7	32.6
of which: General government	9.0	16.0	24.3	30.1	31.3	32.6
Private sector guaranteed by public sector	..	..	..	..	..	..
Private sector not guaranteed	..	..	..	..	..	..
Interest payments (long-term)	**10.7**	**5.9**	**18.4**	**20.6**	**16.3**	**16.5**
Public and publicly guaranteed sector	10.7	5.9	18.4	20.6	16.3	16.5
Public sector	10.7	5.9	18.4	20.6	16.3	16.5
of which: General government	10.6	5.9	18.4	20.6	16.3	16.5
Private sector guaranteed by public sector	..	..	..	..	..	..
Private sector not guaranteed	..	..	..	..	..	..
Summary external debt stock by creditor type						
Long-term external debt stocks	**477.8**	**537.4**	**531.7**	**476.8**	**494.5**	**500.8**
Public and publicly guaranteed debt from:	477.8	537.4	531.7	476.8	494.5	500.8
Official creditors	274.9	350.0	355.9	356.0	383.9	399.7
Multilateral	183.1	244.3	251.0	256.0	278.7	273.6
of which: World Bank	50.2	89.8	89.5	102.0	131.1	131.4
Bilateral	91.8	105.6	104.9	100.0	105.2	126.0
Private creditors	202.8	187.4	175.7	120.8	110.6	101.1
Bondholders	193.2	184.8	175.4	117.5	108.5	99.4
Commercial banks and others	9.6	2.6	0.3	3.3	2.1	1.7
Private nonguaranteed debt from:	..	..	..	..	..	..
Bondholders	..	..	..	..	..	..
Commercial banks and others	..	..	..	..	..	..
Use of IMF credit	40.5	44.8	43.9	44.5	38.6	35.6
Net financial inflows						
Net debt inflows						
Use of IMF credit	9.7	1.1	0.5	-2.0	-4.9	-2.8
Long-term	16.4	37.8	-1.0	-16.2	20.2	7.4
Official creditors	16.4	38.8	8.4	-6.4	30.3	16.8
Multilateral	12.7	37.8	9.2	-0.4	24.8	-4.0
of which: World Bank	1.8	18.1	2.1	7.3	31.3	1.2
Bilateral	3.7	1.0	-0.8	-6.1	5.5	20.8
Private creditors	0.0	-1.1	-9.4	-9.8	-10.2	-9.4
Bondholders	..	..	-9.4	-9.0	-9.0	-9.0
Banks and others	0.0	-1.1	..	-0.8	-1.2	-0.4
Short-term	-28.0	-9.0	5.9	-5.3	-5.8	-3.3
Net equity inflows						
Foreign direct investment	82.8	156.8	91.6	138.7	143.4	131.0
Portfolio equity	..	0.0	0.0	0.0	0.0	..
Debt ratios						
External debt stocks to exports (%)	284.9	114.8	112.4	92.2	83.1	..
External debt stocks to GNI (%)	78.6	68.1	62.5	53.2	52.0	49.5
Debt service to exports (%)	11.7	5.2	9.0	9.5	8.0	..
Short-term to external debt stocks (%)	6.9	3.2	4.4	4.1	3.0	2.5
Multilateral to external debt stocks (%)	32.9	40.6	41.7	47.1	50.7	49.7
Reserves to external debt stocks (%)	23.2	32.9	34.5	36.6	42.5	43.0
Gross national income (GNI)	708.2	882.8	964.6	1,021.2	1,057.5	1,111.6

GUATEMALA
(US$ million, unless otherwise indicated)

	2009	2015	2016	2017	2018	2019
Summary external debt data by debtor type						
Total external debt stocks	14,824	20,378	21,480	23,945	23,408	26,574
Use of IMF credit	315	278	270	286	279	278
Long-term external debt	13,283	19,256	20,289	22,616	22,430	25,589
Public and publicly guaranteed sector	4,926	7,544	8,148	8,366	8,428	9,326
Public sector	4,926	7,544	8,148	8,366	8,428	9,326
of which: General government	4,413	7,237	7,878	8,134	8,234	9,170
Private sector guaranteed by public sector	..	..	..	..	..	..
Private sector not guaranteed	8,358	11,711	12,142	14,250	14,002	16,263
Short-term external debt	1,226	844	920	1,042	698	707
Disbursements (long-term)	942	2,423	3,212	5,527	3,001	6,381
Public and publicly guaranteed sector	807	906	953	662	406	1,312
Public sector	807	906	953	662	406	1,312
of which: General government	767	906	953	662	406	1,312
Private sector guaranteed by public sector	..	..	..	..	..	..
Private sector not guaranteed	135	1,516	2,260	4,866	2,594	5,069
Principal repayments (long-term)	1,086	1,424	2,116	3,225	3,182	3,202
Public and publicly guaranteed sector	269	350	352	457	342	395
Public sector	269	350	352	457	342	395
of which: General government	257	312	314	419	305	357
Private sector guaranteed by public sector	..	..	..	..	..	..
Private sector not guaranteed	817	1,074	1,765	2,768	2,839	2,807
Interest payments (long-term)	657	676	953	950	752	574
Public and publicly guaranteed sector	258	288	354	376	267	408
Public sector	258	288	354	376	267	408
of which: General government	227	271	338	362	255	397
Private sector guaranteed by public sector	..	..	..	..	..	..
Private sector not guaranteed	399	388	600	574	485	166
Summary external debt stock by creditor type						
Long-term external debt stocks	13,283	19,256	20,289	22,616	22,430	25,589
Public and publicly guaranteed debt from:	4,926	7,544	8,148	8,366	8,428	9,326
Official creditors	3,968	5,783	5,684	5,406	5,470	5,171
Multilateral	3,612	5,353	5,197	4,911	4,977	4,686
of which: World Bank	1,112	1,765	1,679	1,555	1,718	1,641
Bilateral	356	430	486	496	493	485
Private creditors	957	1,762	2,464	2,960	2,958	4,155
Bondholders	955	1,730	2,430	2,930	2,930	4,130
Commercial banks and others	2	32	34	30	28	25
Private nonguaranteed debt from:	8,358	11,711	12,142	14,250	14,002	16,263
Bondholders	5	1,150	1,500	2,330	2,330	2,330
Commercial banks and others	8,353	10,561	10,642	11,920	11,672	13,933
Use of IMF credit	315	278	270	286	279	278
Net financial inflows						
Net debt inflows						
Use of IMF credit	..	..	..	..	..	..
Long-term	-144	998	1,096	2,302	-181	3,179
Official creditors	537	548	-101	-290	65	-281
Multilateral	548	508	-154	-289	68	-289
of which: World Bank	306	269	-86	-124	163	-78
Bilateral	-11	39	53	-1	-2	8
Private creditors	-682	451	1,197	2,593	-246	3,460
Bondholders	-50	-5	1,050	1,330	..	1,200
Banks and others	-632	456	147	1,263	-246	2,260
Short-term	-925	-107	76	122	-344	9
Net equity inflows						
Foreign direct investment	348	1,486	782	880	1,050	944
Portfolio equity	0	0	0	0	0	0
Debt ratios						
External debt stocks to exports (%)	168	158	164	171	164	182
External debt stocks to GNI (%)	40	34	33	34	33	35
Debt service to exports (%)	20	16	24	30	28	26
Short-term to external debt stocks (%)	8	4	4	4	3	3
Multilateral to external debt stocks (%)	24	26	24	21	21	18
Reserves to external debt stocks (%)	33	37	41	48	53	54
Gross national income (GNI)	36,772	60,700	64,628	70,111	71,598	75,435

GUINEA

(US$ million, unless otherwise indicated)

	2009	2015	2016	2017	2018	2019
Summary external debt data by debtor type						
Total external debt stocks	3,502	2,151	2,198	2,382	2,578	2,931
Use of IMF credit	220	340	379	426	464	481
Long-term external debt	3,246	1,686	1,723	1,832	1,957	2,240
Public and publicly guaranteed sector	3,246	1,686	1,723	1,832	1,957	2,240
Public sector	3,246	1,686	1,723	1,832	1,957	2,240
of which: General government	2,876	1,565	1,603	1,707	1,845	2,135
Private sector guaranteed by public sector	..	..	..	..	..	..
Private sector not guaranteed	..	..	..	..	..	..
Short-term external debt	37	124	96	124	158	210
Disbursements (long-term)	63	188	124	121	225	354
Public and publicly guaranteed sector	63	188	124	121	225	354
Public sector	63	188	124	121	225	354
of which: General government	37	159	115	121	224	352
Private sector guaranteed by public sector	..	..	..	..	..	..
Private sector not guaranteed	..	..	..	..	..	..
Principal repayments (long-term)	98	65	59	70	72	62
Public and publicly guaranteed sector	98	65	59	70	72	62
Public sector	98	65	59	70	72	62
of which: General government	89	58	51	61	62	55
Private sector guaranteed by public sector	..	..	..	..	..	..
Private sector not guaranteed	..	..	..	..	..	..
Interest payments (long-term)	32	14	23	24	30	31
Public and publicly guaranteed sector	32	14	23	24	30	31
Public sector	32	14	23	24	30	31
of which: General government	21	11	20	20	26	28
Private sector guaranteed by public sector	..	..	..	..	..	..
Private sector not guaranteed	..	..	..	..	..	..
Summary external debt stock by creditor type						
Long-term external debt stocks	3,246	1,686	1,723	1,832	1,957	2,240
Public and publicly guaranteed debt from:	3,246	1,686	1,723	1,832	1,957	2,240
Official creditors	3,090	1,632	1,680	1,798	1,935	2,177
Multilateral	1,897	603	618	677	822	1,018
of which: World Bank	1,269	186	222	252	344	471
Bilateral	1,193	1,029	1,063	1,121	1,113	1,159
Private creditors	156	54	43	34	22	63
Bondholders	..	..	..	..	..	..
Commercial banks and others	156	54	43	34	22	63
Private nonguaranteed debt from:	..	..	..	..	..	..
Bondholders	..	..	..	..	..	..
Commercial banks and others	..	..	..	..	..	..
Use of IMF credit	220	340	379	426	464	481
Net financial inflows						
Net debt inflows						
Use of IMF credit	-13	33	51	24	49	20
Long-term	-36	124	65	51	153	292
Official creditors	-22	135	76	62	165	251
Multilateral	-40	-13	29	27	160	201
of which: World Bank	-27	-2	43	17	98	129
Bilateral	18	148	47	35	5	50
Private creditors	-14	-11	-11	-11	-12	41
Bondholders	..	..	..	..	..	..
Banks and others	-14	-11	-11	-11	-12	41
Short-term	-104	39	-28	28	34	52
Net equity inflows						
Foreign direct investment	91	9	3	40	-28	13
Portfolio equity	..	-2	0	1	0	0
Debt ratios						
External debt stocks to exports (%)	306	113	88	51	62	71
External debt stocks to GNI (%)	53	25	26	23	22	23
Debt service to exports (%)	13	6	3	2	3	3
Short-term to external debt stocks (%)	1	6	4	5	6	7
Multilateral to external debt stocks (%)	54	28	28	28	32	35
Reserves to external debt stocks (%)	12	27	36	39	44	42
Gross national income (GNI)	6,549	8,651	8,501	10,286	11,521	12,819

79

GUINEA-BISSAU

(US$ million, unless otherwise indicated)

	2009	2015	2016	2017	2018	2019
Summary external debt data by debtor type						
Total external debt stocks	1,164.0	355.7	336.3	436.9	543.1	634.8
Use of IMF credit	31.3	37.7	42.5	51.6	52.6	50.3
Long-term external debt	978.5	264.9	261.2	351.7	448.2	525.3
Public and publicly guaranteed sector	978.5	264.9	261.2	351.7	424.2	507.0
Public sector	978.5	264.9	261.2	351.7	424.2	507.0
of which: General government	968.3	264.9	261.2	351.7	424.2	507.0
Private sector guaranteed by public sector	..	..	..	..	..	..
Private sector not guaranteed	..	0.0	0.0	0.0	24.0	18.4
Short-term external debt	154.3	53.0	32.6	33.6	42.3	59.2
Disbursements (long-term)	**16.2**	**34.9**	**4.6**	**88.7**	**129.8**	**90.0**
Public and publicly guaranteed sector	16.2	34.9	4.6	88.7	105.8	90.0
Public sector	16.2	34.9	4.6	88.7	105.8	90.0
of which: General government	16.2	34.9	4.6	88.7	105.8	90.0
Private sector guaranteed by public sector	..	..	..	..	..	..
Private sector not guaranteed	..	..	0.0	..	24.0	..
Principal repayments (long-term)	**5.7**	**4.2**	**4.7**	**6.6**	**5.4**	**5.3**
Public and publicly guaranteed sector	5.7	4.2	4.7	6.6	5.4	5.3
Public sector	5.7	4.2	4.7	6.6	5.4	5.3
of which: General government	5.3	4.2	4.7	6.6	5.4	5.3
Private sector guaranteed by public sector	..	..	..	..	..	..
Private sector not guaranteed	..	0.0	..	..	..	..
Interest payments (long-term)	**4.1**	**2.0**	**1.9**	**3.3**	**6.5**	**8.5**
Public and publicly guaranteed sector	4.1	2.0	1.9	3.3	5.1	7.1
Public sector	4.1	2.0	1.9	3.3	5.1	7.1
of which: General government	4.0	2.0	1.9	3.3	5.1	7.1
Private sector guaranteed by public sector	..	..	..	..	..	..
Private sector not guaranteed	..	..	..	..	1.4	1.4
Summary external debt stock by creditor type						
Long-term external debt stocks	978.5	264.9	261.2	351.7	448.2	525.3
Public and publicly guaranteed debt from:	978.5	264.9	261.2	351.7	424.2	507.0
Official creditors	978.5	236.5	233.3	283.1	327.4	380.8
Multilateral	521.2	115.7	114.7	162.5	203.5	258.9
of which: World Bank	303.8	53.0	54.1	67.0	111.1	126.1
Bilateral	457.3	120.8	118.7	120.6	124.0	121.9
Private creditors	..	28.4	27.9	68.5	96.7	126.2
Bondholders	..	28.4	27.9	68.5	96.7	126.2
Commercial banks and others	..	..	..	..	..	..
Private nonguaranteed debt from:	..	0.0	0.0	0.0	24.0	18.4
Bondholders	..	..	..	..	..	..
Commercial banks and others	..	0.0	0.0	0.0	24.0	18.4
Use of IMF credit	31.3	37.7	42.5	51.6	52.6	50.3
Net financial inflows						
Net debt inflows						
Use of IMF credit	1.2	4.0	6.1	6.4	2.2	-2.0
Long-term	10.5	30.6	-0.1	82.1	124.4	84.7
Official creditors	10.5	22.9	0.4	41.5	72.2	55.2
Multilateral	1.3	24.8	2.3	36.5	68.6	57.3
of which: World Bank	0.0	2.2	2.8	9.4	46.1	15.7
Bilateral	9.3	-1.9	-1.9	4.9	3.5	-2.1
Private creditors	..	7.7	-0.5	40.6	52.2	29.5
Bondholders	..	7.8	-0.5	40.6	28.2	29.5
Banks and others	..	0.0	0.0	..	24.0	..
Short-term	5.0	20.7	-20.4	1.0	8.7	16.9
Net equity inflows						
Foreign direct investment	18.9	18.6	14.2	15.7	16.7	30.6
Portfolio equity	-0.2	..	..	..	..	..
Debt ratios						
External debt stocks to exports (%)	712.4	103.9	154.4	103.9	124.6	..
External debt stocks to GNI (%)	142.5	33.1	27.8	32.4	37.3	44.2
Debt service to exports (%)	7.1	1.9	3.5	2.8	3.3	..
Short-term to external debt stocks (%)	13.3	14.9	9.7	7.7	7.8	9.3
Multilateral to external debt stocks (%)	44.8	32.5	34.1	37.2	37.5	40.8
Reserves to external debt stocks (%)	14.5	93.4	..	..	..	..
Gross national income (GNI)	816.6	1,073.4	1,207.9	1,349.6	1,456.1	1,437.3

GUYANA

(US$ million, unless otherwise indicated)

	2009	2015	2016	2017	2018	2019
Summary external debt data by debtor type						
Total external debt stocks	1,427.9	1,636.9	1,643.9	1,582.9	1,608.0	1,597.4
Use of IMF credit	194.6	124.5	117.1	124.0	121.1	120.4
Long-term external debt	781.3	1,201.3	1,283.6	1,342.6	1,361.8	1,357.4
Public and publicly guaranteed sector	779.6	1,031.3	1,049.0	1,135.0	1,204.8	1,251.1
Public sector	779.6	1,031.3	1,049.0	1,135.0	1,204.8	1,251.1
of which: General government	710.1	995.1	1,013.2	1,099.3	1,169.5	1,216.1
Private sector guaranteed by public sector	..	..	..	..	..	..
Private sector not guaranteed	1.7	170.0	234.5	207.7	157.0	106.3
Short-term external debt	452.0	311.1	243.2	116.2	125.1	119.6
Disbursements (long-term)	**104.6**	**73.9**	**140.9**	**109.4**	**137.6**	**104.8**
Public and publicly guaranteed sector	104.6	73.9	60.9	109.4	137.6	104.8
Public sector	104.6	73.9	60.9	109.4	137.6	104.8
of which: General government	104.6	73.9	60.9	109.4	137.6	104.8
Private sector guaranteed by public sector	..	..	..	..	..	..
Private sector not guaranteed	..	..	80.0		..	..
Principal repayments (long-term)	**8.5**	**43.7**	**47.7**	**65.6**	**105.5**	**105.0**
Public and publicly guaranteed sector	8.2	28.7	32.2	38.7	54.8	54.3
Public sector	8.2	28.7	32.2	38.7	54.8	54.3
of which: General government	7.9	28.4	31.9	38.4	54.5	54.0
Private sector guaranteed by public sector	..	..	..	..	..	..
Private sector not guaranteed	0.3	15.0	15.5	26.9	50.7	50.7
Interest payments (long-term)	**10.6**	**16.9**	**28.2**	**31.6**	**33.5**	**32.6**
Public and publicly guaranteed sector	10.4	16.9	17.5	19.1	22.1	23.2
Public sector	10.4	16.9	17.5	19.1	22.1	23.2
of which: General government	10.3	16.8	17.4	19.0	22.0	23.1
Private sector guaranteed by public sector	..	..	..	..	..	..
Private sector not guaranteed	0.2	..	10.7	12.5	11.3	9.4
Summary external debt stock by creditor type						
Long-term external debt stocks	781.3	1,201.3	1,283.6	1,342.6	1,361.8	1,357.4
Public and publicly guaranteed debt from:	779.6	1,031.3	1,049.0	1,135.0	1,204.8	1,251.1
Official creditors	763.1	1,014.9	1,032.8	1,101.4	1,172.0	1,219.1
Multilateral	479.0	688.4	693.8	725.5	787.9	815.3
of which: World Bank	9.7	20.4	25.0	35.6	75.5	83.0
Bilateral	284.1	326.6	339.0	375.9	384.1	403.8
Private creditors	16.5	16.4	16.2	33.6	32.8	32.1
Bondholders	0.0	0.0	0.0	0.0	0.0	0.0
Commercial banks and others	16.5	16.3	16.2	33.5	32.8	32.0
Private nonguaranteed debt from:	1.7	170.0	234.5	207.7	157.0	106.3
Bondholders	..	..	..	..	..	..
Commercial banks and others	1.7	170.0	234.5	207.7	157.0	106.3
Use of IMF credit	194.6	124.5	117.1	124.0	121.1	120.4
Net financial inflows						
Net debt inflows						
Use of IMF credit	0.0	-9.1	-3.9	..	..	..
Long-term	96.1	30.3	93.3	43.8	32.1	-0.2
Official creditors	96.4	45.3	28.8	53.4	83.5	51.3
Multilateral	63.5	26.1	6.9	26.3	64.4	28.0
of which: World Bank	-0.1	6.9	5.4	8.7	41.1	7.9
Bilateral	32.9	19.1	21.9	27.0	19.1	23.2
Private creditors	-0.3	-15.0	64.5	-9.6	-51.4	-51.4
Bondholders	..	..	..	..	..	0.0
Banks and others	-0.3	-15.0	64.5	-9.6	-51.4	-51.4
Short-term	215.0	-608.2	-80.3	-121.7	5.7	-6.8
Net equity inflows						
Foreign direct investment	31.1	113.4	137.1	274.2	956.6	1,713.3
Portfolio equity	..	0.0	0.0	0.0	..	..
Debt ratios						
External debt stocks to exports (%)	146.0	119.8	95.4	93.1	98.2	88.0
External debt stocks to GNI (%)	68.7	50.8	47.5	45.6	42.5	38.1
Debt service to exports (%)	2.1	5.3	4.8	5.7	8.5	7.6
Short-term to external debt stocks (%)	31.7	19.0	14.8	7.3	7.8	7.5
Multilateral to external debt stocks (%)	33.5	42.1	42.2	45.8	49.0	51.0
Reserves to external debt stocks (%)	44.2	32.5	35.3	35.7	32.2	35.9
Gross national income (GNI)	2,078.1	3,221.9	3,458.0	3,472.5	3,779.7	4,192.1

HAITI
(US$ million, unless otherwise indicated)

	2009	2015	2016	2017	2018	2019
Summary external debt data by debtor type						
Total external debt stocks	**1,448**	**2,096**	**2,168**	**2,170**	**2,214**	**2,214**
Use of IMF credit	291	178	216	213	201	185
Long-term external debt	1,158	1,915	1,951	1,955	2,013	2,012
Public and publicly guaranteed sector	1,158	1,914	1,947	1,954	2,013	2,012
Public sector	1,158	1,914	1,947	1,954	2,013	2,012
of which: General government	1,110	1,877	1,913	1,923	1,988	1,987
Private sector guaranteed by public sector	..	..	..	..	..	..
Private sector not guaranteed	..	1	4	1	0	0
Short-term external debt	0	4	1	2	0	16
Disbursements (long-term)	**212**	**173**	**106**	**16**	**40**	**4**
Public and publicly guaranteed sector	212	173	102	16	40	4
Public sector	212	173	102	16	40	4
of which: General government	212	173	102	16	40	3
Private sector guaranteed by public sector	..	..	..	..	..	..
Private sector not guaranteed	..	..	4	..	..	..
Principal repayments (long-term)	**26**	**27**	**68**	**9**	**8**	**8**
Public and publicly guaranteed sector	26	27	67	6	7	7
Public sector	26	27	67	6	7	7
of which: General government	21	25	64	3	4	4
Private sector guaranteed by public sector	..	..	..	..	..	..
Private sector not guaranteed	..	0	0	4	0	0
Interest payments (long-term)	**15**	**8**	**19**	**5**	**3**	**3**
Public and publicly guaranteed sector	15	8	19	5	3	3
Public sector	15	8	19	5	3	3
of which: General government	13	8	18	4	3	2
Private sector guaranteed by public sector	..	..	..	..	..	..
Private sector not guaranteed	..	0	0	0	0	0
Summary external debt stock by creditor type						
Long-term external debt stocks	**1,158**	**1,915**	**1,951**	**1,955**	**2,013**	**2,012**
Public and publicly guaranteed debt from:	1,158	1,914	1,947	1,954	2,013	2,012
Official creditors	1,107	1,868	1,901	1,909	1,970	1,968
Multilateral	520	81	89	101	99	96
of which: World Bank	39	..	..	..	..	..
Bilateral	588	1,787	1,812	1,808	1,871	1,872
Private creditors	50	45	45	45	43	44
Bondholders	..	..	..	..	..	..
Commercial banks and others	50	45	45	45	43	44
Private nonguaranteed debt from:	..	1	4	1	0	0
Bondholders	..	..	..	..	..	..
Commercial banks and others	..	1	4	1	0	0
Use of IMF credit	291	178	216	213	201	185
Net financial inflows						
Net debt inflows						
Use of IMF credit	57	10	39	-6	-10	-11
Long-term	185	146	38	7	32	-3
Official creditors	185	146	35	11	35	-1
Multilateral	76	8	10	15	-2	1
of which: World Bank	-11	..	..	..	..	..
Bilateral	109	138	25	-4	37	-2
Private creditors	..	0	4	-4	-3	-3
Bondholders	..	..	..	..	..	..
Banks and others	..	0	4	-4	-3	-3
Short-term	0	0	0	0	0	0
Net equity inflows						
Foreign direct investment	55	106	105	375	105	75
Portfolio equity	0	..	..	..	..	..
Debt ratios						
External debt stocks to exports (%)	136	116	129	136	120	134
External debt stocks to GNI (%)	22	24	27	26	23	26
Debt service to exports (%)	4	2	5	1	1	1
Short-term to external debt stocks (%)	0	0	0	0	0	1
Multilateral to external debt stocks (%)	36	4	4	5	4	4
Reserves to external debt stocks (%)	73	91	97	108	104	..
Gross national income (GNI)	6,597	8,760	8,014	8,463	9,712	8,446

HONDURAS
(US$ million, unless otherwise indicated)

	2009	2015	2016	2017	2018	2019
Summary external debt data by debtor type						
Total external debt stocks	**3,836**	**7,627**	**7,614**	**8,742**	**9,167**	**9,767**
Use of IMF credit	226	173	166	176	172	171
Long-term external debt	3,361	6,963	7,009	8,072	8,293	8,820
Public and publicly guaranteed sector	2,481	5,921	6,084	7,126	7,350	7,776
Public sector	2,481	5,921	6,084	7,126	7,350	7,776
of which: General government	2,318	5,746	5,848	6,793	6,967	7,404
Private sector guaranteed by public sector	0	..	..	..	..	..
Private sector not guaranteed	880	1,042	925	946	942	1,044
Short-term external debt	249	491	439	493	702	776
Disbursements (long-term)	**719**	**1,457**	**775**	**1,695**	**1,013**	**1,079**
Public and publicly guaranteed sector	263	565	387	1,160	523	693
Public sector	263	565	387	1,160	523	693
of which: General government	258	517	311	1,061	466	671
Private sector guaranteed by public sector	..	..	..	..	..	..
Private sector not guaranteed	457	893	388	535	490	386
Principal repayments (long-term)	**355**	**1,061**	**685**	**713**	**731**	**527**
Public and publicly guaranteed sector	121	138	179	203	257	250
Public sector	121	138	179	203	257	250
of which: General government	112	126	167	199	251	217
Private sector guaranteed by public sector	..	..	..	..	..	..
Private sector not guaranteed	234	922	506	510	474	277
Interest payments (long-term)	**68**	**215**	**237**	**238**	**285**	**324**
Public and publicly guaranteed sector	41	193	218	220	267	301
Public sector	41	193	218	220	267	301
of which: General government	37	189	213	206	256	282
Private sector guaranteed by public sector	..	..	..	..	..	..
Private sector not guaranteed	27	22	20	19	18	23
Summary external debt stock by creditor type						
Long-term external debt stocks	**3,361**	**6,963**	**7,009**	**8,072**	**8,293**	**8,820**
Public and publicly guaranteed debt from:	2,481	5,921	6,084	7,126	7,350	7,776
Official creditors	2,375	4,595	4,715	4,980	5,196	5,631
Multilateral	1,532	3,792	3,894	4,135	4,395	4,564
of which: World Bank	502	965	940	985	937	908
Bilateral	844	802	822	846	801	1,067
Private creditors	105	1,326	1,369	2,146	2,155	2,145
Bondholders	..	1,000	1,000	1,700	1,700	1,700
Commercial banks and others	105	326	369	446	455	445
Private nonguaranteed debt from:	880	1,042	925	946	942	1,044
Bondholders	..	..	..	..	..	..
Commercial banks and others	880	1,042	925	946	942	1,044
Use of IMF credit	226	173	166	176	172	171
Net financial inflows						
Net debt inflows						
Use of IMF credit	0	-4	-1	..	..	..
Long-term	364	397	90	982	282	552
Official creditors	145	384	162	194	252	451
Multilateral	77	292	131	183	284	178
of which: World Bank	49	68	1	-4	-28	-23
Bilateral	67	91	31	12	-32	273
Private creditors	220	13	-72	787	30	101
Bondholders	..	..	..	700	0	0
Banks and others	220	13	-72	87	30	101
Short-term	-223	-13	-54	55	210	74
Net equity inflows						
Foreign direct investment	443	974	1,181	862	766	716
Portfolio equity	0	0	0	0	0	0
Debt ratios						
External debt stocks to exports (%)	89	109	112	117	126	133
External debt stocks to GNI (%)	27	39	38	40	41	42
Debt service to exports (%)	10	18	14	13	14	12
Short-term to external debt stocks (%)	6	6	6	6	8	8
Multilateral to external debt stocks (%)	40	50	51	47	48	47
Reserves to external debt stocks (%)	54	49	50	54	52	58
Gross national income (GNI)	13,952	19,543	20,199	21,721	22,130	23,181

83

INDIA

(US$ million, unless otherwise indicated)

	2009	2015	2016	2017	2018	2019
Summary external debt data by debtor type						
Total external debt stocks	256,312	478,826	455,502	511,475	521,034	560,035
Use of IMF credit	6,237	5,513	5,348	5,666	5,533	5,501
Long-term external debt	203,473	391,750	366,221	408,200	411,577	447,754
Public and publicly guaranteed sector	85,293	162,305	152,973	182,916	180,399	191,797
Public sector	85,225	162,305	152,973	182,916	180,399	191,797
of which: General government	67,070	116,713	111,062	141,987	134,213	140,060
Private sector guaranteed by public sector	68	..	..	..	..	..
Private sector not guaranteed	118,180	229,445	213,248	225,284	231,179	255,957
Short-term external debt	46,603	81,563	83,933	97,609	103,924	106,780
Disbursements (long-term)	**26,646**	**66,337**	**41,942**	**78,143**	**52,134**	**71,863**
Public and publicly guaranteed sector	10,396	23,113	11,570	39,422	18,992	24,616
Public sector	10,396	23,113	11,570	39,422	18,992	24,616
of which: General government	6,320	12,562	6,194	33,036	7,866	11,596
Private sector guaranteed by public sector	0	..	..	..	..	..
Private sector not guaranteed	16,250	43,224	30,372	38,721	33,141	47,247
Principal repayments (long-term)	**10,990**	**38,773**	**65,971**	**38,667**	**46,229**	**34,949**
Public and publicly guaranteed sector	5,336	11,774	20,472	11,982	21,016	13,287
Public sector	5,311	11,774	20,472	11,982	21,016	13,287
of which: General government	2,391	3,746	11,409	4,189	15,244	5,821
Private sector guaranteed by public sector	25	..	..	..	..	..
Private sector not guaranteed	5,654	26,998	45,499	26,684	25,213	21,662
Interest payments (long-term)	**4,942**	**9,814**	**9,540**	**10,348**	**13,975**	**12,888**
Public and publicly guaranteed sector	1,322	1,898	2,105	2,153	2,615	3,283
Public sector	1,319	1,898	2,105	2,153	2,615	3,283
of which: General government	818	623	770	954	1,217	1,496
Private sector guaranteed by public sector	3	..	..	..	..	..
Private sector not guaranteed	3,620	7,916	7,435	8,195	11,361	9,605
Summary external debt stock by creditor type						
Long-term external debt stocks	203,473	391,750	366,221	408,200	411,577	447,754
Public and publicly guaranteed debt from:	85,293	162,305	152,973	182,916	180,399	191,797
Official creditors	65,914	71,691	73,229	78,046	81,005	84,359
Multilateral	42,327	50,462	50,789	52,976	54,165	56,404
of which: World Bank	34,432	36,509	36,348	37,234	36,464	36,809
Bilateral	23,587	21,229	22,440	25,070	26,840	27,955
Private creditors	19,379	90,615	79,744	104,870	99,394	107,438
Bondholders	9,521	59,512	53,246	81,997	73,809	81,351
Commercial banks and others	9,858	31,103	26,499	22,873	25,585	26,087
Private nonguaranteed debt from:	118,180	229,445	213,248	225,284	231,179	255,957
Bondholders	15,326	7,783	10,040	14,645	13,962	19,199
Commercial banks and others	102,854	221,661	203,208	210,639	217,216	236,757
Use of IMF credit	6,237	5,513	5,348	5,666	5,533	5,501
Net financial inflows						
Net debt inflows						
Use of IMF credit	..	..	..	..	..	..
Long-term	15,656	27,564	-24,029	39,476	5,905	36,914
Official creditors	3,034	1,434	1,978	2,452	3,422	3,290
Multilateral	2,686	843	1,014	885	1,747	2,381
of which: World Bank	1,418	260	506	-369	-243	465
Bilateral	348	591	965	1,566	1,675	910
Private creditors	12,622	26,130	-26,008	37,025	2,482	33,624
Bondholders	1,972	10,705	-3,796	33,310	-8,417	12,939
Banks and others	10,650	15,424	-22,211	3,715	10,899	20,685
Short-term	2,782	-4,012	2,370	13,676	6,315	2,856
Net equity inflows						
Foreign direct investment	34,111	39,663	41,987	37,098	39,234	43,136
Portfolio equity	24,689	1,933	2,337	5,928	-4,361	13,769
Debt ratios						
External debt stocks to exports (%)	93	108	102	101	93	98
External debt stocks to GNI (%)	19	23	20	19	19	20
Debt service to exports (%)	6	11	17	10	11	9
Short-term to external debt stocks (%)	18	17	18	19	20	19
Multilateral to external debt stocks (%)	17	11	11	10	10	10
Reserves to external debt stocks (%)	103	70	75	76	72	77
Gross national income (GNI)	1,333,877	2,079,182	2,247,940	2,624,082	2,684,230	2,843,902

INDONESIA
(US$ million, unless otherwise indicated)

	2009	2015	2016	2017	2018	2019
Summary external debt data by debtor type						
Total external debt stocks	**179,405**	**307,749**	**318,942**	**353,564**	**379,589**	**402,084**
Use of IMF credit	3,105	2,744	2,662	2,820	2,754	2,739
Long-term external debt	152,250	266,574	275,595	304,013	328,875	354,547
Public and publicly guaranteed sector	97,457	159,571	177,073	194,953	215,072	233,505
Public sector	97,457	159,571	177,073	194,953	215,072	233,505
of which: General government	90,511	135,948	154,762	175,600	183,262	199,054
Private sector guaranteed by public sector	..	..	..	..	..	..
Private sector not guaranteed	54,793	107,003	98,522	109,059	113,802	121,041
Short-term external debt	24,050	38,431	40,685	46,731	47,960	44,799
Disbursements (long-term)	**34,913**	**67,974**	**68,083**	**78,616**	**72,086**	**94,779**
Public and publicly guaranteed sector	16,217	27,261	26,669	27,535	31,060	31,656
Public sector	16,217	27,261	26,669	27,535	31,060	31,656
of which: General government	12,757	20,160	23,903	24,690	15,822	25,950
Private sector guaranteed by public sector	..	..	..	..	..	..
Private sector not guaranteed	18,695	40,713	41,414	51,081	41,026	63,122
Principal repayments (long-term)	**20,431**	**43,131**	**53,835**	**46,884**	**42,905**	**68,404**
Public and publicly guaranteed sector	7,063	9,026	10,029	11,765	10,614	13,246
Public sector	7,063	9,026	10,029	11,765	10,614	13,246
of which: General government	6,747	5,568	5,951	5,961	7,858	10,190
Private sector guaranteed by public sector	..	..	..	..	..	..
Private sector not guaranteed	13,368	34,105	43,806	35,119	32,291	55,157
Interest payments (long-term)	**4,301**	**16,356**	**9,730**	**10,595**	**10,703**	**12,046**
Public and publicly guaranteed sector	2,802	5,201	5,959	6,579	6,767	7,867
Public sector	2,802	5,201	5,959	6,579	6,767	7,867
of which: General government	2,582	4,235	4,906	5,520	5,873	6,281
Private sector guaranteed by public sector	..	..	..	..	..	..
Private sector not guaranteed	1,499	11,155	3,771	4,015	3,936	4,179
Summary external debt stock by creditor type						
Long-term external debt stocks	152,250	266,574	275,595	304,013	328,875	354,547
Public and publicly guaranteed debt from:	97,457	159,571	177,073	194,953	215,072	233,505
Official creditors	62,933	50,863	51,549	51,666	53,072	52,254
Multilateral	21,052	25,202	26,720	27,499	29,118	30,420
of which: World Bank	10,111	16,044	17,224	17,941	18,507	19,109
Bilateral	41,880	25,662	24,829	24,167	23,955	21,834
Private creditors	34,525	108,708	125,524	143,287	162,000	181,251
Bondholders	25,833	96,484	114,376	135,396	151,001	173,224
Commercial banks and others	8,691	12,224	11,149	7,891	10,999	8,027
Private nonguaranteed debt from:	54,793	107,003	98,522	109,059	113,802	121,041
Bondholders	7,856	14,279	13,306	14,383	15,038	16,515
Commercial banks and others	46,937	92,724	85,216	94,677	98,764	104,526
Use of IMF credit	3,105	2,744	2,662	2,820	2,754	2,739
Net financial inflows						
Net debt inflows						
Use of IMF credit	..	..	..	..	..	..
Long-term	14,481	24,844	14,248	31,732	29,182	26,375
Official creditors	33	726	-472	-905	1,401	-938
Multilateral	1,111	2,614	1,576	659	1,663	1,309
of which: World Bank	1,121	2,060	1,221	645	594	617
Bilateral	-1,078	-1,888	-2,048	-1,564	-262	-2,247
Private creditors	14,449	24,118	14,720	32,637	27,780	27,313
Bondholders	8,600	15,320	17,144	21,257	16,496	23,767
Banks and others	5,848	8,798	-2,424	11,380	11,284	3,546
Short-term	3,561	-7,529	2,254	6,046	1,229	-3,161
Net equity inflows						
Foreign direct investment	4,982	18,822	4,684	18,839	19,993	24,739
Portfolio equity	787	-1,547	1,319	-2,538	-3,668	-397
Debt ratios						
External debt stocks to exports (%)	141	177	186	177	172	194
External debt stocks to GNI (%)	34	37	35	36	37	37
Debt service to exports (%)	20	35	37	29	25	39
Short-term to external debt stocks (%)	13	12	13	13	13	11
Multilateral to external debt stocks (%)	12	8	8	8	8	8
Reserves to external debt stocks (%)	35	34	36	36	31	31
Gross national income (GNI)	520,695	832,299	902,045	983,438	1,012,284	1,085,709

85

IRAN, ISLAMIC REPUBLIC OF

(US$ million, unless otherwise indicated)

	2009	2015	2016	2017	2018	2019
Summary external debt data by debtor type						
Total external debt stocks	18,610.0	6,453.3	6,058.4	6,819.1	5,773.7	4,833.7
Use of IMF credit	2,235.6	1,976.1	1,917.1	2,030.9	1,983.4	1,972.0
Long-term external debt	7,587.4	2,457.8	826.8	589.3	1,636.8	1,263.1
Public and publicly guaranteed sector	7,587.4	2,457.8	826.8	589.3	437.2	348.4
Public sector	7,577.3	2,457.8	826.8	589.3	437.2	348.4
of which: General government	956.3	462.0	378.1	280.3	206.1	141.0
Private sector guaranteed by public sector	10.0	..	..	..	..	..
Private sector not guaranteed	0.0	0.0	0.0	0.0	1,199.7	914.7
Short-term external debt	8,787.0	2,019.4	3,314.5	4,198.9	2,153.5	1,598.6
Disbursements (long-term)	**398.0**	**7.3**	**36.6**	**123.0**	**0.0**	**7.6**
Public and publicly guaranteed sector	398.0	7.3	36.6	123.0	0.0	7.6
Public sector	388.3	7.3	36.6	123.0	0.0	7.6
of which: General government	158.8	0.0	0.0	0.0	0.0	..
Private sector guaranteed by public sector	9.7	..	..	..	..	..
Private sector not guaranteed	..	..	..	..	..	..
Principal repayments (long-term)	**2,027.3**	**650.0**	**1,933.7**	**387.2**	**137.7**	**256.0**
Public and publicly guaranteed sector	2,027.3	650.0	1,933.7	387.2	137.7	93.4
Public sector	2,024.4	650.0	1,933.7	387.2	137.7	93.4
of which: General government	99.6	90.9	98.9	99.2	74.5	65.1
Private sector guaranteed by public sector	3.0	..	..	..	..	..
Private sector not guaranteed	..	..	..	..	..	162.5
Interest payments (long-term)	**271.5**	**40.1**	**87.6**	**22.4**	**18.1**	**32.6**
Public and publicly guaranteed sector	271.5	40.1	87.6	22.4	18.1	14.9
Public sector	271.3	40.1	87.6	22.4	18.1	14.9
of which: General government	19.9	5.0	6.5	7.4	5.8	6.8
Private sector guaranteed by public sector	0.1	..	..	..	..	..
Private sector not guaranteed	..	..	..	..	..	17.7
Summary external debt stock by creditor type						
Long-term external debt stocks	**7,587.4**	**2,457.8**	**826.8**	**589.3**	**1,636.8**	**1,263.1**
Public and publicly guaranteed debt from:	7,587.4	2,457.8	826.8	589.3	437.2	348.4
Official creditors	2,313.7	738.4	592.7	519.7	413.3	324.9
Multilateral	855.0	477.8	406.8	342.5	272.2	198.8
of which: World Bank	835.8	438.0	354.7	271.1	206.1	141.0
Bilateral	1,458.7	260.6	185.9	177.2	141.2	126.1
Private creditors	5,273.6	1,719.4	234.2	69.5	23.8	23.5
Bondholders	..	..	..	..	..	..
Commercial banks and others	5,273.6	1,719.4	234.2	69.5	23.8	23.5
Private nonguaranteed debt from:	0.0	0.0	0.0	0.0	1,199.7	914.7
Bondholders	..	..	..	..	..	..
Commercial banks and others	0.0	0.0	0.0	0.0	1,199.7	914.7
Use of IMF credit	2,235.6	1,976.1	1,917.1	2,030.9	1,983.4	1,972.0
Net financial inflows						
Net debt inflows						
Use of IMF credit	..	..	..	..	..	..
Long-term	-1,629.4	-642.7	-1,897.1	-264.1	-137.7	-248.4
Official creditors	-169.3	-239.6	-161.6	-87.7	-93.1	-85.8
Multilateral	93.2	-76.0	-71.6	-72.2	-67.1	-72.1
of which: World Bank	74.7	-82.5	-83.3	-83.6	-65.1	-65.1
Bilateral	-262.5	-163.6	-90.0	-15.5	-26.0	-13.7
Private creditors	-1,460.1	-403.1	-1,735.4	-176.4	-44.7	-162.5
Bondholders	..	..	..	..	..	..
Banks and others	-1,460.1	-403.1	-1,735.4	-176.4	-44.7	-162.5
Short-term	2,188.0	1,587.7	1,292.1	886.0	-2,046.5	-612.0
Net equity inflows						
Foreign direct investment	2,983.4	2,050.0	3,372.0	5,019.0	2,373.0	1,508.0
Portfolio equity	..	..	..	..	..	..
Debt ratios						
External debt stocks to exports (%)	16.6	6.3	6.3	7.0	5.5	6.7
External debt stocks to GNI (%)	4.5	1.7	1.4	1.5	..	..
Debt service to exports (%)	2.1	0.7	2.2	0.5	0.2	0.5
Short-term to external debt stocks (%)	47.2	31.3	54.7	61.6	37.3	33.1
Multilateral to external debt stocks (%)	4.6	7.4	6.7	5.0	4.7	4.1
Reserves to external debt stocks (%)	..	..	..	..	..	..
Gross national income (GNI)	416,274.6	385,924.9	419,284.3	446,174.0	..	..

JAMAICA
(US$ million, unless otherwise indicated)

	2009	2015	2016	2017	2018	2019
Summary external debt data by debtor type						
Total external debt stocks	**11,124**	**14,134**	**14,127**	**14,808**	**16,505**	**15,862**
Use of IMF credit	410	1,025	1,103	1,152	1,074	978
Long-term external debt	9,965	11,597	11,363	11,862	13,227	12,615
Public and publicly guaranteed sector	6,724	9,648	9,507	9,929	9,759	9,407
Public sector	6,723	9,648	9,507	9,929	9,759	9,407
of which: General government	5,600	8,497	8,398	9,190	9,115	8,798
Private sector guaranteed by public sector	1	..	..	..	..	..
Private sector not guaranteed	3,241	1,949	1,856	1,932	3,468	3,208
Short-term external debt	749	1,513	1,662	1,794	2,205	2,269
Disbursements (long-term)	**1,546**	**3,322**	**1,097**	**1,184**	**1,389**	**1,613**
Public and publicly guaranteed sector	461	2,394	1,054	1,079	294	1,009
Public sector	461	2,394	1,054	1,079	294	1,009
of which: General government	408	2,373	1,018	1,073	285	993
Private sector guaranteed by public sector	..	..	..	..	..	..
Private sector not guaranteed	1,085	928	44	105	1,096	604
Principal repayments (long-term)	**736**	**3,246**	**1,206**	**712**	**460**	**1,405**
Public and publicly guaranteed sector	727	707	1,170	683	456	1,355
Public sector	727	707	1,170	683	456	1,355
of which: General government	511	508	1,093	595	352	1,305
Private sector guaranteed by public sector	0	..	..	..	..	..
Private sector not guaranteed	9	2,539	37	28	4	50
Interest payments (long-term)	**748**	**666**	**667**	**652**	**688**	**775**
Public and publicly guaranteed sector	523	427	575	558	591	607
Public sector	523	427	575	558	591	607
of which: General government	437	357	514	503	541	559
Private sector guaranteed by public sector	..	..	..	..	..	..
Private sector not guaranteed	225	239	92	94	96	168
Summary external debt stock by creditor type						
Long-term external debt stocks	**9,965**	**11,597**	**11,363**	**11,862**	**13,227**	**12,615**
Public and publicly guaranteed debt from:	6,724	9,648	9,507	9,929	9,759	9,407
Official creditors	2,423	3,601	3,643	3,609	3,645	3,585
Multilateral	1,525	2,878	2,967	2,922	2,940	2,915
of which: World Bank	398	826	809	862	865	886
Bilateral	898	723	677	687	705	670
Private creditors	4,302	6,047	5,863	6,320	6,114	5,822
Bondholders	3,890	5,736	5,632	6,163	6,064	5,810
Commercial banks and others	411	311	232	157	50	12
Private nonguaranteed debt from:	3,241	1,949	1,856	1,932	3,468	3,208
Bondholders	3,215	1,175	1,175	1,175	1,175	1,775
Commercial banks and others	26	774	681	757	2,293	1,433
Use of IMF credit	410	1,025	1,103	1,152	1,074	978
Net financial inflows						
Net debt inflows						
Use of IMF credit	..	25	113	-16	-53	-90
Long-term	810	76	-109	472	929	208
Official creditors	97	178	51	-50	42	-54
Multilateral	182	189	90	-49	18	-22
of which: World Bank	71	72	-16	53	3	21
Bilateral	-85	-11	-39	-1	24	-32
Private creditors	714	-102	-160	522	887	263
Bondholders	740	-20	-90	532	-100	347
Banks and others	-27	-82	-70	-9	987	-84
Short-term	-471	6	119	130	409	64
Net equity inflows						
Foreign direct investment	440	925	928	889	775	665
Portfolio equity	0	72	33	251	181	..
Debt ratios						
External debt stocks to exports (%)	260	306	300	285	268	252
External debt stocks to GNI (%)	98	103	105	103	110	100
Debt service to exports (%)	35	88	41	27	20	37
Short-term to external debt stocks (%)	7	11	12	12	13	14
Multilateral to external debt stocks (%)	14	20	21	20	18	18
Reserves to external debt stocks (%)	19	21	23	26	21	23
Gross national income (GNI)	11,402	13,755	13,481	14,370	14,998	15,814

JORDAN

(US$ million, unless otherwise indicated)

	2009	2015	2016	2017	2018	2019
Summary external debt data by debtor type						
Total external debt stocks	**14,444**	**25,792**	**27,292**	**30,233**	**32,157**	**33,683**
Use of IMF credit	266	2,070	1,820	1,500	981	729
Long-term external debt	5,660	13,415	15,003	17,800	19,665	20,702
Public and publicly guaranteed sector	5,461	11,048	12,689	15,340	16,595	17,088
Public sector	5,323	10,963	12,612	15,270	16,561	17,058
of which: General government	5,156	10,350	12,021	14,660	15,965	16,389
Private sector guaranteed by public sector	139	85	76	69	34	30
Private sector not guaranteed	198	2,367	2,314	2,460	3,071	3,614
Short-term external debt	8,518	10,307	10,470	10,933	11,511	12,252
Disbursements (long-term)	**787**	**3,267**	**3,502**	**3,241**	**2,817**	**2,841**
Public and publicly guaranteed sector	762	2,975	3,242	2,994	2,049	2,066
Public sector	762	2,975	3,242	2,994	2,049	2,066
of which: General government	709	2,964	3,233	2,949	1,920	1,957
Private sector guaranteed by public sector	0	0	0	0	0	0
Private sector not guaranteed	25	292	259	247	769	775
Principal repayments (long-term)	**425**	**1,602**	**1,653**	**663**	**762**	**1,791**
Public and publicly guaranteed sector	405	1,538	1,578	565	604	1,560
Public sector	401	1,530	1,570	557	596	1,556
of which: General government	386	1,496	1,544	520	555	1,520
Private sector guaranteed by public sector	4	8	8	8	8	4
Private sector not guaranteed	20	64	75	98	158	231
Interest payments (long-term)	**155**	**312**	**326**	**443**	**606**	**739**
Public and publicly guaranteed sector	147	283	285	389	506	585
Public sector	141	279	281	386	503	584
of which: General government	134	259	260	366	483	561
Private sector guaranteed by public sector	6	4	4	3	3	1
Private sector not guaranteed	8	29	42	55	99	153
Summary external debt stock by creditor type						
Long-term external debt stocks	**5,660**	**13,415**	**15,003**	**17,800**	**19,665**	**20,702**
Public and publicly guaranteed debt from:	5,461	11,048	12,689	15,340	16,595	17,088
Official creditors	5,154	5,481	6,096	6,745	7,329	8,449
Multilateral	2,361	2,881	3,290	3,449	3,822	4,786
of which: World Bank	1,109	1,550	1,857	1,876	2,252	2,985
Bilateral	2,792	2,600	2,806	3,296	3,507	3,663
Private creditors	308	5,567	6,593	8,595	9,266	8,638
Bondholders	145	5,458	6,444	8,429	9,115	8,500
Commercial banks and others	163	109	149	166	152	138
Private nonguaranteed debt from:	198	2,367	2,314	2,460	3,071	3,614
Bondholders	..	..	..	..	..	..
Commercial banks and others	198	2,367	2,314	2,460	3,071	3,614
Use of IMF credit	266	2,070	1,820	1,500	981	729
Net financial inflows						
Net debt inflows						
Use of IMF credit	-16	552	-195	-416	-493	-246
Long-term	362	1,665	1,848	2,578	2,056	1,050
Official creditors	360	206	636	438	770	1,133
Multilateral	427	6	428	101	397	971
of which: World Bank	237	155	308	19	376	733
Bilateral	-67	200	209	337	373	162
Private creditors	2	1,459	1,212	2,140	1,286	-83
Bondholders	..	1,236	986	1,986	686	-615
Banks and others	2	224	227	155	600	531
Short-term	-78	-581	163	463	578	742
Net equity inflows						
Foreign direct investment	2,413	1,600	1,553	2,030	950	825
Portfolio equity	-30	15	334	-476	41	-31
Debt ratios						
External debt stocks to exports (%)	120	174	190	199	200	192
External debt stocks to GNI (%)	59	69	70	75	77	78
Debt service to exports (%)	6	14	17	12	14	19
Short-term to external debt stocks (%)	59	40	38	36	36	36
Multilateral to external debt stocks (%)	16	11	12	11	12	14
Reserves to external debt stocks (%)	81	59	51	..	..	..
Gross national income (GNI)	24,529	37,611	38,892	40,503	42,032	43,429

88

KAZAKHSTAN
(US$ million, unless otherwise indicated)

	2009	2015	2016	2017	2018	2019
Summary external debt data by debtor type						
Total external debt stocks	109,741	153,180	163,488	158,949	156,979	156,263
Use of IMF credit	539	476	462	489	478	475
Long-term external debt	102,217	146,443	156,294	150,781	148,135	146,800
Public and publicly guaranteed sector	2,487	20,114	21,425	21,295	24,181	24,716
Public sector	2,487	20,114	21,425	21,295	24,181	24,716
of which: General government	2,196	13,001	14,071	13,806	14,652	15,220
Private sector guaranteed by public sector	..	..	..	..	..	..
Private sector not guaranteed	99,731	126,329	134,869	129,486	123,954	122,084
Short-term external debt	6,985	6,260	6,732	7,678	8,366	8,989
Disbursements (long-term)	30,471	34,595	30,505	31,525	33,912	31,801
Public and publicly guaranteed sector	717	5,375	1,712	892	3,504	1,975
Public sector	717	5,375	1,712	892	3,504	1,975
of which: General government	689	5,375	1,454	243	1,447	1,581
Private sector guaranteed by public sector	..	..	..	..	..	..
Private sector not guaranteed	29,754	29,220	28,793	30,632	30,408	29,826
Principal repayments (long-term)	20,033	31,267	17,415	24,529	29,807	29,334
Public and publicly guaranteed sector	131	326	418	1,042	581	1,433
Public sector	131	326	418	1,042	581	1,433
of which: General government	90	313	401	528	565	1,003
Private sector guaranteed by public sector	..	..	..	..	..	..
Private sector not guaranteed	19,902	30,941	16,997	23,487	29,226	27,901
Interest payments (long-term)	5,366	3,468	2,668	3,185	3,518	3,177
Public and publicly guaranteed sector	58	526	801	859	902	1,079
Public sector	58	526	801	859	902	1,079
of which: General government	47	166	434	489	525	586
Private sector guaranteed by public sector	..	..	..	..	..	..
Private sector not guaranteed	5,307	2,942	1,866	2,325	2,617	2,098
Summary external debt stock by creditor type						
Long-term external debt stocks	102,217	146,443	156,294	150,781	148,135	146,800
Public and publicly guaranteed debt from:	2,487	20,114	21,425	21,295	24,181	24,716
Official creditors	2,486	6,679	7,990	8,361	8,372	7,634
Multilateral	1,349	6,094	7,175	6,925	6,638	6,010
of which: World Bank	547	3,261	4,313	4,185	3,977	3,802
Bilateral	1,137	585	815	1,435	1,734	1,624
Private creditors	1	13,435	13,435	12,935	15,810	17,082
Bondholders	..	13,435	13,435	12,935	15,810	17,082
Commercial banks and others	1	..	..	..	..	..
Private nonguaranteed debt from:	99,731	126,329	134,869	129,486	123,954	122,084
Bondholders	22,097	6,683	6,273	9,272	7,908	6,415
Commercial banks and others	77,634	119,647	128,596	120,213	116,046	115,669
Use of IMF credit	539	476	462	489	478	475
Net financial inflows						
Net debt inflows						
Use of IMF credit	..	..	..	..	..	..
Long-term	10,437	3,328	13,090	6,995	4,105	2,467
Official creditors	587	1,049	1,294	350	9	-746
Multilateral	600	1,093	1,082	-250	-281	-629
of which: World Bank	84	-168	1,053	-128	-208	-175
Bilateral	-13	-44	212	600	290	-117
Private creditors	9,851	2,280	11,796	6,645	4,096	3,213
Bondholders	-2,108	-2,998	-482	1,499	2,797	-101
Banks and others	11,958	5,277	12,278	5,146	1,299	3,314
Short-term	-2,502	-3,453	300	929	661	617
Net equity inflows						
Foreign direct investment	4,183	1,979	9,042	5,748	2,765	6,831
Portfolio equity	38	6	-27	22	-1,520	479
Debt ratios						
External debt stocks to exports (%)	214	288	373	283	225	229
External debt stocks to GNI (%)	107	89	132	107	100	99
Debt service to exports (%)	50	65	46	50	48	48
Short-term to external debt stocks (%)	6	4	4	5	5	6
Multilateral to external debt stocks (%)	1	4	4	4	4	4
Reserves to external debt stocks (%)	19	13	12	11	11	6
Gross national income (GNI)	102,891	172,771	123,828	148,657	157,279	157,872

89

KENYA

(US$ million, unless otherwise indicated)

	2009	2015	2016	2017	2018	2019
Summary external debt data by debtor type						
Total external debt stocks	**8,559**	**19,777**	**21,061**	**26,198**	**30,688**	**34,217**
Use of IMF credit	858	1,205	1,103	1,047	879	720
Long-term external debt	6,741	15,874	17,824	22,494	27,263	30,886
Public and publicly guaranteed sector	6,741	15,139	17,150	21,646	26,242	30,069
Public sector	6,741	15,139	17,150	21,646	26,242	30,069
of which: General government	6,337	14,744	16,653	21,085	25,483	29,264
Private sector guaranteed by public sector	..	..	..	..	..	..
Private sector not guaranteed	..	735	673	849	1,021	817
Short-term external debt	961	2,698	2,134	2,657	2,546	2,611
Disbursements (long-term)	**538**	**3,149**	**2,798**	**4,463**	**6,629**	**6,723**
Public and publicly guaranteed sector	538	2,609	2,663	4,429	6,255	6,713
Public sector	538	2,609	2,663	4,429	6,255	6,713
of which: General government	515	2,574	2,548	4,341	6,024	6,638
Private sector guaranteed by public sector	..	..	..	..	..	..
Private sector not guaranteed	..	540	135	34	374	10
Principal repayments (long-term)	**259**	**436**	**533**	**713**	**1,566**	**3,010**
Public and publicly guaranteed sector	259	344	336	572	1,370	2,800
Public sector	259	344	336	572	1,370	2,800
of which: General government	228	326	315	525	1,331	2,763
Private sector guaranteed by public sector	..	..	..	..	..	..
Private sector not guaranteed	..	91	196	141	196	210
Interest payments (long-term)	**85**	**364**	**479**	**657**	**976**	**1,222**
Public and publicly guaranteed sector	85	350	438	606	921	1,162
Public sector	85	350	438	606	921	1,162
of which: General government	78	346	435	603	918	1,157
Private sector guaranteed by public sector	..	..	..	..	..	..
Private sector not guaranteed	..	14	42	51	55	61
Summary external debt stock by creditor type						
Long-term external debt stocks	**6,741**	**15,874**	**17,824**	**22,494**	**27,263**	**30,886**
Public and publicly guaranteed debt from:	6,741	15,139	17,150	21,646	26,242	30,069
Official creditors	6,407	11,376	13,289	16,779	19,609	22,968
Multilateral	3,946	6,370	6,981	8,778	10,116	12,716
of which: World Bank	3,156	4,382	4,568	5,303	5,802	7,125
Bilateral	2,461	5,006	6,308	8,001	9,493	10,252
Private creditors	334	3,763	3,861	4,867	6,634	7,101
Bondholders	..	2,750	2,750	2,750	4,750	6,100
Commercial banks and others	334	1,013	1,111	2,117	1,884	1,001
Private nonguaranteed debt from:	..	735	673	849	1,021	817
Bondholders	..	..	..	..	..	..
Commercial banks and others	..	735	673	849	1,021	817
Use of IMF credit	858	1,205	1,103	1,047	879	720
Net financial inflows						
Net debt inflows						
Use of IMF credit	191	-66	-68	-119	-146	-154
Long-term	278	2,714	2,266	3,750	5,063	3,712
Official creditors	273	1,505	2,176	2,895	3,090	3,432
Multilateral	183	615	813	1,421	1,510	2,641
of which: World Bank	83	365	334	455	631	1,359
Bilateral	90	891	1,363	1,474	1,580	791
Private creditors	5	1,208	90	855	1,973	280
Bondholders	..	..	..	..	2,000	1,350
Banks and others	5	1,208	90	855	-27	-1,070
Short-term	4	696	-593	457	-132	139
Net equity inflows						
Foreign direct investment	32	90	432	793	627	901
Portfolio equity	3	11	57	-126	-293	14
Debt ratios						
External debt stocks to exports (%)	113	185	210	247	261	292
External debt stocks to GNI (%)	23	31	31	34	36	37
Debt service to exports (%)	5	8	11	15	24	38
Short-term to external debt stocks (%)	11	14	10	10	8	8
Multilateral to external debt stocks (%)	46	32	33	34	33	37
Reserves to external debt stocks (%)	45	38	36	28	27	27
Gross national income (GNI)	36,977	63,195	68,178	77,456	86,329	93,578

KOSOVO

(US$ million, unless otherwise indicated)

	2009	2015	2016	2017	2018	2019
Summary external debt data by debtor type						
Total external debt stocks	1,725.7	2,158.5	2,124.8	2,504.2	2,320.7	2,428.2
Use of IMF credit	86.8	215.8	194.6	271.7	260.4	224.9
Long-term external debt	817.8	1,263.3	1,309.2	1,396.6	1,260.3	1,357.2
Public and publicly guaranteed sector	358.5	265.1	274.2	313.4	299.6	319.7
Public sector	358.5	265.1	274.2	313.4	297.3	319.7
of which: General government	358.5	248.0	239.8	263.2	249.8	267.4
Private sector guaranteed by public sector	..	0.0	0.0	0.0	2.3	0.0
Private sector not guaranteed	459.3	998.2	1,035.0	1,083.2	960.7	1,037.5
Short-term external debt	821.1	679.3	621.0	836.0	800.0	846.0
Disbursements (long-term)	90.1	111.3	193.1	196.1	220.2	282.9
Public and publicly guaranteed sector	..	33.3	36.5	24.7	20.3	43.6
Public sector	..	33.3	36.5	24.7	18.0	43.6
of which: General government	..	24.9	14.0	9.5	12.8	38.9
Private sector guaranteed by public sector	..	..	..	..	2.4	..
Private sector not guaranteed	90.1	78.0	156.6	171.4	199.9	239.4
Principal repayments (long-term)	269.0	79.0	107.5	97.5	208.6	170.9
Public and publicly guaranteed sector	207.7	13.9	18.7	19.8	21.6	23.4
Public sector	207.7	13.9	18.7	19.8	21.6	23.4
of which: General government	207.7	12.4	14.9	15.1	16.1	17.2
Private sector guaranteed by public sector	..	..	..	..	..	..
Private sector not guaranteed	61.2	65.2	88.8	77.6	187.0	147.5
Interest payments (long-term)	44.1	62.1	55.8	49.8	55.3	47.4
Public and publicly guaranteed sector	22.5	10.0	10.6	10.6	10.8	10.4
Public sector	22.5	10.0	10.6	10.6	10.8	10.4
of which: General government	22.5	9.3	9.6	9.2	9.2	8.6
Private sector guaranteed by public sector	..	..	..	..	..	..
Private sector not guaranteed	21.5	52.2	45.2	39.2	44.5	37.0
Summary external debt stock by creditor type						
Long-term external debt stocks	817.8	1,263.3	1,309.2	1,396.6	1,260.3	1,357.2
Public and publicly guaranteed debt from:	358.5	265.1	274.2	313.4	299.6	319.7
Official creditors	358.5	261.9	267.3	304.9	291.5	303.7
Multilateral	358.5	228.5	217.1	239.2	235.3	253.6
of which: World Bank	358.5	228.5	217.1	239.1	225.0	220.1
Bilateral	..	33.3	50.2	65.7	56.3	50.1
Private creditors	..	3.2	6.8	8.4	8.1	16.0
Bondholders	..	..	..	..	..	..
Commercial banks and others	..	3.2	6.8	8.4	8.1	16.0
Private nonguaranteed debt from:	459.3	998.2	1,035.0	1,083.2	960.7	1,037.5
Bondholders	..	..	..	..	..	..
Commercial banks and others	459.3	998.2	1,035.0	1,083.2	960.7	1,037.5
Use of IMF credit	86.8	215.8	194.6	271.7	260.4	224.9
Net financial inflows						
Net debt inflows						
Use of IMF credit	..	21.1	-15.3	63.8	-5.0	-34.0
Long-term	-178.8	32.3	85.6	98.6	11.7	112.0
Official creditors	-207.7	18.4	13.9	4.2	-1.2	12.1
Multilateral	-207.7	-5.1	-5.0	-3.9	5.4	17.2
of which: World Bank	-207.7	-5.1	-5.0	-4.0	-5.0	-1.4
Bilateral	..	23.5	18.8	8.1	-6.7	-5.1
Private creditors	28.9	13.9	71.7	94.4	12.9	99.9
Bondholders	..	..	..	..	..	..
Banks and others	28.9	13.9	71.7	94.4	12.9	99.9
Short-term	626.9	-100.8	-58.3	215.0	-36.0	46.0
Net equity inflows						
Foreign direct investment	371.0	253.3	202.2	262.1	309.3	281.3
Portfolio equity	0.0	0.0	0.0	0.0	0.0	0.0
Debt ratios						
External debt stocks to exports (%)	140.6	130.0	116.0	111.3	89.6	92.5
External debt stocks to GNI (%)	30.1	33.0	31.2	33.9	28.7	30.0
Debt service to exports (%)	25.5	9.7	12.0	8.7	10.5	9.8
Short-term to external debt stocks (%)	47.6	31.5	29.2	33.4	34.5	34.8
Multilateral to external debt stocks (%)	20.8	10.6	10.2	9.6	10.1	10.4
Reserves to external debt stocks (%)	48.1	35.7	30.0	32.7	38.0	39.8
Gross national income (GNI)	5,738.0	6,545.8	6,801.0	7,393.0	8,076.8	8,092.8

91

KYRGYZ REPUBLIC

(US$ million, unless otherwise indicated)

	2009	2015	2016	2017	2018	2019
Summary external debt data by debtor type						
Total external debt stocks	**4,119**	**7,720**	**7,975**	**8,131**	**8,171**	**8,339**
Use of IMF credit	300	306	302	321	285	258
Long-term external debt	3,395	7,063	7,312	7,454	7,429	7,562
Public and publicly guaranteed sector	2,319	3,431	3,609	3,892	3,660	3,720
Public sector	2,319	3,431	3,609	3,892	3,660	3,720
of which: General government	2,319	3,431	3,609	3,892	3,660	3,720
Private sector guaranteed by public sector	..	..	..	..	..	..
Private sector not guaranteed	1,076	3,632	3,702	3,562	3,769	3,843
Short-term external debt	424	352	362	356	457	519
Disbursements (long-term)	**635**	**780**	**901**	**529**	**687**	**580**
Public and publicly guaranteed sector	378	316	343	286	150	190
Public sector	378	316	343	286	150	190
of which: General government	378	316	343	286	150	190
Private sector guaranteed by public sector	..	..	..	..	..	..
Private sector not guaranteed	257	464	558	243	537	390
Principal repayments (long-term)	**200**	**320**	**574**	**465**	**432**	**438**
Public and publicly guaranteed sector	38	73	86	82	102	122
Public sector	38	73	86	82	102	122
of which: General government	36	73	86	82	102	122
Private sector guaranteed by public sector	..	..	..	..	..	..
Private sector not guaranteed	162	247	488	383	331	316
Interest payments (long-term)	**37**	**71**	**75**	**83**	**84**	**87**
Public and publicly guaranteed sector	19	44	47	51	54	56
Public sector	19	44	47	51	54	56
of which: General government	19	44	47	51	54	56
Private sector guaranteed by public sector	..	..	..	..	..	..
Private sector not guaranteed	18	27	28	32	30	31
Summary external debt stock by creditor type						
Long-term external debt stocks	**3,395**	**7,063**	**7,312**	**7,454**	**7,429**	**7,562**
Public and publicly guaranteed debt from:	2,319	3,431	3,609	3,892	3,660	3,720
Official creditors	2,319	3,431	3,609	3,892	3,660	3,720
Multilateral	1,309	1,356	1,352	1,452	1,450	1,464
of which: World Bank	656	652	631	667	660	657
Bilateral	1,010	2,075	2,257	2,440	2,211	2,256
Private creditors	..	..	..	..	..	..
Bondholders	..	..	..	..	..	..
Commercial banks and others	..	..	..	..	..	..
Private nonguaranteed debt from:	1,076	3,632	3,702	3,562	3,769	3,843
Bondholders	..	..	..	..	0	0
Commercial banks and others	1,076	3,632	3,702	3,562	3,768	3,842
Use of IMF credit	300	306	302	321	285	258
Net financial inflows						
Net debt inflows						
Use of IMF credit	0	11	6	1	-29	-26
Long-term	435	460	327	64	254	142
Official creditors	340	242	257	204	48	68
Multilateral	8	41	31	19	32	23
of which: World Bank	-4	9	-2	-1	8	1
Bilateral	332	201	226	185	16	45
Private creditors	96	218	71	-141	206	74
Bondholders	..	..	..	..	..	0
Banks and others	96	218	71	-141	206	74
Short-term	37	40	10	-6	101	61
Net equity inflows						
Foreign direct investment	178	890	446	-17	86	332
Portfolio equity	1	0	-1	0	0	0
Debt ratios						
External debt stocks to exports (%)	175	315	328	312	294	267
External debt stocks to GNI (%)	91	120	124	111	102	106
Debt service to exports (%)	11	17	28	22	20	18
Short-term to external debt stocks (%)	10	5	5	4	6	6
Multilateral to external debt stocks (%)	32	18	17	18	18	18
Reserves to external debt stocks (%)	36	21	23	23	21	21
Gross national income (GNI)	4,509	6,417	6,455	7,331	8,020	7,837

LAO PEOPLE'S DEMOCRATIC REPUBLIC

(US$ million, unless otherwise indicated)

	2009	2015	2016	2017	2018	2019
Summary external debt data by debtor type						
Total external debt stocks	6,383	11,642	13,535	14,696	15,377	16,686
Use of IMF credit	95	70	68	72	70	70
Long-term external debt	6,084	10,873	12,745	13,879	14,903	16,031
Public and publicly guaranteed sector	3,460	6,689	7,313	8,419	9,315	10,314
Public sector	3,460	6,689	7,313	8,419	9,315	10,314
of which: General government	3,237	6,489	7,117	8,252	9,151	10,155
Private sector guaranteed by public sector	..	0	0	0	0	0
Private sector not guaranteed	2,625	4,183	5,433	5,461	5,588	5,717
Short-term external debt	204	699	722	745	404	585
Disbursements (long-term)	738	2,517	2,308	1,332	1,650	1,331
Public and publicly guaranteed sector	292	1,384	968	1,156	1,402	1,208
Public sector	292	1,384	968	1,156	1,402	1,208
of which: General government	286	1,384	968	1,156	1,377	1,208
Private sector guaranteed by public sector	..	..	..	..	..	..
Private sector not guaranteed	447	1,133	1,340	176	248	124
Principal repayments (long-term)	150	238	326	446	536	276
Public and publicly guaranteed sector	61	145	236	298	416	274
Public sector	61	145	236	298	416	274
of which: General government	57	140	231	269	389	269
Private sector guaranteed by public sector	..	..	..	..	..	..
Private sector not guaranteed	89	92	91	148	120	2
Interest payments (long-term)	72	176	223	281	328	244
Public and publicly guaranteed sector	29	104	138	176	222	211
Public sector	29	104	138	176	222	211
of which: General government	28	103	138	176	222	211
Private sector guaranteed by public sector	..	..	..	..	..	..
Private sector not guaranteed	43	72	85	105	106	33
Summary external debt stock by creditor type						
Long-term external debt stocks	6,084	10,873	12,745	13,879	14,903	16,031
Public and publicly guaranteed debt from:	3,460	6,689	7,313	8,419	9,315	10,314
Official creditors	3,378	5,703	6,050	6,696	7,428	8,380
Multilateral	2,032	1,546	1,478	1,600	1,577	1,701
of which: World Bank	680	511	493	582	588	659
Bilateral	1,347	4,157	4,572	5,097	5,851	6,679
Private creditors	81	987	1,263	1,722	1,887	1,934
Bondholders	..	838	1,082	1,484	1,596	1,671
Commercial banks and others	81	148	181	238	291	263
Private nonguaranteed debt from:	2,625	4,183	5,433	5,461	5,588	5,717
Bondholders	..	246	558	510	560	691
Commercial banks and others	2,625	3,937	4,874	4,951	5,028	5,026
Use of IMF credit	95	70	68	72	70	70
Net financial inflows						
Net debt inflows						
Use of IMF credit	-6	..	..	..	..	..
Long-term	589	2,280	1,982	886	1,113	1,055
Official creditors	231	627	451	461	819	959
Multilateral	17	-44	-25	36	13	133
of which: World Bank	-10	-21	-4	60	19	74
Bilateral	214	671	475	425	806	827
Private creditors	358	1,652	1,531	425	294	96
Bondholders	..	538	560	309	158	124
Banks and others	358	1,114	971	116	137	-28
Short-term	55	-125	23	23	-341	181
Net equity inflows						
Foreign direct investment	319	1,078	935	1,693	1,320	557
Portfolio equity	0	0	-5	-34	2	..
Debt ratios						
External debt stocks to exports (%)	428	252	260	254	242	237
External debt stocks to GNI (%)	113	85	89	92	90	94
Debt service to exports (%)	15	9	11	13	14	7
Short-term to external debt stocks (%)	3	6	5	5	3	4
Multilateral to external debt stocks (%)	32	13	11	11	10	10
Reserves to external debt stocks (%)	11	9	7	7	6	6
Gross national income (GNI)	5,668	13,750	15,126	15,964	17,116	17,746

LEBANON

(US$ million, unless otherwise indicated)

	2009	2015	2016	2017	2018	2019
Summary external debt data by debtor type						
Total external debt stocks	**46,144**	**68,226**	**69,515**	**74,169**	**79,706**	**73,985**
Use of IMF credit	422	268	260	275	269	267
Long-term external debt	42,723	59,579	61,401	65,130	73,890	68,755
Public and publicly guaranteed sector	20,764	26,729	27,708	29,991	33,077	33,325
Public sector	20,764	26,729	27,708	29,991	33,077	33,325
of which: General government	20,764	26,729	27,708	29,991	33,077	33,325
Private sector guaranteed by public sector	..	..	..	..	..	..
Private sector not guaranteed	21,959	32,849	33,693	35,140	40,813	35,430
Short-term external debt	2,999	8,379	7,854	8,764	5,547	4,963
Disbursements (long-term)	**10,325**	**14,037**	**13,374**	**16,061**	**20,797**	**8,647**
Public and publicly guaranteed sector	3,150	3,962	3,651	5,152	5,716	3,173
Public sector	3,150	3,962	3,651	5,152	5,716	3,173
of which: General government	3,150	3,962	3,651	5,152	5,716	3,173
Private sector guaranteed by public sector	..	..	..	..	..	..
Private sector not guaranteed	7,176	10,075	9,724	10,909	15,080	5,474
Principal repayments (long-term)	**8,401**	**10,451**	**11,308**	**12,493**	**11,995**	**13,774**
Public and publicly guaranteed sector	3,107	2,287	2,627	3,031	2,588	2,917
Public sector	3,107	2,287	2,627	3,031	2,588	2,917
of which: General government	3,107	2,287	2,627	3,031	2,588	2,917
Private sector guaranteed by public sector	..	..	..	..	..	..
Private sector not guaranteed	5,294	8,165	8,680	9,462	9,407	10,858
Interest payments (long-term)	**2,651**	**3,480**	**3,689**	**3,779**	**4,275**	**4,600**
Public and publicly guaranteed sector	1,432	1,623	1,718	1,760	2,150	2,142
Public sector	1,432	1,623	1,718	1,760	2,150	2,142
of which: General government	1,432	1,623	1,718	1,760	2,150	2,142
Private sector guaranteed by public sector	..	..	..	..	..	..
Private sector not guaranteed	1,220	1,856	1,971	2,018	2,125	2,458
Summary external debt stock by creditor type						
Long-term external debt stocks	**42,723**	**59,579**	**61,401**	**65,130**	**73,890**	**68,755**
Public and publicly guaranteed debt from:	20,764	26,729	27,708	29,991	33,077	33,325
Official creditors	2,472	1,835	1,765	2,030	1,949	1,881
Multilateral	1,399	991	1,039	1,337	1,375	1,379
of which: World Bank	318	189	254	441	510	536
Bilateral	1,073	844	726	692	574	502
Private creditors	18,292	24,895	25,944	27,961	31,128	31,444
Bondholders	17,704	24,628	25,727	27,768	30,964	31,314
Commercial banks and others	588	266	217	193	164	130
Private nonguaranteed debt from:	21,959	32,849	33,693	35,140	40,813	35,430
Bondholders	670	700	500	300	600	600
Commercial banks and others	21,289	32,149	33,193	34,840	40,213	34,830
Use of IMF credit	422	268	260	275	269	267
Net financial inflows						
Net debt inflows						
Use of IMF credit	..	..	..	..	..	..
Long-term	1,924	3,586	2,067	3,568	8,802	-5,128
Official creditors	-103	-122	-43	177	-50	-61
Multilateral	-1	-30	63	264	54	7
of which: World Bank	-50	13	67	186	70	26
Bilateral	-102	-92	-106	-86	-105	-68
Private creditors	2,027	3,708	2,110	3,390	8,852	-5,066
Bondholders	388	1,846	1,114	1,776	3,504	350
Banks and others	1,639	1,862	996	1,614	5,348	-5,416
Short-term	-78	373	-525	909	-3,217	-584
Net equity inflows						
Foreign direct investment	4,804	2,158	2,568	2,519	2,650	2,220
Portfolio equity	929	-1,002	-135	-294	-266	344
Debt ratios						
External debt stocks to exports (%)	199	312	326	336	363	352
External debt stocks to GNI (%)	131	138	138	140	146	139
Debt service to exports (%)	48	64	71	75	75	88
Short-term to external debt stocks (%)	6	12	11	12	7	7
Multilateral to external debt stocks (%)	3	1	1	2	2	2
Reserves to external debt stocks (%)	63	57	62	59	51	52
Gross national income (GNI)	35,174	49,403	50,390	52,931	54,647	53,147

LESOTHO

(US$ million, unless otherwise indicated)

	2009	2015	2016	2017	2018	2019
Summary external debt data by debtor type						
Total external debt stocks	**766.5**	**921.4**	**921.5**	**936.0**	**904.6**	**938.8**
Use of IMF credit	75.7	114.6	108.3	108.1	93.8	79.3
Long-term external debt	687.8	773.8	774.8	827.5	810.3	859.1
Public and publicly guaranteed sector	687.8	773.8	774.8	827.5	810.3	859.1
Public sector	687.8	773.8	774.8	827.5	810.3	859.1
of which: General government	676.6	773.4	774.1	826.4	808.0	854.5
Private sector guaranteed by public sector	..	..	..	..	..	..
Private sector not guaranteed	..	..	..	..	..	..
Short-term external debt	3.0	33.1	38.4	0.4	0.5	0.4
Disbursements (long-term)	**40.8**	**70.6**	**59.6**	**38.9**	**43.7**	**73.6**
Public and publicly guaranteed sector	40.8	70.6	59.6	38.9	43.7	73.6
Public sector	40.8	70.6	59.6	38.9	43.7	73.6
of which: General government	40.8	70.4	59.3	38.5	42.5	71.2
Private sector guaranteed by public sector	..	..	..	..	..	..
Private sector not guaranteed	..	..	..	..	..	..
Principal repayments (long-term)	**24.6**	**31.3**	**40.2**	**33.2**	**42.0**	**41.5**
Public and publicly guaranteed sector	24.6	31.3	40.2	33.2	42.0	41.5
Public sector	24.6	31.3	40.2	33.2	42.0	41.5
of which: General government	23.4	27.0	40.1	33.2	42.0	41.5
Private sector guaranteed by public sector	..	..	..	..	..	..
Private sector not guaranteed	..	..	..	..	..	..
Interest payments (long-term)	**7.4**	**20.3**	**14.2**	**16.1**	**16.9**	**23.8**
Public and publicly guaranteed sector	7.4	20.3	14.2	16.1	16.9	23.8
Public sector	7.4	20.3	14.2	16.1	16.9	23.8
of which: General government	6.6	19.7	14.2	16.1	16.9	23.8
Private sector guaranteed by public sector	..	..	..	..	..	..
Private sector not guaranteed	..	..	..	..	..	..
Summary external debt stock by creditor type						
Long-term external debt stocks	**687.8**	**773.8**	**774.8**	**827.5**	**810.3**	**859.1**
Public and publicly guaranteed debt from:	687.8	773.8	774.8	827.5	810.3	859.1
Official creditors	672.6	770.1	771.5	824.1	807.1	856.2
Multilateral	614.0	655.8	648.5	703.5	697.9	724.5
of which: World Bank	313.2	283.7	284.1	321.4	338.3	362.8
Bilateral	58.6	114.3	123.0	120.6	109.2	131.7
Private creditors	15.2	3.7	3.3	3.5	3.1	2.9
Bondholders	..	..	..	..	..	..
Commercial banks and others	15.2	3.7	3.3	3.5	3.1	2.9
Private nonguaranteed debt from:	..	..	..	..	..	..
Bondholders	..	..	..	..	..	..
Commercial banks and others	..	..	..	..	..	..
Use of IMF credit	75.7	114.6	108.3	108.1	93.8	79.3
Net financial inflows						
Net debt inflows						
Use of IMF credit	-5.9	-1.1	-3.0	-6.5	-11.9	-14.0
Long-term	16.2	39.3	19.4	5.7	1.6	32.1
Official creditors	17.1	43.9	19.8	5.9	1.8	32.3
Multilateral	4.1	33.9	7.5	12.3	10.6	19.8
of which: World Bank	5.2	2.4	8.7	20.9	24.6	27.7
Bilateral	13.0	10.0	12.3	-6.4	-8.8	12.5
Private creditors	-0.9	-4.5	-0.3	-0.2	-0.2	-0.2
Bondholders	..	..	..	..	..	..
Banks and others	-0.9	-4.5	-0.3	-0.2	-0.2	-0.2
Short-term	1.0	33.0	5.2	-37.9	-0.3	0.3
Net equity inflows						
Foreign direct investment	85.6	52.9	45.7	45.9	50.6	46.5
Portfolio equity	0.0	0.3	0.2	0.2	0.3	0.2
Debt ratios						
External debt stocks to exports (%)	52.0	64.5	62.5	55.9	48.6	58.7
External debt stocks to GNI (%)	33.0	34.6	37.7	34.4	30.9	33.5
Debt service to exports (%)	2.6	3.7	3.9	3.3	3.8	5.0
Short-term to external debt stocks (%)	0.4	3.6	4.2	0.0	0.1	0.0
Multilateral to external debt stocks (%)	80.1	71.2	70.4	75.2	77.2	77.2
Reserves to external debt stocks (%)	153.9	108.2	100.4	70.3	80.5	82.5
Gross national income (GNI)	2,325.4	2,666.6	2,442.9	2,722.7	2,927.0	2,805.7

95

LIBERIA

(US$ million, unless otherwise indicated)

	2009	2015	2016	2017	2018	2019
Summary external debt data by debtor type						
Total external debt stocks	**1,850.3**	**839.1**	**952.6**	**1,122.2**	**1,228.5**	**1,357.4**
Use of IMF credit	1,085.5	332.1	359.4	401.8	389.5	396.3
Long-term external debt	673.1	507.0	593.2	720.4	839.0	961.1
Public and publicly guaranteed sector	673.1	436.0	528.3	661.6	787.9	917.6
Public sector	673.1	436.0	528.3	659.7	783.8	912.6
of which: General government	660.8	436.0	528.3	659.7	783.8	912.6
Private sector guaranteed by public sector	..	..	0.0	2.0	4.0	5.0
Private sector not guaranteed	..	71.0	64.9	58.8	51.2	43.5
Short-term external debt	91.6	0.0	0.0	0.0	0.0	0.1
Disbursements (long-term)	**0.0**	**166.9**	**103.7**	**112.4**	**155.8**	**142.6**
Public and publicly guaranteed sector	0.0	150.9	103.7	112.4	155.8	142.6
Public sector	0.0	150.9	103.7	110.3	153.4	141.3
of which: General government	0.0	150.9	103.7	110.3	153.4	141.3
Private sector guaranteed by public sector	..	..	..	2.1	2.5	1.3
Private sector not guaranteed	..	16.0	..	..	..	..
Principal repayments (long-term)	**4.3**	**5.4**	**7.7**	**9.3**	**23.9**	**16.3**
Public and publicly guaranteed sector	4.3	2.4	1.6	3.2	16.2	8.7
Public sector	4.3	2.4	1.6	3.0	16.0	8.5
of which: General government	4.3	2.4	1.6	3.0	16.0	8.5
Private sector guaranteed by public sector	..	..	..	0.2	0.2	0.2
Private sector not guaranteed	..	3.0	6.1	6.1	7.6	7.6
Interest payments (long-term)	**11.8**	**3.8**	**4.2**	**5.6**	**8.4**	**8.4**
Public and publicly guaranteed sector	11.8	2.7	3.0	4.8	7.4	7.0
Public sector	11.8	2.7	3.0	4.7	7.3	6.9
of which: General government	10.8	2.7	3.0	4.7	7.3	6.9
Private sector guaranteed by public sector	..	..	..	0.0	0.1	0.1
Private sector not guaranteed	..	1.1	1.2	0.9	1.0	1.4
Summary external debt stock by creditor type						
Long-term external debt stocks	**673.1**	**507.0**	**593.2**	**720.4**	**839.0**	**961.1**
Public and publicly guaranteed debt from:	673.1	436.0	528.3	661.6	787.9	917.6
Official creditors	652.6	436.0	528.3	661.6	787.9	917.6
Multilateral	154.5	321.6	395.6	506.0	590.2	706.4
of which: World Bank	69.0	164.3	231.3	306.4	367.6	454.9
Bilateral	498.1	114.4	132.7	155.6	197.6	211.2
Private creditors	20.5	..	..	..	0.0	..
Bondholders	..	..	..	..	..	..
Commercial banks and others	20.5	..	..	..	0.0	..
Private nonguaranteed debt from:	..	71.0	64.9	58.8	51.2	43.5
Bondholders	..	..	..	..	..	..
Commercial banks and others	..	71.0	64.9	58.8	51.2	43.5
Use of IMF credit	1,085.5	332.1	359.4	401.8	389.5	396.3
Net financial inflows						
Net debt inflows						
Use of IMF credit	17.6	19.4	38.5	20.5	-3.0	9.0
Long-term	-4.3	161.6	95.9	103.1	132.0	126.3
Official creditors	-4.3	148.6	102.0	109.2	139.6	133.9
Multilateral	-4.3	148.5	83.6	87.1	95.3	119.4
of which: World Bank	-3.3	67.2	74.3	59.6	69.3	89.4
Bilateral	..	0.1	18.4	22.1	44.3	14.6
Private creditors	..	13.0	-6.1	-6.1	-7.6	-7.6
Bondholders	..	..	..	..	..	..
Banks and others	..	13.0	-6.1	-6.1	-7.6	-7.6
Short-term	0.0	0.0	0.0	0.0	0.0	0.0
Net equity inflows						
Foreign direct investment	2.9	53.1	141.7	188.4	59.1	100.7
Portfolio equity	0.0	0.0	0.0	0.0	..	..
Debt ratios						
External debt stocks to exports (%)	391.9	161.0	240.0	249.5	219.8	235.6
External debt stocks to GNI (%)	114.0	29.0	31.8	37.6	43.5	50.0
Debt service to exports (%)	5.8	8.7	3.0	3.4	6.3	7.1
Short-term to external debt stocks (%)	5.0	0.0	0.0	0.0	0.0	0.0
Multilateral to external debt stocks (%)	8.4	38.3	41.5	45.1	48.0	52.0
Reserves to external debt stocks (%)	20.1	68.5	62.5	53.5	45.6	25.7
Gross national income (GNI)	1,623.4	2,897.0	2,996.8	2,982.6	2,827.0	2,717.6

MADAGASCAR
(US$ million, unless otherwise indicated)

	2009	2015	2016	2017	2018	2019
Summary external debt data by debtor type						
Total external debt stocks	2,847	3,007	2,976	3,382	3,730	4,065
Use of IMF credit	284	281	301	440	465	545
Long-term external debt	1,914	2,522	2,470	2,765	2,994	3,239
Public and publicly guaranteed sector	1,895	2,509	2,465	2,735	2,902	3,120
Public sector	1,893	2,509	2,465	2,735	2,902	3,120
of which: General government	1,870	2,422	2,387	2,670	2,826	2,990
Private sector guaranteed by public sector	2	..	..	..	..	..
Private sector not guaranteed	19	13	5	30	92	119
Short-term external debt	649	204	204	177	271	281
Disbursements (long-term)	124	323	133	272	363	328
Public and publicly guaranteed sector	124	323	133	246	297	302
Public sector	124	323	133	246	297	302
of which: General government	121	251	133	246	285	247
Private sector guaranteed by public sector	0	..	..	..	..	..
Private sector not guaranteed	..	..	..	26	66	26
Principal repayments (long-term)	29	96	84	93	72	67
Public and publicly guaranteed sector	27	95	76	92	72	67
Public sector	26	95	76	92	72	67
of which: General government	18	85	68	77	71	67
Private sector guaranteed by public sector	1	..	..	..	..	..
Private sector not guaranteed	1	1	8	1	..	..
Interest payments (long-term)	15	26	20	23	30	32
Public and publicly guaranteed sector	15	25	20	23	29	30
Public sector	15	25	20	23	29	30
of which: General government	14	25	20	22	29	29
Private sector guaranteed by public sector	0	..	..	..	..	..
Private sector not guaranteed	0	0	0	0	1	2
Summary external debt stock by creditor type						
Long-term external debt stocks	1,914	2,522	2,470	2,765	2,994	3,239
Public and publicly guaranteed debt from:	1,895	2,509	2,465	2,735	2,902	3,120
Official creditors	1,887	2,422	2,387	2,609	2,738	2,966
Multilateral	1,486	1,973	2,015	2,254	2,349	2,491
of which: World Bank	1,105	1,412	1,433	1,595	1,648	1,686
Bilateral	401	450	372	355	390	475
Private creditors	8	86	78	127	164	154
Bondholders	..	..	..	..	..	..
Commercial banks and others	8	86	78	127	164	154
Private nonguaranteed debt from:	19	13	5	30	92	119
Bondholders	..	..	..	..	..	..
Commercial banks and others	19	13	5	30	92	119
Use of IMF credit	284	281	301	440	465	545
Net financial inflows						
Net debt inflows						
Use of IMF credit	0	26	29	118	36	83
Long-term	96	227	49	178	291	261
Official creditors	97	166	65	110	185	244
Multilateral	55	133	94	133	145	156
of which: World Bank	30	106	65	77	93	48
Bilateral	42	33	-30	-23	40	88
Private creditors	-1	61	-15	68	106	17
Bondholders	..	..	..	..	..	..
Banks and others	-1	61	-15	68	106	17
Short-term	35	-74	26	-26	94	11
Net equity inflows						
Foreign direct investment	72	20	31	30	36	227
Portfolio equity	0	0	0	0	0	..
Debt ratios						
External debt stocks to exports (%)	146	96	88	82	85	90
External debt stocks to GNI (%)	30	27	26	26	28	30
Debt service to exports (%)	3	4	4	3	3	3
Short-term to external debt stocks (%)	23	7	7	5	7	7
Multilateral to external debt stocks (%)	52	66	68	67	63	61
Reserves to external debt stocks (%)	34	28	40	47	47	42
Gross national income (GNI)	9,503	10,949	11,432	12,817	13,454	13,629

97

MALAWI

(US$ million, unless otherwise indicated)

	2009	2015	2016	2017	2018	2019
Summary external debt data by debtor type						
Total external debt stocks	**1,144.4**	**1,721.2**	**1,847.0**	**2,162.4**	**2,265.8**	**2,433.9**
Use of IMF credit	230.9	254.7	295.9	318.9	314.1	339.5
Long-term external debt	846.5	1,453.9	1,507.0	1,789.8	1,926.2	2,026.1
Public and publicly guaranteed sector	846.5	1,453.9	1,507.0	1,789.8	1,926.2	2,026.1
Public sector	846.5	1,453.9	1,507.0	1,789.8	1,926.2	2,026.1
of which: General government	839.6	1,438.2	1,492.9	1,774.7	1,913.0	2,014.6
Private sector guaranteed by public sector	..	..	..	..	..	..
Private sector not guaranteed	..	..	..	..	..	..
Short-term external debt	67.0	12.7	44.0	53.7	25.4	68.3
Disbursements (long-term)	**107.3**	**175.3**	**134.6**	**240.0**	**223.2**	**176.3**
Public and publicly guaranteed sector	107.3	175.3	134.6	240.0	223.2	176.3
Public sector	107.3	175.3	134.6	240.0	223.2	176.3
of which: General government	107.1	175.3	134.6	240.0	223.2	176.3
Private sector guaranteed by public sector	..	..	..	..	..	..
Private sector not guaranteed	..	..	..	..	..	..
Principal repayments (long-term)	**22.4**	**30.3**	**32.8**	**32.7**	**42.6**	**65.6**
Public and publicly guaranteed sector	22.4	30.3	32.8	32.7	42.6	65.6
Public sector	22.4	30.3	32.8	32.7	42.6	65.6
of which: General government	20.1	28.4	31.7	31.8	41.4	64.1
Private sector guaranteed by public sector	..	..	..	..	..	..
Private sector not guaranteed	..	..	..	..	..	..
Interest payments (long-term)	**14.8**	**15.6**	**17.0**	**15.6**	**12.1**	**17.1**
Public and publicly guaranteed sector	14.8	15.6	17.0	15.6	12.1	17.1
Public sector	14.8	15.6	17.0	15.6	12.1	17.1
of which: General government	14.5	15.3	16.7	15.6	12.1	17.1
Private sector guaranteed by public sector	..	..	..	..	..	..
Private sector not guaranteed	..	..	..	..	..	..
Summary external debt stock by creditor type						
Long-term external debt stocks	**846.5**	**1,453.9**	**1,507.0**	**1,789.8**	**1,926.2**	**2,026.1**
Public and publicly guaranteed debt from:	846.5	1,453.9	1,507.0	1,789.8	1,926.2	2,026.1
Official creditors	840.7	1,453.9	1,507.0	1,789.8	1,926.2	2,026.1
Multilateral	547.0	1,013.0	1,087.9	1,369.4	1,487.0	1,600.2
of which: World Bank	212.8	588.2	642.2	862.2	916.7	969.3
Bilateral	293.7	440.9	419.1	420.4	439.2	425.9
Private creditors	5.8	0.0	..	..	..	..
Bondholders	..	..	..	..	..	..
Commercial banks and others	5.8	0.0	..	..	..	..
Private nonguaranteed debt from:	..	..	..	..	..	..
Bondholders	..	..	..	..	..	..
Commercial banks and others	..	..	..	..	..	..
Use of IMF credit	230.9	254.7	295.9	318.9	314.1	339.5
Net financial inflows						
Net debt inflows						
Use of IMF credit	0.0	-6.1	50.5	5.3	2.7	27.2
Long-term	84.9	145.0	101.8	207.4	180.5	110.8
Official creditors	84.9	147.0	101.8	207.3	180.5	110.8
Multilateral	46.3	126.4	107.6	221.1	150.3	120.0
of which: World Bank	24.2	111.6	75.8	180.3	78.4	57.8
Bilateral	38.6	20.6	-5.8	-13.7	30.2	-9.3
Private creditors	..	-1.9	..	..	..	..
Bondholders	..	..	..	..	..	..
Banks and others	..	-1.9	..	..	..	..
Short-term	-17.0	-8.3	31.3	5.0	-26.0	42.9
Net equity inflows						
Foreign direct investment	69.2	172.5	25.1	81.2	91.3	88.8
Portfolio equity	-0.3	0.5	0.4	0.5	..	..
Debt ratios						
External debt stocks to exports (%)	84.9	135.2	156.0	203.9	200.6	207.1
External debt stocks to GNI (%)	18.7	28.0	34.1	35.2	33.6	32.5
Debt service to exports (%)	2.9	5.5	6.4	6.7	7.5	8.7
Short-term to external debt stocks (%)	5.9	0.7	2.4	2.5	1.1	2.8
Multilateral to external debt stocks (%)	47.8	58.9	58.9	63.3	65.6	65.7
Reserves to external debt stocks (%)	13.1	39.4	32.9	35.6	33.5	33.9
Gross national income (GNI)	6,132.2	6,153.4	5,409.9	6,149.8	6,752.5	7,485.1

MALDIVES
(US$ million, unless otherwise indicated)

	2009	2015	2016	2017	2018	2019
Summary external debt data by debtor type						
Total external debt stocks	1,383.5	1,006.2	1,222.0	1,515.7	2,339.7	2,679.2
Use of IMF credit	20.9	13.1	12.1	12.3	11.4	10.8
Long-term external debt	758.5	836.0	1,080.0	1,392.1	2,089.9	2,331.9
Public and publicly guaranteed sector	542.7	685.3	911.8	1,234.1	2,003.9	2,228.2
Public sector	527.7	685.3	911.8	1,234.1	1,949.6	2,121.4
of which: General government	515.3	653.8	760.5	1,078.3	1,321.0	1,432.6
Private sector guaranteed by public sector	15.0	..	0.0	0.0	54.3	106.8
Private sector not guaranteed	215.8	150.7	168.2	158.1	86.0	103.7
Short-term external debt	604.0	157.2	129.8	111.3	238.4	336.5
Disbursements (long-term)	156.8	48.4	387.7	420.1	1,124.0	612.7
Public and publicly guaranteed sector	112.0	48.4	330.4	388.1	1,124.0	562.1
Public sector	112.0	48.4	330.4	388.1	1,069.7	509.6
of which: General government	111.5	41.5	198.9	349.8	330.2	179.1
Private sector guaranteed by public sector	..	..	..	..	54.3	52.5
Private sector not guaranteed	44.8	..	57.3	32.0	..	50.7
Principal repayments (long-term)	64.7	120.1	122.9	144.6	373.9	364.1
Public and publicly guaranteed sector	44.4	81.4	83.1	102.4	333.9	331.1
Public sector	41.4	81.4	83.1	102.4	333.9	331.1
of which: General government	37.0	64.7	71.6	68.5	67.3	60.7
Private sector guaranteed by public sector	3.0	..	..	..	0.0	0.0
Private sector not guaranteed	20.3	38.7	39.7	42.2	40.1	33.0
Interest payments (long-term)	16.4	14.6	17.4	19.1	58.0	83.6
Public and publicly guaranteed sector	12.1	13.5	14.5	15.0	54.6	80.4
Public sector	11.3	13.5	14.5	15.0	53.8	75.4
of which: General government	10.8	11.8	12.3	11.6	31.5	40.0
Private sector guaranteed by public sector	0.8	..	..	..	0.8	5.0
Private sector not guaranteed	4.2	1.1	2.9	4.1	3.5	3.3
Summary external debt stock by creditor type						
Long-term external debt stocks	758.5	836.0	1,080.0	1,392.1	2,089.9	2,331.9
Public and publicly guaranteed debt from:	542.7	685.3	911.8	1,234.1	2,003.9	2,228.2
Official creditors	461.3	625.1	866.2	934.4	1,294.1	1,446.1
Multilateral	279.7	268.9	252.6	275.9	339.7	383.8
of which: World Bank	84.2	92.6	87.5	90.1	85.4	92.2
Bilateral	181.7	356.2	613.5	658.6	954.4	1,062.4
Private creditors	81.4	60.2	45.7	299.6	709.8	782.0
Bondholders	..	..	..	250.0	350.0	350.0
Commercial banks and others	81.4	60.2	45.7	49.6	359.8	432.0
Private nonguaranteed debt from:	215.8	150.7	168.2	158.1	86.0	103.7
Bondholders	..	..	..	..	..	..
Commercial banks and others	215.8	150.7	168.2	158.1	86.0	103.7
Use of IMF credit	20.9	13.1	12.1	12.3	11.4	10.8
Net financial inflows						
Net debt inflows						
Use of IMF credit	4.7	-1.1	-0.6	-0.6	-0.6	-0.6
Long-term	92.1	-71.7	264.8	275.5	750.0	248.6
Official creditors	85.9	-37.8	261.0	34.9	379.2	158.4
Multilateral	2.3	-9.0	-8.8	7.5	69.9	45.5
of which: World Bank	4.4	-1.9	-2.5	-2.5	-2.7	7.2
Bilateral	83.5	-28.8	269.9	27.4	309.2	112.9
Private creditors	6.2	-34.0	3.8	240.6	370.9	90.2
Bondholders	..	..	..	250.0	100.0	..
Banks and others	6.2	-34.0	3.8	-9.4	270.9	90.2
Short-term	140.0	12.0	-26.3	-17.6	126.0	96.7
Net equity inflows						
Foreign direct investment	158.0	298.0	456.6	457.8	575.7	891.1
Portfolio equity	-14.5	1.9	-0.7	-0.8	31.8	0.0
Debt ratios						
External debt stocks to exports (%)	80.5	31.9	38.7	45.5	64.9	71.2
External debt stocks to GNI (%)	66.2	26.6	30.4	34.8	48.4	51.5
Debt service to exports (%)	5.7	4.4	4.6	5.0	12.3	12.2
Short-term to external debt stocks (%)	43.7	15.6	10.6	7.3	10.2	12.6
Multilateral to external debt stocks (%)	20.2	26.7	20.7	18.2	14.5	14.3
Reserves to external debt stocks (%)	19.9	57.2	39.1	39.5	30.9	28.5
Gross national income (GNI)	2,090.0	3,777.0	4,026.2	4,361.0	4,835.3	5,199.4

MALI

(US$ million, unless otherwise indicated)

	2009	2015	2016	2017	2018	2019
Summary external debt data by debtor type						
Total external debt stocks	**2,210**	**3,692**	**3,789**	**4,294**	**4,675**	**5,192**
Use of IMF credit	184	256	288	334	441	447
Long-term external debt	2,002	3,354	3,420	3,866	4,123	4,636
Public and publicly guaranteed sector	2,002	3,354	3,420	3,866	4,123	4,636
Public sector	2,002	3,354	3,420	3,866	4,123	4,636
of which: General government	1,997	3,352	3,419	3,865	4,121	4,634
Private sector guaranteed by public sector	..	..	..	..	..	..
Private sector not guaranteed	..	..	..	..	..	..
Short-term external debt	25	82	80	94	111	110
Disbursements (long-term)	**494**	**453**	**244**	**299**	**520**	**712**
Public and publicly guaranteed sector	494	453	244	299	520	712
Public sector	494	453	244	299	520	712
of which: General government	494	453	244	299	520	712
Private sector guaranteed by public sector	..	..	..	..	..	..
Private sector not guaranteed	..	..	..	..	..	..
Principal repayments (long-term)	**46**	**65**	**72**	**91**	**147**	**152**
Public and publicly guaranteed sector	46	65	72	91	147	152
Public sector	46	65	72	91	147	152
of which: General government	45	65	71	91	147	152
Private sector guaranteed by public sector	..	..	..	..	..	..
Private sector not guaranteed	..	..	..	..	..	..
Interest payments (long-term)	**22**	**33**	**35**	**35**	**42**	**51**
Public and publicly guaranteed sector	22	33	35	35	42	51
Public sector	22	33	35	35	42	51
of which: General government	22	33	35	35	42	51
Private sector guaranteed by public sector	..	..	..	..	..	..
Private sector not guaranteed	..	..	..	..	..	..
Summary external debt stock by creditor type						
Long-term external debt stocks	**2,002**	**3,354**	**3,420**	**3,866**	**4,123**	**4,636**
Public and publicly guaranteed debt from:	2,002	3,354	3,420	3,866	4,123	4,636
Official creditors	1,995	3,353	3,420	3,866	4,122	4,635
Multilateral	1,565	2,490	2,505	2,910	3,124	3,537
of which: World Bank	698	1,349	1,364	1,574	1,682	1,970
Bilateral	430	863	915	956	999	1,098
Private creditors	7	1	0	0	0	0
Bondholders	..	..	..	..	..	..
Commercial banks and others	7	1	0	0	0	0
Private nonguaranteed debt from:	..	..	..	..	..	..
Bondholders	..	..	..	..	..	..
Commercial banks and others	..	..	..	..	..	..
Use of IMF credit	184	256	288	334	441	447
Net financial inflows						
Net debt inflows						
Use of IMF credit	3	3	41	28	116	9
Long-term	448	389	173	208	373	560
Official creditors	446	389	173	208	373	560
Multilateral	352	236	87	210	302	444
of which: World Bank	159	172	57	123	149	298
Bilateral	94	153	86	-2	71	116
Private creditors	1	-1	0	0	0	0
Bondholders	..	..	..	..	..	..
Banks and others	1	-1	0	0	0	0
Short-term	24	23	-3	12	19	10
Net equity inflows						
Foreign direct investment	645	92	237	365	358	494
Portfolio equity	-3	4	5	2	-1	..
Debt ratios						
External debt stocks to exports (%)	100	114	112	122	107	..
External debt stocks to GNI (%)	23	29	28	29	28	30
Debt service to exports (%)	3	3	4	4	5	..
Short-term to external debt stocks (%)	1	2	2	2	2	2
Multilateral to external debt stocks (%)	71	67	66	68	67	68
Reserves to external debt stocks (%)	73	17	..	..	..	..
Gross national income (GNI)	9,725	12,809	13,645	14,875	16,716	17,055

MAURITANIA
(US$ million, unless otherwise indicated)

	2009	2015	2016	2017	2018	2019
Summary external debt data by debtor type						
Total external debt stocks	3,142	4,993	5,080	5,241	5,226	5,370
Use of IMF credit	113	196	180	200	221	244
Long-term external debt	1,989	3,712	3,865	4,002	3,952	4,043
Public and publicly guaranteed sector	1,989	3,712	3,865	4,002	3,952	4,043
Public sector	1,989	3,712	3,865	4,002	3,952	4,043
of which: General government	1,733	2,779	3,011	3,214	3,238	3,383
Private sector guaranteed by public sector	..	..	..	..	..	..
Private sector not guaranteed	..	..	..	..	..	..
Short-term external debt	1,040	1,086	1,035	1,040	1,052	1,083
Disbursements (long-term)	**410**	**681**	**390**	**250**	**270**	**367**
Public and publicly guaranteed sector	410	681	390	250	270	367
Public sector	410	681	390	250	270	367
of which: General government	398	381	390	248	270	345
Private sector guaranteed by public sector	..	..	..	..	..	..
Private sector not guaranteed	..	..	..	..	..	..
Principal repayments (long-term)	**54**	**140**	**173**	**224**	**270**	**266**
Public and publicly guaranteed sector	54	140	173	224	270	266
Public sector	54	140	173	224	270	266
of which: General government	30	62	96	149	198	190
Private sector guaranteed by public sector	..	..	..	..	..	..
Private sector not guaranteed	..	..	..	..	..	..
Interest payments (long-term)	**23**	**95**	**75**	**80**	**92**	**88**
Public and publicly guaranteed sector	23	95	75	80	92	88
Public sector	23	95	75	80	92	88
of which: General government	16	41	42	50	62	60
Private sector guaranteed by public sector	..	..	..	..	..	..
Private sector not guaranteed	..	..	..	..	..	..
Summary external debt stock by creditor type						
Long-term external debt stocks	1,989	3,712	3,865	4,002	3,952	4,043
Public and publicly guaranteed debt from:	1,989	3,712	3,865	4,002	3,952	4,043
Official creditors	1,977	3,712	3,865	4,002	3,952	4,043
Multilateral	1,232	2,093	2,239	2,358	2,284	2,379
of which: World Bank	282	369	366	390	382	388
Bilateral	745	1,618	1,627	1,644	1,668	1,664
Private creditors	12	..	..	..	..	..
Bondholders	..	..	..	..	..	..
Commercial banks and others	12	..	..	..	..	..
Private nonguaranteed debt from:	..	..	..	..	..	..
Bondholders	..	..	..	..	..	..
Commercial banks and others	..	..	..	..	..	..
Use of IMF credit	113	196	180	200	221	244
Net financial inflows						
Net debt inflows						
Use of IMF credit	0	-4	-10	9	26	24
Long-term	356	541	217	27	0	101
Official creditors	357	541	217	27	0	101
Multilateral	180	135	181	48	-45	99
of which: World Bank	38	6	9	2	2	8
Bilateral	178	406	36	-21	45	2
Private creditors	-1	..	..	..	..	..
Bondholders	..	..	..	..	..	..
Banks and others	-1	..	..	..	..	..
Short-term	-108	63	-50	4	13	30
Net equity inflows						
Foreign direct investment	-3	502	271	588	773	885
Portfolio equity	..	0	..	..	..	..
Debt ratios						
External debt stocks to exports (%)	191	292	294	257	235	198
External debt stocks to GNI (%)	66	83	81	79	75	72
Debt service to exports (%)	5	14	15	16	17	14
Short-term to external debt stocks (%)	33	22	20	20	20	20
Multilateral to external debt stocks (%)	39	42	44	45	44	44
Reserves to external debt stocks (%)	7	16	16	16	18	19
Gross national income (GNI)	4,777	5,987	6,282	6,662	7,011	7,503

MEXICO
(US$ million, unless otherwise indicated)

	2009	2015	2016	2017	2018	2019
Summary external debt data by debtor type						
Total external debt stocks	193,343	426,914	421,904	441,577	453,158	469,729
Use of IMF credit	4,470	3,951	3,833	4,060	3,965	3,943
Long-term external debt	163,318	352,708	364,975	385,083	388,045	403,093
Public and publicly guaranteed sector	118,878	259,358	266,772	286,640	295,157	303,817
Public sector	118,878	259,358	266,772	286,440	294,957	303,617
of which: General government	67,110	180,944	176,253	185,818	191,327	201,787
Private sector guaranteed by public sector	0	..	0	200	200	200
Private sector not guaranteed	44,440	93,349	98,203	98,443	92,888	99,276
Short-term external debt	25,555	70,255	53,096	52,433	61,147	62,693
Disbursements (long-term)	37,074	49,799	60,842	59,298	37,523	55,065
Public and publicly guaranteed sector	26,995	27,849	40,967	34,933	25,468	37,407
Public sector	26,995	27,849	40,967	34,733	25,468	37,407
of which: General government	17,117	9,705	12,806	13,424	8,417	18,303
Private sector guaranteed by public sector	..	..	..	200	0	0
Private sector not guaranteed	10,079	21,950	19,875	24,365	12,054	17,658
Principal repayments (long-term)	22,318	31,761	59,133	38,066	32,422	36,290
Public and publicly guaranteed sector	11,873	11,709	28,386	17,516	14,910	25,037
Public sector	11,872	11,709	28,386	17,516	14,910	25,037
of which: General government	3,827	6,479	12,933	4,769	1,498	4,386
Private sector guaranteed by public sector	1	..	0	0	0	0
Private sector not guaranteed	10,446	20,052	30,747	20,550	17,512	11,253
Interest payments (long-term)	8,792	18,790	17,302	24,910	22,875	22,626
Public and publicly guaranteed sector	6,019	14,475	12,297	18,563	15,728	16,955
Public sector	6,019	14,475	12,297	18,561	15,721	16,948
of which: General government	3,648	11,533	8,886	14,347	10,923	11,964
Private sector guaranteed by public sector	..	..	0	2	6	7
Private sector not guaranteed	2,773	4,315	5,005	6,347	7,148	5,671
Summary external debt stock by creditor type						
Long-term external debt stocks	163,318	352,708	364,975	385,083	388,045	403,093
Public and publicly guaranteed debt from:	118,878	259,358	266,772	286,640	295,157	303,817
Official creditors	20,121	31,553	31,139	32,723	32,605	33,509
Multilateral	17,104	28,077	27,927	29,304	29,794	31,022
of which: World Bank	10,143	14,748	14,656	14,887	14,611	14,942
Bilateral	3,016	3,476	3,212	3,419	2,810	2,487
Private creditors	98,757	227,806	235,633	253,918	262,552	270,308
Bondholders	78,522	195,362	208,310	225,580	237,164	247,179
Commercial banks and others	20,236	32,443	27,322	28,338	25,388	23,129
Private nonguaranteed debt from:	44,440	93,349	98,203	98,443	92,888	99,276
Bondholders	21,444	77,863	78,753	80,120	74,589	77,355
Commercial banks and others	22,996	15,486	19,450	18,323	18,299	21,921
Use of IMF credit	4,470	3,951	3,833	4,060	3,965	3,943
Net financial inflows						
Net debt inflows						
Use of IMF credit	..	..	..	..	..	..
Long-term	14,756	18,038	1,709	21,232	5,101	18,775
Official creditors	6,921	291	-1	1,344	-276	820
Multilateral	6,311	674	231	1,297	269	1,118
of which: World Bank	4,213	15	27	178	-278	298
Bilateral	610	-383	-233	46	-544	-298
Private creditors	7,835	17,747	1,711	19,889	5,376	17,955
Bondholders	12,716	16,806	15,654	20,062	7,974	16,370
Banks and others	-4,881	940	-13,944	-173	-2,597	1,585
Short-term	1,377	-21,672	-17,159	-663	8,714	1,546
Net equity inflows						
Foreign direct investment	16,377	25,271	21,561	23,862	25,654	30,814
Portfolio equity	4,155	3,601	9,477	10,320	2,421	-10
Debt ratios						
External debt stocks to exports (%)	77	104	104	99	92	93
External debt stocks to GNI (%)	22	37	40	39	38	38
Debt service to exports (%)	13	13	19	15	12	12
Short-term to external debt stocks (%)	13	16	13	12	13	13
Multilateral to external debt stocks (%)	9	7	7	7	7	7
Reserves to external debt stocks (%)	52	41	41	39	38	38
Gross national income (GNI)	884,929	1,141,656	1,049,496	1,128,748	1,189,362	1,221,112

MOLDOVA
(US$ million, unless otherwise indicated)

	2009	2015	2016	2017	2018	2019
Summary external debt data by debtor type						
Total external debt stocks	3,715	6,107	6,235	6,988	7,451	7,536
Use of IMF credit	338	628	574	562	496	458
Long-term external debt	2,011	4,255	4,313	4,756	4,925	5,074
Public and publicly guaranteed sector	809	1,072	1,212	1,442	1,450	1,464
Public sector	809	1,072	1,212	1,442	1,450	1,464
of which: General government	780	1,066	1,209	1,437	1,442	1,450
Private sector guaranteed by public sector	..	..	..	..	..	..
Private sector not guaranteed	1,203	3,183	3,101	3,315	3,476	3,610
Short-term external debt	1,366	1,224	1,348	1,670	2,030	2,005
Disbursements (long-term)	284	312	381	596	551	549
Public and publicly guaranteed sector	54	139	207	183	138	130
Public sector	54	139	207	183	138	130
of which: General government	41	139	207	180	134	122
Private sector guaranteed by public sector	..	..	..	..	..	..
Private sector not guaranteed	230	173	174	413	413	419
Principal repayments (long-term)	303	312	265	249	375	427
Public and publicly guaranteed sector	55	41	37	50	89	101
Public sector	55	41	37	50	89	101
of which: General government	52	35	34	48	88	100
Private sector guaranteed by public sector	..	..	..	..	..	..
Private sector not guaranteed	248	271	229	200	286	325
Interest payments (long-term)	54	43	61	55	67	63
Public and publicly guaranteed sector	22	15	15	20	22	23
Public sector	22	15	15	20	22	23
of which: General government	20	14	15	20	22	22
Private sector guaranteed by public sector	..	..	..	..	..	..
Private sector not guaranteed	32	28	45	35	44	40
Summary external debt stock by creditor type						
Long-term external debt stocks	2,011	4,255	4,313	4,756	4,925	5,074
Public and publicly guaranteed debt from:	809	1,072	1,212	1,442	1,450	1,464
Official creditors	780	1,050	1,189	1,417	1,425	1,440
Multilateral	524	876	960	1,086	1,152	1,226
of which: World Bank	443	570	634	696	712	716
Bilateral	256	173	229	331	273	214
Private creditors	29	22	23	25	25	24
Bondholders	0	..	..	..	..	..
Commercial banks and others	29	22	23	25	25	24
Private nonguaranteed debt from:	1,203	3,183	3,101	3,315	3,476	3,610
Bondholders	..	..	..	..	..	..
Commercial banks and others	1,203	3,183	3,101	3,315	3,476	3,610
Use of IMF credit	338	628	574	562	496	458
Net financial inflows						
Net debt inflows						
Use of IMF credit	-15	-41	-37	-44	-54	-35
Long-term	-19	1	116	347	175	122
Official creditors	-4	101	169	134	48	29
Multilateral	16	79	111	51	100	85
of which: World Bank	0	29	81	28	31	8
Bilateral	-20	23	58	83	-52	-57
Private creditors	-15	-101	-53	213	127	94
Bondholders	-6	..	..	..	..	..
Banks and others	-9	-101	-53	213	127	94
Short-term	-8	-272	130	342	357	-18
Net equity inflows						
Foreign direct investment	150	167	135	66	186	503
Portfolio equity	2	4	0	0	-1	0
Debt ratios						
External debt stocks to exports (%)	162	185	185	175	167	161
External debt stocks to GNI (%)	64	75	73	68	62	..
Debt service to exports (%)	17	13	13	11	13	13
Short-term to external debt stocks (%)	37	20	22	24	27	27
Multilateral to external debt stocks (%)	14	14	15	16	15	16
Reserves to external debt stocks (%)	40	29	35	40	40	41
Gross national income (GNI)	5,762	8,195	8,517	10,227	12,015	..

103

MONGOLIA
(US$ million, unless otherwise indicated)

	2009	2015	2016	2017	2018	2019
Summary external debt data by debtor type						
Total external debt stocks	2,988	21,940	24,597	27,946	29,684	31,445
Use of IMF credit	258	68	66	189	287	285
Long-term external debt	2,481	19,437	21,943	24,595	26,299	28,200
Public and publicly guaranteed sector	1,819	3,993	5,122	7,494	7,902	8,150
Public sector	1,819	3,993	5,122	7,494	7,902	8,150
of which: General government	1,726	3,986	5,116	7,488	7,896	8,144
Private sector guaranteed by public sector	..	..	..	..	..	..
Private sector not guaranteed	662	15,444	16,821	17,101	18,398	20,050
Short-term external debt	248	2,435	2,589	3,163	3,098	2,960
Disbursements (long-term)	520	2,066	5,103	4,325	8,323	12,639
Public and publicly guaranteed sector	212	258	1,187	2,327	1,058	410
Public sector	212	258	1,187	2,327	1,058	410
of which: General government	212	258	1,187	2,327	1,058	410
Private sector guaranteed by public sector	..	..	..	..	..	..
Private sector not guaranteed	308	1,808	3,916	1,997	7,265	12,229
Principal repayments (long-term)	70	1,323	938	2,788	6,614	11,130
Public and publicly guaranteed sector	62	61	84	68	630	164
Public sector	62	61	84	68	630	164
of which: General government	61	61	83	68	629	164
Private sector guaranteed by public sector	..	..	..	..	..	..
Private sector not guaranteed	8	1,262	855	2,720	5,984	10,966
Interest payments (long-term)	41	464	471	826	1,036	503
Public and publicly guaranteed sector	26	95	112	217	244	307
Public sector	26	95	112	217	244	307
of which: General government	19	95	112	217	244	307
Private sector guaranteed by public sector	..	..	..	..	..	..
Private sector not guaranteed	15	369	358	609	793	196
Summary external debt stock by creditor type						
Long-term external debt stocks	2,481	19,437	21,943	24,595	26,299	28,200
Public and publicly guaranteed debt from:	1,819	3,993	5,122	7,494	7,902	8,150
Official creditors	1,735	2,475	2,843	3,797	4,230	4,539
Multilateral	1,069	1,152	1,205	1,644	1,876	2,096
of which: World Bank	392	434	423	579	570	579
Bilateral	666	1,323	1,637	2,153	2,354	2,444
Private creditors	84	1,518	2,280	3,697	3,672	3,611
Bondholders	75	1,500	2,000	3,400	3,400	3,400
Commercial banks and others	9	18	280	297	272	211
Private nonguaranteed debt from:	662	15,444	16,821	17,101	18,398	20,050
Bondholders	..	1,119	1,495	1,317	1,865	2,228
Commercial banks and others	662	14,325	15,326	15,783	16,533	17,822
Use of IMF credit	258	68	66	189	287	285
Net financial inflows						
Net debt inflows						
Use of IMF credit	159	-3	..	116	104	0
Long-term	450	743	4,165	1,536	1,709	1,509
Official creditors	153	186	340	848	451	305
Multilateral	96	106	85	377	261	228
of which: World Bank	51	4	2	130	5	13
Bilateral	57	80	255	471	190	78
Private creditors	297	557	3,825	688	1,258	1,203
Bondholders	..	200	500	1,232	525	440
Banks and others	297	357	3,325	-544	733	763
Short-term	179	61	154	574	-64	-138
Net equity inflows						
Foreign direct investment	488	95	-399	828	799	1,231
Portfolio equity	4	0	4	-10	-7	7
Debt ratios						
External debt stocks to exports (%)	129	422	434	406	374	357
External debt stocks to GNI (%)	68	203	240	285	252	256
Debt service to exports (%)	5	35	26	54	98	133
Short-term to external debt stocks (%)	8	11	11	11	10	9
Multilateral to external debt stocks (%)	36	5	5	6	6	7
Reserves to external debt stocks (%)	43	6	5	10	9	10
Gross national income (GNI)	4,388	10,786	10,265	9,817	11,765	12,291

MONTENEGRO

(US$ million, unless otherwise indicated)

	2009	2015	2016	2017	2018	2019
Summary external debt data by debtor type						
Total external debt stocks	2,357	6,226	6,261	7,190	7,972	8,199
Use of IMF credit	40	36	35	37	36	36
Long-term external debt	1,109	5,955	6,083	7,008	7,729	7,953
Public and publicly guaranteed sector	1,094	2,556	2,428	2,978	3,443	3,726
Public sector	1,094	2,493	2,380	2,935	3,417	3,717
of which: General government	842	2,188	2,088	2,644	3,163	3,479
Private sector guaranteed by public sector	0	63	49	44	26	9
Private sector not guaranteed	15	3,399	3,655	4,029	4,286	4,227
Short-term external debt	1,207	235	143	146	207	210
Disbursements (long-term)	**248**	**1,051**	**1,391**	**1,608**	**1,969**	**797**
Public and publicly guaranteed sector	242	805	414	456	1,175	788
Public sector	242	805	414	456	1,175	788
of which: General government	224	796	384	438	1,156	765
Private sector guaranteed by public sector	..	..	..	..	..	..
Private sector not guaranteed	7	246	977	1,152	794	8
Principal repayments (long-term)	**25**	**1,125**	**1,094**	**993**	**1,449**	**510**
Public and publicly guaranteed sector	23	388	375	197	591	444
Public sector	23	373	362	186	575	428
of which: General government	17	341	327	142	527	392
Private sector guaranteed by public sector	..	15	13	11	17	16
Private sector not guaranteed	2	737	718	795	858	65
Interest payments (long-term)	**28**	**150**	**172**	**218**	**265**	**226**
Public and publicly guaranteed sector	28	88	88	96	102	105
Public sector	28	85	86	94	101	105
of which: General government	20	77	79	87	95	100
Private sector guaranteed by public sector	..	2	2	2	1	0
Private sector not guaranteed	0	63	84	122	163	121
Summary external debt stock by creditor type						
Long-term external debt stocks	1,109	5,955	6,083	7,008	7,729	7,953
Public and publicly guaranteed debt from:	1,094	2,556	2,428	2,978	3,443	3,726
Official creditors	873	1,127	1,091	1,323	1,459	1,551
Multilateral	592	633	600	634	589	556
of which: World Bank	336	311	287	297	271	243
Bilateral	281	493	490	689	871	995
Private creditors	221	1,429	1,337	1,655	1,984	2,175
Bondholders	..	1,043	1,138	1,295	1,394	1,740
Commercial banks and others	221	386	199	360	589	435
Private nonguaranteed debt from:	15	3,399	3,655	4,029	4,286	4,227
Bondholders	..	..	..	..	..	..
Commercial banks and others	15	3,399	3,655	4,029	4,286	4,227
Use of IMF credit	40	36	35	37	36	36
Net financial inflows						
Net debt inflows						
Use of IMF credit	..	..	..	..	..	..
Long-term	224	-73	298	615	520	287
Official creditors	37	145	-10	133	167	116
Multilateral	26	-32	-14	-44	-22	-12
of which: World Bank	-5	-15	-17	-26	-18	-12
Bilateral	11	177	3	177	190	128
Private creditors	186	-218	308	483	352	171
Bondholders	..	344	135	0	163	370
Banks and others	186	-563	173	483	189	-200
Short-term	605	-45	-92	2	61	3
Net equity inflows						
Foreign direct investment	1,360	465	91	386	342	277
Portfolio equity	-5	10	17	14	0	3
Debt ratios						
External debt stocks to exports (%)	142	313	303	308	295	297
External debt stocks to GNI (%)	57	150	142	145	143	149
Debt service to exports (%)	4	64	61	52	64	27
Short-term to external debt stocks (%)	51	4	2	2	3	3
Multilateral to external debt stocks (%)	25	10	10	9	7	7
Reserves to external debt stocks (%)	24	11	13	14	15	19
Gross national income (GNI)	4,166	4,144	4,414	4,958	5,571	5,514

MOROCCO

(US$ million, unless otherwise indicated)

	2009	2015	2016	2017	2018	2019
Summary external debt data by debtor type						
Total external debt stocks	24,725	44,391	47,626	51,150	50,314	54,968
Use of IMF credit	880	778	755	800	781	776
Long-term external debt	21,635	36,746	37,949	42,823	42,088	45,501
Public and publicly guaranteed sector	19,281	31,131	31,460	34,712	33,387	36,466
Public sector	19,275	31,131	31,460	34,712	33,387	36,466
of which: General government	11,506	18,981	19,594	21,644	20,677	23,579
Private sector guaranteed by public sector	6	..	..	..	..	..
Private sector not guaranteed	2,354	5,615	6,489	8,111	8,700	9,036
Short-term external debt	2,210	6,867	8,923	7,527	7,446	8,690
Disbursements (long-term)	4,563	7,190	4,633	4,477	3,134	6,691
Public and publicly guaranteed sector	3,480	4,840	3,040	2,964	1,672	5,438
Public sector	3,480	4,840	3,040	2,964	1,672	5,438
of which: General government	2,404	2,832	2,119	1,825	882	4,338
Private sector guaranteed by public sector	0	..	..	..	..	..
Private sector not guaranteed	1,083	2,350	1,593	1,513	1,462	1,253
Principal repayments (long-term)	2,709	2,474	2,659	2,797	2,729	2,873
Public and publicly guaranteed sector	1,137	1,670	2,102	2,389	2,047	1,993
Public sector	1,134	1,670	2,102	2,389	2,047	1,993
of which: General government	649	1,035	1,076	1,611	1,197	1,178
Private sector guaranteed by public sector	3	..	..	..	..	..
Private sector not guaranteed	1,572	804	557	408	682	880
Interest payments (long-term)	678	990	1,023	1,017	1,088	1,054
Public and publicly guaranteed sector	613	880	929	929	932	948
Public sector	612	880	929	929	932	948
of which: General government	363	470	512	523	519	558
Private sector guaranteed by public sector	1	..	..	..	..	..
Private sector not guaranteed	66	110	94	88	155	106
Summary external debt stock by creditor type						
Long-term external debt stocks	21,635	36,746	37,949	42,823	42,088	45,501
Public and publicly guaranteed debt from:	19,281	31,131	31,460	34,712	33,387	36,466
Official creditors	16,753	20,361	21,013	24,230	23,102	23,650
Multilateral	10,078	13,197	13,589	16,110	15,613	16,639
of which: World Bank	2,601	4,155	4,565	5,560	5,529	6,414
Bilateral	6,675	7,164	7,425	8,119	7,489	7,011
Private creditors	2,528	10,769	10,447	10,483	10,286	12,816
Bondholders	..	6,277	6,208	6,499	6,390	7,590
Commercial banks and others	2,528	4,492	4,238	3,984	3,896	5,226
Private nonguaranteed debt from:	2,354	5,615	6,489	8,111	8,700	9,036
Bondholders	..	..	..	..	..	..
Commercial banks and others	2,354	5,615	6,489	8,111	8,700	9,036
Use of IMF credit	880	778	755	800	781	776
Net financial inflows						
Net debt inflows						
Use of IMF credit	..	..	..	..	..	..
Long-term	1,854	4,716	1,974	1,680	405	3,818
Official creditors	1,882	986	1,089	1,229	-421	825
Multilateral	1,303	699	715	1,166	11	1,237
of which: World Bank	-3	529	521	532	146	957
Bilateral	579	287	373	63	-433	-411
Private creditors	-27	3,730	885	451	826	2,993
Bondholders	..	1,110	0	0	0	1,239
Banks and others	-27	2,620	885	451	826	1,754
Short-term	579	-740	2,055	-1,395	-82	1,244
Net equity inflows						
Foreign direct investment	2,456	2,240	1,626	1,952	2,926	1,391
Portfolio equity	-4	..	-26	-33	-184	280
Debt ratios						
External debt stocks to exports (%)	99	131	136	129	114	123
External debt stocks to GNI (%)	27	45	47	48	44	47
Debt service to exports (%)	14	11	11	10	9	9
Short-term to external debt stocks (%)	9	15	19	15	15	16
Multilateral to external debt stocks (%)	41	30	29	31	31	30
Reserves to external debt stocks (%)	92	50	51	49	47	46
Gross national income (GNI)	91,616	99,245	101,326	107,564	115,442	116,445

MOZAMBIQUE

(US$ million, unless otherwise indicated)

	2009	2015	2016	2017	2018	2019
Summary external debt data by debtor type						
Total external debt stocks	**6,088**	**14,446**	**14,500**	**16,103**	**18,932**	**20,516**
Use of IMF credit	342	399	355	343	303	375
Long-term external debt	5,114	13,249	13,569	14,671	17,399	18,493
Public and publicly guaranteed sector	3,400	9,821	10,003	10,794	10,929	10,888
Public sector	3,400	9,821	10,003	10,794	10,929	10,888
of which: General government	3,302	7,867	8,283	9,178	9,433	9,597
Private sector guaranteed by public sector	..	..	..	..	..	..
Private sector not guaranteed	1,714	3,428	3,566	3,877	6,470	7,606
Short-term external debt	632	798	576	1,089	1,230	1,647
Disbursements (long-term)	**636**	**985**	**965**	**1,070**	**3,307**	**1,823**
Public and publicly guaranteed sector	532	890	771	733	668	687
Public sector	532	890	771	733	668	687
of which: General government	527	890	771	733	668	687
Private sector guaranteed by public sector	..	..	..	..	..	..
Private sector not guaranteed	103	95	194	338	2,639	1,136
Principal repayments (long-term)	**348**	**394**	**351**	**328**	**414**	**681**
Public and publicly guaranteed sector	17	272	294	301	368	681
Public sector	17	272	294	301	368	681
of which: General government	17	163	186	191	250	476
Private sector guaranteed by public sector	..	..	..	..	..	..
Private sector not guaranteed	331	122	57	27	47	..
Interest payments (long-term)	**159**	**205**	**152**	**139**	**167**	**206**
Public and publicly guaranteed sector	25	154	109	119	155	155
Public sector	25	154	109	119	155	155
of which: General government	24	96	105	116	151	137
Private sector guaranteed by public sector	..	..	..	..	..	..
Private sector not guaranteed	134	51	43	20	13	51
Summary external debt stock by creditor type						
Long-term external debt stocks	**5,114**	**13,249**	**13,569**	**14,671**	**17,399**	**18,493**
Public and publicly guaranteed debt from:	3,400	9,821	10,003	10,794	10,929	10,888
Official creditors	3,373	7,759	8,183	9,051	9,265	9,390
Multilateral	1,967	3,590	3,716	4,073	4,214	4,432
of which: World Bank	1,356	2,461	2,555	2,822	2,904	3,039
Bilateral	1,406	4,168	4,466	4,978	5,051	4,958
Private creditors	27	2,062	1,820	1,743	1,664	1,498
Bondholders	..	850	727	727	727	727
Commercial banks and others	27	1,212	1,094	1,016	937	771
Private nonguaranteed debt from:	1,714	3,428	3,566	3,877	6,470	7,606
Bondholders	..	..	..	..	..	..
Commercial banks and others	1,714	3,428	3,566	3,877	6,470	7,606
Use of IMF credit	342	399	355	343	303	375
Net financial inflows						
Net debt inflows						
Use of IMF credit	153	87	-33	-32	-32	73
Long-term	288	591	614	743	2,893	1,142
Official creditors	495	725	589	536	368	168
Multilateral	287	346	227	162	232	240
of which: World Bank	197	280	174	113	153	154
Bilateral	209	379	362	374	136	-73
Private creditors	-207	-134	26	207	2,525	975
Bondholders	..	..	..	..	..	..
Banks and others	-207	-134	26	207	2,525	975
Short-term	36	280	-223	445	77	418
Net equity inflows						
Foreign direct investment	242	1,128	805	668	491	382
Portfolio equity	0	0	0	-5	0	0
Debt ratios						
External debt stocks to exports (%)	209	340	374	290	304	347
External debt stocks to GNI (%)	52	92	124	126	131	141
Debt service to exports (%)	18	15	14	9	10	16
Short-term to external debt stocks (%)	10	6	4	7	6	8
Multilateral to external debt stocks (%)	32	25	26	25	22	22
Reserves to external debt stocks (%)	34	17	14	20	16	18
Gross national income (GNI)	11,623	15,654	11,678	12,825	14,422	14,573

MYANMAR
(US$ million, unless otherwise indicated)

	2009	2015	2016	2017	2018	2019
Summary external debt data by debtor type						
Total external debt stocks	**9,495**	**10,293**	**10,107**	**10,759**	**10,685**	**11,114**
Use of IMF credit	385	341	330	350	342	340
Long-term external debt	8,023	9,853	9,685	10,312	10,238	10,709
Public and publicly guaranteed sector	8,023	9,787	9,638	10,284	10,224	10,681
Public sector	7,895	9,787	9,638	10,284	10,224	10,681
of which: General government	1,824	4,560	4,815	5,490	5,938	6,755
Private sector guaranteed by public sector	129	..	..	..	..	..
Private sector not guaranteed	..	66	47	28	14	28
Short-term external debt	1,087	99	91	97	105	66
Disbursements (long-term)	**231**	**689**	**446**	**400**	**757**	**1,017**
Public and publicly guaranteed sector	231	604	446	400	757	953
Public sector	231	604	446	400	757	953
of which: General government	25	151	368	381	696	864
Private sector guaranteed by public sector	0	..	..	..	..	..
Private sector not guaranteed	..	85	..	..	..	65
Principal repayments (long-term)	**82**	**260**	**493**	**430**	**530**	**501**
Public and publicly guaranteed sector	82	241	475	411	516	450
Public sector	82	241	475	411	516	450
of which: General government	24	78	94	41	84	52
Private sector guaranteed by public sector	..	..	..	..	..	..
Private sector not guaranteed	..	19	19	19	14	51
Interest payments (long-term)	**29**	**263**	**280**	**226**	**309**	**207**
Public and publicly guaranteed sector	29	263	279	225	309	197
Public sector	29	263	279	225	309	197
of which: General government	3	98	112	53	150	46
Private sector guaranteed by public sector	..	..	..	..	..	..
Private sector not guaranteed	..	0	1	1	..	10
Summary external debt stock by creditor type						
Long-term external debt stocks	**8,023**	**9,853**	**9,685**	**10,312**	**10,238**	**10,709**
Public and publicly guaranteed debt from:	8,023	9,787	9,638	10,284	10,224	10,681
Official creditors	6,878	9,412	9,278	9,931	9,911	10,396
Multilateral	1,372	1,381	1,462	1,788	1,859	2,081
of which: World Bank	777	833	914	1,192	1,266	1,468
Bilateral	5,506	8,030	7,816	8,144	8,053	8,314
Private creditors	1,145	375	360	353	312	285
Bondholders	..	..	..	..	..	..
Commercial banks and others	1,145	375	360	353	312	285
Private nonguaranteed debt from:	..	66	47	28	14	28
Bondholders	..	..	..	..	..	..
Commercial banks and others	..	66	47	28	14	28
Use of IMF credit	385	341	330	350	342	340
Net financial inflows						
Net debt inflows						
Use of IMF credit	..	..	..	..	..	..
Long-term	149	429	-47	-30	227	516
Official creditors	151	358	-14	1	281	530
Multilateral	2	47	120	226	207	232
of which: World Bank	..	53	108	214	181	208
Bilateral	149	311	-134	-224	74	298
Private creditors	-2	71	-33	-31	-53	-14
Bondholders	..	..	..	..	..	..
Banks and others	-2	71	-33	-31	-53	-14
Short-term	..	..	..	..	..	..
Net equity inflows						
Foreign direct investment	1,079	4,053	3,319	3,094	1,435	2,522
Portfolio equity	..	0	0	0	0	0
Debt ratios						
External debt stocks to exports (%)	150	70	72	72	62	59
External debt stocks to GNI (%)	26	16	15	16	15	15
Debt service to exports (%)	2	4	6	4	5	4
Short-term to external debt stocks (%)	11	1	1	1	1	1
Multilateral to external debt stocks (%)	14	13	14	17	17	19
Reserves to external debt stocks (%)	55	42	46	46	50	49
Gross national income (GNI)	36,896	65,776	65,411	66,983	73,469	73,292

NEPAL

(US$ million, unless otherwise indicated)

	2009	2015	2016	2017	2018	2019
Summary external debt data by debtor type						
Total external debt stocks	3,777	4,143	4,297	4,963	5,511	6,513
Use of IMF credit	183	194	171	168	156	147
Long-term external debt	3,550	3,600	3,748	4,374	5,103	5,963
Public and publicly guaranteed sector	3,550	3,543	3,665	4,299	4,974	5,845
Public sector	3,550	3,543	3,665	4,299	4,974	5,845
of which: General government	3,534	3,536	3,660	4,294	4,969	5,840
Private sector guaranteed by public sector	..	..	..	..	..	..
Private sector not guaranteed	..	57	83	75	129	118
Short-term external debt	44	349	379	421	252	403
Disbursements (long-term)	114	425	431	606	1,017	1,096
Public and publicly guaranteed sector	114	408	397	591	955	1,096
Public sector	114	408	397	591	955	1,096
of which: General government	114	408	397	591	955	1,096
Private sector guaranteed by public sector	..	..	..	..	..	..
Private sector not guaranteed	..	17	34	15	63	..
Principal repayments (long-term)	140	169	177	195	181	205
Public and publicly guaranteed sector	140	165	170	172	174	194
Public sector	140	165	170	172	174	194
of which: General government	138	164	169	172	173	194
Private sector guaranteed by public sector	..	..	..	..	..	..
Private sector not guaranteed	..	4	8	23	8	11
Interest payments (long-term)	32	33	37	38	45	57
Public and publicly guaranteed sector	32	32	35	36	41	52
Public sector	32	32	35	36	41	52
of which: General government	32	32	35	36	41	52
Private sector guaranteed by public sector	..	..	..	..	..	..
Private sector not guaranteed	..	1	1	2	4	6
Summary external debt stock by creditor type						
Long-term external debt stocks	3,550	3,600	3,748	4,374	5,103	5,963
Public and publicly guaranteed debt from:	3,550	3,543	3,665	4,299	4,974	5,845
Official creditors	3,547	3,543	3,665	4,299	4,974	5,845
Multilateral	3,198	3,215	3,318	3,901	4,458	5,080
of which: World Bank	1,483	1,640	1,708	2,022	2,477	2,877
Bilateral	349	328	347	399	516	764
Private creditors	4	0	0	0	0	0
Bondholders	..	..	..	..	..	..
Commercial banks and others	4	0	0	0	0	0
Private nonguaranteed debt from:	..	57	83	75	129	118
Bondholders	..	..	..	..	..	..
Commercial banks and others	..	57	83	75	129	118
Use of IMF credit	183	194	171	168	156	147
Net financial inflows						
Net debt inflows						
Use of IMF credit	-2	36	-18	-12	-8	-8
Long-term	-25	256	254	411	836	891
Official creditors	-25	243	228	419	781	902
Multilateral	-14	239	203	386	658	651
of which: World Bank	-33	185	120	211	512	415
Bilateral	-11	4	25	34	123	251
Private creditors	-1	13	26	-8	55	-11
Bondholders	..	..	..	..	..	..
Banks and others	-1	13	26	-8	55	-11
Short-term	-13	17	29	43	-170	151
Net equity inflows						
Foreign direct investment	39	52	106	196	68	186
Portfolio equity	..	..	..	..	..	..
Debt ratios						
External debt stocks to exports (%)	216	155	167	166	163	188
External debt stocks to GNI (%)	29	19	20	19	19	21
Debt service to exports (%)	10	8	9	8	7	8
Short-term to external debt stocks (%)	1	8	9	8	5	6
Multilateral to external debt stocks (%)	85	78	77	79	81	78
Reserves to external debt stocks (%)	73	192	198	185	146	129
Gross national income (GNI)	13,008	21,755	21,506	25,472	29,390	30,996

NICARAGUA
(US$ million, unless otherwise indicated)

	2009	2015	2016	2017	2018	2019
Summary external debt data by debtor type						
Total external debt stocks	**5,901**	**10,514**	**11,011**	**11,496**	**11,652**	**11,691**
Use of IMF credit	346	264	228	219	195	181
Long-term external debt	4,563	8,981	9,376	9,845	10,094	10,345
Public and publicly guaranteed sector	2,514	3,949	4,205	4,696	5,094	5,414
Public sector	2,514	3,949	4,205	4,696	5,094	5,414
of which: General government	1,791	3,125	3,397	3,912	4,137	4,503
Private sector guaranteed by public sector	0	..	..	..	..	..
Private sector not guaranteed	2,049	5,032	5,171	5,149	5,000	4,931
Short-term external debt	993	1,269	1,407	1,432	1,363	1,165
Disbursements (long-term)	**845**	**1,147**	**988**	**1,235**	**1,057**	**1,022**
Public and publicly guaranteed sector	292	385	373	540	572	509
Public sector	292	385	373	540	572	509
of which: General government	286	385	373	540	372	509
Private sector guaranteed by public sector	..	..	..	..	..	..
Private sector not guaranteed	553	763	615	695	485	513
Principal repayments (long-term)	**335**	**564**	**575**	**849**	**776**	**835**
Public and publicly guaranteed sector	62	72	89	122	135	177
Public sector	62	72	89	122	135	177
of which: General government	40	58	74	96	110	131
Private sector guaranteed by public sector	..	..	..	..	..	..
Private sector not guaranteed	273	492	486	727	640	658
Interest payments (long-term)	**121**	**189**	**213**	**262**	**265**	**297**
Public and publicly guaranteed sector	37	61	74	83	94	119
Public sector	37	61	74	83	94	119
of which: General government	29	57	70	79	89	102
Private sector guaranteed by public sector	..	..	..	..	..	..
Private sector not guaranteed	84	128	138	179	172	178
Summary external debt stock by creditor type						
Long-term external debt stocks	**4,563**	**8,981**	**9,376**	**9,845**	**10,094**	**10,345**
Public and publicly guaranteed debt from:	2,514	3,949	4,205	4,696	5,094	5,414
Official creditors	2,502	3,944	4,194	4,682	5,070	5,388
Multilateral	1,465	2,841	3,081	3,529	3,914	4,215
of which: World Bank	418	532	531	595	624	692
Bilateral	1,037	1,103	1,113	1,153	1,156	1,173
Private creditors	12	5	11	14	24	26
Bondholders	..	..	..	..	..	..
Commercial banks and others	12	5	11	14	24	26
Private nonguaranteed debt from:	2,049	5,032	5,171	5,149	5,000	4,931
Bondholders	..	..	..	..	..	..
Commercial banks and others	2,049	5,032	5,171	5,149	5,000	4,931
Use of IMF credit	346	264	228	219	195	181
Net financial inflows						
Net debt inflows						
Use of IMF credit	37	-27	-29	-22	-19	-13
Long-term	510	584	413	386	281	187
Official creditors	231	314	278	417	425	330
Multilateral	220	318	261	404	411	306
of which: World Bank	67	32	15	33	44	71
Bilateral	10	-4	17	13	14	24
Private creditors	279	270	135	-31	-144	-143
Bondholders	..	..	..	..	..	..
Banks and others	279	270	135	-31	-144	-143
Short-term	-173	-243	129	15	-105	-221
Net equity inflows						
Foreign direct investment	434	950	899	772	359	515
Portfolio equity	..	..	..	..	..	..
Debt ratios						
External debt stocks to exports (%)	207	205	212	200	208	202
External debt stocks to GNI (%)	73	85	85	86	91	96
Debt service to exports (%)	16	15	16	20	19	20
Short-term to external debt stocks (%)	17	12	13	12	12	10
Multilateral to external debt stocks (%)	25	27	28	31	34	36
Reserves to external debt stocks (%)	27	24	22	24	19	21
Gross national income (GNI)	8,042	12,411	12,929	13,422	12,754	12,200

NIGER
(US$ million, unless otherwise indicated)

	2009	2015	2016	2017	2018	2019
Summary external debt data by debtor type						
Total external debt stocks	**1,255**	**2,228**	**2,522**	**3,045**	**3,188**	**3,608**
Use of IMF credit	155	237	239	287	311	346
Long-term external debt	969	1,969	2,242	2,688	2,808	3,167
Public and publicly guaranteed sector	963	1,969	2,242	2,688	2,808	3,167
Public sector	963	1,969	2,242	2,688	2,808	3,167
of which: General government	963	1,969	2,242	2,688	2,808	3,167
Private sector guaranteed by public sector	..	..	..	..	..	..
Private sector not guaranteed	7	..	..	..	..	..
Short-term external debt	131	23	40	70	69	95
Disbursements (long-term)	**211**	**402**	**399**	**358**	**278**	**428**
Public and publicly guaranteed sector	211	402	399	358	278	428
Public sector	211	402	399	358	278	428
of which: General government	211	402	399	358	278	428
Private sector guaranteed by public sector	..	..	..	..	..	..
Private sector not guaranteed	..	..	..	..	..	..
Principal repayments (long-term)	**28**	**53**	**72**	**87**	**71**	**92**
Public and publicly guaranteed sector	21	53	72	87	71	92
Public sector	21	53	72	87	71	92
of which: General government	21	53	72	87	71	92
Private sector guaranteed by public sector	..	..	..	..	..	..
Private sector not guaranteed	7	..	..	..	..	..
Interest payments (long-term)	**8**	**24**	**32**	**38**	**44**	**50**
Public and publicly guaranteed sector	8	24	32	38	44	50
Public sector	8	24	32	38	44	50
of which: General government	8	24	32	38	44	50
Private sector guaranteed by public sector	..	..	..	..	..	..
Private sector not guaranteed	0	..	..	..	..	..
Summary external debt stock by creditor type						
Long-term external debt stocks	**969**	**1,969**	**2,242**	**2,688**	**2,808**	**3,167**
Public and publicly guaranteed debt from:	963	1,969	2,242	2,688	2,808	3,167
Official creditors	962	1,969	2,242	2,688	2,808	3,167
Multilateral	622	1,418	1,632	2,019	2,078	2,456
of which: World Bank	266	626	773	988	1,044	1,347
Bilateral	340	551	610	669	730	711
Private creditors	1	..	..	..	..	..
Bondholders	..	..	..	..	..	..
Commercial banks and others	1	..	..	..	..	..
Private nonguaranteed debt from:	7	..	..	..	..	..
Bondholders	..	..	..	..	..	..
Commercial banks and others	7	..	..	..	..	..
Use of IMF credit	**155**	**237**	**239**	**287**	**311**	**346**
Net financial inflows						
Net debt inflows						
Use of IMF credit	5	44	10	32	32	36
Long-term	183	348	327	272	206	336
Official creditors	190	348	327	272	206	336
Multilateral	44	361	259	238	127	349
of which: World Bank	16	76	170	159	87	257
Bilateral	146	-13	68	34	79	-13
Private creditors	-7	..	..	..	..	..
Bondholders	..	..	..	..	..	..
Banks and others	-7	..	..	..	..	..
Short-term	40	-32	9	21	-11	16
Net equity inflows						
Foreign direct investment	-6	228	146	128	211	593
Portfolio equity	9	12	18	16	21	..
Debt ratios						
External debt stocks to exports (%)	105	157	188	197	201	..
External debt stocks to GNI (%)	17	23	25	28	25	28
Debt service to exports (%)	3	6	8	9	8	..
Short-term to external debt stocks (%)	10	1	2	2	2	3
Multilateral to external debt stocks (%)	50	64	65	66	65	68
Reserves to external debt stocks (%)	52	47	..	..	..	..
Gross national income (GNI)	7,244	9,515	10,122	10,985	12,634	12,735

NIGERIA

(US$ million, unless otherwise indicated)

	2009	2015	2016	2017	2018	2019
Summary external debt data by debtor type						
Total external debt stocks	19,286	32,413	34,396	43,193	50,452	54,832
Use of IMF credit	2,626	2,322	2,252	2,386	2,330	2,317
Long-term external debt	16,659	30,092	32,144	40,807	48,122	52,516
Public and publicly guaranteed sector	4,221	10,677	11,317	18,822	25,232	27,531
Public sector	4,214	10,677	11,317	18,822	25,232	27,531
of which: General government	4,200	10,464	11,059	18,496	24,840	27,131
Private sector guaranteed by public sector	7	..	..	..	..	..
Private sector not guaranteed	12,438	19,415	20,827	21,985	22,890	24,984
Short-term external debt	0	0	0	0	0	0
Disbursements (long-term)	953	5,321	4,216	10,854	11,487	7,735
Public and publicly guaranteed sector	519	1,431	1,134	7,126	7,363	2,660
Public sector	519	1,431	1,134	7,126	7,363	2,660
of which: General government	519	1,288	1,082	7,075	7,289	2,649
Private sector guaranteed by public sector	0	..	..	..	..	..
Private sector not guaranteed	434	3,890	3,082	3,727	4,124	5,075
Principal repayments (long-term)	666	1,125	1,850	2,706	3,955	3,274
Public and publicly guaranteed sector	342	115	180	136	736	293
Public sector	335	115	180	136	736	293
of which: General government	299	115	180	136	736	293
Private sector guaranteed by public sector	7	..	..	..	..	..
Private sector not guaranteed	325	1,010	1,670	2,570	3,219	2,980
Interest payments (long-term)	85	476	640	822	1,411	1,832
Public and publicly guaranteed sector	85	282	175	207	698	1,095
Public sector	84	282	175	207	698	1,095
of which: General government	81	281	173	205	696	1,092
Private sector guaranteed by public sector	1	..	..	..	..	..
Private sector not guaranteed	..	194	465	615	713	737
Summary external debt stock by creditor type						
Long-term external debt stocks	16,659	30,092	32,144	40,807	48,122	52,516
Public and publicly guaranteed debt from:	4,221	10,677	11,317	18,822	25,232	27,531
Official creditors	4,135	9,177	9,817	12,522	14,063	16,363
Multilateral	3,521	7,494	7,885	10,110	10,932	12,516
of which: World Bank	2,852	6,226	6,640	7,913	8,557	9,959
Bilateral	614	1,683	1,932	2,412	3,131	3,846
Private creditors	87	1,500	1,500	6,300	11,168	11,168
Bondholders	..	1,500	1,500	6,300	11,168	11,168
Commercial banks and others	87	..	..	..	..	..
Private nonguaranteed debt from:	12,438	19,415	20,827	21,985	22,890	24,984
Bondholders	..	5,275	5,942	6,942	6,017	6,367
Commercial banks and others	12,438	14,140	14,885	15,042	16,873	18,617
Use of IMF credit	2,626	2,322	2,252	2,386	2,330	2,317
Net financial inflows						
Net debt inflows						
Use of IMF credit	..	..	..	..	..	..
Long-term	287	4,196	2,366	8,148	7,532	4,461
Official creditors	204	1,316	954	2,190	1,759	2,367
Multilateral	305	1,071	706	1,714	1,040	1,655
of which: World Bank	380	726	650	858	851	1,475
Bilateral	-102	245	248	476	719	712
Private creditors	83	2,880	1,412	5,958	5,774	2,095
Bondholders	..	800	667	5,800	3,943	350
Banks and others	83	2,080	745	158	1,830	1,745
Short-term	0	0	0	0	0	0
Net equity inflows						
Foreign direct investment	8,536	3,060	4,448	3,501	1,812	3,287
Portfolio equity	487	-477	325	2,924	1,259	-1,548
Debt ratios						
External debt stocks to exports (%)	33	65	87	82	74	76
External debt stocks to GNI (%)	7	7	9	12	13	13
Debt service to exports (%)	1	3	6	7	8	7
Short-term to external debt stocks (%)	0	0	0	0	0	0
Multilateral to external debt stocks (%)	18	23	23	23	22	23
Reserves to external debt stocks (%)	232	87	79	92	85	70
Gross national income (GNI)	277,317	481,571	395,951	364,253	379,792	433,449

112

NORTH MACEDONIA
(US$ million, unless otherwise indicated)

	2009	2015	2016	2017	2018	2019
Summary external debt data by debtor type						
Total external debt stocks	**5,247**	**6,767**	**7,513**	**8,544**	**8,666**	**8,986**
Use of IMF credit	103	91	88	93	91	91
Long-term external debt	3,731	5,662	6,320	7,133	7,237	7,499
Public and publicly guaranteed sector	1,874	3,109	3,473	3,829	4,061	4,163
Public sector	1,873	3,109	3,473	3,829	4,061	4,163
of which: General government	1,704	2,375	2,655	2,920	3,142	3,152
Private sector guaranteed by public sector	0	..	..	..	..	..
Private sector not guaranteed	1,858	2,553	2,847	3,304	3,176	3,336
Short-term external debt	1,413	1,014	1,105	1,318	1,339	1,396
Disbursements (long-term)	**1,012**	**1,094**	**1,465**	**1,020**	**1,400**	**821**
Public and publicly guaranteed sector	347	583	777	221	794	383
Public sector	347	583	777	221	794	383
of which: General government	319	395	604	110	672	181
Private sector guaranteed by public sector	..	..	..	..	..	..
Private sector not guaranteed	665	512	688	798	606	438
Principal repayments (long-term)	**375**	**699**	**702**	**645**	**1,077**	**513**
Public and publicly guaranteed sector	88	327	309	262	406	219
Public sector	87	327	309	262	406	219
of which: General government	72	255	235	177	317	118
Private sector guaranteed by public sector	0	..	..	..	..	..
Private sector not guaranteed	287	373	394	383	671	293
Interest payments (long-term)	**93**	**128**	**124**	**177**	**159**	**151**
Public and publicly guaranteed sector	47	78	86	112	105	115
Public sector	47	78	86	112	105	115
of which: General government	40	67	75	100	92	101
Private sector guaranteed by public sector	0	..	..	..	..	..
Private sector not guaranteed	46	51	38	65	54	36
Summary external debt stock by creditor type						
Long-term external debt stocks	**3,731**	**5,662**	**6,320**	**7,133**	**7,237**	**7,499**
Public and publicly guaranteed debt from:	1,874	3,109	3,473	3,829	4,061	4,163
Official creditors	1,321	1,680	1,737	1,921	1,865	2,051
Multilateral	1,081	1,282	1,232	1,336	1,245	1,387
of which: World Bank	653	656	620	658	614	732
Bilateral	240	397	505	585	620	664
Private creditors	552	1,429	1,736	1,907	2,196	2,112
Bondholders	468	838	1,286	1,463	1,864	1,829
Commercial banks and others	84	591	450	444	332	283
Private nonguaranteed debt from:	1,858	2,553	2,847	3,304	3,176	3,336
Bondholders	..	..	..	..	..	..
Commercial banks and others	1,858	2,553	2,847	3,304	3,176	3,336
Use of IMF credit	103	91	88	93	91	91
Net financial inflows						
Net debt inflows						
Use of IMF credit	..	-172	..	..	..	..
Long-term	637	395	763	375	323	309
Official creditors	22	125	99	22	1	206
Multilateral	16	69	-10	-40	-39	161
of which: World Bank	26	-6	-16	-24	-21	125
Bilateral	6	55	109	62	39	46
Private creditors	615	271	664	352	323	102
Bondholders	244	133	498	0	482	0
Banks and others	371	137	166	352	-160	102
Short-term	100	-210	68	230	8	50
Net equity inflows						
Foreign direct investment	57	89	325	246	471	362
Portfolio equity	-14	-9	-8	-12	-34	-15
Debt ratios						
External debt stocks to exports (%)	165	133	134	133	111	113
External debt stocks to GNI (%)	56	69	73	79	72	74
Debt service to exports (%)	17	21	16	14	17	9
Short-term to external debt stocks (%)	27	15	15	15	15	16
Multilateral to external debt stocks (%)	21	19	16	16	14	15
Reserves to external debt stocks (%)	39	33	33	29	35	37
Gross national income (GNI)	9,335	9,747	10,248	10,859	12,097	12,193

PAKISTAN

(US$ million, unless otherwise indicated)

	2009	2015	2016	2017	2018	2019
Summary external debt data by debtor type						
Total external debt stocks	56,634	66,691	73,041	86,032	93,532	100,819
Use of IMF credit	9,045	6,359	7,235	7,664	7,276	8,097
Long-term external debt	46,124	53,858	58,686	69,658	78,168	83,195
Public and publicly guaranteed sector	42,859	49,119	52,561	61,068	67,261	71,113
Public sector	42,812	49,089	52,532	61,038	67,235	71,089
of which: General government	42,667	48,274	51,772	60,226	64,929	68,258
Private sector guaranteed by public sector	46	30	29	29	26	24
Private sector not guaranteed	3,265	4,739	6,125	8,591	10,906	12,083
Short-term external debt	1,466	6,474	7,121	8,709	8,088	9,526
Disbursements (long-term)	4,431	5,876	8,148	14,017	12,452	12,683
Public and publicly guaranteed sector	3,750	5,503	6,388	11,189	9,697	10,900
Public sector	3,750	5,503	6,388	11,189	9,697	10,900
of which: General government	3,750	5,197	6,258	10,883	7,938	10,152
Private sector guaranteed by public sector	0	0	0	0	0	0
Private sector not guaranteed	681	373	1,760	2,828	2,755	1,782
Principal repayments (long-term)	2,247	2,565	2,984	4,957	3,309	7,476
Public and publicly guaranteed sector	1,641	2,204	2,609	4,595	2,870	6,870
Public sector	1,640	2,202	2,607	4,594	2,868	6,868
of which: General government	1,591	2,073	2,421	4,339	2,603	6,644
Private sector guaranteed by public sector	2	1	1	1	2	2
Private sector not guaranteed	606	361	375	362	439	606
Interest payments (long-term)	911	1,008	1,222	1,562	2,196	2,627
Public and publicly guaranteed sector	806	942	1,112	1,322	1,762	2,084
Public sector	806	942	1,111	1,322	1,761	2,084
of which: General government	801	916	1,093	1,304	1,711	1,984
Private sector guaranteed by public sector	0	0	0	0	0	0
Private sector not guaranteed	105	66	111	240	434	543
Summary external debt stock by creditor type						
Long-term external debt stocks	46,124	53,858	58,686	69,658	78,168	83,195
Public and publicly guaranteed debt from:	42,859	49,119	52,561	61,068	67,261	71,113
Official creditors	40,534	42,842	45,241	50,375	56,410	62,193
Multilateral	23,712	24,766	25,533	27,845	27,880	30,141
of which: World Bank	11,844	13,784	14,049	15,300	15,162	15,305
Bilateral	16,822	18,076	19,708	22,530	28,529	32,053
Private creditors	2,324	6,277	7,320	10,693	10,852	8,920
Bondholders	2,150	5,050	5,550	7,300	7,300	5,300
Commercial banks and others	174	1,227	1,770	3,393	3,552	3,620
Private nonguaranteed debt from:	3,265	4,739	6,125	8,591	10,906	12,083
Bondholders	850	12	12	12	12	12
Commercial banks and others	2,415	4,727	6,113	8,579	10,894	12,071
Use of IMF credit	9,045	6,359	7,235	7,664	7,276	8,097
Net financial inflows						
Net debt inflows						
Use of IMF credit	3,016	1,591	1,102	0	-212	862
Long-term	2,184	3,311	5,165	9,059	9,143	5,207
Official creditors	2,658	2,276	2,737	3,220	6,668	5,963
Multilateral	1,600	1,417	1,073	1,173	482	2,418
of which: World Bank	825	1,285	654	491	183	223
Bilateral	1,057	859	1,663	2,047	6,186	3,545
Private creditors	-474	1,036	2,428	5,839	2,475	-756
Bondholders	-500	500	500	1,750	0	-2,000
Banks and others	26	536	1,928	4,089	2,475	1,244
Short-term	96	987	647	1,588	-621	1,438
Net equity inflows						
Foreign direct investment	2,338	1,623	2,484	2,583	1,479	1,972
Portfolio equity	-37	529	-339	-391	-528	22
Debt ratios						
External debt stocks to exports (%)	247	228	265	285	297	324
External debt stocks to GNI (%)	33	23	25	27	28	34
Debt service to exports (%)	15	14	16	22	19	35
Short-term to external debt stocks (%)	3	10	10	10	9	9
Multilateral to external debt stocks (%)	42	37	35	32	30	30
Reserves to external debt stocks (%)	20	27	27	18	10	13
Gross national income (GNI)	172,564	287,068	295,741	321,203	331,344	296,935

114

PAPUA NEW GUINEA
(US$ million, unless otherwise indicated)

	2009	2015	2016	2017	2018	2019
Summary external debt data by debtor type						
Total external debt stocks	**1,769**	**20,387**	**19,245**	**17,221**	**17,721**	**18,744**
Use of IMF credit	197	174	169	179	175	174
Long-term external debt	1,460	19,902	18,414	16,966	17,082	17,914
Public and publicly guaranteed sector	1,045	1,501	1,919	2,303	3,408	4,313
Public sector	1,045	1,501	1,919	2,303	3,408	4,313
of which: General government	1,040	1,498	1,916	2,300	3,405	4,310
Private sector guaranteed by public sector	..	..	..	..	..	..
Private sector not guaranteed	415	18,400	16,494	14,663	13,674	13,601
Short-term external debt	112	311	663	77	464	657
Disbursements (long-term)	**516**	**562**	**1,538**	**1,320**	**3,046**	**1,344**
Public and publicly guaranteed sector	33	242	534	394	1,234	1,044
Public sector	33	242	534	394	1,234	1,044
of which: General government	33	242	534	394	1,234	1,044
Private sector guaranteed by public sector	..	..	..	..	..	..
Private sector not guaranteed	483	320	1,004	926	1,812	300
Principal repayments (long-term)	**513**	**519**	**2,662**	**2,111**	**2,030**	**1,567**
Public and publicly guaranteed sector	62	67	76	84	93	281
Public sector	62	67	76	84	93	281
of which: General government	62	66	75	84	93	281
Private sector guaranteed by public sector	..	..	..	..	..	..
Private sector not guaranteed	451	452	2,586	2,027	1,937	1,286
Interest payments (long-term)	**28**	**575**	**651**	**673**	**741**	**772**
Public and publicly guaranteed sector	21	21	25	51	88	149
Public sector	21	21	25	51	88	149
of which: General government	21	21	25	51	88	149
Private sector guaranteed by public sector	..	..	..	..	..	..
Private sector not guaranteed	7	555	626	622	653	623
Summary external debt stock by creditor type						
Long-term external debt stocks	**1,460**	**19,902**	**18,414**	**16,966**	**17,082**	**17,914**
Public and publicly guaranteed debt from:	1,045	1,501	1,919	2,303	3,408	4,313
Official creditors	1,008	1,500	1,703	1,954	2,371	3,160
Multilateral	724	1,087	1,168	1,278	1,633	1,853
of which: World Bank	231	250	262	277	446	446
Bilateral	285	413	535	676	739	1,307
Private creditors	36	1	216	349	1,037	1,152
Bondholders	..	..	..	..	500	500
Commercial banks and others	36	1	216	349	537	652
Private nonguaranteed debt from:	415	18,400	16,494	14,663	13,674	13,601
Bondholders	..	..	..	..	..	..
Commercial banks and others	415	18,400	16,494	14,663	13,674	13,601
Use of IMF credit	197	174	169	179	175	174
Net financial inflows						
Net debt inflows						
Use of IMF credit	..	..	..	..	..	..
Long-term	3	43	-1,124	-791	1,017	-223
Official creditors	-22	176	242	181	452	679
Multilateral	-2	103	101	68	373	229
of which: World Bank	2	5	17	4	174	8
Bilateral	-20	73	141	114	79	450
Private creditors	25	-133	-1,366	-972	565	-902
Bondholders	..	..	..	..	500	..
Banks and others	25	-133	-1,366	-972	65	-902
Short-term	102	-497	144	-383	235	334
Net equity inflows						
Foreign direct investment	420	214	19	99	168	334
Portfolio equity	0	-1	-1	0	0	..
Debt ratios						
External debt stocks to exports (%)	38	237	231	168	167	159
External debt stocks to GNI (%)	16	96	94	77	78	77
Debt service to exports (%)	12	13	40	27	26	20
Short-term to external debt stocks (%)	6	2	3	0	3	4
Multilateral to external debt stocks (%)	41	5	6	7	9	10
Reserves to external debt stocks (%)	145	8	8	10	12	12
Gross national income (GNI)	10,764	21,328	20,529	22,294	22,795	24,426

PARAGUAY

(US$ million, unless otherwise indicated)

	2009	2015	2016	2017	2018	2019
Summary external debt data by debtor type						
Total external debt stocks	**13,941**	**16,125**	**16,228**	**15,929**	**15,799**	**16,388**
Use of IMF credit	149	132	128	136	132	132
Long-term external debt	9,731	11,218	11,503	11,173	11,026	11,543
Public and publicly guaranteed sector	2,269	4,024	4,828	5,609	6,402	7,183
Public sector	2,269	4,024	4,825	5,605	6,383	7,148
of which: General government	2,025	3,883	4,662	5,421	6,196	6,978
Private sector guaranteed by public sector	..	0	4	4	19	35
Private sector not guaranteed	7,462	7,194	6,675	5,564	4,625	4,360
Short-term external debt	4,061	4,775	4,596	4,620	4,640	4,713
Disbursements (long-term)	**1,572**	**1,471**	**1,217**	**996**	**1,535**	**1,453**
Public and publicly guaranteed sector	249	496	1,041	978	1,003	994
Public sector	249	496	1,037	978	988	978
of which: General government	249	468	1,002	945	969	973
Private sector guaranteed by public sector	..	0	4	0	15	16
Private sector not guaranteed	1,323	975	176	18	533	459
Principal repayments (long-term)	**310**	**1,592**	**914**	**1,338**	**1,680**	**1,507**
Public and publicly guaranteed sector	264	183	234	209	208	207
Public sector	264	183	234	209	208	207
of which: General government	231	166	218	194	193	187
Private sector guaranteed by public sector	..	0	0	0	0	0
Private sector not guaranteed	46	1,409	681	1,129	1,472	1,300
Interest payments (long-term)	**122**	**312**	**371**	**356**	**553**	**404**
Public and publicly guaranteed sector	97	135	178	211	254	330
Public sector	97	135	178	211	254	329
of which: General government	88	131	174	206	249	323
Private sector guaranteed by public sector	..	0	0	0	0	1
Private sector not guaranteed	25	177	194	145	299	74
Summary external debt stock by creditor type						
Long-term external debt stocks	**9,731**	**11,218**	**11,503**	**11,173**	**11,026**	**11,543**
Public and publicly guaranteed debt from:	2,269	4,024	4,828	5,609	6,402	7,183
Official creditors	1,987	2,140	2,384	2,690	2,979	3,273
Multilateral	1,362	1,869	2,167	2,501	2,790	3,062
of which: World Bank	296	431	544	605	636	619
Bilateral	625	272	217	189	189	211
Private creditors	282	1,883	2,445	2,919	3,423	3,910
Bondholders	..	1,780	2,380	2,880	3,410	3,910
Commercial banks and others	282	103	65	39	13	0
Private nonguaranteed debt from:	7,462	7,194	6,675	5,564	4,625	4,360
Bondholders	..	800	800	600	600	600
Commercial banks and others	7,462	6,394	5,875	4,964	4,025	3,760
Use of IMF credit	149	132	128	136	132	132
Net financial inflows						
Net debt inflows						
Use of IMF credit	..	..	..	..	..	..
Long-term	1,262	-121	303	-342	-145	-54
Official creditors	27	45	246	295	290	300
Multilateral	40	90	306	330	293	280
of which: World Bank	67	51	113	62	31	-11
Bilateral	-13	-44	-60	-35	-2	20
Private creditors	1,235	-167	57	-637	-435	-354
Bondholders	..	280	600	300	530	500
Banks and others	1,235	-447	-543	-937	-965	-854
Short-term	-7	-39	-178	24	20	72
Net equity inflows						
Foreign direct investment	129	451	355	337	376	381
Portfolio equity	..	..	..	..	..	..
Debt ratios						
External debt stocks to exports (%)	166	136	127	112	109	122
External debt stocks to GNI (%)	66	46	47	42	40	45
Debt service to exports (%)	6	17	11	12	16	15
Short-term to external debt stocks (%)	29	30	28	29	29	29
Multilateral to external debt stocks (%)	10	12	13	16	18	19
Reserves to external debt stocks (%)	28	35	41	47	47	45
Gross national income (GNI)	21,281	34,808	34,608	37,802	39,024	36,747

116

PERU

(US$ million, unless otherwise indicated)

	2009	2015	2016	2017	2018	2019
Summary external debt data by debtor type						
Total external debt stocks	**37,390**	**67,186**	**69,613**	**67,604**	**66,769**	**64,204**
Use of IMF credit	956	845	820	869	848	843
Long-term external debt	31,649	59,266	61,028	58,040	55,923	54,820
Public and publicly guaranteed sector	20,788	19,411	19,733	18,978	18,145	18,606
Public sector	20,225	19,411	19,733	18,978	18,145	18,606
of which: General government	20,212	19,405	19,728	16,823	15,990	16,451
Private sector guaranteed by public sector	563	..	..	..	..	..
Private sector not guaranteed	10,862	39,855	41,295	39,062	37,778	36,214
Short-term external debt	4,784	7,075	7,765	8,695	9,998	8,541
Disbursements (long-term)	**4,772**	**10,451**	**7,982**	**5,371**	**3,513**	**3,291**
Public and publicly guaranteed sector	3,232	4,866	1,978	2,631	569	1,866
Public sector	3,232	4,866	1,978	2,631	569	1,866
of which: General government	3,232	4,866	1,978	481	569	1,866
Private sector guaranteed by public sector	0	..	..	..	..	..
Private sector not guaranteed	1,539	5,585	6,004	2,740	2,945	1,425
Principal repayments (long-term)	**2,221**	**3,220**	**5,545**	**8,718**	**4,583**	**4,345**
Public and publicly guaranteed sector	1,833	907	980	3,746	1,263	1,356
Public sector	1,723	907	980	3,746	1,263	1,356
of which: General government	1,719	906	979	3,745	1,263	1,356
Private sector guaranteed by public sector	109	..	..	..	..	..
Private sector not guaranteed	389	2,313	4,565	4,973	3,320	2,989
Interest payments (long-term)	**1,976**	**2,204**	**2,090**	**2,151**	**2,328**	**2,103**
Public and publicly guaranteed sector	1,084	811	876	969	982	979
Public sector	1,047	811	876	969	982	979
of which: General government	1,046	811	876	914	872	870
Private sector guaranteed by public sector	37	..	..	..	..	..
Private sector not guaranteed	892	1,393	1,214	1,182	1,346	1,124
Summary external debt stock by creditor type						
Long-term external debt stocks	**31,649**	**59,266**	**61,028**	**58,040**	**55,923**	**54,820**
Public and publicly guaranteed debt from:	20,788	19,411	19,733	18,978	18,145	18,606
Official creditors	11,843	7,913	8,130	4,919	4,447	4,916
Multilateral	8,395	6,411	6,729	3,867	3,426	3,843
of which: World Bank	2,846	2,714	2,610	1,093	1,145	1,564
Bilateral	3,448	1,502	1,401	1,053	1,021	1,074
Private creditors	8,945	11,498	11,604	14,059	13,698	13,690
Bondholders	8,911	11,496	11,604	14,059	13,698	13,690
Commercial banks and others	34	1	0	0	..	..
Private nonguaranteed debt from:	10,862	39,855	41,295	39,062	37,778	36,214
Bondholders	4,428	15,250	13,875	16,340	15,510	16,285
Commercial banks and others	6,434	24,606	27,420	22,723	22,268	19,929
Use of IMF credit	956	845	820	869	848	843
Net financial inflows						
Net debt inflows						
Use of IMF credit	..	..	..	..	..	..
Long-term	2,550	7,231	2,437	-3,347	-1,070	-1,053
Official creditors	-591	716	190	-3,265	-448	474
Multilateral	386	802	315	-2,822	-431	419
of which: World Bank	134	877	-104	-1,516	51	423
Bilateral	-978	-86	-125	-442	-16	55
Private creditors	3,142	6,514	2,247	-83	-622	-1,527
Bondholders	2,828	4,723	-566	4,615	-1,077	812
Banks and others	314	1,792	2,813	-4,698	455	-2,339
Short-term	-615	97	690	930	1,304	-1,457
Net equity inflows						
Foreign direct investment	7,213	7,043	6,179	7,571	6,257	8,892
Portfolio equity	47	-60	-307	-172	-442	..
Debt ratios						
External debt stocks to exports (%)	118	162	157	125	115	111
External debt stocks to GNI (%)	33	37	38	34	32	30
Debt service to exports (%)	13	13	18	21	12	11
Short-term to external debt stocks (%)	13	11	11	13	15	13
Multilateral to external debt stocks (%)	22	10	10	6	5	6
Reserves to external debt stocks (%)	86	90	87	92	88	103
Gross national income (GNI)	113,308	183,306	183,939	201,299	211,136	216,266

117

PHILIPPINES

(US$ million, unless otherwise indicated)

	2009	2015	2016	2017	2018	2019
Summary external debt data by debtor type						
Total external debt stocks	**55,984**	**76,266**	**74,739**	**73,414**	**78,997**	**83,661**
Use of IMF credit	1,314	1,161	1,127	1,193	1,165	1,159
Long-term external debt	50,668	60,005	59,086	57,946	61,764	65,294
Public and publicly guaranteed sector	42,196	38,860	35,757	36,500	38,344	41,679
Public sector	42,125	38,785	35,719	36,464	38,311	41,649
of which: General government	33,162	33,364	30,695	31,703	33,769	37,002
Private sector guaranteed by public sector	71	75	37	35	33	30
Private sector not guaranteed	8,472	21,145	23,330	21,447	23,420	23,615
Short-term external debt	4,002	15,099	14,526	14,275	16,068	17,208
Disbursements (long-term)	**8,767**	**12,243**	**5,878**	**6,808**	**9,856**	**10,411**
Public and publicly guaranteed sector	8,125	6,529	3,321	3,472	4,980	6,990
Public sector	8,125	6,529	3,321	3,472	4,980	6,990
of which: General government	5,527	6,303	2,973	3,420	4,922	6,153
Private sector guaranteed by public sector	0	0	0	0	0	0
Private sector not guaranteed	642	5,714	2,557	3,336	4,876	3,421
Principal repayments (long-term)	**5,675**	**7,411**	**7,811**	**8,245**	**6,236**	**7,366**
Public and publicly guaranteed sector	3,841	3,151	4,079	3,026	2,381	4,106
Public sector	3,838	3,144	4,041	3,023	2,378	4,103
of which: General government	2,296	2,615	3,290	2,829	2,200	2,708
Private sector guaranteed by public sector	4	8	39	3	3	3
Private sector not guaranteed	1,833	4,259	3,732	5,219	3,855	3,259
Interest payments (long-term)	**3,266**	**3,161**	**3,174**	**2,952**	**2,553**	**3,079**
Public and publicly guaranteed sector	2,841	2,431	2,430	2,236	2,290	2,309
Public sector	2,839	2,429	2,428	2,236	2,289	2,308
of which: General government	2,341	2,061	2,076	1,931	2,001	2,092
Private sector guaranteed by public sector	2	2	2	1	1	1
Private sector not guaranteed	425	729	744	716	264	771
Summary external debt stock by creditor type						
Long-term external debt stocks	**50,668**	**60,005**	**59,086**	**57,946**	**61,764**	**65,294**
Public and publicly guaranteed debt from:	42,196	38,860	35,757	36,500	38,344	41,679
Official creditors	22,052	18,286	18,573	19,074	20,034	21,475
Multilateral	8,449	10,166	10,487	11,015	12,051	13,169
of which: World Bank	2,669	4,661	4,672	5,132	5,842	6,456
Bilateral	13,603	8,120	8,086	8,059	7,982	8,306
Private creditors	20,144	20,574	17,184	17,426	18,310	20,204
Bondholders	18,901	19,989	16,460	16,713	17,632	19,077
Commercial banks and others	1,243	585	724	713	679	1,127
Private nonguaranteed debt from:	8,472	21,145	23,330	21,447	23,420	23,615
Bondholders	956	5,362	5,262	4,012	5,187	6,091
Commercial banks and others	7,516	15,783	18,067	17,434	18,233	17,524
Use of IMF credit	1,314	1,161	1,127	1,193	1,165	1,159
Net financial inflows						
Net debt inflows						
Use of IMF credit	..	..	..	..	..	..
Long-term	3,092	4,833	-1,934	-1,437	3,621	3,045
Official creditors	627	880	-31	121	873	1,388
Multilateral	1,052	1,199	321	481	1,037	1,149
of which: World Bank	-40	700	10	443	709	615
Bilateral	-425	-319	-352	-361	-164	239
Private creditors	2,465	3,953	-1,903	-1,557	2,747	1,657
Bondholders	3,527	2,057	-962	-879	2,932	1,948
Banks and others	-1,063	1,895	-941	-678	-184	-291
Short-term	-2,998	-1,149	-573	-252	1,793	1,140
Net equity inflows						
Foreign direct investment	1,886	2,563	3,302	4,261	3,242	2,495
Portfolio equity	308	-743	131	496	-1,031	1,764
Debt ratios						
External debt stocks to exports (%)	113	93	90	76	77	78
External debt stocks to GNI (%)	28	22	21	20	21	20
Debt service to exports (%)	18	13	13	12	9	10
Short-term to external debt stocks (%)	7	20	19	19	20	21
Multilateral to external debt stocks (%)	15	13	14	15	15	16
Reserves to external debt stocks (%)	69	97	98	100	90	95
Gross national income (GNI)	196,472	341,467	354,013	364,719	383,817	414,269

RUSSIAN FEDERATION
(US$ million, unless otherwise indicated)

	2009	2015	2016	2017	2018	2019
Summary external debt data by debtor type						
Total external debt stocks	406,431	467,699	533,204	518,191	453,808	490,726
Use of IMF credit	8,892	7,860	7,625	8,077	7,888	7,843
Long-term external debt	344,443	417,740	480,479	459,079	397,620	425,183
Public and publicly guaranteed sector	145,865	194,185	189,423	220,079	177,150	194,171
Public sector	145,865	194,185	189,423	220,079	177,150	194,171
of which: General government	30,964	30,807	39,035	55,179	43,550	69,611
Private sector guaranteed by public sector	..	..	..	..	..	..
Private sector not guaranteed	198,578	223,555	291,056	239,000	220,470	231,012
Short-term external debt	53,096	42,100	45,100	51,035	48,300	57,700
Disbursements (long-term)	45,374	12,163	89,772	83,355	29,285	81,078
Public and publicly guaranteed sector	21,229	5,579	20,007	50,928	10,406	48,137
Public sector	21,229	5,579	20,007	50,928	10,406	48,137
of which: General government	4,956	81	9,925	17,045	5,205	27,815
Private sector guaranteed by public sector	..	..	..	..	..	..
Private sector not guaranteed	24,145	6,584	69,765	32,427	18,878	32,941
Principal repayments (long-term)	74,281	81,730	51,103	61,790	90,537	76,535
Public and publicly guaranteed sector	19,318	40,610	24,728	20,552	53,040	31,105
Public sector	19,318	40,610	24,728	20,552	53,040	31,105
of which: General government	2,552	10,378	1,660	1,051	16,741	1,711
Private sector guaranteed by public sector	..	..	..	..	..	..
Private sector not guaranteed	54,963	41,120	26,374	41,238	37,497	45,430
Interest payments (long-term)	16,293	19,036	20,121	19,008	19,049	17,258
Public and publicly guaranteed sector	2,357	3,548	5,643	6,554	8,928	7,306
Public sector	2,357	3,548	5,643	6,554	8,928	7,306
of which: General government	789	2,349	1,249	1,657	2,761	1,922
Private sector guaranteed by public sector	..	..	..	..	..	..
Private sector not guaranteed	13,936	15,489	14,478	12,455	10,121	9,953
Summary external debt stock by creditor type						
Long-term external debt stocks	344,443	417,740	480,479	459,079	397,620	425,183
Public and publicly guaranteed debt from:	145,865	194,185	189,423	220,079	177,150	194,171
Official creditors	7,333	2,472	2,135	1,149	950	761
Multilateral	3,724	873	733	589	460	341
of which: World Bank	3,211	731	646	551	428	315
Bilateral	3,609	1,599	1,402	559	489	420
Private creditors	138,532	191,714	187,289	218,930	176,200	193,410
Bondholders	21,689	30,567	40,124	62,020	53,534	82,629
Commercial banks and others	116,843	161,147	147,165	156,910	122,666	110,781
Private nonguaranteed debt from:	198,578	223,555	291,056	239,000	220,470	231,012
Bondholders	2,286	11,639	18,156	16,879	19,890	27,126
Commercial banks and others	196,292	211,915	272,900	222,121	200,580	203,885
Use of IMF credit	8,892	7,860	7,625	8,077	7,888	7,843
Net financial inflows						
Net debt inflows						
Use of IMF credit	..	..	..	..	..	..
Long-term	-28,907	-69,567	38,669	21,565	-61,252	4,543
Official creditors	-1,075	-388	-336	-986	-199	-187
Multilateral	-764	-198	-139	-144	-129	-117
of which: World Bank	-635	-145	-85	-95	-123	-111
Bilateral	-311	-189	-197	-842	-70	-70
Private creditors	-27,832	-69,179	39,005	22,551	-61,053	4,730
Bondholders	-9,324	-9,155	16,109	20,326	-5,159	36,345
Banks and others	-18,508	-60,025	22,895	2,225	-55,894	-31,615
Short-term	-20,883	-19,600	3,000	5,935	-2,735	9,400
Net equity inflows						
Foreign direct investment	23,161	10,719	35,715	26,601	9,913	28,847
Portfolio equity	3,763	-5,538	-1,788	-7,940	-4,164	-4,320
Debt ratios						
External debt stocks to exports (%)	108	109	143	113	81	91
External debt stocks to GNI (%)	34	35	43	34	28	30
Debt service to exports (%)	24	23	19	18	20	18
Short-term to external debt stocks (%)	13	9	8	10	11	12
Multilateral to external debt stocks (%)	1	0	0	0	0	0
Reserves to external debt stocks (%)	103	68	60	69	84	90
Gross national income (GNI)	1,182,905	1,325,731	1,241,289	1,532,144	1,627,790	1,646,524

119

RWANDA
(US$ million, unless otherwise indicated)

	2009	2015	2016	2017	2018	2019
Summary external debt data by debtor type						
Total external debt stocks	1,101.4	3,452.0	4,318.7	4,833.4	5,422.6	6,211.4
Use of IMF credit	135.7	111.6	203.3	290.7	307.9	305.6
Long-term external debt	955.5	3,329.1	3,888.8	4,474.5	5,010.1	5,677.3
Public and publicly guaranteed sector	715.5	2,057.3	2,353.3	2,829.1	3,240.6	3,907.9
Public sector	715.5	2,057.3	2,353.3	2,829.1	3,240.6	3,907.9
of which: General government	714.6	2,056.6	2,352.6	2,828.4	3,239.9	3,907.2
Private sector guaranteed by public sector	..	..	..	..	..	..
Private sector not guaranteed	240.0	1,271.7	1,535.5	1,645.4	1,769.5	1,769.4
Short-term external debt	10.1	11.3	226.6	68.2	104.7	228.5
Disbursements (long-term)	96.8	659.4	774.9	713.5	847.1	714.5
Public and publicly guaranteed sector	72.8	375.7	368.1	407.2	492.0	714.5
Public sector	72.8	375.7	368.1	407.2	492.0	714.5
of which: General government	72.8	375.7	368.1	407.2	492.0	714.5
Private sector guaranteed by public sector	..	..	..	..	..	..
Private sector not guaranteed	24.0	283.8	406.8	306.3	355.1	..
Principal repayments (long-term)	29.3	125.7	148.2	155.4	155.5	31.5
Public and publicly guaranteed sector	5.3	17.4	23.0	27.7	29.2	31.5
Public sector	5.3	17.4	23.0	27.7	29.2	31.5
of which: General government	5.3	17.4	22.9	27.6	29.2	31.5
Private sector guaranteed by public sector	..	..	..	..	..	..
Private sector not guaranteed	24.0	108.4	125.2	127.8	126.3	0.1
Interest payments (long-term)	9.7	56.1	68.8	83.3	101.2	133.2
Public and publicly guaranteed sector	5.7	39.2	41.8	45.7	51.1	55.7
Public sector	5.7	39.2	41.8	45.7	51.1	55.7
of which: General government	5.7	39.2	41.8	45.7	51.1	55.7
Private sector guaranteed by public sector	..	..	..	..	..	..
Private sector not guaranteed	4.0	16.9	27.0	37.6	50.2	77.5
Summary external debt stock by creditor type						
Long-term external debt stocks	955.5	3,329.1	3,888.8	4,474.5	5,010.1	5,677.3
Public and publicly guaranteed debt from:	715.5	2,057.3	2,353.3	2,829.1	3,240.6	3,907.9
Official creditors	715.5	1,657.3	1,953.3	2,429.1	2,840.6	3,443.8
Multilateral	615.3	1,362.8	1,645.5	2,076.6	2,458.6	2,957.6
of which: World Bank	254.2	861.9	1,048.5	1,403.5	1,610.5	1,897.3
Bilateral	100.3	294.6	307.8	352.5	382.1	486.2
Private creditors	..	400.0	400.0	400.0	400.0	464.1
Bondholders	..	400.0	400.0	400.0	400.0	421.0
Commercial banks and others	..	..	..	..	..	43.1
Private nonguaranteed debt from:	240.0	1,271.7	1,535.5	1,645.4	1,769.5	1,769.4
Bondholders	..	..	..	..	..	..
Commercial banks and others	240.0	1,271.7	1,535.5	1,645.4	1,769.5	1,769.4
Use of IMF credit	135.7	111.6	203.3	290.7	307.9	305.6
Net financial inflows						
Net debt inflows						
Use of IMF credit	3.6	-2.6	98.2	73.4	24.4	-0.5
Long-term	67.5	533.7	626.8	558.1	691.6	683.0
Official creditors	67.5	358.3	345.1	379.6	462.8	618.9
Multilateral	53.6	309.0	322.8	345.1	424.6	511.3
of which: World Bank	10.5	284.5	216.6	287.8	241.2	295.0
Bilateral	14.0	49.3	22.4	34.5	38.2	107.6
Private creditors	0.0	175.4	281.6	178.5	228.8	64.0
Bondholders	..	..	..	..	0.0	21.0
Banks and others	0.0	175.4	281.6	178.5	228.8	43.0
Short-term	4.0	-13.7	215.3	-158.4	36.5	123.8
Net equity inflows						
Foreign direct investment	118.7	88.3	171.0	176.4	185.9	420.2
Portfolio equity	..	2.5	3.0	0.3	5.8	..
Debt ratios						
External debt stocks to exports (%)	182.9	232.9	279.8	241.6	263.1	270.0
External debt stocks to GNI (%)	19.5	41.2	50.7	54.0	58.2	63.4
Debt service to exports (%)	6.6	12.5	14.4	12.1	12.6	7.4
Short-term to external debt stocks (%)	0.9	0.3	5.2	1.4	1.9	3.7
Multilateral to external debt stocks (%)	55.9	39.5	38.1	43.0	45.3	47.6
Reserves to external debt stocks (%)	91.7	26.6	23.5	24.4	25.0	23.6
Gross national income (GNI)	5,657.3	8,381.9	8,523.0	8,944.5	9,315.4	9,798.0

120

SAMOA

(US$ million, unless otherwise indicated)

	2009	2015	2016	2017	2018	2019
Summary external debt data by debtor type						
Total external debt stocks	**252.9**	**437.4**	**417.5**	**443.1**	**427.5**	**408.6**
Use of IMF credit	26.5	29.8	27.4	27.4	24.3	21.0
Long-term external debt	226.4	407.6	390.1	415.7	403.2	387.6
Public and publicly guaranteed sector	226.4	407.6	390.1	415.7	403.2	387.6
Public sector	226.4	407.6	390.1	415.7	403.2	387.6
of which: General government	224.5	407.0	389.7	415.5	403.1	387.6
Private sector guaranteed by public sector	..	..	..	..	..	..
Private sector not guaranteed	..	..	..	..	..	..
Short-term external debt	0.0	0.0	0.0	0.0	0.0	0.0
Disbursements (long-term)	**25.2**	**23.3**	**14.3**	**21.0**	**22.0**	**9.3**
Public and publicly guaranteed sector	25.2	23.3	14.3	21.0	22.0	9.3
Public sector	25.2	23.3	14.3	21.0	22.0	9.3
of which: General government	25.2	23.3	14.3	21.0	22.0	9.3
Private sector guaranteed by public sector	..	..	..	..	..	..
Private sector not guaranteed	..	..	..	..	..	..
Principal repayments (long-term)	**6.0**	**13.7**	**15.6**	**18.3**	**21.9**	**21.3**
Public and publicly guaranteed sector	6.0	13.7	15.6	18.3	21.9	21.3
Public sector	6.0	13.7	15.6	18.3	21.9	21.3
of which: General government	5.8	13.6	15.4	18.1	21.7	21.3
Private sector guaranteed by public sector	..	..	..	..	..	..
Private sector not guaranteed	..	..	..	..	..	..
Interest payments (long-term)	**2.5**	**5.6**	**5.8**	**5.7**	**6.1**	**5.6**
Public and publicly guaranteed sector	2.5	5.6	5.8	5.7	6.1	5.6
Public sector	2.5	5.6	5.8	5.7	6.1	5.6
of which: General government	2.5	5.6	5.7	5.7	6.1	5.6
Private sector guaranteed by public sector	..	..	..	..	..	..
Private sector not guaranteed	..	..	..	..	..	..
Summary external debt stock by creditor type						
Long-term external debt stocks	**226.4**	**407.6**	**390.1**	**415.7**	**403.2**	**387.6**
Public and publicly guaranteed debt from:	226.4	407.6	390.1	415.7	403.2	387.6
Official creditors	226.4	407.6	390.1	415.7	403.2	387.6
Multilateral	180.1	214.0	203.7	215.0	208.1	205.8
of which: World Bank	79.9	96.1	92.8	103.4	104.9	110.3
Bilateral	46.3	193.6	186.4	200.7	195.1	181.8
Private creditors	..	..	..	..	..	..
Bondholders	..	..	..	..	..	..
Commercial banks and others	..	..	..	..	..	..
Private nonguaranteed debt from:	..	..	..	..	..	..
Bondholders	..	..	..	..	..	..
Commercial banks and others	..	..	..	..	..	..
Use of IMF credit	26.5	29.8	27.4	27.4	24.3	21.0
Net financial inflows						
Net debt inflows						
Use of IMF credit	8.9	-1.6	-1.6	-1.6	-2.5	-3.2
Long-term	19.2	9.5	-1.3	2.8	0.1	-12.0
Official creditors	19.2	9.5	-1.3	2.8	0.1	-12.0
Multilateral	2.6	1.6	-4.3	-0.1	-2.0	-1.2
of which: World Bank	0.4	4.5	-0.6	5.2	4.0	6.0
Bilateral	16.6	7.9	3.0	2.9	2.1	-10.9
Private creditors	..	..	..	..	..	..
Bondholders	..	..	..	..	..	..
Banks and others	..	..	..	..	..	..
Short-term	0.0	0.0	0.0	0.0	0.0	0.0
Net equity inflows						
Foreign direct investment	9.9	26.9	2.5	9.2	16.7	2.8
Portfolio equity	..	-0.1	0.0	0.0	0.0	..
Debt ratios						
External debt stocks to exports (%)	139.4	182.6	162.7	155.8	137.4	122.1
External debt stocks to GNI (%)	45.6	56.6	53.5	55.0	54.1	50.2
Debt service to exports (%)	4.7	8.8	9.0	9.0	9.8	9.1
Short-term to external debt stocks (%)	0.0	0.0	0.0	0.0	0.0	0.0
Multilateral to external debt stocks (%)	71.2	48.9	48.8	48.5	48.7	50.4
Reserves to external debt stocks (%)	57.1	28.0	23.8	29.6	39.8	45.3
Gross national income (GNI)	554.5	772.3	780.8	805.3	790.5	813.4

121

SÃO TOMÉ AND PRÍNCIPE

(US$ million, unless otherwise indicated)

	2009	2015	2016	2017	2018	2019
Summary external debt data by debtor type						
Total external debt stocks	**157.0**	**241.7**	**248.3**	**269.5**	**252.6**	**251.6**
Use of IMF credit	15.6	14.2	14.7	16.8	16.8	18.8
Long-term external debt	125.0	219.2	224.5	245.5	226.3	225.2
Public and publicly guaranteed sector	125.0	219.2	224.5	245.5	226.3	225.2
Public sector	120.0	215.0	220.3	241.2	222.1	220.6
of which: General government	120.0	215.0	220.3	241.2	222.1	220.6
Private sector guaranteed by public sector	5.0	4.2	4.2	4.2	4.2	4.6
Private sector not guaranteed	..	..	..	..	..	..
Short-term external debt	16.4	8.3	9.1	7.2	9.6	7.6
Disbursements (long-term)	**18.8**	**25.1**	**9.6**	**12.2**	**5.6**	**4.4**
Public and publicly guaranteed sector	18.8	25.1	9.6	12.2	5.6	4.4
Public sector	13.8	25.1	9.6	12.2	5.6	4.4
of which: General government	13.8	25.1	9.6	12.2	5.6	4.4
Private sector guaranteed by public sector	5.0	..	..	..	..	..
Private sector not guaranteed	..	..	..	..	..	..
Principal repayments (long-term)	**1.7**	**0.8**	**0.7**	**2.1**	**2.7**	**4.8**
Public and publicly guaranteed sector	1.7	0.8	0.7	2.1	2.7	4.8
Public sector	1.7	0.8	0.7	2.1	2.7	4.8
of which: General government	1.7	0.8	0.7	2.1	2.7	4.8
Private sector guaranteed by public sector	..	..	..	..	..	..
Private sector not guaranteed	..	..	..	..	..	..
Interest payments (long-term)	**0.3**	**1.0**	**1.1**	**1.1**	**1.3**	**3.4**
Public and publicly guaranteed sector	0.3	1.0	1.1	1.1	1.3	3.4
Public sector	0.3	1.0	1.1	1.1	1.3	3.4
of which: General government	0.3	1.0	1.1	1.1	1.3	3.4
Private sector guaranteed by public sector	..	..	..	..	..	..
Private sector not guaranteed	..	..	..	..	..	..
Summary external debt stock by creditor type						
Long-term external debt stocks	**125.0**	**219.2**	**224.5**	**245.5**	**226.3**	**225.2**
Public and publicly guaranteed debt from:	125.0	219.2	224.5	245.5	226.3	225.2
Official creditors	125.0	219.2	224.5	245.5	226.3	225.2
Multilateral	36.7	37.9	40.1	44.9	46.9	46.2
of which: World Bank	14.4	12.2	11.6	12.0	11.5	11.1
Bilateral	88.3	181.3	184.4	200.6	179.4	179.0
Private creditors	..	..	..	..	..	..
Bondholders	..	..	..	..	..	..
Commercial banks and others	..	..	..	..	..	..
Private nonguaranteed debt from:	..	..	..	..	..	..
Bondholders	..	..	..	..	..	..
Commercial banks and others	..	..	..	..	..	..
Use of IMF credit	15.6	14.2	14.7	16.8	16.8	18.8
Net financial inflows						
Net debt inflows						
Use of IMF credit	0.6	-0.1	1.0	1.2	0.4	2.2
Long-term	17.1	24.4	8.8	10.1	2.9	-0.4
Official creditors	17.1	24.4	8.8	10.1	2.9	-0.4
Multilateral	2.4	1.4	2.9	2.9	2.9	-0.4
of which: World Bank	1.0	-0.3	-0.3	-0.3	-0.3	-0.3
Bilateral	14.7	23.0	5.9	7.2	..	0.0
Private creditors	..	..	..	..	..	..
Bondholders	..	..	..	..	..	..
Banks and others	..	..	..	..	..	..
Short-term	1.0	-3.0	0.9	-2.1	2.4	0.1
Net equity inflows						
Foreign direct investment	15.5	24.8	23.3	32.9	22.7	24.7
Portfolio equity	0.0	0.0	-0.1	0.1	0.0	7.7
Debt ratios						
External debt stocks to exports (%)	738.6	249.4	241.4	284.3	257.1	328.9
External debt stocks to GNI (%)	83.7	76.2	71.2	72.1	59.5	59.2
Debt service to exports (%)	9.9	2.9	2.6	4.1	4.7	11.6
Short-term to external debt stocks (%)	10.5	3.4	3.6	2.7	3.8	3.0
Multilateral to external debt stocks (%)	23.4	15.7	16.2	16.7	18.6	18.3
Reserves to external debt stocks (%)	42.5	30.1	25.5	21.9	17.3	18.7
Gross national income (GNI)	187.5	317.2	348.5	373.9	424.8	424.8

SENEGAL

(US$ million, unless otherwise indicated)

	2009	2015	2016	2017	2018	2019
Summary external debt data by debtor type						
Total external debt stocks	3,721	5,905	6,690	8,899	11,892	13,583
Use of IMF credit	409	344	299	283	242	219
Long-term external debt	3,312	5,561	6,390	8,616	11,650	13,365
Public and publicly guaranteed sector	2,954	5,332	6,151	8,367	11,208	12,845
Public sector	2,954	5,332	6,151	8,367	11,208	12,845
of which: General government	2,948	5,332	6,151	8,367	11,208	12,845
Private sector guaranteed by public sector	..	..	..	..	..	..
Private sector not guaranteed	357	229	239	250	442	520
Short-term external debt	0	0	0	0	0	0
Disbursements (long-term)	837	643	1,229	2,083	4,030	2,365
Public and publicly guaranteed sector	628	595	1,096	1,919	3,634	2,288
Public sector	628	595	1,096	1,919	3,634	2,288
of which: General government	628	595	1,096	1,919	3,634	2,288
Private sector guaranteed by public sector	..	..	..	..	..	
Private sector not guaranteed	208	49	133	165	396	78
Principal repayments (long-term)	146	193	207	327	483	547
Public and publicly guaranteed sector	97	101	121	147	316	547
Public sector	97	101	121	147	316	547
of which: General government	96	101	121	147	316	547
Private sector guaranteed by public sector	..	..	..	..	..	..
Private sector not guaranteed	49	92	86	180	167	..
Interest payments (long-term)	50	150	155	298	304	374
Public and publicly guaranteed sector	41	138	145	292	292	359
Public sector	41	138	145	292	292	359
of which: General government	41	138	145	292	292	359
Private sector guaranteed by public sector	..	..	..	..	..	..
Private sector not guaranteed	9	12	10	6	11	16
Summary external debt stock by creditor type						
Long-term external debt stocks	3,312	5,561	6,390	8,616	11,650	13,365
Public and publicly guaranteed debt from:	2,954	5,332	6,151	8,367	11,208	12,845
Official creditors	2,752	4,272	5,107	6,120	6,674	7,645
Multilateral	1,806	2,779	3,056	3,620	3,719	4,746
of which: World Bank	927	1,598	1,670	1,999	2,070	2,657
Bilateral	946	1,493	2,051	2,501	2,955	2,899
Private creditors	202	1,060	1,044	2,246	4,534	5,200
Bondholders	200	886	874	2,025	4,151	4,122
Commercial banks and others	2	174	170	221	383	1,078
Private nonguaranteed debt from:	357	229	239	250	442	520
Bondholders	..	..	..	..	..	..
Commercial banks and others	357	229	239	250	442	520
Use of IMF credit	409	344	299	283	242	219
Net financial inflows						
Net debt inflows						
Use of IMF credit	100	-34	-36	-34	-34	-22
Long-term	691	450	1,022	1,756	3,547	1,818
Official creditors	334	493	972	646	959	1,041
Multilateral	206	189	368	314	208	1,070
of which: World Bank	134	162	124	224	123	604
Bilateral	128	305	605	332	751	-30
Private creditors	357	-43	49	1,110	2,588	777
Bondholders	200	..	..	1,100	2,181	0
Banks and others	157	-43	49	10	407	777
Short-term	-197	0	0	0	0	0
Net equity inflows						
Foreign direct investment	245	259	272	368	439	983
Portfolio equity	-2	20	25	13	15	..
Debt ratios						
External debt stocks to exports (%)	113	137	152	181	208	..
External debt stocks to GNI (%)	23	34	36	44	53	59
Debt service to exports (%)	6	9	9	13	14	..
Short-term to external debt stocks (%)	0	0	0	0	0	0
Multilateral to external debt stocks (%)	49	47	46	41	31	35
Reserves to external debt stocks (%)	57	34	..	..	..	..
Gross national income (GNI)	16,078	17,383	18,542	20,409	22,635	22,963

123

SERBIA
(US$ million, unless otherwise indicated)

	2009	2015	2016	2017	2018	2019
Summary external debt data by debtor type						
Total external debt stocks	**33,809**	**31,301**	**29,533**	**34,279**	**34,223**	**35,896**
Use of IMF credit	2,299	633	598	634	619	615
Long-term external debt	27,910	29,780	27,811	32,120	31,553	32,669
Public and publicly guaranteed sector	8,835	16,276	16,215	16,422	15,088	15,343
Public sector	8,833	16,137	16,084	16,308	15,088	15,343
of which: General government	7,133	14,823	14,879	15,140	14,183	14,467
Private sector guaranteed by public sector	2	139	131	114	0	..
Private sector not guaranteed	19,076	13,505	11,595	15,698	16,465	17,326
Short-term external debt	3,600	888	1,124	1,526	2,051	2,611
Disbursements (long-term)	**4,529**	**3,112**	**3,698**	**7,339**	**4,709**	**8,694**
Public and publicly guaranteed sector	966	1,378	1,207	1,439	1,502	3,125
Public sector	966	1,378	1,207	1,439	1,502	3,125
of which: General government	824	1,182	934	1,294	1,394	2,992
Private sector guaranteed by public sector	0	0	..	..	..	..
Private sector not guaranteed	3,562	1,734	2,492	5,899	3,207	5,569
Principal repayments (long-term)	**3,613**	**2,980**	**5,016**	**4,086**	**4,813**	**6,385**
Public and publicly guaranteed sector	158	827	1,030	2,195	2,501	2,743
Public sector	157	819	1,027	2,162	2,389	2,743
of which: General government	116	588	678	1,862	2,056	2,594
Private sector guaranteed by public sector	1	8	3	34	112	..
Private sector not guaranteed	3,454	2,153	3,986	1,891	2,312	3,643
Interest payments (long-term)	**916**	**1,117**	**917**	**869**	**908**	**912**
Public and publicly guaranteed sector	348	594	588	576	546	515
Public sector	348	586	582	571	542	515
of which: General government	288	532	536	542	522	502
Private sector guaranteed by public sector	0	8	6	5	4	..
Private sector not guaranteed	568	523	330	292	361	396
Summary external debt stock by creditor type						
Long-term external debt stocks	**27,910**	**29,780**	**27,811**	**32,120**	**31,553**	**32,669**
Public and publicly guaranteed debt from:	8,835	16,276	16,215	16,422	15,088	15,343
Official creditors	7,499	10,188	10,355	11,708	11,565	11,770
Multilateral	4,404	5,373	5,313	6,246	5,861	5,743
of which: World Bank	2,459	2,515	2,384	2,939	2,799	2,708
Bilateral	3,095	4,815	5,042	5,462	5,704	6,027
Private creditors	1,336	6,087	5,860	4,714	3,523	3,573
Bondholders	..	5,250	5,250	4,500	3,500	3,552
Commercial banks and others	1,336	837	610	214	23	22
Private nonguaranteed debt from:	19,076	13,505	11,595	15,698	16,465	17,326
Bondholders	165	1,041	1,206	2,825	2,752	3,336
Commercial banks and others	18,911	12,464	10,389	12,872	13,713	13,990
Use of IMF credit	2,299	633	598	634	619	615
Net financial inflows						
Net debt inflows						
Use of IMF credit	1,575	-162	-16	..	..	..
Long-term	916	132	-1,318	3,252	-105	2,308
Official creditors	673	656	391	421	191	337
Multilateral	329	453	114	206	-117	-9
of which: World Bank	72	274	-56	226	-17	-38
Bilateral	344	204	277	216	308	346
Private creditors	243	-524	-1,709	2,831	-295	1,971
Bondholders	..	162	166	775	-1,000	656
Banks and others	243	-686	-1,874	2,056	705	1,315
Short-term	-95	217	378	300	624	529
Net equity inflows						
Foreign direct investment	1,592	2,107	1,521	1,657	3,515	3,415
Portfolio equity	23	-90	-14	-7	-28	-64
Debt ratios						
External debt stocks to exports (%)	284	172	148	152	134	134
External debt stocks to GNI (%)	76	83	77	83	71	74
Debt service to exports (%)	39	23	30	22	22	27
Short-term to external debt stocks (%)	11	3	4	4	6	7
Multilateral to external debt stocks (%)	13	17	18	18	17	16
Reserves to external debt stocks (%)	44	34	34	32	35	38
Gross national income (GNI)	44,463	37,789	38,393	41,227	48,021	48,636

124

SIERRA LEONE
(US$ million, unless otherwise indicated)

	2009	2015	2016	2017	2018	2019
Summary external debt data by debtor type						
Total external debt stocks	856.9	1,553.5	1,612.5	1,734.6	1,735.5	1,808.1
Use of IMF credit	229.2	391.0	443.9	509.5	501.1	502.9
Long-term external debt	604.7	948.6	967.6	1,030.0	1,045.9	1,118.7
Public and publicly guaranteed sector	604.7	948.6	967.6	1,030.0	1,045.9	1,118.7
Public sector	604.7	948.6	967.6	1,030.0	1,045.9	1,118.7
of which: General government	604.7	948.6	967.6	1,030.0	1,045.9	1,118.7
Private sector guaranteed by public sector	..	..	..	..	..	..
Private sector not guaranteed	..	..	..	..	..	..
Short-term external debt	23.0	213.9	201.0	195.1	188.5	186.5
Disbursements (long-term)	**62.2**	**79.6**	**53.4**	**72.3**	**57.3**	**106.7**
Public and publicly guaranteed sector	62.2	79.6	53.4	72.3	57.3	106.7
Public sector	62.2	79.6	53.4	72.3	57.3	106.7
of which: General government	62.2	79.6	53.4	72.3	57.3	106.7
Private sector guaranteed by public sector	..	..	..	..	..	..
Private sector not guaranteed	..	..	..	..	..	..
Principal repayments (long-term)	**3.3**	**13.9**	**19.7**	**24.4**	**28.3**	**30.8**
Public and publicly guaranteed sector	3.3	13.9	19.7	24.4	28.3	30.8
Public sector	3.3	13.9	19.7	24.4	28.3	30.8
of which: General government	3.3	13.9	19.7	24.4	28.3	30.8
Private sector guaranteed by public sector	..	..	..	..	..	..
Private sector not guaranteed	..	..	..	..	..	..
Interest payments (long-term)	**3.7**	**7.6**	**12.3**	**12.9**	**5.4**	**9.5**
Public and publicly guaranteed sector	3.7	7.6	12.3	12.9	5.4	9.5
Public sector	3.7	7.6	12.3	12.9	5.4	9.5
of which: General government	3.7	7.6	12.3	12.9	5.4	9.5
Private sector guaranteed by public sector	..	..	..	..	..	..
Private sector not guaranteed	..	..	..	..	..	..
Summary external debt stock by creditor type						
Long-term external debt stocks	604.7	948.6	967.6	1,030.0	1,045.9	1,118.7
Public and publicly guaranteed debt from:	604.7	948.6	967.6	1,030.0	1,045.9	1,118.7
Official creditors	393.6	755.2	774.2	836.6	852.4	925.3
Multilateral	322.2	590.9	601.6	671.6	683.2	757.2
of which: World Bank	124.3	225.7	224.3	275.7	284.3	348.0
Bilateral	71.3	164.3	172.5	165.0	169.2	168.0
Private creditors	211.1	193.4	193.4	193.4	193.4	193.4
Bondholders	..	..	..	..	..	..
Commercial banks and others	211.1	193.4	193.4	193.4	193.4	193.4
Private nonguaranteed debt from:	..	..	..	..	..	..
Bondholders	..	..	..	..	..	..
Commercial banks and others	..	..	..	..	..	..
Use of IMF credit	229.2	391.0	443.9	509.5	501.1	502.9
Net financial inflows						
Net debt inflows						
Use of IMF credit	18.8	102.0	66.8	38.1	3.6	4.7
Long-term	58.8	65.7	33.7	47.9	29.0	75.9
Official creditors	58.8	65.7	33.7	47.9	29.0	75.9
Multilateral	49.0	50.2	21.8	45.6	22.3	76.5
of which: World Bank	15.1	5.3	5.6	37.2	15.7	65.2
Bilateral	9.9	15.5	11.9	2.4	6.7	-0.6
Private creditors	..	..	..	..	..	..
Bondholders	..	..	..	..	..	..
Banks and others	..	..	..	..	..	..
Short-term	14.0	0.7	-12.9	-5.9	-6.6	-2.0
Net equity inflows						
Foreign direct investment	84.6	231.9	121.5	176.2	189.3	367.7
Portfolio equity	5.6	..	..	..	..	..
Debt ratios						
External debt stocks to exports (%)	225.7	197.2	171.8	225.0	225.9	..
External debt stocks to GNI (%)	32.2	37.3	49.2	47.8	45.7	49.3
Debt service to exports (%)	2.1	6.6	4.0	7.6	7.7	..
Short-term to external debt stocks (%)	2.7	13.8	12.5	11.2	10.9	10.3
Multilateral to external debt stocks (%)	37.6	38.0	37.3	38.7	39.4	41.9
Reserves to external debt stocks (%)	47.3	37.3	30.8	31.7	29.0	29.5
Gross national income (GNI)	2,665.0	4,162.1	3,277.0	3,629.6	3,798.5	3,668.4

125

SOLOMON ISLANDS
(US$ million, unless otherwise indicated)

	2009	2015	2016	2017	2018	2019
Summary external debt data by debtor type						
Total external debt stocks	**172.4**	**207.5**	**263.8**	**376.7**	**323.5**	**350.5**
Use of IMF credit	15.5	27.7	23.6	21.0	17.1	15.0
Long-term external debt	154.4	158.0	205.6	327.8	263.4	299.3
Public and publicly guaranteed sector	132.9	81.2	86.7	96.5	96.0	98.1
Public sector	132.9	81.2	86.7	96.5	96.0	98.1
of which: General government	132.9	81.2	86.7	96.5	96.0	98.1
Private sector guaranteed by public sector	..	..	..	..	..	..
Private sector not guaranteed	21.5	76.8	118.9	231.3	167.4	201.3
Short-term external debt	2.5	21.7	34.7	27.9	43.0	36.2
Disbursements (long-term)	**13.7**	**32.6**	**38.4**	**177.0**	**36.8**	**18.0**
Public and publicly guaranteed sector	0.0	0.0	13.1	11.1	6.1	7.6
Public sector	0.0	0.0	13.1	11.1	6.1	7.6
of which: General government	0.0	0.0	13.1	11.1	6.1	7.6
Private sector guaranteed by public sector	..	..	..	..	..	..
Private sector not guaranteed	13.7	32.5	25.2	165.9	30.7	10.4
Principal repayments (long-term)	**7.6**	**8.5**	**13.2**	**17.1**	**29.5**	**9.8**
Public and publicly guaranteed sector	6.5	5.3	6.5	5.2	4.8	5.1
Public sector	6.5	5.3	6.5	5.2	4.8	5.1
of which: General government	6.5	5.3	6.5	5.2	4.8	5.1
Private sector guaranteed by public sector	..	..	..	..	..	..
Private sector not guaranteed	1.1	3.2	6.7	11.9	24.7	4.7
Interest payments (long-term)	**2.4**	**2.2**	**5.1**	**4.0**	**6.0**	**3.2**
Public and publicly guaranteed sector	1.8	1.1	1.1	1.1	1.1	1.1
Public sector	1.8	1.1	1.1	1.1	1.1	1.1
of which: General government	1.8	1.1	1.1	1.1	1.1	1.1
Private sector guaranteed by public sector	..	..	..	..	..	..
Private sector not guaranteed	0.5	1.1	4.0	3.0	4.9	2.1
Summary external debt stock by creditor type						
Long-term external debt stocks	**154.4**	**158.0**	**205.6**	**327.8**	**263.4**	**299.3**
Public and publicly guaranteed debt from:	132.9	81.2	86.7	96.5	96.0	98.1
Official creditors	132.7	81.2	86.7	96.5	96.0	98.1
Multilateral	111.5	69.3	75.9	86.8	87.5	90.7
of which: World Bank	43.7	31.2	33.6	36.1	36.6	38.5
Bilateral	21.2	11.9	10.8	9.7	8.5	7.4
Private creditors	0.2	..	..	..	..	..
Bondholders	..	..	..	..	..	..
Commercial banks and others	0.2	..	..	..	..	..
Private nonguaranteed debt from:	21.5	76.8	118.9	231.3	167.4	201.3
Bondholders	..	..	..	..	..	..
Commercial banks and others	21.5	76.8	118.9	231.3	167.4	201.3
Use of IMF credit	15.5	27.7	23.6	21.0	17.1	15.0
Net financial inflows						
Net debt inflows						
Use of IMF credit	..	-2.7	-3.4	-3.8	-3.5	-2.0
Long-term	6.1	24.0	25.1	159.9	7.3	8.1
Official creditors	-6.3	-5.3	6.6	6.0	1.3	2.5
Multilateral	-4.6	-4.2	7.7	7.1	2.4	3.6
of which: World Bank	-1.1	-1.5	3.5	0.5	1.4	2.2
Bilateral	-1.6	-1.1	-1.1	-1.1	-1.1	-1.1
Private creditors	12.4	29.3	18.5	154.0	6.0	5.7
Bondholders	..	..	..	..	..	..
Banks and others	12.4	29.3	18.5	154.0	6.0	5.7
Short-term	1.0	6.8	13.0	-6.8	15.2	-6.9
Net equity inflows						
Foreign direct investment	35.0	6.9	28.6	31.4	32.4	35.1
Portfolio equity	..	..	..	0.0	0.0	0.0
Debt ratios						
External debt stocks to exports (%)	72.7	35.9	44.2	59.3	44.7	54.9
External debt stocks to GNI (%)	39.8	18.5	22.7	30.2	24.2	25.8
Debt service to exports (%)	4.2	2.4	3.8	4.0	5.6	2.6
Short-term to external debt stocks (%)	1.5	10.5	13.2	7.4	13.3	10.3
Multilateral to external debt stocks (%)	64.6	33.4	28.8	23.1	27.0	25.9
Reserves to external debt stocks (%)	84.7	238.2	184.4	144.2	181.2	152.7
Gross national income (GNI)	432.9	1,121.1	1,164.6	1,246.5	1,334.8	1,356.1

126

SOMALIA

(US$ million, unless otherwise indicated)

	2009	2015	2016	2017	2018	2019
Summary external debt data by debtor type						
Total external debt stocks	**2,935**	**2,762**	**2,737**	**2,825**	**5,563**	**5,616**
Use of IMF credit	248	219	212	225	220	219
Long-term external debt	1,876	1,751	1,736	1,779	2,085	2,082
Public and publicly guaranteed sector	1,876	1,751	1,736	1,779	2,085	2,082
Public sector	1,876	1,751	1,736	1,779	2,085	2,082
of which: General government	1,852	1,728	1,713	1,756	2,060	2,058
Private sector guaranteed by public sector	..	..	..	..	..	..
Private sector not guaranteed	..	..	..	..	..	..
Short-term external debt	811	793	788	821	3,259	3,315
Disbursements (long-term)	**0**	**0**	**0**	**0**	**0**	**0**
Public and publicly guaranteed sector	0	0	0	0	0	0
Public sector	0	0	0	0	0	0
of which: General government	0	0	0	0	0	0
Private sector guaranteed by public sector	..	..	..	..	..	..
Private sector not guaranteed	..	..	..	..	..	..
Principal repayments (long-term)	**0**	**0**	**0**	**0**	**0**	**0**
Public and publicly guaranteed sector	0	0	0	0	0	0
Public sector	0	0	0	0	0	0
of which: General government	0	0	0	0	0	0
Private sector guaranteed by public sector	..	..	..	..	..	..
Private sector not guaranteed	..	..	..	..	..	..
Interest payments (long-term)	**0**	**0**	**0**	**0**	**0**	**0**
Public and publicly guaranteed sector	0	0	0	0	0	0
Public sector	0	0	0	0	0	0
of which: General government	0	0	0	0	0	0
Private sector guaranteed by public sector	..	..	..	..	..	..
Private sector not guaranteed	..	..	..	..	..	..
Summary external debt stock by creditor type						
Long-term external debt stocks	**1,876**	**1,751**	**1,736**	**1,779**	**2,085**	**2,082**
Public and publicly guaranteed debt from:	1,876	1,751	1,736	1,779	2,085	2,082
Official creditors	1,842	1,719	1,705	1,747	2,038	2,037
Multilateral	780	710	698	725	716	714
of which: World Bank	448	412	404	420	413	411
Bilateral	1,062	1,009	1,006	1,022	1,322	1,322
Private creditors	35	31	31	32	46	46
Bondholders	..	..	..	..	..	..
Commercial banks and others	35	31	31	32	46	46
Private nonguaranteed debt from:	..	..	..	..	..	..
Bondholders	..	..	..	..	..	..
Commercial banks and others	..	..	..	..	..	..
Use of IMF credit	248	219	212	225	220	219
Net financial inflows						
Net debt inflows						
Use of IMF credit	..	..	..	..	..	..
Long-term	0	0	0	0	0	0
Official creditors	0	0	0	0	0	0
Multilateral	0	0	0	0	0	0
of which: World Bank	0	0	0	0	0	..
Bilateral	0	0	0	0	0	0
Private creditors	0	0	0	0	..	..
Bondholders	..	..	..	..	..	..
Banks and others	0	0	0	0	..	..
Short-term	0	0	0	0	0	0
Net equity inflows						
Foreign direct investment	108	303	330	369	408	447
Portfolio equity	..	..	..	..	..	..
Debt ratios						
External debt stocks to exports (%)	..	..	250	267	478	477
External debt stocks to GNI (%)	..	..	..	..	..	..
Debt service to exports (%)	..	..	0	0	0	0
Short-term to external debt stocks (%)	28	29	29	29	59	59
Multilateral to external debt stocks (%)	27	26	26	26	13	13
Reserves to external debt stocks (%)	..	..	..	..	..	..
Gross national income (GNI)	..	..	..	..	..	..

127

SOUTH AFRICA

(US$ million, unless otherwise indicated)

	2009	2015	2016	2017	2018	2019
Summary external debt data by debtor type						
Total external debt stocks	**79,903**	**124,354**	**142,259**	**177,583**	**172,995**	**188,102**
Use of IMF credit	2,799	2,474	2,400	2,543	2,483	2,469
Long-term external debt	55,818	92,805	110,068	138,411	133,758	151,214
Public and publicly guaranteed sector	23,201	44,065	58,413	78,678	71,647	86,307
Public sector	22,695	43,824	58,140	78,375	71,387	86,003
of which: General government	19,003	41,136	54,666	71,646	63,701	78,266
Private sector guaranteed by public sector	506	240	273	303	260	304
Private sector not guaranteed	32,617	48,740	51,655	59,732	62,111	64,907
Short-term external debt	21,286	29,075	29,791	36,630	36,754	34,419
Disbursements (long-term)	**4,379**	**14,509**	**17,410**	**30,812**	**21,536**	**15,415**
Public and publicly guaranteed sector	2,209	1,830	10,422	15,873	6,198	12,584
Public sector	2,209	1,830	10,422	15,873	6,198	12,584
of which: General government	2,209	1,193	9,897	12,750	4,484	11,336
Private sector guaranteed by public sector	..	..	..	..	..	..
Private sector not guaranteed	2,170	12,679	6,988	14,939	15,338	2,831
Principal repayments (long-term)	**2,773**	**15,372**	**8,043**	**8,627**	**21,945**	**10,312**
Public and publicly guaranteed sector	2,065	12,906	1,978	1,750	10,437	764
Public sector	2,065	12,906	1,978	1,750	10,437	760
of which: General government	433	12,847	1,919	1,610	10,265	590
Private sector guaranteed by public sector	..	..	..	..	..	4
Private sector not guaranteed	708	2,465	6,065	6,877	11,509	9,548
Interest payments (long-term)	**1,766**	**5,323**	**5,376**	**5,252**	**6,230**	**5,601**
Public and publicly guaranteed sector	1,114	2,661	2,696	2,752	3,752	3,405
Public sector	1,064	2,628	2,667	2,720	3,720	3,376
of which: General government	965	2,424	2,446	2,452	3,400	2,877
Private sector guaranteed by public sector	50	33	28	31	32	30
Private sector not guaranteed	652	2,661	2,680	2,500	2,478	2,196
Summary external debt stock by creditor type						
Long-term external debt stocks	**55,818**	**92,805**	**110,068**	**138,411**	**133,758**	**151,214**
Public and publicly guaranteed debt from:	23,201	44,065	58,413	78,678	71,647	86,307
Official creditors	227	3,783	4,602	7,999	8,298	7,783
Multilateral	227	3,495	4,175	5,466	4,794	4,631
of which: World Bank	21	1,785	2,343	2,686	2,277	2,239
Bilateral	0	288	426	2,534	3,504	3,153
Private creditors	22,974	40,282	53,811	70,679	63,349	78,523
Bondholders	17,097	28,807	40,271	55,713	46,626	55,075
Commercial banks and others	5,876	11,474	13,540	14,966	16,723	23,448
Private nonguaranteed debt from:	32,617	48,740	51,655	59,732	62,111	64,907
Bondholders	8,485	10,309	9,878	10,116	11,187	11,634
Commercial banks and others	24,132	38,431	41,776	49,616	50,923	53,273
Use of IMF credit	2,799	2,474	2,400	2,543	2,483	2,469
Net financial inflows						
Net debt inflows						
Use of IMF credit	..	..	..	..	..	..
Long-term	1,606	-863	9,368	22,186	-410	5,103
Official creditors	-6	617	463	2,986	980	999
Multilateral	-6	340	370	930	-69	-214
of which: World Bank	-5	357	324	230	-46	-90
Bilateral	..	277	92	2,055	1,048	1,214
Private creditors	1,611	-1,480	8,905	19,200	-1,389	4,104
Bondholders	1,809	-10,295	5,477	10,044	-5,928	6,732
Banks and others	-198	8,815	3,428	9,156	4,538	-2,628
Short-term	-4,176	1,033	716	6,839	124	-2,335
Net equity inflows						
Foreign direct investment	4,957	-596	364	-266	1,378	1,486
Portfolio equity	9,364	8,499	1,640	7,588	2,946	-4,289
Debt ratios						
External debt stocks to exports (%)	91	120	147	162	147	167
External debt stocks to GNI (%)	28	40	49	52	49	55
Debt service to exports (%)	6	21	15	13	25	15
Short-term to external debt stocks (%)	27	23	21	21	21	18
Multilateral to external debt stocks (%)	0	3	3	3	3	2
Reserves to external debt stocks (%)	44	33	30	26	27	26
Gross national income (GNI)	289,309	309,749	288,167	339,071	356,649	341,523

SRI LANKA
(US$ million, unless otherwise indicated)

	2009	2015	2016	2017	2018	2019
Summary external debt data by debtor type						
Total external debt stocks	19,504	43,925	46,661	50,766	52,909	56,095
Use of IMF credit	1,341	1,240	1,086	1,329	1,545	1,864
Long-term external debt	14,609	35,098	38,163	41,426	43,184	45,790
Public and publicly guaranteed sector	13,643	27,453	30,114	32,624	34,345	36,964
Public sector	13,643	27,453	30,114	32,624	34,345	36,964
of which: General government	13,548	24,820	27,441	30,847	33,776	36,633
Private sector guaranteed by public sector	..	..	..	..	..	..
Private sector not guaranteed	967	7,645	8,049	8,802	8,839	8,826
Short-term external debt	3,554	7,588	7,413	8,011	8,181	8,442
Disbursements (long-term)	2,214	4,507	4,606	5,338	7,245	7,059
Public and publicly guaranteed sector	1,827	3,757	3,986	4,357	5,087	6,223
Public sector	1,827	3,757	3,986	4,357	5,087	6,223
of which: General government	1,826	3,677	3,806	4,247	5,006	6,172
Private sector guaranteed by public sector	..	..	..	..	..	..
Private sector not guaranteed	387	750	620	981	2,158	836
Principal repayments (long-term)	978	2,115	1,702	2,713	5,523	4,431
Public and publicly guaranteed sector	824	1,718	1,186	2,486	3,190	3,582
Public sector	824	1,718	1,186	2,486	3,190	3,582
of which: General government	816	1,421	1,048	1,477	1,902	3,294
Private sector guaranteed by public sector	..	..	..	..	..	..
Private sector not guaranteed	154	397	516	227	2,333	849
Interest payments (long-term)	325	778	990	1,030	1,546	1,542
Public and publicly guaranteed sector	285	730	924	970	1,247	1,383
Public sector	285	730	924	970	1,247	1,383
of which: General government	285	644	786	852	1,153	1,365
Private sector guaranteed by public sector	..	..	..	..	..	..
Private sector not guaranteed	40	48	65	59	300	159
Summary external debt stock by creditor type						
Long-term external debt stocks	14,609	35,098	38,163	41,426	43,184	45,790
Public and publicly guaranteed debt from:	13,643	27,453	30,114	32,624	34,345	36,964
Official creditors	11,740	17,111	17,604	18,817	18,942	19,373
Multilateral	5,880	6,901	7,186	7,853	8,050	8,231
of which: World Bank	2,487	2,784	2,970	3,244	3,210	3,226
Bilateral	5,860	10,209	10,418	10,964	10,892	11,142
Private creditors	1,903	10,342	12,511	13,807	15,403	17,590
Bondholders	1,000	8,650	10,150	11,150	12,400	15,050
Commercial banks and others	903	1,692	2,361	2,657	3,003	2,540
Private nonguaranteed debt from:	967	7,645	8,049	8,802	8,839	8,826
Bondholders	0	305	362	362	262	175
Commercial banks and others	967	7,340	7,687	8,440	8,577	8,651
Use of IMF credit	1,341	1,240	1,086	1,329	1,545	1,864
Net financial inflows						
Net debt inflows						
Use of IMF credit	541	-506	-122	174	252	327
Long-term	1,236	2,392	2,904	2,625	1,723	2,628
Official creditors	614	555	623	644	279	445
Multilateral	267	273	452	340	333	216
of which: World Bank	91	60	270	118	34	33
Bilateral	348	282	171	304	-54	229
Private creditors	622	1,837	2,281	1,980	1,444	2,183
Bondholders	400	1,517	1,558	1,000	1,150	2,563
Banks and others	222	320	723	980	294	-380
Short-term	828	314	-234	490	166	251
Net equity inflows						
Foreign direct investment	173	439	710	532	463	384
Portfolio equity	-382	-60	24	359	-4	-15
Debt ratios						
External debt stocks to exports (%)	214	257	266	264	258	285
External debt stocks to GNI (%)	47	56	58	60	62	69
Debt service to exports (%)	16	21	19	22	36	32
Short-term to external debt stocks (%)	18	17	16	16	15	15
Multilateral to external debt stocks (%)	30	16	15	15	15	15
Reserves to external debt stocks (%)	24	15	11	14	12	12
Gross national income (GNI)	41,581	78,582	80,205	85,114	86,028	81,591

ST. LUCIA

(US$ million, unless otherwise indicated)

	2009	2015	2016	2017	2018	2019
Summary external debt data by debtor type						
Total external debt stocks	433.1	530.2	542.2	622.1	615.8	639.0
Use of IMF credit	33.6	33.4	29.8	28.5	24.8	21.7
Long-term external debt	314.9	420.0	430.9	489.8	499.8	542.3
Public and publicly guaranteed sector	314.9	420.0	430.9	489.8	499.8	542.3
Public sector	298.5	399.8	410.9	467.5	475.8	508.7
of which: General government	289.0	396.7	408.4	462.0	469.8	496.5
Private sector guaranteed by public sector	16.4	20.2	20.0	22.3	24.0	33.5
Private sector not guaranteed	..	..	..	..	..	..
Short-term external debt	84.6	76.8	81.5	103.8	91.1	75.0
Disbursements (long-term)	25.8	21.4	7.3	13.5	6.5	35.9
Public and publicly guaranteed sector	25.8	21.4	7.3	13.5	6.5	35.9
Public sector	24.3	21.4	7.3	13.5	6.5	35.9
of which: General government	24.3	21.3	7.3	10.0	5.6	29.1
Private sector guaranteed by public sector	1.5	0.0	0.0	0.0	0.0	0.0
Private sector not guaranteed	..	..	..	..	..	..
Principal repayments (long-term)	27.8	46.7	23.8	18.0	17.8	18.5
Public and publicly guaranteed sector	27.8	46.7	23.8	18.0	17.8	18.5
Public sector	25.9	44.5	21.7	16.6	16.5	17.2
of which: General government	23.5	43.9	21.1	16.0	16.0	16.7
Private sector guaranteed by public sector	1.9	2.2	2.1	1.4	1.3	1.3
Private sector not guaranteed	..	..	..	..	..	..
Interest payments (long-term)	13.4	18.9	19.9	23.5	25.0	26.2
Public and publicly guaranteed sector	13.4	18.9	19.9	23.5	25.0	26.2
Public sector	12.8	18.1	19.1	22.7	24.1	25.2
of which: General government	12.4	18.0	19.0	22.5	23.9	25.0
Private sector guaranteed by public sector	0.7	0.8	0.8	0.8	0.9	1.0
Private sector not guaranteed	..	..	..	..	..	..
Summary external debt stock by creditor type						
Long-term external debt stocks	314.9	420.0	430.9	489.8	499.8	542.3
Public and publicly guaranteed debt from:	314.9	420.0	430.9	489.8	499.8	542.3
Official creditors	239.8	259.8	248.0	253.2	242.9	270.7
Multilateral	215.7	219.7	211.0	218.4	211.5	222.8
of which: World Bank	69.2	81.3	79.5	85.6	85.6	86.6
Bilateral	24.1	40.2	37.0	34.7	31.3	48.0
Private creditors	75.1	160.2	182.9	236.6	256.9	271.5
Bondholders	75.1	160.2	182.9	236.6	256.9	271.5
Commercial banks and others	..	..	..	..	..	..
Private nonguaranteed debt from:	..	..	..	..	..	..
Bondholders	..	..	..	..	..	..
Commercial banks and others	..	..	..	..	..	..
Use of IMF credit	33.6	33.4	29.8	28.5	24.8	21.7
Net financial inflows						
Net debt inflows						
Use of IMF credit	10.6	-3.0	-2.7	-3.0	-3.0	-3.0
Long-term	-2.0	-25.3	-16.5	-4.4	-11.3	17.4
Official creditors	6.5	0.9	-11.1	-3.8	-11.1	17.6
Multilateral	9.9	-6.3	-8.1	-0.8	-7.9	0.9
of which: World Bank	1.5	0.0	0.4	1.7	2.0	1.4
Bilateral	-3.4	7.2	-3.0	-3.0	-3.2	16.7
Private creditors	-8.5	-26.1	-5.4	-0.6	-0.2	-0.2
Bondholders	-8.5	-26.1	-5.4	-0.6	-0.2	-0.2
Banks and others	..	..	..	..	..	..
Short-term	-432.0	-40.9	4.8	22.3	-12.7	-16.1
Net equity inflows						
Foreign direct investment	72.6	142.7	149.1	49.0	44.7	30.6
Portfolio equity	..	0.6	0.5	0.5	3.3	..
Debt ratios						
External debt stocks to exports (%)	77.3	50.9	55.5	55.7	49.1	..
External debt stocks to GNI (%)	31.9	32.1	31.0	32.9	31.7	32.0
Debt service to exports (%)	7.6	6.7	4.9	4.2	3.9	..
Short-term to external debt stocks (%)	19.5	14.5	15.0	16.7	14.8	11.7
Multilateral to external debt stocks (%)	49.8	41.4	38.9	35.1	34.4	34.9
Reserves to external debt stocks (%)	40.4	59.9	56.4	51.7	46.4	40.8
Gross national income (GNI)	1,356.3	1,653.7	1,750.1	1,891.3	1,942.0	1,997.2

ST. VINCENT AND THE GRENADINES
(US$ million, unless otherwise indicated)

	2009	2015	2016	2017	2018	2019
Summary external debt data by debtor type						
Total external debt stocks	**246.0**	**343.9**	**333.5**	**337.1**	**326.3**	**356.6**
Use of IMF credit	18.3	24.9	22.9	21.9	18.0	15.4
Long-term external debt	227.3	318.9	306.5	314.9	308.3	341.2
Public and publicly guaranteed sector	227.3	318.9	306.5	314.9	308.3	341.2
Public sector	227.3	318.9	306.5	314.9	308.3	341.2
of which: General government	207.9	310.2	299.3	308.3	301.9	335.7
Private sector guaranteed by public sector	..	..	..	..	..	..
Private sector not guaranteed	..	..	..	..	..	..
Short-term external debt	0.5	0.1	4.1	0.3	0.0	0.0
Disbursements (long-term)	**20.2**	**28.9**	**13.3**	**31.0**	**23.3**	**59.0**
Public and publicly guaranteed sector	20.2	28.9	13.3	31.0	23.3	59.0
Public sector	20.2	28.9	13.3	31.0	23.3	59.0
of which: General government	17.9	28.8	12.7	29.7	20.9	57.5
Private sector guaranteed by public sector	..	..	..	..	..	..
Private sector not guaranteed	..	..	..	..	..	..
Principal repayments (long-term)	**24.9**	**24.8**	**24.6**	**24.7**	**29.0**	**25.9**
Public and publicly guaranteed sector	24.9	24.8	24.6	24.7	29.0	25.9
Public sector	24.9	24.8	24.6	24.7	29.0	25.9
of which: General government	22.8	22.9	22.7	22.7	26.5	23.6
Private sector guaranteed by public sector	..	..	..	..	..	..
Private sector not guaranteed	..	..	..	..	..	..
Interest payments (long-term)	**11.2**	**7.7**	**6.0**	**6.2**	**7.1**	**8.2**
Public and publicly guaranteed sector	11.2	7.7	6.0	6.2	7.1	8.2
Public sector	11.2	7.7	6.0	6.2	7.1	8.2
of which: General government	10.1	7.2	5.7	6.0	6.7	8.0
Private sector guaranteed by public sector	..	..	..	..	..	..
Private sector not guaranteed	..	..	..	..	..	..
Summary external debt stock by creditor type						
Long-term external debt stocks	**227.3**	**318.9**	**306.5**	**314.9**	**308.3**	**341.2**
Public and publicly guaranteed debt from:	227.3	318.9	306.5	314.9	308.3	341.2
Official creditors	167.4	308.2	299.2	300.6	297.9	333.3
Multilateral	145.1	265.7	258.6	252.1	244.1	276.2
of which: World Bank	23.7	32.0	31.5	32.7	31.8	69.1
Bilateral	22.4	42.5	40.6	48.5	53.8	57.2
Private creditors	59.8	10.7	7.3	14.3	10.5	7.9
Bondholders	..	..	..	10.4	9.1	7.9
Commercial banks and others	59.8	10.7	7.3	3.9	1.3	0.0
Private nonguaranteed debt from:	..	..	..	..	..	..
Bondholders	..	..	..	..	..	..
Commercial banks and others	..	..	..	..	..	..
Use of IMF credit	18.3	24.9	22.9	21.9	18.0	15.4
Net financial inflows						
Net debt inflows						
Use of IMF credit	5.8	-1.0	-1.3	-2.3	-3.5	-2.5
Long-term	-4.6	4.1	-11.3	6.3	-5.7	33.1
Official creditors	6.1	10.5	-8.0	-0.7	-1.9	35.7
Multilateral	9.3	2.8	-6.1	-8.3	-7.2	32.3
of which: World Bank	1.3	0.2	0.5	-0.5	-0.2	37.5
Bilateral	-3.2	7.7	-1.8	7.7	5.3	3.4
Private creditors	-10.7	-6.4	-3.4	7.0	-3.8	-2.6
Bondholders	..	..	..	10.4	-1.2	-1.2
Banks and others	-10.7	-6.4	-3.4	-3.4	-2.6	-1.3
Short-term	0.0	0.0	0.0	0.0	0.0	0.0
Net equity inflows						
Foreign direct investment	60.2	114.4	95.8	143.8	100.3	113.1
Portfolio equity	..	-0.4	-0.8	-0.1	-0.1	..
Debt ratios						
External debt stocks to exports (%)	119.4	118.7	109.5	112.0	101.0	..
External debt stocks to GNI (%)	37.2	46.7	43.4	42.9	40.6	43.6
Debt service to exports (%)	17.6	11.6	10.5	11.1	12.3	..
Short-term to external debt stocks (%)	0.2	0.0	1.2	0.1	0.0	0.0
Multilateral to external debt stocks (%)	59.0	77.3	77.5	74.8	74.8	77.4
Reserves to external debt stocks (%)	35.7	48.3	57.6	54.0	52.0	54.2
Gross national income (GNI)	661.9	737.2	769.2	786.5	803.1	818.8

SUDAN

(US$ million, unless otherwise indicated)

	2009	2015	2016	2017	2018	2019
Summary external debt data by debtor type						
Total external debt stocks	**21,113**	**21,401**	**21,092**	**21,701**	**21,529**	**22,264**
Use of IMF credit	682	557	531	555	542	528
Long-term external debt	13,752	15,772	15,506	15,806	15,579	16,309
Public and publicly guaranteed sector	13,752	15,772	15,506	15,806	15,579	16,309
Public sector	13,752	15,772	15,506	15,806	15,579	16,309
of which: General government	13,719	15,752	15,485	15,785	15,558	16,289
Private sector guaranteed by public sector	..	..	..	..	..	..
Private sector not guaranteed	..	..	..	..	..	..
Short-term external debt	6,679	5,072	5,055	5,340	5,408	5,427
Disbursements (long-term)	**972**	**541**	**134**	**89**	**62**	**853**
Public and publicly guaranteed sector	972	541	134	89	62	853
Public sector	972	541	134	89	62	853
of which: General government	959	541	134	89	62	853
Private sector guaranteed by public sector	..	..	..	..	..	..
Private sector not guaranteed	..	..	..	..	..	..
Principal repayments (long-term)	**366**	**414**	**224**	**139**	**159**	**139**
Public and publicly guaranteed sector	366	414	224	139	159	139
Public sector	366	414	224	139	159	139
of which: General government	366	414	224	139	159	139
Private sector guaranteed by public sector	..	..	..	..	..	..
Private sector not guaranteed	..	..	..	..	..	..
Interest payments (long-term)	**113**	**100**	**59**	**86**	**50**	**39**
Public and publicly guaranteed sector	113	100	59	86	50	39
Public sector	113	100	59	86	50	39
of which: General government	113	100	59	86	50	39
Private sector guaranteed by public sector	..	..	..	..	..	..
Private sector not guaranteed	..	..	..	..	..	..
Summary external debt stock by creditor type						
Long-term external debt stocks	**13,752**	**15,772**	**15,506**	**15,806**	**15,579**	**16,309**
Public and publicly guaranteed debt from:	13,752	15,772	15,506	15,806	15,579	16,309
Official creditors	11,287	11,190	10,969	11,190	10,982	11,679
Multilateral	3,365	3,351	3,338	3,455	3,411	3,672
of which: World Bank	1,306	1,203	1,180	1,225	1,206	1,201
Bilateral	7,922	7,839	7,631	7,734	7,571	8,007
Private creditors	2,465	4,583	4,537	4,616	4,597	4,630
Bondholders	..	..	..	..	..	..
Commercial banks and others	2,465	4,583	4,537	4,616	4,597	4,630
Private nonguaranteed debt from:	..	..	..	..	..	..
Bondholders	..	..	..	..	..	..
Commercial banks and others	..	..	..	..	..	..
Use of IMF credit	682	557	531	555	542	528
Net financial inflows						
Net debt inflows						
Use of IMF credit	-11	-8	-10	-7	..	-11
Long-term	605	127	-90	-50	-96	714
Official creditors	605	127	-90	-50	-96	714
Multilateral	51	-21	39	2	1	268
of which: World Bank	0	0	0	0	0	..
Bilateral	554	147	-128	-52	-98	445
Private creditors	..	..	..	0	0	0
Bondholders	..	..	..	..	..	..
Banks and others	..	..	..	0	0	0
Short-term	-332	-43	-21	60	51	-78
Net equity inflows						
Foreign direct investment	-846	1,728	1,064	1,065	1,136	825
Portfolio equity	0	..	..	..	..	..
Debt ratios						
External debt stocks to exports (%)	245	436	455	369	420	560
External debt stocks to GNI (%)	46	29	41	50	89	122
Debt service to exports (%)	6	11	6	4	4	5
Short-term to external debt stocks (%)	32	24	24	25	25	24
Multilateral to external debt stocks (%)	16	16	16	16	16	16
Reserves to external debt stocks (%)	5	1	1	1	..	..
Gross national income (GNI)	45,862	73,131	50,906	43,728	24,193	18,286

SYRIAN ARAB REPUBLIC

(US$ million, unless otherwise indicated)

	2009	2015	2016	2017	2018	2019
Summary external debt data by debtor type						
Total external debt stocks	5,689	4,419	4,368	4,604	4,584	4,590
Use of IMF credit	438	387	375	398	388	386
Long-term external debt	4,491	3,528	3,497	3,654	3,647	3,635
Public and publicly guaranteed sector	4,491	3,528	3,497	3,654	3,647	3,635
Public sector	4,491	3,528	3,497	3,654	3,647	3,635
of which: General government	3,861	3,035	3,013	3,144	3,150	3,142
Private sector guaranteed by public sector	..	..	..	..	..	..
Private sector not guaranteed	..	..	..	..	..	..
Short-term external debt	760	504	495	553	548	569
Disbursements (long-term)	281	0	0	0	60	0
Public and publicly guaranteed sector	281	0	0	0	60	0
Public sector	281	0	0	0	60	0
of which: General government	255	0	0	0	60	0
Private sector guaranteed by public sector	..	..	..	..	..	..
Private sector not guaranteed	..	..	..	..	..	..
Principal repayments (long-term)	499	0	0	0	19	1
Public and publicly guaranteed sector	499	0	0	0	19	1
Public sector	499	0	0	0	19	1
of which: General government	446	0	0	0	17	..
Private sector guaranteed by public sector	..	..	..	..	..	..
Private sector not guaranteed	..	..	..	..	..	..
Interest payments (long-term)	119	0	0	0	1	0
Public and publicly guaranteed sector	119	0	0	0	1	0
Public sector	119	0	0	0	1	0
of which: General government	99	0	0	0	1	..
Private sector guaranteed by public sector	..	..	..	..	..	..
Private sector not guaranteed	..	..	..	..	..	..
Summary external debt stock by creditor type						
Long-term external debt stocks	4,491	3,528	3,497	3,654	3,647	3,635
Public and publicly guaranteed debt from:	4,491	3,528	3,497	3,654	3,647	3,635
Official creditors	4,464	3,510	3,479	3,635	3,630	3,619
Multilateral	1,660	1,434	1,403	1,512	1,472	1,459
of which: World Bank	16	14	14	14	14	14
Bilateral	2,803	2,076	2,076	2,123	2,158	2,160
Private creditors	27	18	18	19	17	16
Bondholders	..	..	..	..	..	..
Commercial banks and others	27	18	18	19	17	16
Private nonguaranteed debt from:	..	..	..	..	..	..
Bondholders	..	..	..	..	..	..
Commercial banks and others	..	..	..	..	..	..
Use of IMF credit	438	387	375	398	388	386
Net financial inflows						
Net debt inflows						
Use of IMF credit	..	..	..	..	..	..
Long-term	-219	0	0	0	41	-1
Official creditors	-216	0	0	0	43	0
Multilateral	106	0	0	0	1	0
of which: World Bank	-1	0	0	0	0	..
Bilateral	-322	0	0	0	41	0
Private creditors	-2	0	0	0	-2	-1
Bondholders	..	..	..	..	..	..
Banks and others	-2	0	0	0	-2	-1
Short-term	114	-46	-25	0	1	-1
Net equity inflows						
Foreign direct investment	2,570	..	..	..	..	..
Portfolio equity	0	..	..	..	..	..
Debt ratios						
External debt stocks to exports (%)	35	..	..	..	..	..
External debt stocks to GNI (%)	..	..	..	..	..	..
Debt service to exports (%)	4	..	..	..	..	..
Short-term to external debt stocks (%)	13	11	11	12	12	12
Multilateral to external debt stocks (%)	29	32	32	33	32	32
Reserves to external debt stocks (%)	306	..	..	..	..	..
Gross national income (GNI)	..	..	..	..	..	..

133

TAJIKISTAN
(US$ million, unless otherwise indicated)

	2009	2015	2016	2017	2018	2019
Summary external debt data by debtor type						
Total external debt stocks	2,666	5,144	5,181	6,029	5,975	6,631
Use of IMF credit	170	244	217	204	170	144
Long-term external debt	2,422	3,940	4,150	5,079	4,923	5,128
Public and publicly guaranteed sector	1,606	2,093	2,169	2,825	2,848	2,830
Public sector	1,606	2,093	2,169	2,825	2,848	2,830
of which: General government	1,592	2,089	2,164	2,821	2,842	2,824
Private sector guaranteed by public sector	..	..	..	..	..	..
Private sector not guaranteed	816	1,847	1,981	2,254	2,076	2,298
Short-term external debt	74	961	814	745	881	1,359
Disbursements (long-term)	514	645	730	979	538	260
Public and publicly guaranteed sector	207	252	225	708	184	122
Public sector	207	252	225	708	184	122
of which: General government	204	251	223	708	182	121
Private sector guaranteed by public sector	..	..	..	..	..	..
Private sector not guaranteed	307	392	505	271	354	139
Principal repayments (long-term)	409	197	487	603	401	383
Public and publicly guaranteed sector	35	96	113	112	128	129
Public sector	35	96	113	112	128	129
of which: General government	33	95	111	112	127	129
Private sector guaranteed by public sector	..	..	..	..	..	..
Private sector not guaranteed	374	101	374	490	273	254
Interest payments (long-term)	41	89	108	60	120	108
Public and publicly guaranteed sector	24	30	35	38	72	75
Public sector	24	30	35	38	72	75
of which: General government	24	30	35	37	72	75
Private sector guaranteed by public sector	..	..	..	..	..	..
Private sector not guaranteed	17	59	73	23	48	33
Summary external debt stock by creditor type						
Long-term external debt stocks	2,422	3,940	4,150	5,079	4,923	5,128
Public and publicly guaranteed debt from:	1,606	2,093	2,169	2,825	2,848	2,830
Official creditors	1,599	2,070	2,147	2,301	2,325	2,308
Multilateral	827	909	881	969	1,015	1,038
of which: World Bank	373	316	305	326	333	342
Bilateral	772	1,161	1,267	1,332	1,309	1,269
Private creditors	7	22	21	524	523	522
Bondholders	..	..	..	500	500	500
Commercial banks and others	7	22	21	24	23	22
Private nonguaranteed debt from:	816	1,847	1,981	2,254	2,076	2,298
Bondholders	..	..	..	..	..	..
Commercial banks and others	816	1,847	1,981	2,254	2,076	2,298
Use of IMF credit	170	244	217	204	170	144
Net financial inflows						
Net debt inflows						
Use of IMF credit	25	-11	-20	-25	-30	-25
Long-term	104	448	243	376	137	-123
Official creditors	168	154	112	96	56	-7
Multilateral	84	10	-6	46	65	27
of which: World Bank	5	-7	-1	3	15	10
Bilateral	84	144	119	49	-9	-35
Private creditors	-63	294	130	281	81	-115
Bondholders	..	..	..	500	0	0
Banks and others	-63	294	130	-219	81	-115
Short-term	-16	-204	-147	-69	136	478
Net equity inflows						
Foreign direct investment	41	201	108	68	142	104
Portfolio equity	0	0	0	0	0	-73
Debt ratios						
External debt stocks to exports (%)	160	201	230	223	225	230
External debt stocks to GNI (%)	45	55	64	72	68	70
Debt service to exports (%)	28	12	28	26	22	19
Short-term to external debt stocks (%)	3	19	16	12	15	20
Multilateral to external debt stocks (%)	31	18	17	16	17	16
Reserves to external debt stocks (%)	7	1	2	11	6	8
Gross national income (GNI)	5,953	9,381	8,117	8,373	8,749	9,447

TANZANIA

(US$ million, unless otherwise indicated)

	2009	2015	2016	2017	2018	2019
Summary external debt data by debtor type						
Total external debt stocks	**7,685**	**15,412**	**16,360**	**18,272**	**18,481**	**19,598**
Use of IMF credit	628	592	515	459	364	301
Long-term external debt	5,656	12,961	13,809	15,765	16,317	17,484
Public and publicly guaranteed sector	4,640	10,765	11,135	12,670	12,854	14,115
Public sector	4,640	10,765	11,135	12,670	12,854	14,115
of which: General government	4,571	10,731	11,102	12,614	12,777	14,017
Private sector guaranteed by public sector	0	..	..	..	..	..
Private sector not guaranteed	1,016	2,197	2,674	3,095	3,463	3,369
Short-term external debt	1,402	1,859	2,037	2,049	1,800	1,814
Disbursements (long-term)	**1,065**	**1,586**	**1,366**	**2,156**	**1,533**	**2,391**
Public and publicly guaranteed sector	919	1,170	890	1,638	1,065	2,025
Public sector	919	1,170	890	1,638	1,065	2,025
of which: General government	889	1,170	890	1,616	1,044	2,004
Private sector guaranteed by public sector	0	..	..	..	..	..
Private sector not guaranteed	146	416	476	519	468	365
Principal repayments (long-term)	**106**	**172**	**426**	**422**	**768**	**1,176**
Public and publicly guaranteed sector	27	93	288	324	668	716
Public sector	27	93	288	324	668	716
of which: General government	20	93	288	324	668	716
Private sector guaranteed by public sector	0	..	..	..	..	..
Private sector not guaranteed	79	78	138	98	100	460
Interest payments (long-term)	**45**	**111**	**183**	**182**	**217**	**200**
Public and publicly guaranteed sector	27	101	167	167	202	185
Public sector	27	101	167	167	202	185
of which: General government	24	101	167	167	202	185
Private sector guaranteed by public sector	0	..	..	..	..	..
Private sector not guaranteed	18	10	16	15	16	15
Summary external debt stock by creditor type						
Long-term external debt stocks	**5,656**	**12,961**	**13,809**	**15,765**	**16,317**	**17,484**
Public and publicly guaranteed debt from:	4,640	10,765	11,135	12,670	12,854	14,115
Official creditors	4,520	9,469	10,023	11,246	11,857	12,560
Multilateral	3,573	7,490	7,795	8,930	9,432	10,121
of which: World Bank	2,598	5,399	5,621	6,467	6,815	7,341
Bilateral	947	1,979	2,228	2,316	2,425	2,439
Private creditors	119	1,295	1,111	1,424	997	1,555
Bondholders	..	..	..	..	..	..
Commercial banks and others	119	1,295	1,111	1,424	997	1,555
Private nonguaranteed debt from:	1,016	2,197	2,674	3,095	3,463	3,369
Bondholders	..	..	..	..	..	..
Commercial banks and others	1,016	2,197	2,674	3,095	3,463	3,369
Use of IMF credit	628	592	515	459	364	301
Net financial inflows						
Net debt inflows						
Use of IMF credit	307	-61	-62	-84	-85	-61
Long-term	959	1,414	939	1,734	765	1,215
Official creditors	875	1,114	781	1,017	818	748
Multilateral	871	832	514	747	697	735
of which: World Bank	608	581	398	519	517	568
Bilateral	4	282	267	271	122	14
Private creditors	84	301	159	717	-54	466
Bondholders	..	..	..	..	..	..
Banks and others	84	301	159	717	-54	466
Short-term	-15	-211	193	-17	-237	17
Net equity inflows						
Foreign direct investment	664	347	631	856	822	1,112
Portfolio equity	3	4	4	1	4	..
Debt ratios						
External debt stocks to exports (%)	145	174	189	215	216	199
External debt stocks to GNI (%)	27	33	34	35	33	32
Debt service to exports (%)	3	4	8	8	13	15
Short-term to external debt stocks (%)	18	12	12	11	10	9
Multilateral to external debt stocks (%)	46	49	48	49	51	52
Reserves to external debt stocks (%)	45	26	27	32	27	..
Gross national income (GNI)	28,784	46,478	48,664	52,107	56,211	61,578

135

THAILAND
(US$ million, unless otherwise indicated)

	2009	2015	2016	2017	2018	2019
Summary external debt data by debtor type						
Total external debt stocks	**80,824**	**132,209**	**139,244**	**161,654**	**172,498**	**180,230**
Use of IMF credit	1,521	1,345	1,304	1,382	1,349	1,342
Long-term external debt	46,019	78,289	83,477	91,551	107,763	118,939
Public and publicly guaranteed sector	10,668	22,420	23,192	29,544	35,901	39,497
Public sector	10,668	22,420	23,192	29,544	35,901	39,497
of which: General government	5,567	19,415	20,363	26,552	32,831	36,480
Private sector guaranteed by public sector	..	..	..	..	..	..
Private sector not guaranteed	35,351	55,869	60,285	62,007	71,862	79,442
Short-term external debt	33,284	52,576	54,462	68,721	63,385	59,949
Disbursements (long-term)	**12,989**	**13,723**	**16,799**	**21,092**	**40,537**	**27,924**
Public and publicly guaranteed sector	1,716	184	1,133	6,600	7,189	3,876
Public sector	1,716	184	1,133	6,600	7,189	3,876
of which: General government	1,578	143	1,113	6,324	6,886	3,874
Private sector guaranteed by public sector	..	..	..	..	..	..
Private sector not guaranteed	11,273	13,539	15,666	14,492	33,348	24,049
Principal repayments (long-term)	**11,313**	**17,304**	**12,332**	**13,452**	**16,891**	**24,660**
Public and publicly guaranteed sector	830	1,154	482	396	913	673
Public sector	830	1,154	482	396	913	673
of which: General government	370	769	196	194	645	251
Private sector guaranteed by public sector	..	..	..	..	..	..
Private sector not guaranteed	10,483	16,149	11,850	13,056	15,979	23,986
Interest payments (long-term)	**1,086**	**786**	**1,531**	**819**	**1,163**	**1,606**
Public and publicly guaranteed sector	201	235	309	390	695	1,025
Public sector	201	235	309	390	695	1,025
of which: General government	79	176	250	340	638	951
Private sector guaranteed by public sector	..	..	..	..	..	..
Private sector not guaranteed	885	551	1,221	429	467	581
Summary external debt stock by creditor type						
Long-term external debt stocks	**46,019**	**78,289**	**83,477**	**91,551**	**107,763**	**118,939**
Public and publicly guaranteed debt from:	10,668	22,420	23,192	29,544	35,901	39,497
Official creditors	6,509	5,392	5,483	5,592	5,094	4,711
Multilateral	208	1,344	1,304	1,261	1,313	1,191
of which: World Bank	133	1,039	1,032	1,025	1,018	927
Bilateral	6,301	4,048	4,179	4,331	3,781	3,521
Private creditors	4,158	17,028	17,709	23,952	30,807	34,786
Bondholders	3,074	17,000	17,685	23,929	30,783	34,762
Commercial banks and others	1,085	28	24	23	23	23
Private nonguaranteed debt from:	35,351	55,869	60,285	62,007	71,862	79,442
Bondholders	5,125	8,888	9,188	10,043	12,723	13,193
Commercial banks and others	30,226	46,981	51,097	51,964	59,139	66,249
Use of IMF credit	1,521	1,345	1,304	1,382	1,349	1,342
Net financial inflows						
Net debt inflows						
Use of IMF credit	..	..	..	..	..	..
Long-term	1,676	-3,581	4,467	7,640	23,646	3,265
Official creditors	-393	-160	-31	-39	-579	-442
Multilateral	-56	-20	-40	-43	52	-122
of which: World Bank	6	-7	-7	-7	-7	-90
Bilateral	-337	-140	9	4	-630	-319
Private creditors	2,069	-3,421	4,498	7,679	24,224	3,707
Bondholders	827	-1,956	985	7,099	9,538	4,114
Banks and others	1,242	-1,465	3,513	580	14,686	-407
Short-term	12,825	-3,472	1,886	14,259	-5,337	-3,436
Net equity inflows						
Foreign direct investment	7,136	9,874	4,327	9,059	13,333	6,826
Portfolio equity	9,548	-8,969	-786	598	-7,101	56
Debt ratios						
External debt stocks to exports (%)	43	48	49	52	51	53
External debt stocks to GNI (%)	30	35	35	37	36	34
Debt service to exports (%)	7	7	5	5	6	8
Short-term to external debt stocks (%)	41	40	39	43	37	33
Multilateral to external debt stocks (%)	0	1	1	1	1	1
Reserves to external debt stocks (%)	168	114	119	121	116	120
Gross national income (GNI)	271,839	380,595	394,013	435,851	482,006	523,598

TIMOR-LESTE
(US$ million, unless otherwise indicated)

	2009	2015	2016	2017	2018	2019
Summary external debt data by debtor type						
Total external debt stocks	..	116.7	80.9	124.5	158.1	203.4
Use of IMF credit	..	10.7	10.4	11.0	10.7	10.7
Long-term external debt	..	45.7	70.5	110.5	144.7	191.2
Public and publicly guaranteed sector	..	45.7	70.5	110.5	144.7	191.2
Public sector	..	45.7	70.5	110.5	144.7	191.2
of which: General government	..	45.7	70.5	110.5	144.7	191.2
Private sector guaranteed by public sector	..	..	..	..	..	..
Private sector not guaranteed	..	..	..	..	..	..
Short-term external debt	..	60.3	0.0	3.0	2.6	1.5
Disbursements (long-term)	..	24.0	25.1	35.7	40.0	49.7
Public and publicly guaranteed sector	..	24.0	25.1	35.7	40.0	49.7
Public sector	..	24.0	25.1	35.7	40.0	49.7
of which: General government	..	24.0	25.1	35.7	40.0	49.7
Private sector guaranteed by public sector	..	..	..	..	..	..
Private sector not guaranteed	..	..	..	..	..	..
Principal repayments (long-term)	..	0.0	0.0	0.3	0.7	3.3
Public and publicly guaranteed sector	..	0.0	0.0	0.3	0.7	3.3
Public sector	..	0.0	0.0	0.3	0.7	3.3
of which: General government	..	0.0	0.0	0.3	0.7	3.3
Private sector guaranteed by public sector	..	..	..	..	..	..
Private sector not guaranteed	..	..	..	..	..	..
Interest payments (long-term)	..	0.3	0.8	1.5	2.5	3.8
Public and publicly guaranteed sector	..	0.3	0.8	1.5	2.5	3.8
Public sector	..	0.3	0.8	1.5	2.5	3.8
of which: General government	..	0.3	0.8	1.5	2.5	3.8
Private sector guaranteed by public sector	..	..	..	..	..	..
Private sector not guaranteed	..	..	..	..	..	..
Summary external debt stock by creditor type						
Long-term external debt stocks	..	45.7	70.5	110.5	144.7	191.2
Public and publicly guaranteed debt from:	..	45.7	70.5	110.5	144.7	191.2
Official creditors	..	45.7	70.5	110.5	144.7	191.2
Multilateral	..	43.4	68.1	101.4	131.5	166.3
of which: World Bank	..	10.0	15.6	27.0	33.5	43.2
Bilateral	..	2.3	2.4	9.1	13.2	24.9
Private creditors	..	..	..	..	..	..
Bondholders	..	..	..	..	..	..
Commercial banks and others	..	..	..	..	..	..
Private nonguaranteed debt from:	..	..	..	..	..	..
Bondholders	..	..	..	..	..	..
Commercial banks and others	..	..	..	..	..	..
Use of IMF credit	..	10.7	10.4	11.0	10.7	10.7
Net financial inflows						
Net debt inflows						
Use of IMF credit	..	..	..	..	..	..
Long-term	..	24.0	25.1	35.5	39.3	46.4
Official creditors	..	24.0	25.1	35.5	39.3	46.4
Multilateral	..	24.0	25.1	28.7	35.4	34.9
of which: World Bank	..	7.1	5.6	11.4	7.5	9.7
Bilateral	..	..	..	6.7	3.9	11.5
Private creditors	..	..	..	..	..	..
Bondholders	..	..	..	..	..	..
Banks and others	..	..	..	..	..	..
Short-term	..	-11.0	-60.3	3.0	-0.4	-1.1
Net equity inflows						
Foreign direct investment	49.9	43.0	5.5	6.7	47.9	74.6
Portfolio equity	0.0	..	..	0.0	0.0	0.0
Debt ratios						
External debt stocks to exports (%)	..	8.3	12.3	14.2	15.7	15.5
External debt stocks to GNI (%)	..	4.2	3.6	5.5	7.0	8.4
Debt service to exports (%)	..	0.1	0.1	0.2	0.3	0.5
Short-term to external debt stocks (%)	0.0	51.7	0.0	2.4	1.6	0.7
Multilateral to external debt stocks (%)	0.0	37.2	84.2	81.4	83.2	81.8
Reserves to external debt stocks (%)	..	375.0	347.3	437.2	426.4	322.6
Gross national income (GNI)	2,523.5	2,794.8	2,236.0	2,282.4	2,248.6	2,432.0

137

TOGO
(US$ million, unless otherwise indicated)

	2009	2015	2016	2017	2018	2019
Summary external debt data by debtor type						
Total external debt stocks	**1,727.2**	**1,109.3**	**1,230.0**	**1,685.6**	**1,739.5**	**1,993.3**
Use of IMF credit	201.2	200.6	171.3	226.0	266.0	318.9
Long-term external debt	1,479.0	844.8	1,000.0	1,191.1	1,194.6	1,349.6
Public and publicly guaranteed sector	1,479.0	844.8	1,000.0	1,191.1	1,194.6	1,349.6
Public sector	1,479.0	844.8	1,000.0	1,191.1	1,194.6	1,349.6
of which: General government	1,453.9	840.0	995.9	1,187.1	1,190.9	1,346.2
Private sector guaranteed by public sector	..	..	..	..	..	..
Private sector not guaranteed	..	..	..	..	..	..
Short-term external debt	47.0	63.9	58.7	268.5	278.8	324.8
Disbursements (long-term)	**34.6**	**188.6**	**222.8**	**167.3**	**113.9**	**260.6**
Public and publicly guaranteed sector	34.6	188.6	222.8	167.3	113.9	260.6
Public sector	34.6	188.6	222.8	167.3	113.9	260.6
of which: General government	34.6	188.6	222.8	167.3	113.9	260.6
Private sector guaranteed by public sector	..	..	..	..	..	..
Private sector not guaranteed	..	..	..	..	..	..
Principal repayments (long-term)	**39.5**	**24.8**	**42.2**	**40.6**	**74.0**	**65.4**
Public and publicly guaranteed sector	39.5	24.8	42.2	40.6	74.0	65.4
Public sector	39.5	24.8	42.2	40.6	74.0	65.4
of which: General government	38.9	24.5	41.6	40.3	73.8	65.1
Private sector guaranteed by public sector	..	..	..	..	..	..
Private sector not guaranteed	..	..	..	..	..	..
Interest payments (long-term)	**13.1**	**19.4**	**23.5**	**19.9**	**26.6**	**25.2**
Public and publicly guaranteed sector	13.1	19.4	23.5	19.9	26.6	25.2
Public sector	13.1	19.4	23.5	19.9	26.6	25.2
of which: General government	12.9	19.3	23.5	19.8	26.6	25.2
Private sector guaranteed by public sector	..	..	..	..	..	..
Private sector not guaranteed	..	..	..	..	..	..
Summary external debt stock by creditor type						
Long-term external debt stocks	**1,479.0**	**844.8**	**1,000.0**	**1,191.1**	**1,194.6**	**1,349.6**
Public and publicly guaranteed debt from:	1,479.0	844.8	1,000.0	1,191.1	1,194.6	1,349.6
Official creditors	1,479.0	813.8	980.4	1,180.0	1,190.9	1,233.2
Multilateral	829.3	352.0	425.5	538.9	555.5	625.4
of which: World Bank	586.1	30.8	38.7	50.5	66.0	165.3
Bilateral	649.7	461.8	554.9	641.1	635.4	607.8
Private creditors	..	31.0	19.5	11.1	3.6	116.4
Bondholders	..	..	..	..	..	..
Commercial banks and others	..	31.0	19.5	11.1	3.6	116.4
Private nonguaranteed debt from:	..	..	..	..	..	..
Bondholders	..	..	..	..	..	..
Commercial banks and others	..	..	..	..	..	..
Use of IMF credit	201.2	200.6	171.3	226.0	266.0	318.9
Net financial inflows						
Net debt inflows						
Use of IMF credit	41.3	-16.2	-24.1	43.3	46.1	54.3
Long-term	-4.9	163.8	180.7	126.7	39.9	195.2
Official creditors	-4.9	162.2	191.6	137.2	47.2	82.7
Multilateral	-27.1	60.8	84.2	69.1	35.8	96.8
of which: World Bank	-21.8	4.2	9.2	9.1	17.3	99.6
Bilateral	22.2	101.4	107.5	68.1	11.4	-14.1
Private creditors	..	1.6	-11.0	-10.4	-7.2	112.5
Bondholders	..	..	..	..	..	..
Banks and others	..	1.6	-11.0	-10.4	-7.2	112.5
Short-term	-67.0	-25.5	-4.9	210.2	10.4	45.9
Net equity inflows						
Foreign direct investment	32.8	88.0	28.5	-87.0	-87.8	133.3
Portfolio equity	2.1	-0.2	-3.3	-89.2	-183.5	..
Debt ratios						
External debt stocks to exports (%)	136.0	59.7	66.3	90.9	89.0	..
External debt stocks to GNI (%)	51.6	25.7	27.1	34.9	32.4	36.4
Debt service to exports (%)	4.2	3.3	4.9	5.0	6.8	..
Short-term to external debt stocks (%)	2.7	5.8	4.8	15.9	16.0	16.3
Multilateral to external debt stocks (%)	48.0	31.7	34.6	32.0	31.9	31.4
Reserves to external debt stocks (%)	40.7	51.7	..	..	..	..
Gross national income (GNI)	3,346.7	4,321.5	4,530.6	4,824.9	5,375.8	5,480.7

TONGA

(US$ million, unless otherwise indicated)

	2009	2015	2016	2017	2018	2019
Summary external debt data by debtor type						
Total external debt stocks	**114.9**	**184.3**	**174.4**	**193.1**	**186.8**	**186.5**
Use of IMF credit	10.3	9.1	8.8	9.4	9.2	9.1
Long-term external debt	104.6	175.2	165.6	183.7	177.7	177.4
Public and publicly guaranteed sector	104.6	175.2	165.6	183.7	177.7	177.4
Public sector	104.6	175.2	165.6	183.7	177.7	177.4
of which: General government	104.6	175.2	165.6	183.7	177.7	177.4
Private sector guaranteed by public sector	..	..	..	..	..	..
Private sector not guaranteed	..	..	..	..	..	..
Short-term external debt	0.0	0.0	0.0	0.0	0.0	0.0
Disbursements (long-term)	**17.4**	**2.2**	**7.1**	**10.1**	**7.3**	**4.9**
Public and publicly guaranteed sector	17.4	2.2	7.1	10.1	7.3	4.9
Public sector	17.4	2.2	7.1	10.1	7.3	4.9
of which: General government	17.4	2.2	7.1	10.1	7.3	4.9
Private sector guaranteed by public sector	..	..	..	..	..	..
Private sector not guaranteed	..	..	..	..	..	..
Principal repayments (long-term)	**2.4**	**3.6**	**3.5**	**2.8**	**6.2**	**2.7**
Public and publicly guaranteed sector	2.4	3.6	3.5	2.8	6.2	2.7
Public sector	2.4	3.6	3.5	2.8	6.2	2.7
of which: General government	2.3	3.6	3.5	2.8	6.2	2.7
Private sector guaranteed by public sector	..	..	..	..	..	..
Private sector not guaranteed	..	..	..	..	..	..
Interest payments (long-term)	**1.4**	**2.9**	**2.7**	**2.7**	**4.1**	**2.7**
Public and publicly guaranteed sector	1.4	2.9	2.7	2.7	4.1	2.7
Public sector	1.4	2.9	2.7	2.7	4.1	2.7
of which: General government	1.4	2.9	2.7	2.7	4.1	2.7
Private sector guaranteed by public sector	..	..	..	..	..	..
Private sector not guaranteed	..	..	..	..	..	..
Summary external debt stock by creditor type						
Long-term external debt stocks	**104.6**	**175.2**	**165.6**	**183.7**	**177.7**	**177.4**
Public and publicly guaranteed debt from:	104.6	175.2	165.6	183.7	177.7	177.4
Official creditors	103.7	175.2	165.6	183.7	177.7	177.4
Multilateral	72.9	58.1	60.4	71.4	74.1	75.8
of which: World Bank	23.2	26.5	29.1	37.2	39.1	42.9
Bilateral	30.8	117.1	105.2	112.3	103.6	101.6
Private creditors	0.9	0.0	..	..	..	..
Bondholders	..	..	..	..	..	..
Commercial banks and others	0.9	0.0	..	..	..	..
Private nonguaranteed debt from:	..	..	..	..	..	..
Bondholders	..	..	..	..	..	..
Commercial banks and others	..	..	..	..	..	..
Use of IMF credit	10.3	9.1	8.8	9.4	9.2	9.1
Net financial inflows						
Net debt inflows						
Use of IMF credit	..	..	..	..	..	..
Long-term	14.9	-1.4	3.6	7.3	1.2	2.2
Official creditors	14.2	-1.3	3.6	7.3	1.2	2.2
Multilateral	0.1	-0.6	4.2	7.3	4.4	2.2
of which: World Bank	1.5	1.7	3.5	6.2	2.8	4.1
Bilateral	14.1	-0.7	-0.6	..	-3.2	..
Private creditors	0.8	-0.1	..	..	..	..
Bondholders	..	..	..	..	..	..
Banks and others	0.8	-0.1	..	..	..	..
Short-term	..	0.0	0.0	0.0	0.0	0.0
Net equity inflows						
Foreign direct investment	0.0	7.0	6.8	-2.6	14.2	1.4
Portfolio equity	..	0.0	0.0	0.0	0.0	0.0
Debt ratios						
External debt stocks to exports (%)	213.1	208.5	142.8	138.3	120.9	112.0
External debt stocks to GNI (%)	35.0	41.9	43.2	44.2	40.9	..
Debt service to exports (%)	7.2	7.3	5.1	4.0	6.6	3.3
Short-term to external debt stocks (%)	0.0	0.0	0.0	0.0	0.0	0.0
Multilateral to external debt stocks (%)	63.5	31.5	34.6	37.0	39.6	40.6
Reserves to external debt stocks (%)	83.3	84.7	101.2	102.8	121.6	123.0
Gross national income (GNI)	328.0	440.0	403.6	436.9	457.2	..

139

TUNISIA

(US$ million, unless otherwise indicated)

	2009	2015	2016	2017	2018	2019
Summary external debt data by debtor type						
Total external debt stocks	**22,818**	**27,741**	**28,893**	**34,022**	**35,116**	**37,764**
Use of IMF credit	428	1,768	1,987	2,105	2,280	2,132
Long-term external debt	17,555	19,398	20,212	24,458	24,743	26,415
Public and publicly guaranteed sector	14,948	18,216	18,719	22,386	22,606	23,857
Public sector	14,714	17,933	18,451	22,088	22,362	23,655
of which: General government	11,808	13,864	14,577	15,417	15,899	16,863
Private sector guaranteed by public sector	234	283	268	298	245	203
Private sector not guaranteed	2,607	1,182	1,493	2,072	2,136	2,558
Short-term external debt	4,835	6,575	6,694	7,458	8,093	9,217
Disbursements (long-term)	**1,565**	**3,349**	**1,949**	**3,909**	**2,182**	**3,719**
Public and publicly guaranteed sector	1,388	3,349	1,949	3,909	2,182	3,297
Public sector	1,345	3,346	1,916	3,862	2,182	3,297
of which: General government	904	2,524	1,515	1,128	1,745	2,251
Private sector guaranteed by public sector	43	3	33	47	..	..
Private sector not guaranteed	177	..	..	..	..	422
Principal repayments (long-term)	**1,364**	**1,470**	**1,291**	**1,926**	**1,409**	**1,828**
Public and publicly guaranteed sector	1,247	1,138	1,189	1,784	1,263	1,828
Public sector	1,231	1,091	1,149	1,732	1,222	1,791
of which: General government	967	643	653	1,278	795	1,153
Private sector guaranteed by public sector	16	47	40	52	42	37
Private sector not guaranteed	117	332	102	142	146	..
Interest payments (long-term)	**702**	**444**	**559**	**588**	**684**	**665**
Public and publicly guaranteed sector	600	444	463	455	547	571
Public sector	593	437	457	450	543	567
of which: General government	483	328	356	334	353	393
Private sector guaranteed by public sector	7	7	6	5	4	4
Private sector not guaranteed	102	..	96	133	137	94
Summary external debt stock by creditor type						
Long-term external debt stocks	**17,555**	**19,398**	**20,212**	**24,458**	**24,743**	**26,415**
Public and publicly guaranteed debt from:	14,948	18,216	18,719	22,386	22,606	23,857
Official creditors	10,049	12,655	12,717	14,844	14,635	15,931
Multilateral	6,673	9,214	9,305	11,104	11,025	11,398
of which: World Bank	1,405	2,482	2,447	3,275	3,515	3,489
Bilateral	3,376	3,441	3,412	3,740	3,610	4,533
Private creditors	4,899	5,561	6,002	7,542	7,971	7,926
Bondholders	3,776	4,729	5,268	6,705	7,239	7,278
Commercial banks and others	1,123	832	734	837	732	648
Private nonguaranteed debt from:	2,607	1,182	1,493	2,072	2,136	2,558
Bondholders	..	..	..	..	..	..
Commercial banks and others	2,607	1,182	1,493	2,072	2,136	2,558
Use of IMF credit	428	1,768	1,987	2,105	2,280	2,132
Net financial inflows						
Net debt inflows						
Use of IMF credit	..	301	282	0	228	-135
Long-term	201	1,879	658	1,983	773	1,891
Official creditors	476	986	343	849	407	1,495
Multilateral	439	928	325	814	447	545
of which: World Bank	30	520	20	581	486	31
Bilateral	37	59	19	35	-40	949
Private creditors	-275	893	314	1,134	367	396
Bondholders	-313	1,000	500	1,260	591	49
Banks and others	38	-107	-186	-126	-224	347
Short-term	505	-271	119	764	635	1,124
Net equity inflows						
Foreign direct investment	1,529	971	631	815	998	817
Portfolio equity	-89	153	-57	-64	-41	13
Debt ratios						
External debt stocks to exports (%)	113	155	166	188	176	191
External debt stocks to GNI (%)	55	66	71	88	91	101
Debt service to exports (%)	11	11	12	17	14	16
Short-term to external debt stocks (%)	21	24	23	22	23	24
Multilateral to external debt stocks (%)	29	33	32	33	31	30
Reserves to external debt stocks (%)	48	26	20	17	15	20
Gross national income (GNI)	41,370	41,813	40,575	38,539	38,421	37,391

TURKEY
(US$ million, unless otherwise indicated)

	2009	2015	2016	2017	2018	2019
Summary external debt data by debtor type						
Total external debt stocks	278,830	399,949	409,421	456,562	445,973	440,783
Use of IMF credit	9,638	1,485	1,440	1,526	1,490	1,481
Long-term external debt	220,215	293,333	306,738	335,174	327,989	316,199
Public and publicly guaranteed sector	87,185	103,283	107,727	117,843	121,211	124,923
Public sector	87,009	102,876	107,375	117,497	120,925	124,679
of which: General government	69,826	82,798	84,350	92,236	93,203	99,590
Private sector guaranteed by public sector	176	407	352	346	286	244
Private sector not guaranteed	133,030	190,050	199,011	217,331	206,778	191,277
Short-term external debt	48,977	105,131	101,243	119,863	116,494	123,102
Disbursements (long-term)	**39,668**	**37,297**	**81,760**	**88,318**	**68,568**	**58,895**
Public and publicly guaranteed sector	9,822	9,067	14,324	17,579	15,844	17,226
Public sector	9,812	9,067	14,324	17,579	15,844	17,226
of which: General government	8,605	4,751	7,142	12,046	9,467	13,423
Private sector guaranteed by public sector	10	..	..	0	0	0
Private sector not guaranteed	29,846	28,230	67,436	70,739	52,725	41,669
Principal repayments (long-term)	**49,661**	**41,978**	**61,603**	**69,197**	**67,974**	**69,202**
Public and publicly guaranteed sector	6,474	6,532	8,437	11,339	10,822	12,899
Public sector	6,474	6,503	8,393	11,288	10,777	12,862
of which: General government	5,365	5,675	5,010	7,595	7,387	6,614
Private sector guaranteed by public sector	..	29	45	51	45	37
Private sector not guaranteed	43,188	35,446	53,166	57,858	57,152	56,303
Interest payments (long-term)	**10,589**	**10,194**	**10,934**	**12,098**	**11,509**	**12,558**
Public and publicly guaranteed sector	4,954	4,396	4,499	4,875	4,876	5,492
Public sector	4,949	4,392	4,495	4,871	4,872	5,488
of which: General government	4,173	3,963	4,001	4,284	4,290	4,579
Private sector guaranteed by public sector	5	4	4	4	4	4
Private sector not guaranteed	5,635	5,798	6,435	7,223	6,632	7,066
Summary external debt stock by creditor type						
Long-term external debt stocks	220,215	293,333	306,738	335,174	327,989	316,199
Public and publicly guaranteed debt from:	87,185	103,283	107,727	117,843	121,211	124,923
Official creditors	23,315	30,714	30,880	34,596	34,503	34,252
Multilateral	16,801	25,144	25,593	28,505	28,269	26,845
of which: World Bank	9,816	11,731	10,860	12,039	11,685	11,362
Bilateral	6,513	5,570	5,287	6,091	6,233	7,407
Private creditors	63,870	72,569	76,848	83,247	86,709	90,670
Bondholders	42,432	64,243	67,141	74,436	77,326	82,205
Commercial banks and others	21,439	8,326	9,706	8,811	9,383	8,466
Private nonguaranteed debt from:	133,030	190,050	199,011	217,331	206,778	191,277
Bondholders	6,606	29,666	34,475	41,602	38,894	38,383
Commercial banks and others	126,424	160,384	164,536	175,729	167,884	152,893
Use of IMF credit	9,638	1,485	1,440	1,526	1,490	1,481
Net financial inflows						
Net debt inflows						
Use of IMF credit	-706	..	..	..	..	..
Long-term	-9,993	-4,681	20,157	19,121	594	-10,307
Official creditors	3,006	904	765	925	941	148
Multilateral	2,671	995	1,080	461	745	-1,024
of which: World Bank	1,613	-265	-644	185	5	-172
Bilateral	336	-91	-314	464	196	1,172
Private creditors	-12,999	-5,585	19,391	18,196	-347	-10,455
Bondholders	1,265	3,017	4,307	9,466	1,753	3,112
Banks and others	-14,264	-8,602	15,085	8,730	-2,100	-13,567
Short-term	-3,535	-29,944	-3,889	18,620	-3,369	6,608
Net equity inflows						
Foreign direct investment	7,966	15,973	10,796	10,175	12,219	10,221
Portfolio equity	2,827	-2,395	823	2,971	-1,131	406
Debt ratios						
External debt stocks to exports (%)	184	186	200	201	183	174
External debt stocks to GNI (%)	44	47	48	54	59	59
Debt service to exports (%)	42	26	37	38	35	34
Short-term to external debt stocks (%)	18	26	25	26	26	28
Multilateral to external debt stocks (%)	6	6	6	6	6	6
Reserves to external debt stocks (%)	25	23	22	18	16	18
Gross national income (GNI)	636,983	850,113	854,542	841,585	759,425	741,899

141

TURKMENISTAN

(US$ million, unless otherwise indicated)

	2009	2015	2016	2017	2018	2019
Summary external debt data by debtor type						
Total external debt stocks	**674.2**	**367.0**	**507.7**	**783.7**	**907.3**	**567.6**
Use of IMF credit	109.5	96.7	93.9	99.4	97.1	96.5
Long-term external debt	480.0	269.5	259.9	267.3	503.6	470.3
Public and publicly guaranteed sector	466.1	231.4	231.4	220.6	468.9	427.0
Public sector	466.1	231.4	231.4	220.6	468.9	427.0
of which: General government	67.1	119.7	135.1	127.3	389.4	358.0
Private sector guaranteed by public sector	..	..	..	..	..	..
Private sector not guaranteed	13.9	38.1	28.5	46.8	34.6	43.4
Short-term external debt	84.8	0.8	153.9	417.0	306.7	0.8
Disbursements (long-term)	**34.3**	**22.0**	**29.4**	**29.4**	**276.2**	**20.7**
Public and publicly guaranteed sector	21.4	9.8	23.8	0.5	269.6	0.6
Public sector	21.4	9.8	23.8	0.5	269.6	0.6
of which: General government	0.0	6.3	21.3	0.1	269.6	0.6
Private sector guaranteed by public sector	..	..	..	..	..	..
Private sector not guaranteed	12.8	12.2	5.6	28.9	6.6	20.1
Principal repayments (long-term)	**146.4**	**49.5**	**33.9**	**32.6**	**39.9**	**53.0**
Public and publicly guaranteed sector	146.4	32.1	17.7	18.0	17.4	41.5
Public sector	146.4	32.1	17.7	18.0	17.4	41.5
of which: General government	15.2	3.7	6.7	8.7	7.8	32.3
Private sector guaranteed by public sector	..	..	..	..	..	..
Private sector not guaranteed	..	17.3	16.2	14.5	22.6	11.5
Interest payments (long-term)	**17.6**	**5.5**	**4.7**	**5.2**	**5.5**	**14.1**
Public and publicly guaranteed sector	17.1	4.6	4.3	4.6	4.8	13.3
Public sector	17.1	4.6	4.3	4.6	4.8	13.3
of which: General government	2.0	1.1	1.5	2.1	2.6	11.4
Private sector guaranteed by public sector	..	..	..	..	..	..
Private sector not guaranteed	0.4	0.9	0.4	0.7	0.7	0.8
Summary external debt stock by creditor type						
Long-term external debt stocks	**480.0**	**269.5**	**259.9**	**267.3**	**503.6**	**470.3**
Public and publicly guaranteed debt from:	466.1	231.4	231.4	220.6	468.9	427.0
Official creditors	450.7	231.4	231.4	220.6	199.3	181.9
Multilateral	17.4	97.9	114.5	107.9	102.0	96.8
of which: World Bank	12.8	3.0	1.0	0.0	..	..
Bilateral	433.4	133.5	116.9	112.7	97.3	85.0
Private creditors	15.4	..	..	..	269.6	245.1
Bondholders	..	..	..	..	..	..
Commercial banks and others	15.4	..	..	..	269.6	245.1
Private nonguaranteed debt from:	13.9	38.1	28.5	46.8	34.6	43.4
Bondholders	..	..	..	..	..	..
Commercial banks and others	13.9	38.1	28.5	46.8	34.6	43.4
Use of IMF credit	109.5	96.7	93.9	99.4	97.1	96.5
Net financial inflows						
Net debt inflows						
Use of IMF credit	..	..	..	..	..	..
Long-term	-112.2	-27.4	-4.5	-3.2	236.3	-32.3
Official creditors	-109.6	-22.3	6.0	-17.6	-17.4	-16.3
Multilateral	-2.8	4.4	16.6	-6.6	-5.8	-5.2
of which: World Bank	-1.3	-1.9	-2.0	-1.0	..	..
Bilateral	-106.8	-26.7	-10.6	-10.9	-11.5	-11.1
Private creditors	-2.6	-5.1	-10.6	14.4	253.7	-15.9
Bondholders	..	..	..	..	..	..
Banks and others	-2.6	-5.1	-10.6	14.4	253.7	-15.9
Short-term	41.0	0.0	153.1	263.0	-110.3	-305.9
Net equity inflows						
Foreign direct investment	4,553.0	3,043.0	2,243.2	2,085.9	1,985.1	2,165.9
Portfolio equity	..	..	..	..	..	..
Debt ratios						
External debt stocks to exports (%)	..	..	..	..	..	..
External debt stocks to GNI (%)	3.6	1.1	1.4	2.2	2.3	..
Debt service to exports (%)	..	..	..	..	..	..
Short-term to external debt stocks (%)	12.6	0.2	30.3	53.2	33.8	0.1
Multilateral to external debt stocks (%)	2.6	26.7	22.6	13.8	11.2	17.1
Reserves to external debt stocks (%)	..	..	..	..	..	..
Gross national income (GNI)	18,957.5	33,705.6	35,225.9	36,352.3	39,044.2	..

UGANDA

(US$ million, unless otherwise indicated)

	2009	2015	2016	2017	2018	2019
Summary external debt data by debtor type						
Total external debt stocks	**2,763**	**9,571**	**10,086**	**11,673**	**12,315**	**13,969**
Use of IMF credit	281	240	233	246	241	239
Long-term external debt	2,247	8,776	9,352	10,953	11,566	12,778
Public and publicly guaranteed sector	2,247	4,869	5,446	6,890	7,701	8,635
Public sector	2,243	4,865	5,442	6,886	7,697	8,632
of which: General government	2,242	4,865	5,441	6,885	7,697	8,631
Private sector guaranteed by public sector	5	4	4	4	4	3
Private sector not guaranteed	..	3,907	3,906	4,064	3,865	4,142
Short-term external debt	235	554	502	473	509	952
Disbursements (long-term)	**494**	**1,135**	**936**	**1,568**	**1,167**	**1,408**
Public and publicly guaranteed sector	494	881	785	1,259	1,167	1,131
Public sector	491	881	785	1,259	1,167	1,131
of which: General government	491	881	785	1,259	1,167	1,131
Private sector guaranteed by public sector	3	..	..	..	..	..
Private sector not guaranteed	..	254	151	309	..	277
Principal repayments (long-term)	**49**	**45**	**779**	**97**	**422**	**166**
Public and publicly guaranteed sector	49	45	46	97	223	166
Public sector	49	45	46	97	223	166
of which: General government	49	45	46	97	223	166
Private sector guaranteed by public sector	..	0	0	0	..	0
Private sector not guaranteed	..	..	733	..	199	..
Interest payments (long-term)	**18**	**41**	**57**	**80**	**98**	**115**
Public and publicly guaranteed sector	18	41	55	80	98	115
Public sector	18	41	55	80	98	115
of which: General government	18	41	55	80	98	115
Private sector guaranteed by public sector	..	..	..	..	..	..
Private sector not guaranteed	..	..	1	..	..	..
Summary external debt stock by creditor type						
Long-term external debt stocks	**2,247**	**8,776**	**9,352**	**10,953**	**11,566**	**12,778**
Public and publicly guaranteed debt from:	2,247	4,869	5,446	6,890	7,701	8,635
Official creditors	2,247	4,869	5,445	6,881	7,651	8,552
Multilateral	2,017	3,884	4,077	4,867	5,039	5,653
of which: World Bank	1,379	2,510	2,576	2,980	3,095	3,443
Bilateral	230	985	1,368	2,014	2,612	2,899
Private creditors	0	..	1	8	50	83
Bondholders	..	..	..	..	..	..
Commercial banks and others	0	..	1	8	50	83
Private nonguaranteed debt from:	..	3,907	3,906	4,064	3,865	4,142
Bondholders	..	..	..	..	..	..
Commercial banks and others	..	3,907	3,906	4,064	3,865	4,142
Use of IMF credit	281	240	233	246	241	239
Net financial inflows						
Net debt inflows						
Use of IMF credit	0	-1	0	..	..	..
Long-term	445	1,090	157	1,471	746	1,242
Official creditors	445	836	738	1,155	900	931
Multilateral	435	398	338	538	285	640
of which: World Bank	363	212	163	245	190	366
Bilateral	10	438	400	617	615	291
Private creditors	0	254	-581	316	-155	311
Bondholders	..	..	..	..	..	..
Banks and others	0	254	-581	316	-155	311
Short-term	-223	22	-52	-29	36	443
Net equity inflows						
Foreign direct investment	771	552	396	708	710	955
Portfolio equity	131	10	16	15	66	15
Debt ratios						
External debt stocks to exports (%)	81	201	208	227	217	226
External debt stocks to GNI (%)	11	30	35	39	39	42
Debt service to exports (%)	2	2	17	4	9	5
Short-term to external debt stocks (%)	9	6	5	4	4	7
Multilateral to external debt stocks (%)	73	41	40	42	41	40
Reserves to external debt stocks (%)	108	30	31	32	27	..
Gross national income (GNI)	24,628	31,636	28,455	30,033	31,846	33,471

143

UKRAINE

(US$ million, unless otherwise indicated)

	2009	2015	2016	2017	2018	2019
Summary external debt data by debtor type						
Total external debt stocks	**105,306**	**117,450**	**114,998**	**122,684**	**121,040**	**123,843**
Use of IMF credit	13,027	12,486	13,075	14,001	12,997	11,328
Long-term external debt	72,406	84,951	81,699	86,423	87,352	90,489
Public and publicly guaranteed sector	19,011	32,426	33,097	36,052	36,156	38,396
Public sector	19,011	32,426	33,097	36,052	36,156	38,396
of which: General government	18,249	30,426	31,042	33,702	35,418	35,510
Private sector guaranteed by public sector	..	..	..	..	..	..
Private sector not guaranteed	53,395	52,526	48,602	50,371	51,197	52,093
Short-term external debt	19,873	20,013	20,223	22,259	20,690	22,025
Disbursements (long-term)	**22,368**	**18,690**	**5,018**	**8,166**	**9,453**	**12,493**
Public and publicly guaranteed sector	5,651	15,514	2,749	5,748	4,016	5,331
Public sector	5,651	15,514	2,749	5,748	4,016	5,331
of which: General government	5,603	15,482	2,678	5,437	3,676	3,029
Private sector guaranteed by public sector	..	..	..	..	..	..
Private sector not guaranteed	16,717	3,176	2,268	2,418	5,437	7,163
Principal repayments (long-term)	**18,226**	**23,820**	**8,608**	**8,507**	**8,846**	**8,270**
Public and publicly guaranteed sector	2,093	13,580	1,898	3,456	3,603	2,995
Public sector	2,093	13,580	1,898	3,456	3,603	2,995
of which: General government	1,678	13,565	1,882	3,439	1,657	2,846
Private sector guaranteed by public sector	..	..	..	..	..	..
Private sector not guaranteed	16,134	10,239	6,710	5,051	5,243	5,275
Interest payments (long-term)	**4,263**	**4,012**	**3,116**	**2,975**	**2,808**	**3,170**
Public and publicly guaranteed sector	773	1,289	1,435	1,502	1,463	1,681
Public sector	773	1,289	1,435	1,502	1,463	1,681
of which: General government	690	1,142	1,286	1,347	1,436	1,650
Private sector guaranteed by public sector	..	..	..	..	..	..
Private sector not guaranteed	3,490	2,723	1,681	1,473	1,345	1,488
Summary external debt stock by creditor type						
Long-term external debt stocks	**72,406**	**84,951**	**81,699**	**86,423**	**87,352**	**90,489**
Public and publicly guaranteed debt from:	19,011	32,426	33,097	36,052	36,156	38,396
Official creditors	11,355	12,914	12,298	13,817	12,927	12,342
Multilateral	9,805	11,921	10,985	12,225	11,355	10,715
of which: World Bank	3,294	5,585	5,504	5,346	5,284	5,282
Bilateral	1,551	993	1,312	1,592	1,573	1,627
Private creditors	7,655	19,512	20,800	22,235	23,228	26,054
Bondholders	6,107	19,352	20,643	22,067	22,467	24,485
Commercial banks and others	1,548	159	156	167	761	1,569
Private nonguaranteed debt from:	53,395	52,526	48,602	50,371	51,197	52,093
Bondholders	5,114	4,495	3,831	4,419	4,519	4,489
Commercial banks and others	48,281	48,031	44,771	45,952	46,678	47,604
Use of IMF credit	13,027	12,486	13,075	14,001	12,997	11,328
Net financial inflows						
Net debt inflows						
Use of IMF credit	6,082	5,260	995	146	-689	-1,593
Long-term	4,142	-5,129	-3,591	-341	606	4,223
Official creditors	5,148	868	-432	869	-610	-490
Multilateral	5,303	721	-763	633	-605	-533
of which: World Bank	275	885	-81	-158	-62	-2
Bilateral	-155	147	330	235	-5	43
Private creditors	-1,006	-5,998	-3,158	-1,210	1,217	4,713
Bondholders	-1,181	-1,812	541	1,589	-275	2,551
Banks and others	175	-4,185	-3,699	-2,799	1,492	2,162
Short-term	-1,078	-3,299	-974	1,114	-2,088	1,191
Net equity inflows						
Foreign direct investment	4,456	584	4,076	3,025	4,069	4,909
Portfolio equity	105	177	69	110	-9	49
Debt ratios						
External debt stocks to exports (%)	186	219	217	194	170	161
External debt stocks to GNI (%)	92	128	121	107	90	78
Debt service to exports (%)	41	55	23	21	21	18
Short-term to external debt stocks (%)	19	17	18	18	17	18
Multilateral to external debt stocks (%)	9	10	10	10	9	9
Reserves to external debt stocks (%)	24	11	13	14	16	19
Gross national income (GNI)	114,673	91,406	94,833	114,769	134,250	158,534

144

UZBEKISTAN
(US$ million, unless otherwise indicated)

	2009	2015	2016	2017	2018	2019
Summary external debt data by debtor type						
Total external debt stocks	7,028	13,955	15,705	16,792	17,541	21,745
Use of IMF credit	412	364	353	374	365	363
Long-term external debt	6,386	12,920	14,752	15,580	16,473	20,171
Public and publicly guaranteed sector	3,269	5,605	6,603	7,545	9,413	11,790
Public sector	3,263	5,605	6,603	7,545	9,413	11,790
of which: General government	2,369	3,899	4,311	5,087	6,768	9,116
Private sector guaranteed by public sector	6	..	..	..	..	..
Private sector not guaranteed	3,117	7,315	8,149	8,035	7,061	8,381
Short-term external debt	229	671	600	838	702	1,211
Disbursements (long-term)	2,612	2,388	2,899	2,102	2,617	5,647
Public and publicly guaranteed sector	475	1,259	1,399	1,121	2,288	2,801
Public sector	475	1,259	1,399	1,121	2,288	2,801
of which: General government	242	868	663	835	1,908	2,579
Private sector guaranteed by public sector	0	..	..	..	..	..
Private sector not guaranteed	2,138	1,130	1,501	981	330	2,846
Principal repayments (long-term)	713	963	1,006	1,436	691	1,951
Public and publicly guaranteed sector	386	286	341	341	383	429
Public sector	384	286	341	341	383	429
of which: General government	141	176	209	178	198	233
Private sector guaranteed by public sector	2	..	..	..	..	..
Private sector not guaranteed	327	677	665	1,095	309	1,521
Interest payments (long-term)	120	281	354	449	285	643
Public and publicly guaranteed sector	82	73	91	118	144	231
Public sector	82	73	91	118	144	231
of which: General government	58	37	49	68	95	169
Private sector guaranteed by public sector	0	..	..	..	..	..
Private sector not guaranteed	38	208	262	331	141	412
Summary external debt stock by creditor type						
Long-term external debt stocks	6,386	12,920	14,752	15,580	16,473	20,171
Public and publicly guaranteed debt from:	3,269	5,605	6,603	7,545	9,413	11,790
Official creditors	2,934	5,350	6,334	7,264	9,214	11,559
Multilateral	1,101	3,039	3,367	3,893	5,441	7,049
of which: World Bank	368	599	779	910	1,907	2,723
Bilateral	1,833	2,311	2,967	3,370	3,773	4,510
Private creditors	335	255	269	281	199	231
Bondholders	..	..	..	..	..	..
Commercial banks and others	335	255	269	281	199	231
Private nonguaranteed debt from:	3,117	7,315	8,149	8,035	7,061	8,381
Bondholders	..	..	..	..	..	300
Commercial banks and others	3,117	7,315	8,149	8,035	7,061	8,081
Use of IMF credit	412	364	353	374	365	363
Net financial inflows						
Net debt inflows						
Use of IMF credit	..	..	..	..	..	..
Long-term	1,899	1,426	1,893	666	1,926	3,697
Official creditors	241	884	1,034	804	1,977	2,336
Multilateral	149	629	361	460	1,580	1,616
of which: World Bank	0	120	196	101	1,013	820
Bilateral	92	255	673	343	397	720
Private creditors	1,658	541	859	-138	-51	1,361
Bondholders	..	..	..	..	..	300
Banks and others	1,658	541	859	-138	-51	1,061
Short-term	49	176	-71	238	-136	499
Net equity inflows						
Foreign direct investment	842	1,047	1,129	1,914	639	2,122
Portfolio equity	..	1	2	3	13	29
Debt ratios						
External debt stocks to exports (%)	..	101	123	112	101	109
External debt stocks to GNI (%)	20	17	19	28	34	37
Debt service to exports (%)	..	9	11	13	6	13
Short-term to external debt stocks (%)	3	5	4	5	4	6
Multilateral to external debt stocks (%)	16	22	21	23	31	32
Reserves to external debt stocks (%)	..	98	90	84	71	59
Gross national income (GNI)	34,586	83,271	82,711	60,371	51,900	58,795

VANUATU

(US$ million, unless otherwise indicated)

	2009	2015	2016	2017	2018	2019
Summary external debt data by debtor type						
Total external debt stocks	**153.3**	**256.8**	**293.4**	**401.4**	**402.2**	**414.8**
Use of IMF credit	25.5	46.1	44.7	47.4	43.3	37.2
Long-term external debt	98.8	172.0	210.9	287.6	313.8	335.5
Public and publicly guaranteed sector	98.8	172.0	210.9	287.6	313.8	335.5
Public sector	98.8	172.0	210.9	287.6	313.8	335.5
of which: General government	98.3	171.7	210.7	287.4	313.8	335.5
Private sector guaranteed by public sector	..	..	..	..	..	..
Private sector not guaranteed	..	..	..	..	..	..
Short-term external debt	29.0	38.7	37.8	66.4	45.1	42.1
Disbursements (long-term)	**11.7**	**84.8**	**53.2**	**68.7**	**46.4**	**36.0**
Public and publicly guaranteed sector	11.7	84.8	53.2	68.7	46.4	36.0
Public sector	11.7	84.8	53.2	68.7	46.4	36.0
of which: General government	11.7	84.8	53.2	68.7	46.4	36.0
Private sector guaranteed by public sector	..	..	..	..	..	..
Private sector not guaranteed	..	..	..	..	..	..
Principal repayments (long-term)	**3.5**	**5.0**	**4.9**	**5.0**	**12.0**	**12.5**
Public and publicly guaranteed sector	3.5	5.0	4.9	5.0	12.0	12.5
Public sector	3.5	5.0	4.9	5.0	12.0	12.5
of which: General government	3.5	5.0	4.9	5.0	11.8	12.5
Private sector guaranteed by public sector	..	..	..	..	..	..
Private sector not guaranteed	..	..	..	..	..	..
Interest payments (long-term)	**1.4**	**1.3**	**3.2**	**3.5**	**4.2**	**4.0**
Public and publicly guaranteed sector	1.4	1.3	3.2	3.5	4.2	4.0
Public sector	1.4	1.3	3.2	3.5	4.2	4.0
of which: General government	1.4	1.3	3.2	3.5	4.2	4.0
Private sector guaranteed by public sector	..	..	..	..	..	..
Private sector not guaranteed	..	..	..	..	..	..
Summary external debt stock by creditor type						
Long-term external debt stocks	**98.8**	**172.0**	**210.9**	**287.6**	**313.8**	**335.5**
Public and publicly guaranteed debt from:	98.8	172.0	210.9	287.6	313.8	335.5
Official creditors	98.8	172.0	210.9	287.6	313.8	335.5
Multilateral	68.6	47.7	53.7	76.1	101.8	135.0
of which: World Bank	12.4	9.1	12.2	29.1	54.7	83.0
Bilateral	30.2	124.3	157.2	211.5	212.0	200.5
Private creditors	..	..	..	..	..	..
Bondholders	..	..	..	..	..	..
Commercial banks and others	..	..	..	..	..	..
Private nonguaranteed debt from:	..	..	..	..	..	..
Bondholders	..	..	..	..	..	..
Commercial banks and others	..	..	..	..	..	..
Use of IMF credit	**25.5**	**46.1**	**44.7**	**47.4**	**43.3**	**37.2**
Net financial inflows						
Net debt inflows						
Use of IMF credit	..	23.8	0.0	0.0	-3.0	-5.9
Long-term	8.1	79.8	48.3	63.7	34.4	23.6
Official creditors	8.1	79.8	48.3	63.7	34.4	23.6
Multilateral	-3.2	1.4	6.1	19.6	27.1	33.5
of which: World Bank	-0.6	0.7	3.4	15.8	26.8	28.7
Bilateral	11.3	78.4	42.1	44.0	7.2	-10.0
Private creditors	..	..	..	..	..	..
Bondholders	..	..	..	..	..	..
Banks and others	..	..	..	..	..	..
Short-term	-5.0	-42.1	-0.9	28.6	-21.3	-3.1
Net equity inflows						
Foreign direct investment	23.8	16.8	38.7	34.2	34.0	41.0
Portfolio equity	0.0	..	..	..	..	..
Debt ratios						
External debt stocks to exports (%)	46.3	72.7	70.8	90.0	71.5	85.3
External debt stocks to GNI (%)	25.9	33.7	36.6	46.2	44.0	44.8
Debt service to exports (%)	1.7	2.0	2.1	2.3	3.6	4.8
Short-term to external debt stocks (%)	18.9	15.1	12.9	16.6	11.2	10.1
Multilateral to external debt stocks (%)	44.7	18.6	18.3	19.0	25.3	32.6
Reserves to external debt stocks (%)	96.9	104.8	91.1	98.4	104.6	123.3
Gross national income (GNI)	591.5	761.8	802.2	869.2	914.6	926.0

VENEZUELA, RB

(US$ million, unless otherwise indicated)

	2009	2015	2016	2017	2018	2019
Summary external debt data by debtor type						
Total external debt stocks	**94,353**	**159,007**	**163,908**	**164,633**	**167,797**	**168,074**
Use of IMF credit	3,987	3,524	3,419	3,622	3,537	3,517
Long-term external debt	69,532	114,385	113,431	113,443	113,402	113,390
Public and publicly guaranteed sector	44,973	67,098	66,145	66,157	66,116	66,104
Public sector	44,973	67,098	66,145	66,157	66,116	66,104
of which: General government	35,185	42,540	41,587	41,599	41,558	41,546
Private sector guaranteed by public sector	..	..	..	..	..	..
Private sector not guaranteed	24,559	47,286	47,286	47,286	47,286	47,286
Short-term external debt	20,834	41,098	47,058	47,568	50,858	51,167
Disbursements (long-term)	**24,099**	**20,257**	**79**	**18**	**0**	**0**
Public and publicly guaranteed sector	9,981	1,683	79	18	0	0
Public sector	9,981	1,683	79	18	0	0
of which: General government	6,068	1,683	79	18	0	0
Private sector guaranteed by public sector	..	..	..	..	..	..
Private sector not guaranteed	14,119	18,574	..	..	..	..
Principal repayments (long-term)	**7,674**	**17,560**	**234**	**108**	**7**	**..**
Public and publicly guaranteed sector	1,173	3,711	234	108	7	..
Public sector	1,173	3,711	234	108	7	..
of which: General government	805	2,310	234	108	7	..
Private sector guaranteed by public sector	..	..	..	..	..	..
Private sector not guaranteed	6,501	13,849	..	..	..	..
Interest payments (long-term)	**4,511**	**9,117**	**77**	**36**	**10**	**..**
Public and publicly guaranteed sector	2,927	5,913	77	36	10	..
Public sector	2,927	5,913	77	36	10	..
of which: General government	2,440	3,759	77	36	10	..
Private sector guaranteed by public sector	..	..	..	..	..	..
Private sector not guaranteed	1,585	3,204	..	..	..	..
Summary external debt stock by creditor type						
Long-term external debt stocks	**69,532**	**114,385**	**113,431**	**113,443**	**113,402**	**113,390**
Public and publicly guaranteed debt from:	44,973	67,098	66,145	66,157	66,116	66,104
Official creditors	4,221	9,214	8,283	8,200	8,194	8,197
Multilateral	3,296	5,295	5,140	5,050	5,044	5,044
of which: World Bank	..	..	..	..	..	..
Bilateral	925	3,918	3,143	3,150	3,151	3,153
Private creditors	40,752	57,885	57,862	57,957	57,921	57,907
Bondholders	38,984	56,828	56,828	56,828	56,828	56,828
Commercial banks and others	1,768	1,057	1,034	1,129	1,094	1,080
Private nonguaranteed debt from:	24,559	47,286	47,286	47,286	47,286	47,286
Bondholders	3,972	2,300	2,300	2,300	2,300	2,300
Commercial banks and others	20,587	44,986	44,986	44,986	44,986	44,986
Use of IMF credit	3,987	3,524	3,419	3,622	3,537	3,517
Net financial inflows						
Net debt inflows						
Use of IMF credit	..	..	..	..	..	..
Long-term	16,425	2,697	-155	-90	-7	0
Official creditors	586	266	-155	-90	-7	0
Multilateral	396	266	-155	-90	-7	0
of which: World Bank	..	..	..	..	..	..
Bilateral	190	0	0	0	0	0
Private creditors	15,839	2,431	0	0	0	0
Bondholders	8,905	-2,595	0	0	0	0
Banks and others	6,934	5,026	0	0	0	0
Short-term	560	10,511	600	-458	3,296	0
Net equity inflows						
Foreign direct investment	-1,350	-282	446	-68	886	934
Portfolio equity	118	5	..	..	..	..
Debt ratios						
External debt stocks to exports (%)	150	400	560	..	..	..
External debt stocks to GNI (%)	29	..	..	..	..	..
Debt service to exports (%)	20	70	4	..	..	..
Short-term to external debt stocks (%)	22	26	29	29	30	30
Multilateral to external debt stocks (%)	3	3	3	3	3	3
Reserves to external debt stocks (%)	23	4	2	2	..	..
Gross national income (GNI)	327,123	..	..	..	..	..

VIETNAM

(US$ million, unless otherwise indicated)

	2009	2015	2016	2017	2018	2019
Summary external debt data by debtor type						
Total external debt stocks	32,742	77,832	85,665	104,092	106,861	118,490
Use of IMF credit	578	436	423	448	438	435
Long-term external debt	27,381	65,405	72,521	81,746	86,838	93,658
Public and publicly guaranteed sector	27,381	46,366	48,038	51,792	52,121	52,935
Public sector	27,381	46,148	47,842	51,622	51,976	52,815
of which: General government	24,357	32,055	33,256	36,161	36,745	37,783
Private sector guaranteed by public sector	..	218	196	170	145	120
Private sector not guaranteed	..	19,039	24,484	29,954	34,717	40,723
Short-term external debt	4,783	11,991	12,720	21,898	19,585	24,397
Disbursements (long-term)	4,731	12,952	13,111	18,661	20,335	19,835
Public and publicly guaranteed sector	4,731	4,427	4,457	4,270	3,210	3,564
Public sector	4,731	4,427	4,457	4,270	3,210	3,564
of which: General government	3,762	2,771	2,846	2,748	2,147	2,571
Private sector guaranteed by public sector	..	0	0	0	0	0
Private sector not guaranteed	..	8,525	8,654	14,391	17,126	16,271
Principal repayments (long-term)	917	4,929	5,734	11,249	14,708	13,052
Public and publicly guaranteed sector	917	1,884	2,524	2,328	2,581	2,787
Public sector	917	1,874	2,502	2,303	2,556	2,762
of which: General government	689	1,046	1,514	1,272	1,402	1,601
Private sector guaranteed by public sector	..	10	23	25	25	25
Private sector not guaranteed	..	3,045	3,210	8,920	12,127	10,265
Interest payments (long-term)	477	1,538	1,412	2,059	2,720	2,738
Public and publicly guaranteed sector	477	822	879	940	1,016	1,122
Public sector	477	818	874	935	1,011	1,116
of which: General government	409	471	505	527	574	657
Private sector guaranteed by public sector	..	4	5	5	5	6
Private sector not guaranteed	..	717	532	1,119	1,704	1,616
Summary external debt stock by creditor type						
Long-term external debt stocks	27,381	65,405	72,521	81,746	86,838	93,658
Public and publicly guaranteed debt from:	27,381	46,366	48,038	51,792	52,121	52,935
Official creditors	23,815	37,587	40,199	44,619	45,741	47,237
Multilateral	10,604	20,174	21,166	23,285	23,723	24,118
of which: World Bank	6,304	12,638	13,110	14,683	14,968	15,327
Bilateral	13,211	17,414	19,033	21,334	22,018	23,118
Private creditors	3,567	8,778	7,839	7,173	6,380	5,698
Bondholders	1,327	1,877	1,521	1,516	1,511	1,506
Commercial banks and others	2,240	6,902	6,318	5,657	4,869	4,192
Private nonguaranteed debt from:	..	19,039	24,484	29,954	34,717	40,723
Bondholders	..	290	235	235	35	1,014
Commercial banks and others	..	18,749	24,248	29,718	34,682	39,709
Use of IMF credit	578	436	423	448	438	435
Net financial inflows						
Net debt inflows						
Use of IMF credit	-38	..	..	..	..	..
Long-term	3,813	8,023	7,377	7,413	5,627	6,783
Official creditors	3,387	2,783	2,857	2,692	1,397	1,450
Multilateral	2,231	1,800	1,443	1,146	846	505
of which: World Bank	1,157	1,054	830	885	592	443
Bilateral	1,155	984	1,415	1,547	552	945
Private creditors	427	5,240	4,520	4,720	4,230	5,333
Bondholders	-39	-23	-411	-5	-205	974
Banks and others	466	5,263	4,931	4,725	4,435	4,359
Short-term	579	-1,613	729	9,178	-2,313	4,812
Net equity inflows						
Foreign direct investment	6,369	8,260	8,820	8,418	13,977	11,980
Portfolio equity	128	134	..	..	..	..
Debt ratios						
External debt stocks to exports (%)	51	45	45	45	41	42
External debt stocks to GNI (%)	35	42	44	50	47	49
Debt service to exports (%)	2	4	4	6	7	6
Short-term to external debt stocks (%)	15	15	15	21	18	21
Multilateral to external debt stocks (%)	32	26	25	22	22	20
Reserves to external debt stocks (%)	50	36	43	47	52	66
Gross national income (GNI)	92,614	183,321	196,687	206,917	228,057	242,274

YEMEN, REPUBLIC OF
(US$ million, unless otherwise indicated)

	2009	2015	2016	2017	2018	2019
Summary external debt data by debtor type						
Total external debt stocks	6,799	7,299	7,063	7,193	7,037	7,055
Use of IMF credit	417	522	497	508	469	440
Long-term external debt	5,875	6,477	6,322	6,317	6,205	6,188
Public and publicly guaranteed sector	5,875	6,477	6,322	6,317	6,205	6,188
Public sector	5,875	6,477	6,322	6,317	6,205	6,188
of which: General government	5,875	5,477	5,322	5,317	5,205	5,188
Private sector guaranteed by public sector	..	..	..	..	..	..
Private sector not guaranteed	..	..	..	..	..	..
Short-term external debt	507	300	243	368	362	427
Disbursements (long-term)	**332**	**60**	**24**	**4**	**19**	**66**
Public and publicly guaranteed sector	332	60	24	4	19	66
Public sector	332	60	24	4	19	66
of which: General government	332	60	24	4	19	66
Private sector guaranteed by public sector	..	..	..	..	..	..
Private sector not guaranteed	..	..	..	..	..	..
Principal repayments (long-term)	**140**	**282**	**98**	**66**	**71**	**72**
Public and publicly guaranteed sector	140	282	98	66	71	72
Public sector	140	282	98	66	71	72
of which: General government	140	282	98	66	71	72
Private sector guaranteed by public sector	..	..	..	..	..	..
Private sector not guaranteed	..	..	..	..	..	..
Interest payments (long-term)	**72**	**74**	**31**	**13**	**13**	**12**
Public and publicly guaranteed sector	72	74	31	13	13	12
Public sector	72	74	31	13	13	12
of which: General government	72	71	28	13	13	12
Private sector guaranteed by public sector	..	..	..	..	..	..
Private sector not guaranteed	..	..	..	..	..	..
Summary external debt stock by creditor type						
Long-term external debt stocks	5,875	6,477	6,322	6,317	6,205	6,188
Public and publicly guaranteed debt from:	5,875	6,477	6,322	6,317	6,205	6,188
Official creditors	5,871	6,477	6,322	6,317	6,205	6,188
Multilateral	3,159	3,182	3,039	3,110	3,004	2,987
of which: World Bank	2,187	1,780	1,668	1,695	1,586	1,505
Bilateral	2,712	3,295	3,283	3,207	3,201	3,201
Private creditors	5	..	..	..	..	..
Bondholders	..	..	..	..	..	..
Commercial banks and others	5	..	..	..	..	..
Private nonguaranteed debt from:	..	..	..	..	..	..
Bondholders	..	..	..	..	..	..
Commercial banks and others	..	..	..	..	..	..
Use of IMF credit	417	522	497	508	469	440
Net financial inflows						
Net debt inflows						
Use of IMF credit	-44	0	-10	-18	-27	-26
Long-term	192	-222	-74	-62	-52	-7
Official creditors	193	-222	-74	-62	-52	-7
Multilateral	128	-166	-72	-62	-51	-7
of which: World Bank	59	-51	-64	-66	-71	-72
Bilateral	65	-56	-2	0	0	0
Private creditors	-1	..	..	..	..	..
Bondholders	..	..	..	..	..	..
Banks and others	-1	..	..	..	..	..
Short-term	109	-23	-109	50	-82	36
Net equity inflows						
Foreign direct investment	129	-15	-561	-270	-282	-371
Portfolio equity	0	0	0	..	..	..
Debt ratios						
External debt stocks to exports (%)	94	386	738	..	..	..
External debt stocks to GNI (%)	28	20	25	29	26	..
Debt service to exports (%)	4	19	15	..	..	..
Short-term to external debt stocks (%)	7	4	3	5	5	6
Multilateral to external debt stocks (%)	46	44	43	43	43	42
Reserves to external debt stocks (%)	102	..	..	..	..	..
Gross national income (GNI)	23,958	35,622	28,085	24,561	27,579	..

149

ZAMBIA

(US$ million, unless otherwise indicated)

	2009	2015	2016	2017	2018	2019
Summary external debt data by debtor type						
Total external debt stocks	**3,646**	**11,779**	**15,221**	**17,381**	**19,005**	**27,341**
Use of IMF credit	1,080	907	813	794	715	667
Long-term external debt	2,120	10,132	13,646	15,686	17,667	25,839
Public and publicly guaranteed sector	1,100	6,487	7,060	8,785	9,920	11,104
Public sector	1,100	6,487	7,060	8,785	9,920	11,104
of which: General government	1,039	6,462	7,039	8,764	9,903	11,091
Private sector guaranteed by public sector	..	0	0	0	0	0
Private sector not guaranteed	1,020	3,645	6,586	6,902	7,748	14,736
Short-term external debt	446	740	762	901	623	835
Disbursements (long-term)	**126**	**3,106**	**3,768**	**2,283**	**2,718**	**9,935**
Public and publicly guaranteed sector	91	1,909	798	1,752	1,487	1,670
Public sector	91	1,909	798	1,752	1,487	1,670
of which: General government	91	1,909	798	1,752	1,487	1,670
Private sector guaranteed by public sector	..	0	0	0	0	..
Private sector not guaranteed	35	1,197	2,970	531	1,231	8,265
Principal repayments (long-term)	**122**	**215**	**209**	**366**	**666**	**1,742**
Public and publicly guaranteed sector	59	96	146	151	282	464
Public sector	59	96	146	151	282	464
of which: General government	48	93	143	148	278	461
Private sector guaranteed by public sector	..	0	0	0	0	0
Private sector not guaranteed	63	118	63	215	385	1,277
Interest payments (long-term)	**36**	**259**	**448**	**386**	**701**	**778**
Public and publicly guaranteed sector	13	189	326	341	445	444
Public sector	13	189	326	341	445	444
of which: General government	12	189	325	341	444	444
Private sector guaranteed by public sector	..	..	..	..	..	..
Private sector not guaranteed	24	69	122	45	256	334
Summary external debt stock by creditor type						
Long-term external debt stocks	**2,120**	**10,132**	**13,646**	**15,686**	**17,667**	**25,839**
Public and publicly guaranteed debt from:	1,100	6,487	7,060	8,785	9,920	11,104
Official creditors	1,095	3,222	3,763	4,226	4,701	5,701
Multilateral	871	1,295	1,408	1,620	1,822	2,117
of which: World Bank	407	698	760	894	1,003	1,108
Bilateral	224	1,927	2,356	2,606	2,879	3,584
Private creditors	5	3,265	3,297	4,558	5,219	5,403
Bondholders	..	3,000	3,000	3,000	3,000	3,000
Commercial banks and others	5	265	297	1,558	2,219	2,403
Private nonguaranteed debt from:	1,020	3,645	6,586	6,902	7,748	14,736
Bondholders	..	..	..	..	..	..
Commercial banks and others	1,020	3,645	6,586	6,902	7,748	14,736
Use of IMF credit	1,080	907	813	794	715	667
Net financial inflows						
Net debt inflows						
Use of IMF credit	244	-61	-69	-66	-61	-44
Long-term	4	2,891	3,558	1,917	2,052	8,193
Official creditors	35	547	621	339	542	1,019
Multilateral	42	136	156	132	239	304
of which: World Bank	33	61	86	86	132	112
Bilateral	-8	411	465	207	303	715
Private creditors	-31	2,344	2,938	1,578	1,509	7,174
Bondholders	..	1,250	0	0	0	0
Banks and others	-31	1,094	2,938	1,578	1,509	7,174
Short-term	-202	-79	22	81	-225	196
Net equity inflows						
Foreign direct investment	472	309	267	547	-502	-466
Portfolio equity	-13	0	3	-3	-5	1
Debt ratios						
External debt stocks to exports (%)	74	143	203	190	190	330
External debt stocks to GNI (%)	24	57	75	70	71	120
Debt service to exports (%)	3	7	10	9	14	31
Short-term to external debt stocks (%)	12	6	5	5	3	3
Multilateral to external debt stocks (%)	24	11	9	9	10	8
Reserves to external debt stocks (%)	52	25	15	12	8	5
Gross national income (GNI)	14,910	20,831	20,308	24,723	26,598	22,767

ZIMBABWE
(US$ million, unless otherwise indicated)

	2009	2015	2016	2017	2018	2019
Summary external debt data by debtor type						
Total external debt stocks	6,163	9,679	11,496	12,540	12,646	12,270
Use of IMF credit	542	464	455	482	471	468
Long-term external debt	3,974	6,129	7,888	8,323	8,786	8,275
Public and publicly guaranteed sector	3,876	4,207	4,248	4,341	4,308	4,386
Public sector	3,876	4,207	4,248	4,341	4,308	4,386
of which: General government	3,198	3,509	3,629	3,736	3,766	3,856
Private sector guaranteed by public sector	..	..	..	..	..	..
Private sector not guaranteed	98	1,922	3,640	3,983	4,478	3,889
Short-term external debt	1,646	3,086	3,153	3,735	3,389	3,527
Disbursements (long-term)	125	1,443	1,132	815	980	972
Public and publicly guaranteed sector	59	502	245	153	280	91
Public sector	59	502	245	153	280	91
of which: General government	13	297	245	153	280	91
Private sector guaranteed by public sector	..	..	..	..	..	..
Private sector not guaranteed	66	941	887	662	700	881
Principal repayments (long-term)	66	426	988	384	281	1,214
Public and publicly guaranteed sector	0	116	108	111	76	52
Public sector	0	116	108	111	76	52
of which: General government	0	69	41	61	26	42
Private sector guaranteed by public sector	..	..	..	..	..	..
Private sector not guaranteed	66	310	880	273	205	1,163
Interest payments (long-term)	30	202	121	267	254	313
Public and publicly guaranteed sector	14	38	44	27	14	13
Public sector	14	38	44	27	14	13
of which: General government	14	24	23	24	13	13
Private sector guaranteed by public sector	..	..	..	..	..	..
Private sector not guaranteed	16	164	78	240	240	301
Summary external debt stock by creditor type						
Long-term external debt stocks	3,974	6,129	7,888	8,323	8,786	8,275
Public and publicly guaranteed debt from:	3,876	4,207	4,248	4,341	4,308	4,386
Official creditors	3,409	3,796	3,828	3,899	3,883	3,967
Multilateral	1,646	1,659	1,575	1,434	1,232	1,226
of which: World Bank	985	912	885	907	896	890
Bilateral	1,764	2,137	2,253	2,466	2,651	2,741
Private creditors	467	411	419	441	425	419
Bondholders	0	0	0	0	0	0
Commercial banks and others	467	411	419	441	425	419
Private nonguaranteed debt from:	98	1,922	3,640	3,983	4,478	3,889
Bondholders	..	..	..	..	..	..
Commercial banks and others	98	1,922	3,640	3,983	4,478	3,889
Use of IMF credit	542	464	455	482	471	468
Net financial inflows						
Net debt inflows						
Use of IMF credit	0	-2	-87	..	..	..
Long-term	59	1,017	144	431	699	-243
Official creditors	58	382	101	53	204	45
Multilateral	0	153	-69	-60	-41	0
of which: World Bank	0	-7	-13	-5	0	-3
Bilateral	58	228	170	113	245	44
Private creditors	0	635	43	378	496	-287
Bondholders	0	0	0	0	..	0
Banks and others	0	635	43	378	496	-287
Short-term	-312	367	30	450	-416	63
Net equity inflows						
Foreign direct investment	105	399	343	247	745	280
Portfolio equity	67	123	-80	-101	..	..
Debt ratios						
External debt stocks to exports (%)	308	232	269	254	262	..
External debt stocks to GNI (%)	73	54	61	62	56	62
Debt service to exports (%)	6	16	29	14	13	..
Short-term to external debt stocks (%)	27	32	27	30	27	29
Multilateral to external debt stocks (%)	27	17	14	11	10	10
Reserves to external debt stocks (%)	13	4	4	2	1	1
Gross national income (GNI)	8,401	17,981	18,773	20,080	22,707	19,836

151

APPENDIX
About the Data

User Guide to Tables

International Debt Statistics 2021 focuses on financial flows, trends in external debt, and other major financial indicators for low- and middle-income countries. This edition of *International Debt Statistics* (IDS) has been reconfigured to offer a more condensed presentation of the principal indicators. The longer version of the report will be found in the online tables.

Tables

Aggregate Tables

The aggregate tables are labeled by region name. Data are shown for all low- and middle-income countries and six regional groups (East Asia and Pacific, Europe and Central Asia, Latin America and the Caribbean, Middle East and North Africa, South Asia, and Sub-Saharan Africa).

Country Tables

Country tables are labeled by country name and ordered alphabetically. Data are shown for 120 low- and middle-income countries that report public and publicly guaranteed external debt to the World Bank's Debtor Reporting System (DRS). The tables also include key debt ratios and the composition of external debt stocks and flows for each country.

Each table shows a time series with the most recent five years, as well as 2009 as a comparison year. Full time series data are available for all countries in the World Bank's Open Data website (https://datacatalog.worldbank.org/dataset/international-debt-statistics).

Statistics

The general cutoff date for countries to report data for this publication was end-August 2020. The economic aggregates presented in the tables are prepared for the convenience of users. Although debt ratios can give useful information about developments in a debt-servicing capacity, conclusions drawn from them will not be valid unless accompanied by careful economic evaluation.

The macroeconomic data provided are collected from national statistical organizations, which in some cases may be subject to a considerable margin of error. The usual care must be taken in interpreting the ratios, particularly for the most recent years, because figures may be preliminary and subject to revision.

Specific country notes describing the sources of information that are not provided by the country are summarized in the "Data Documentation" section. Unless otherwise specified, data on long-term public and publicly guaranteed external debt for 2019 are based on reports provided by the country.

More detailed information on data sources, methodology, and compilation is provided in the appendix at the back of this book.

Aggregate Measures for Income Groups and Regions

Aggregate measures for income groups and regions include the 120 low- and middle-income countries that report public and publicly guaranteed external debt to the World Bank's DRS, whenever data are available. The aggregate "All low- and middle-income countries" is the sum of data for 120 countries.

Classification of Countries

For operational and analytical purposes, the World Bank's main criterion for classifying countries is gross national income (GNI) per capita (calculated by the *World Bank Atlas* method). Every country is classified as low-income, middle-income, or high-income. Low- and middle-income countries are sometimes referred to as developing countries. The term is used for convenience; it is not intended to imply that all countries in the group are experiencing similar development or that other countries have reached a preferred or final stage of development. Because GNI per capita changes over time, the country composition of income groups may change from one edition of *International Debt Statistics* to the next. Once the classification is fixed for an edition, based on GNI per capita in the most recent year for which data are available, all historical data presented are based on the same country grouping.

Symbols

0 or 0.0 means zero or small enough that the number would round to zero at the displayed number of decimal places.

.. means that data are not available or that aggregates cannot be calculated because of missing data in the years shown.

$ indicates current U.S. dollars unless otherwise specified.

User Guide to IDS Online Tables and Database

The country tables that were previously available in the *International Debt Statistics* print edition is now available online. Using an automated query process, these reference tables will be updated based on the revisions to the International Debt Statistics database.

Users can access all the online tables, download the PDF version of the publication, and view the report as an eBook on ISSUU, as well as access the database and download the archived editions of the publication by going to http://data.worldbank.org/products/ids.

How to Access IDS Online Country Tables

To access the IDS online tables, visit http://datatopics.worldbank.org/debt/ids and select from "Country," "Region," "Topic," or "DSSI" options. Click on "Analytical" to view the table with a select number of indicators as reported in the IDS publication, or "Standard" to view the tables with the full list of indicators available in the database. To access the DSSI debt service payments due table, select from "DSSI" and click on "Monthly presentation" for monthly projections or "Annual presentation" for yearly projections.

To access a specific country table directly without going through the above landing page, use the URL http://datatopics.worldbank.org/debt/ids/ and the country code (for example, http://datatopics.worldbank .org/debt/ids/country/DZA to view the table for Algeria). Similarly, to view the regional table, click on the "Region" tab and select one of the listed regions (for example http://datatopics.worldbank.org/debt/ids /region/SAS to view the table for South Asia).

2021 | International Debt Statistics

Data ▸ Data Topics ▸ Debt Data ▸ Country Tables ▸   Albania

	2010	2011	2012	2013	2014	2015	2016	2017	2018
Summary external debt data by debtor type									
Total External debt stocks	5,441.3	6,486.7	7,389.1	9,068.0	8,640.5	8,657.3	8,741.2	10,062.2	10,121.9
Use of IMF Credit	129.4	117.2	107.0	96.8	150.9	243.6	587.1	488.8	470.3
Long-term external debt	4,568.7	5,279.7	5,812.2	6,968.0	6,614.5	6,618.7	6,484.7	7,424.4	7,447.0
Public and publicly guaranteed sector	3,214.8	3,369.6	3,552.5	3,759.3	3,665.9	3,845.7	3,763.1	4,338.9	4,562.9
Public sector	3,214.8	3,369.6	3,552.5	3,759.3	3,665.9	3,845.7	3,763.1	4,338.9	4,562.9
of which: General Government	2,658.2	2,934.2	3,122.1	3,340.1	3,321.9	3,551.9	3,491.0	4,034.5	4,290.2
Private sector guaranteed by public sector	0.0	0.0	0.0	0.0	0.0	0.0	0.0	0.0	0.0
Private sector not guaranteed	1,353.9	1,910.1	2,259.7	3,208.8	2,948.5	2,772.9	2,721.5	3,085.5	2,924.2
Short-term external debt	743.2	1,091.8	1,469.9	2,003.2	1,875.2	1,795.0	1,869.5	2,149.0	2,164.6
Disbursements (long-term)	846.4	863.6	737.3	784.5	633.7	1,321.2	450.4	776.7	1,269.2
Public and publicly guaranteed sector	631.2	418.4	335.7	260.2	442.4	956.2	205.4	421.7	931.1
Public sector	631.2	418.4	335.7	260.2	442.6	956.2	205.4	421.7	931.1
of which: General Government	612.1	293.0	317.4	253.5	442.6	952.4	188.9	420.3	791.7
Private sector guaranteed by public sector	0.0	0.0	0.0	0.0	0.0	0.0	0.0	0.0	0.0
Private sector not guaranteed	215.1	445.2	401.6	524.3	191.2	365.0	245.0	355.1	338.1
Principal repayments (long-term)	250.1	302.0	352.2	347.7	539.3	1,071.7	487.3	406.6	927.3
Public and publicly guaranteed sector	174.2	190.4	189.8	126.1	177.9	498.6	190.7	221.3	553.8
Public sector	174.2	190.4	189.8	126.1	177.9	495.6	190.7	221.3	553.8
of which: General Government	145.6	152.5	163.2	97.3	150.6	477.6	159.9	197.7	455.9
Private sector guaranteed by public sector	0.0	0.0	0.0	0.0	0.0	0.0	0.0	0.0	0.0
Private sector not guaranteed	75.9	111.6	160.4	221.7	361.4	573.1	296.6	185.3	367.5
Interest payments (long-term)	110.0	166.6	176.3	193.5	184.5	96.4	94.8	96.6	142.1
Public and publicly guaranteed sector	66.2	105.3	109.5	72.2	79.2	89.4	83.6	83.3	119.5
Public sector	66.2	105.5	100.5	72.2	79.2	89.6	83.6	83.0	119.5
of which: General Government	59.5	97.8	93.3	67.9	75.1	85.0	82.0	80.2	118.4
Private sector guaranteed by public sector	0.0	0.0	0.0	0.0	0.0	0.0	0.0	0.0	0.0
Private sector not guaranteed	43.8	61.1	72.8	121.3	105.3	8.8	11.3	12.4	27.6
Summary external debt stock by creditor type									
Long-term External debt stocks	4,568.7	5,279.7	5,812.2	6,968.0	6,614.5	6,618.7	6,484.7	7,424.4	7,447.0
Public and publicly guaranteed debt from	3,214.8	3,369.6	3,552.5	3,759.3	3,665.9	3,845.7	3,763.1	4,338.9	4,562.9
Official creditors	2,173.5	2,311.3	2,539.1	2,692.4	2,744.5	2,584.1	2,530.9	2,983.5	3,036.6
Multilateral	1,520.7	1,667.0	1,872.2	2,004.0	2,091.1	1,943.4	1,889.0	2,279.7	2,362.1
of which: World Bank	875.4	903.4	934.5	938.0	1,085.9	1,019.6	990.9	1,300.4	1,300.6
Bilateral	652.8	644.3	667.0	688.4	653.4	640.6	641.9	704.7	674.5
Private creditors	1,041.3	1,058.3	1,013.4	1,066.8	921.4	1,261.7	1,232.3	1,355.4	1,526.3
Bondholders	477.0	556.4	567.3	593.0	522.1	631.4	611.4	695.6	942.3
Commercial banks and others	564.3	501.9	446.1	473.8	399.4	630.2	620.9	659.8	584.0
Private nonguaranteed debt from	1,353.9	1,910.1	2,259.7	3,208.8	2,948.5	2,772.9	2,721.5	3,085.5	2,924.2
Bondholders	69.0	177.9	232.4	265.9	243.7	133.1	148.4	101.9	245.2
Commercial banks and others	1,284.9	1,732.2	2,027.2	2,942.8	2,704.8	2,639.9	2,573.1	2,983.6	2,678.9
Use of IMF Credit	129.4	117.2	107.0	96.8	150.9	243.6	587.1	488.8	470.3
Net financial inflows									
Net debt inflows									

Indicators

The main indicator codes for each of the indicators online and in the publication are listed below. To view a specific indicator online, go to http://data.worldbank.org/indicator/ and add the indicator code at the end of the url; for example, to view a page for total debt stocks, this line should be in your browser: http://data.worldbank.org/indicator/DT.DOD.DECT.CD.

1. SUMMARY EXTERNAL DEBT DATA			
External debt stocks	DT.DOD.DECT.CD	**External debt flows**	
Long-term external debt	DT.DOD.DLXF.CD	**Disbursements**	DT.DIS.DLTF.CD
Public and publicly guaranteed	DT.DOD.DPPG.CD	Long-term external debt	DT.DIS.DLXF.CD
Private nonguaranteed	DT.DOD.DPNG.CD	IMF purchases	DT.DIS.DIMF.CD
Use of IMF credit	DT.DOD.DIMF.CD	**Principal repayments**	DT.AMT.DLTF.CD
Short-term debt	DT.DOD.DSTC.CD	Long-term external debt	DT.AMT.DLXF.CD
interest arrears on long-term	DT.IXA.DPPG.CD	IMF repurchases	DT.AMT.DIMF.CD
		Net flows	DT.NFL.DECT.CD
		Long-term external debt	DT.NFL.DLXF.CD
Memorandum items		Short-term external debt	DT.NFL.DSTC.CD
Principal arrears on long-term	DT.AXA.DPPG.CD	**Interest payments (INT)**	DT.INT.DECT.CD
Long-term public sector debt	DT.DOD.DPPG.CD	Long-term external debt	DT.INT.DLXF.CD
Long-term private sector debt	DT.DOD.PRVS.CD	IMF charges	DT.INT.DIMF.CD
Public & publicly guaranteed commitments	DT.COM.DPPG.CD	Short-term external debt	DT.INT.DSTC.CD

2. OTHER NON-DEBT RESOURCE FLOWS	
Foreign direct investment (net equity inflows)	BX.KLT.DINV.CD.WD
Portfolio equity flows	BX.PEF.TOTL.CD.WD

3. CURRENCY COMPOSITION OF PUBLIC AND PUBLICLY GUARANTEED DEBT (%)	
Euro	DT.CUR.EURO.ZS
Japanese yen	DT.CUR.JYEN.ZS
Pound sterling	DT.CUR.UKPS.ZS
Swiss franc	DT.CUR.SWFR.ZS
U.S. dollars	DT.CUR.USDL.ZS

5. MAJOR ECONOMIC AGGREGATES	
Gross national income (GNI)	NY.GNP.MKTP.CD
Exports of goods, services, and primary income	BX.GSR.TOTL.CD
Personal transfers and compensation of employees	BX.TRF.PWKR.CD.DT
Imports of goods, services, and primary income	BM.GSR.TOTL.CD
Primary income on FDI (payments)	BX.KLT.DREM.CD.DT
International reserves	FI.RES.TOTL.CD

4. AVERAGE TERMS OF NEW COMMITMENTS	
Official creditors	
Interest (%)	DT.INR.OFFT
Maturity (years)	DT.MAT.OFFT
Grace period (years)	DT.GPA.OFFT
Private creditors	
Interest (%)	DT.INR.PRVT
Maturity (years)	DT.MAT.PRVT
Grace period (years)	DT.GPA.PRVT

6. RATIOS	
External debt stocks to exports (%)	DT.DOD.DECT.EX.ZS
External debt stocks to GNI (%)	DT.DOD.DECT.GN.ZS
Debt service to exports (%)	DOD.DECT.GN.ZS
Short-term to external debt stocks (%)	DT.DOD.DSTC.ZS
Multilateral to external debt stocks (%)	DT.DOD.MLAT.ZS
Reserves to external debt stocks (%)	FI.RES.TOTL.DT.ZS
Current account balance	BN.CAB.XOKA.CD
Reserves to imports (months)	FI.RES.TOTL.MO

7. LONG-TERM EXTERNAL DEBT			
Debt outstanding and disbursed	DT.DOD.DLXF.CD	**Interest payments**	DT.INT.DLXF.CD
Public and publicly guaranteed	DT.DOD.DPPG.CD	**Public and publicly guaranteed**	DT.INT.DPPG.CD
Official creditors	DT.DOD.OFFT.CD	Official creditors	DT.INT.OFFT.CD
Multilateral	DT.DOD.MLAT.CD	Multilateral	DT.INT.MLAT.CD
of which: IBRD	DT.DOD.MIBR.CD	of which: IBRD	DT.INT.MIBR.CD
IDA	DT.DOD.MIDA.CD	IDA	DT.INT.MIDA.CD
Bilateral	DT.DOD.BLAT.CD	Bilateral	DT.INT.BLAT.CD
Private creditors	DT.DOD.PRVT.CD	Private creditors	DT.INT.PRVT.CD
of which: Bonds	DT.DOD.PBND.CD	of which: Bonds	DT.INT.PBND.CD
Commercial banks	DT.DOD.PCBK.CD	Commercial banks	DT.INT.PCBK.CD
Private nonguaranteed	DT.DOD.DPNG.CD	Private nonguaranteed	DT.INT.DPNG.CD
of which: Bonds	DT.DOD.PNGB.CD	of which: Bonds	DT.INT.PNGB.CD
Disbursements	DT.DIS.DLXF.CD	**Principal repayments**	DT.AMT.DLXF.CD
Public and publicly guaranteed	DT.DIS.DPPG.CD	Public and publicly guaranteed	DT.AMT.DPPG.CD
Official creditors	DT.DIS.OFFT.CD	Official creditors	DT.AMT.OFFT.CD
Multilateral	DT.DIS.MLAT.CD	Multilateral	DT.AMT.MLAT.CD
of which: IBRD	DT.DIS.MIBR.CD	of which: IBRD	DT.AMT.MIBR.CD
IDA	DT.DIS.MIDA.CD	IDA	DT.AMT.MIDA.CD
Bilateral	DT.DIS.BLAT.CD	Bilateral	DT.AMT.BLAT.CD
Private creditors	DT.DIS.PRVT.CD	Private creditors	DT.AMT.PRVT.CD
of which: Bonds	DT.DIS.PBND.CD	of which: Bonds	DT.AMT.PBND.CD
Commercial banks	DT.DIS.PCBK.CD	Commercial banks	DT.AMT.PCBK.CD
Private nonguaranteed	DT.DIS.DPNG.CD	**Private nonguaranteed**	DT.AMT.DPNG.CD
of which: Bonds	DT.DIS.PNGB.CD	of which: Bonds	DT.AMT.PNGB.CD

8. DEBT STOCK-FLOW RECONCILATION	
Total change in external debt stocks	DT.DOD.DECT.CD.CG
Net flows on external debt	DT.NFL.DECT.CD

9. DEBT STOCK-FLOW RECONCILATION	
Total amount rescheduled	DT.DXR.DPPG.CD
Total amount forgiven	DT.DFR.DPPG.CD
Debt buyback	DT.DSB.DPPG.CD

10. CONTRACTUAL OBLIGATIONS ON OUTSTANDING LONG-TERM EXTERNAL DEBT	
Official creditors	
Principal	DT.AMT.OFFT.CD
Interest	DT.INT.OFFT.CD
Private creditors	
Principal	DT.AMT.PRVT.CD
Interest	DT.INT.PRVT.CD

How to Access the Database

DataBank (http://databank.worldbank.org) is an online web resource that provides simple and quick access to collections of time series data. It has advanced functions for selecting and displaying data, performing customized queries, downloading data, and creating charts and maps. Users can create dynamic, custom reports based on their selection of countries, indicators, and years. All these reports can be easily edited, shared, and embedded as widgets on websites or blogs. For more information, see http://databank .worldbank.org/help.

Actions

Click to share the table using either the embed code or the URL

Click to edit and revise the table in DataBank

Click to export all metadata to Excel

Click to export the table to Excel

Click to export the table and corresponding indicator metadata to PDF

Click to print the table and corresponding indicator metadata

Click to access the IDS Online Tables Help file

Data Sources and Methodology

Data Sources

Debtor reporting system

The principal sources of information for the tables in *International Debt Statistics 2021* are reports to the World Bank through the World Bank's Debtor Reporting System (DRS) from member countries that have received either International Bank for Reconstruction and Development (IBRD) loans or International Development Association (IDA) credits. The DRS has its origin in the World Bank's need to monitor and assess the financial position of its borrowers. Since 1951, borrowers have been required to provide statistics on their public external debt and private sector debt that benefit from a public guarantee. Reporting countries submit reports on the annual status, transactions, and terms of the long-term external debt of public agencies and that of private ones guaranteed by a public agency in the debtor country. The DRS maintains these records on a loan-by-loan basis. In 1973, coverage of the DRS was expanded to include private sector nonguaranteed borrowing, but for this category of debt, data are provided by borrowers in aggregate rather than loan by loan.

Data submitted to the DRS are processed in the World Bank External Debt (WBXD) system, along with additional information received from the African Development Bank, the Asian Development Bank, the Inter-American Development Bank (IDB), the International Monetary Fund (IMF), institutions of the World Bank Group (IBRD and IDA), and the European Bank for Reconstruction and Development (EBRD). The WBXD is an internal system of the World Bank. Among its outputs is the International Debt Statistics (IDS) database, from which the tables in this publication and online database are produced.

Data on exports and imports (on a balance of payments basis), international reserves, current account balances, foreign direct investment (FDI) on equity, portfolio equity flows, and primary income of FDI are drawn mainly from the IMF, supplemented by United Nations Conference on Trade and Development (UNCTAD) reports and country data. Balance of payments data are presented according to the sixth edition of the IMF's *Balance of Payments Manual* (BPM6). Official aid flows come from data collected and published by the Development Assistance Committee (DAC) of the Organisation for Economic Co-operation and Development (OECD). Short-term external debt data are as reported by debtor countries or are estimates based on the Bank for International Settlements (BIS) quarterly series of commercial banks' claims on low- and middle-income countries. For some countries, estimates were prepared by pooling creditor and debtor information. Data on the gross national income of most low- and middle-income countries are collected from national statistical organizations or central banks by visiting and resident World Bank missions.

Every effort has been made to ensure the accuracy and completeness of the external debt statistics. Coverage has been improved through the efforts of the reporting agencies and close collaboration between the Bank and our partners, Commonwealth Secretariat (COMSEC) and UNCTAD, which provide debt recording and reporting systems across the globe, as well as through the work of the World Bank missions, which visit member countries to gather data and to provide technical assistance on debt issues. Nevertheless, quality and coverage vary among debtors and may also vary for the same debtor from year to year. Data on long-term external debt reported by member countries are checked against, and supplemented by, data from several other sources. Among these sources are the statements and reports of several regional development banks, government lending agencies, and official government websites.

Methodology

Aggregations

Total debt stock and other aggregate measures are derived from the summation of loan-level data on stocks and flows after conversion to a common currency. Other tabulations are compiled using terms and conditions reported in the loan-level data, such as currency composition, cancellations, rescheduling of other liabilities into long-term public and publicly guaranteed external debt, and debt buybacks.

Aggregates for regional and income groups are based on the World Bank's operational classifications, which may differ from common geographic usage or income groups used by other organizations. Country classifications of DRS reporting countries in 2019 are shown in the country groups section. The same classification is used for all historical data shown in *International Debt Statistics* and the online tables and online database.

Currency conversion

Data on external obligations are normally reported to the World Bank in the currency of repayment and are converted into a common currency (U.S. dollars) using official exchange rates published by the IMF.

Commitments, disbursements, and debt service payments (flows) are converted to U.S. dollars at the annual average exchange rate for the year. Debt outstanding (disbursed and undisbursed) at the end of a given year (stock) is converted at the exchange rate in effect at the end of the relevant year. Consequently, year-to-year changes in debt outstanding and disbursed may not be equal to net flows (disbursements less principal repayments); similarly, changes in debt outstanding (including undisbursed debt) may not equal commitments less repayments. Discrepancies will be particularly significant when exchange rates have moved sharply during the year. Projected debt service is converted to U.S. dollars at rates in effect at the end of December 2019.

Beginning with 1991, all ruble debt owed to the former Soviet Union has been converted at a rate of US$1 = 0.6 ruble, except in cases where a bilateral agreement specifying a different conversion rate is in place. Adoption of this methodology does not constitute an endorsement by the World Bank staff of the appropriateness or validity of the exchange rate used. That matter must be resolved bilaterally between the Russian Federation and its debtor countries.

Starting with the 1988–89 edition of *World Debt Tables* (a predecessor of IDS), all data pertaining to IBRD loans from 1985 onward are recorded at their current market value. Starting with the 1991–92 edition, all data pertaining to Asian Development Bank loans from 1989 onward are recorded at their current market value. Starting with the 1998 edition, all data pertaining to African Development Bank and African Development Fund loans from 1997 onward are recorded at their current market value.

Debt stock and flow reconciliation

Because of currency conversions and the timing of transactions, there may be differences between the change in aggregate stocks from one period to the next and flows during the relevant period; changes in debt outstanding, including undisbursed amounts, will therefore differ from commitments less repayments.

Changes in the stock of debt from one period to the next can be attributed to five factors: the net flow of debt, the net change in interest arrears, the capitalization of interest, a reduction in debt resulting from debt forgiveness or other debt reduction mechanisms, and cross-currency valuation effects. Any residual difference in the change in stock not explained by one of those five factors may indicate inconsistencies in the reported data or specific phenomena prevailing in an individual country (for example, an incomplete historical series for all categories of debt). Starting in 1989, the IDS includes the debt stock reconciliation, but not all components are shown in the IDS print edition and online tables.

External debt restructuring

Starting in 1985, the WBXD includes information on the restructuring of debt by official creditors in the context of the Paris Club, restructuring by commercial creditors, debt swap operations, buybacks, and bond exchanges. It attempts to capture accurately the effect of debt restructuring on both external debt stocks and external debt flows, consistent with the terms on which the restructuring takes place. In the compilation and presentation of external debt data, a distinction is made between cash flows and imputed flows. According to this criterion, restructured service payments and the shift in liabilities from one financial instrument to another as a result of debt restructuring are considered to be imputed flows. Both cash flows and imputed flows are recorded separately in WBXD.

The imputed flows and stock changes associated with debt restructuring are included in the IDS tables and online database to complement the cash-basis transactions recorded in the main body of the data. Such data encompass information on the debt stock and debt flows restructured each year, the amount of principal forgiven (interest forgiven is shown as a memorandum item), and the amount of external debt stock reduced either by forgiveness or by a debt buyback operation. Changes in creditors and debtors that result from debt restructuring are also reflected. For example, when insured commercial credits are rescheduled, the creditor classification shifts from private to official (bilateral), reflecting the assumption of the assets by the official credit insurance agencies in the creditor country. The IDS data will show a reduction in the external debt owed to the original private creditors equal or similar to the amount of debt restructured and a corresponding increase in the debt owed to the new official creditor. Similarly on the debtor side, when a government accepts responsibility for the payment of restructured debt previously owed by a private enterprise, the relevant change in the debtor category will be reflected. Likewise, if short-term external debt is restructured into a long-term obligation, the stock of short-term external debt will decline and the stock of long-term external debt will rise by the amount of short-term debt restructured. In the event of a debt swap of long-term external debt (external debt to equity, external debt for nature, or external debt for development), the face value of the external debt swapped will be recorded as a decline in long-term external debt stock, but no flow transaction (principal repayment) will be recorded.

Projections of future disbursements and debt service payments

The WBXD system projects future disbursements and future debt service payments on the assumption that every existing loan commitment will be fully used and repaid in full.

Future disbursements

Disbursement projections are made using one of the following methods:

- *Specific schedules.* Debtor countries are requested to submit a schedule of future disbursements, if available, at the time each new loan is first reported.
- *Standard schedules.* In the absence of specific schedules, the WBXD system projects the future disbursement schedule according to the undisbursed balance of each loan at the end of the most recent reporting period.

These projected schedules are based on profiles derived from the disbursement pattern of comparable loans that fully disbursed. Thirty different profiles have been compiled corresponding to each category of creditor and, in the case of official creditors, for concessional and nonconcessional loans. Each profile is derived by applying regression analysis techniques to a body of data on actual disbursements for each fully disbursed loan in the WBXD database. The profiles are periodically updated to take into account the evolving pattern of disbursements observed for fully disbursed loans.

Future principal payments are generated by the WBXD system according to the repayment terms of each loan. Principal repayments (amortization) are based on the amount of the loan commitment. If the amortization schedule follows a set pattern (for example, equal semiannual payments), the WBXD system calculates repayments automatically using the loan commitment amount, the first and final payment dates, and the frequency of the payments. If future payments are irregular, the WBXD system requires a schedule.

Future interest payments are generated by the WBXD system according to the disbursed and outstanding balance of the loan at the beginning of the period. Using the interest rate specified in the loan contract, the first and final interest payment dates, and the frequency of payments, the WBXD system calculates the stream of future interest payments due. If interest payments are irregular, the WBXD system requires a schedule.

Future debt service payments are the sum of future principal and interest payments due on existing commitments, including the undisbursed portion. They do not include debt service payments that may become due as a result of new loans contracted in subsequent years, nor do they take into account the effect of any change to future debt service obligations resulting from actions such as prepayment or rescheduling or from cancellations that occurred after the most recent year-end data reported to the DRS.

Both projected disbursements and future debt service payments are converted into U.S. dollars using end-December 2019 exchange rates. Likewise, future interest payments on loans with a variable interest rate (for example, loans from commercial banks tied to the London Interbank Offered Rate [LIBOR]) are based on the interest rate prevailing at end-December 2019.

Treatment of arrears

The DRS collects information on arrears of both principal and interest. Principal in arrears is included in the amount of long-term external debt outstanding and is shown separately. Interest in arrears on long-term external debt and interest in arrears on the use of IMF credit are included as part of short-term external debt outstanding and are shown separately. Clearance of interest in arrears by repayment will be recorded as an interest payment in the relevant creditor category of the loan (or loans) on which the arrears were incurred, as a corresponding reduction in the level of short-term debt outstanding, and as a net reduction in interest arrears. Clearance of interest arrears through debt restructuring or forgiveness will be recorded as a reduction in the level of short-term debt outstanding and a net reduction in interest arrears. When interests are rescheduled, they will be capitalized: This change will be recorded as an increase in long-term debt outstanding equal to the amount of interest capitalized and the reduction in short-term debt outstanding noted previously.

External Debt and Its Components

This section describes the compilation of the major components of external debt included in the IDS tables and database and the relationship between them, as shown in figure A.1. Information about general methods of compiling external debt data is discussed in the previous section titled "Methodology." For concise definitions, see the glossary.

Total external debt

Total external debt shown in the IDS is the sum of long-term external debt, short-term debt, and IMF credit. It represents the total debt owed to nonresident creditors and is repayable in both foreign and domestic currency.

Short-term debt

Short-term debt is defined as external debt with an original maturity of one year or less. The DRS requires debtor countries to report only on their long-term external debt. However, to gain a comprehensive picture of total external obligations, the World Bank encourages debtor countries to voluntarily provide information on their short-term external obligations.

By its nature, short-term external debt is difficult to monitor: Loan-by-loan registration is normally impractical, and monitoring systems typically rely on information requested periodically by the central bank from the banking sector. The World Bank regards the debtor country as the authoritative source of information on its short-term debt. Unless otherwise specified in the country tables, the data for short-term debt are derived from the data provided by the quarterly external debt statistics database (see QEDS). BIS data on international bank lending is the second source of the short-term debt. These data are reported on the basis of residual maturity, but an estimate of short-term external liabilities by original maturity can be derived by deducting from claims due in one year those that, 12 months earlier, had a maturity of between one and two years. However, not all commercial banks report to the BIS in a way that allows the full maturity distribution to be determined, and the BIS data include liabilities only to banks within the BIS reporting area. Consequently, the results should be interpreted with caution.

The flow of short-term debt may be derived from the change in claims (stock) data in the BIS quarterly series over consecutive periods, but valuation adjustments resulting from exchange rate

Figure A.1. **External Debt and Its Components**

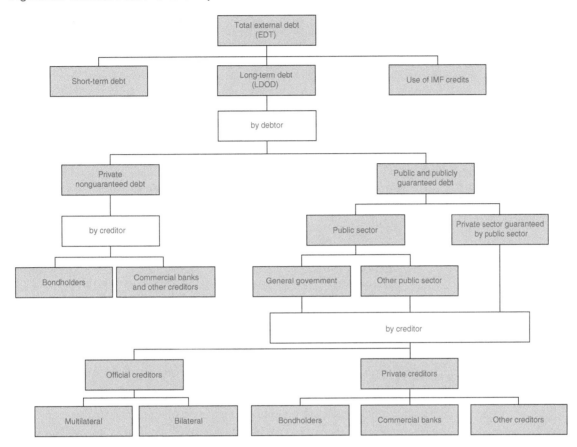

movements will affect the calculations, as will prepayment and refinancing of long-term maturities falling due. When short-term external debt has been rescheduled, lags in reporting and differences in the treatment of the rescheduled external debt by debtors and creditors may result in double counting.

Interest in arrears on long-term external debt and interest in arrears on the use of IMF credit are added to short-term debt and are separately identified.

Use of IMF credit
Data related to the operations of the IMF are provided by the IMF Treasurer's Department. They are converted from special drawing rights (SDR) into dollars using end-of-period exchange rates

for stocks and average-over-the-period exchange rates for flows. IMF trust fund operations under the Enhanced Structural Adjustment Facility, Extended Fund Facility, Poverty Reduction and Growth Facility, and Structural Adjustment Facility (Enhanced Structural Adjustment Facility in 1999) are presented together with all of the IMF's special facilities (buffer stock, supplemental reserve, compensatory and contingency facilities, oil facilities, and other facilities). SDR allocations are also included in this category. According to the BPM6, SDR allocations are recorded as the incurrence of a debt liability of the member receiving them (because of a requirement to repay the allocation in certain circumstances, and also because interest accrues). This debt item was introduced for the first time in IDS 2013 with historical data starting in 1999.

Long-term debt

Long-term debt has an original maturity of more than one year. It comprises the obligations of both public and private debtors. Private nonguaranteed debt comprises the external obligations of private debtors that are not guaranteed for repayment by a public entity in the debtor country.

Public and publicly guaranteed debt comprises the external obligations of public debtors and has two components: (a) public debt, which is borrowing by the national government or agency, by a political subdivision or agency, or by autonomous public bodies, and (b) publicly guaranteed debt, which is borrowing by a private agency that is guaranteed for repayment by a public entity.

Private nonguaranteed debt

The DRS reporting requirements were expanded in 1973 to include long-term private nonguaranteed debt. Data are reported annually on an aggregate basis and include, for the reporting year, the total amount of disbursed and outstanding debt; the amount of disbursements, principal repayments, and interest payments; the principal and interest rescheduled; and the projected principal and interest payments for future years. The aggregate data are usually reported in U.S. dollars, and no information on the underlying currency composition is given.

DRS reporting countries recognize the importance of monitoring borrowing by their private sector, particularly when it constitutes a significant portion of total external debt, but many countries acknowledge the difficulty of this process. Detailed data are available only when countries have registration requirements for private nonguaranteed debt in place, most commonly in connection with exchange controls. When formal registration of private nonguaranteed debt is not mandatory, compilers must rely on balance of payments data and financial surveys.

The data on private nonguaranteed debt in this publication is as reported or as estimated for countries where this type of external debt is known to be significant. The estimation of private nonguaranteed debt is based on the national data on quarterly external debt statistics (QEDS) or IMF data. Flows are derived from the change in stock over consecutive periods and are adjusted for the effects of exchange rate movements (assuming the currency composition mirrors that of public and publicly guaranteed debt)

and for any known debt restructuring. Principal repayments are estimated on the basis of the average maturity observed for loans to private sector borrowers in countries reporting to the DRS and on the basis of the stock of debt outstanding. Interest payments are estimated on the basis of the stock of debt outstanding and interest rates prevailing in international capital markets.

Balance of payments data provide a useful guideline in the estimation process: private nonguaranteed external debt may be derived as a residual between net long-term external borrowing recorded in the balance of payments and net long-term public and publicly guaranteed external debt reported to the DRS.

Public and publicly guaranteed debt

Data related to public and publicly guaranteed debt are reported to the DRS on a loan-by-loan basis. The data provide annual information on the disbursed and outstanding balance and the undisbursed balance of each loan, the cumulative disbursements, the principal and interest paid and principal and interest restructured in the reporting year, and the stock of any outstanding payment's arrears of principal and interest. Detailed information on the terms and conditions of each loan is also reported. Public debt and private debt publicly guaranteed are shown separately in this publication. Public sector debt is disaggregated by government and "other public" and further disaggregated by creditor type.

Official creditors

Official creditors include multilateral and bilateral lenders. In general, official creditors provide loans (and, in some cases, provide grants) to public bodies, although in some cases they may lend to other entities with a public guarantee.

Multilateral creditors are international financial institutions such as the World Bank, regional development banks, and other multilateral and intergovernmental agencies whose lending is administered on a multilateral basis. Funds administered by an international financial organization on behalf of a single donor government constitute bilateral loans (or grants). For lending by a number of multilateral creditors, the data presented in this publication are taken from the creditors' records. Such creditors include the African Development Bank, the Asian Development Bank, the IDB, IBRD, and IDA. (IBRD and IDA are institutions of the World Bank.)

Bilateral creditors are governments and their agencies, including central banks, aid agencies, official export credit agencies, and autonomous agencies such as the U.S. Department of Agriculture or the Federal Home Loan Bank. Member countries of the OECD Development Assistance Committee (DAC) and some other countries also report information on loans extended bilaterally or officially guaranteed to the Creditor Reporting System of the OECD.

Private creditors

Private creditors include commercial banks, bondholders, and other private creditors. This line includes only publicly guaranteed creditors.

Nonguaranteed private creditors are shown separately.

Bonds include publicly issued or privately placed bonds.

Commercial bank loans are loans from private banks and other private financial institutions.

Credits of other private creditors include credits from manufacturers, exporters, and other suppliers of goods, plus bank credits covered by a guarantee of an export credit agency. This line is included in the online database but is not shown in the published tables. It can be obtained as the difference between (a) credits of total private creditors and (b) bonds and commercial bank loans.

Data Documentation
Country Specific Notes on Debt

Country	Country Notes
Afghanistan	Short-term debt before 2015 is based on data from the BIS. Data include the effects of Paris Club debt restructuring agreements signed in 2010 and HIPC and MDRI debt relief.
Angola	Long-term private nonguaranteed debt data are estimates based on Central Bank data and are not available before 2009. Short-term debt before 2012 is based on data from the BIS.
Argentina	Long-term private nonguaranteed debt data before 2008 are World Bank staff estimates. Short-term debt before 2010 is based on data from the BIS.
Azerbaijan	Long-term private nonguaranteed debt data are World Bank staff estimates based on the market data. Short-term debt is based on data from the BIS.
Bangladesh	Short-term debt before 2012 is based on data from the BIS. Long-term private nonguaranteed debt data from 2007 are World Bank staff estimates based on reports provided by the country and are not available prior to 2007.
Belarus	Long-term private nonguaranteed debt data from 2014 are World Bank staff estimates based on reports provided by the country.
Belize	Long-term private nonguaranteed debt data from 2008 are based on Central Bank data.
Benin	Short-term debt is based on data from the BIS. Data include the effects of Paris Club debt restructuring agreement and HIPC and MDRI debt relief.
Bhutan	Short-term debt is based on data from the BIS.
Bosnia and Herzegovina	Long-term private nonguaranteed debt data from 2005 are World Bank staff estimates. Short-term debt is based on data from the BIS.
Botswana	Long-term private nonguaranteed debt data are World Bank staff estimates based on the market data. Short-term debt is based on data from the BIS.
Bulgaria	Long-term private nonguaranteed debt data from 2008 are World Bank staff estimates based on reports provided by the country. Short-term debt before 2009 is World Bank staff estimates based on Central Bank data. The data may include long-term public and publicly guaranteed debt owed by the state-owned railway.
Burkina Faso	Long-term private nonguaranteed debt data are World Bank staff estimates based on reports provided by the country. Data include HIPC and MDRI debt relief.
Burundi	Data include the effects of Paris Club debt restructuring agreement and HIPC and MDRI debt relief. Long-term public and publicly guaranteed debt data for 2019 are World Bank staff estimates based on the original terms of the loans.
Cambodia	Long-term private nonguaranteed debt data are estimates based on Central Bank data. Data include MDRI debt relief.

Country	Country Notes
Cameroon	Short-term debt is based on data from the BIS. Data include the effects of HIPC and MDRI debt relief.
Central African Republic	Short-term debt is based on data from the BIS. Data include the effects of HIPC and MDRI debt relief.
Chad	Short-term debt is based on data from the BIS. Data include the effects of Paris Club debt restructuring agreement and HIPC and MDRI debt relief.
China	Long-term public and publicly guaranteed and long-term private nonguaranteed are World Bank staff estimates based on the aggregate reports provided by the country and market data.
Comoros	Data include the effects of Paris Club debt restructuring agreements signed in 2010 and 2013 and HIPC debt relief.
Congo, Republic of	Short-term debt is based on data from the BIS. Data include the effects of Paris Club debt restructuring agreement and HIPC and MDRI debt relief.
Congo, Democratic Republic of	Short-term debt is based on data from the BIS. Data include the effects of Paris Club debt restructuring agreement and HIPC and MDRI debt relief.
Costa Rica	Long-term private nonguaranteed debt data before 2019 are World Bank staff estimates based on reports provided by the country. Short-term debt before 2005 is based on data from the BIS.
Côte d'Ivoire	Long-term private nonguaranteed debt data are World Bank staff estimates. Short-term debt is based on data from the BIS. Data include the effects of Paris Club agreement signed in 2011, 2012 and HIPC and MDRI debt relief.
Djibouti	Short-term debt before 2017 is based on data from the BIS. Data include the effects of Paris Club debt restructuring agreement signed in 2008.
Dominican Republic	Long-term public and publicly guaranteed debt data for 2019 are World Bank staff estimates based on the original terms of the loans. Long-term private nonguaranteed debt data from 2018 are World Bank staff estimates based on country reports. Short-term debt before 2009 and 2014 onward is based on data from the BIS. Data include the effects of Paris Club debt restructuring agreement signed in 2005.
El Salvador	Long-term private nonguaranteed debt data from 2005 to 2016 are World Bank staff estimates based on reports provided by the country.
Eritrea	Long-term public and publicly guaranteed debt from 2010 are World Bank staff estimates. Short-term debt is based on data from the BIS.
Eswatini	Short-term debt is based on data from the BIS.
Ethiopia	Short-term debt is based on data from the BIS. Data include the effects of HIPC and MDRI debt relief.
Fiji	Short-term debt is based on data from the BIS.
Gabon	Long-term public and publicly guaranteed debt data before 2008 are World Bank staff estimates based on reports provided by the country. Short-term debt is based on data from the BIS. Data include the effects of Paris Club debt buyback agreement signed in 2007.
Gambia, The	Short-term debt is based on data from the BIS. Data include the effects of HIPC and MDRI debt relief.
Ghana	Long-term public and publicly guaranteed debt data for 2019 are World Bank staff estimates based on the original terms of the loans. Short-term debt is based on data from the BIS. Data include the effects of MDRI debt relief.
Grenada	Short-term debt is based on data from the BIS.
Guatemala	Long-term private nonguaranteed debt data are World Bank staff estimates based on market data. Short-term debt before 2012 is based on data from the BIS.
Guinea	Long-term public and publicly guaranteed debt for 2016 are World Bank staff estimates. Short-term debt is based on data from the BIS. Data include the effects of Paris Club debt restructuring agreement signed in 2010, 2012 and HIPC debt relief.
Guinea-Bissau	Long-term public and publicly guaranteed debt for 2019 are World Bank staff estimates. Short-term debt before 2019 is based on data from the BIS. Data include the effects of Paris Club debt restructuring agreement and HIPC and MDRI debt relief.
Guyana	Long-term private nonguaranteed debt data after 2014 are World Bank staff estimates based on market data. Short-term debt is based on data from the BIS. Principal payment shown from 2012 include rice for oil deal. Data include the effects of HIPC and MDRI debt relief.

Country	Country Notes
Haiti	Long-term private nonguaranteed debt data only cover IDB loans. Short-term debt before 2004 is based on data from the BIS. Data include the effects of Paris Club restructuring agreements signed in 2006 and 2009 and HIPC and MDRI debt relief.
Honduras	Data include the effects of HIPC and MDRI debt relief.
India	External debt data prior to 2003 are revised from fiscal year to calendar year. Long-term public and publicly guaranteed bonds include Foreign Institutional Investor debt (FII) as reported by the Reserve Bank of India.
Indonesia	Long-term private nonguaranteed debt data are World Bank staff estimates based on reports provided by the country.
Iran, Islamic Republic of	Short-term debt is based on Central Bank data.
Jamaica	Short-term debt before 2012 is based on data from the BIS.
Jordan	Long-term private nonguaranteed debt data from 2001 are based on reports provided by the country. Short-term debt before 1999 is based on data from the BIS.
Kenya	Long-term private nonguaranteed debt data are World Bank staff estimates based on market data. Short-term debt is based on data from the BIS.
Lao People's Democratic Republic	Long-term public and publicly guaranteed debt data for 2019 are World Bank staff estimates based on the original terms of the loans. Long-term private nonguaranteed debt data are World Bank staff estimates. Short-term debt is based on data from the BIS.
Lebanon	Long-term private nonguaranteed debt data from 2008 to 2012 are World Bank staff estimates based on the 2013–2017 debt stock. Short-term debt before 2013 is based on data from the BIS.
Lesotho	Large interest payment was made during 2007 to a creditor country to settle a long-standing claim. Short-term debt is based on data from the BIS.
Liberia	Long-term private nonguaranteed debt data are World Bank staff estimates based on market data. Data include the effects of Paris Club rescheduling agreement signed in 2008 and 2010, and HIPC and MDRI debt relief.
Madagascar	Long-term private nonguaranteed debt data from 2017 are World Bank staff estimates based on market data. Short-term debt from 2017 is based on data from the BIS. Data include the effects of HIPC and MDRI debt relief.
Malawi	Short-term debt is based on data from the BIS. Data include the effects of Paris Club rescheduling agreement signed in 2006 and HIPC and MDRI debt relief.
Maldives	Long-term private nonguaranteed debt data from 2006 are World Bank staff estimates based on reports provided by the country. Short-term debt is based on data from the BIS.
Mali	Short-term debt is based on data from the BIS. Data include the effects of HIPC and MDRI debt relief.
Mauritania	Short-term debt is based on data from the BIS. Data include the effects of MDRI debt relief.
Mongolia	Long-term private nonguaranteed debt data before 2016 are World Bank staff estimates based on reports provided by the country. Short-term debt before 2008 is based on data from the BIS.
Montenegro	Long-term private nonguaranteed debt data for 2018 and 2017 are World Bank staff estimates; data prior to 2017 are based on country reports. Short-term debt for 2018 are World Bank staff estimates; data prior to 2018 are based on country reports.
Morocco	Short-term debt before 2009 is based on data from the BIS.
Mozambique	Long-term public and publicly guaranteed debt data for 2019 are World Bank staff estimates based on the original terms of the loans. Long-term private nonguaranteed debt data before 2019 are World Bank staff estimates based on reports provided by the country. Short-term debt is based on data from the BIS. Data include HIPC and MDRI debt relief.
Myanmar	Long-term public and publicly guaranteed before 2018 are World Bank staff estimates based on the original terms of the loans. Long-term private nonguaranteed debt data are World Bank staff estimates based on the market data. Data include HIPC debt relief.
Nepal	Long-term private nonguaranteed debt data are World Bank staff estimates based on reports provided by the country.
Nicaragua	Short-term debt before 2007 is based on data from the BIS. Data include the effects of HIPC and MDRI debt relief.

Country	Country Notes
Niger	Short-term debt is based on data from the BIS. Data include the effects of HIPC and MDRI debt relief.
Nigeria	Long-term private nonguaranteed debt data from 2005 are estimates based on market data.
Pakistan	Long-term private nonguaranteed debt data from 2006 to 2015 are World Bank staff estimates based on the reports provided by the country. Short-term debt before 2010 is based on data from the BIS.
Papua New Guinea	Short-term debt is based on data from the BIS.
Peru	Long-term private nonguaranteed debt data are World Bank staff estimates based on reports provided by the country.
Philippines	Long-term private nonguaranteed debt data no longer include unregistered debt and are revised from 2005 based on the reports provided by the country.
Russian Federation	Long-term public and publicly guaranteed and long-term private nonguaranteed debt are World Bank staff estimates based on reports provided by the country.
Rwanda	Data include the effects of HIPC and MDRI debt relief.
Samoa	Short-term debt data are excluded since BIS data include debt liabilities of offshore centers located in the country. BIS short-term debt data for 2017, 2018, and 2019 are $4.2 billion, $4.4 billion, and $4.5 billion, respectively.
São Tomé and Príncipe	Short-term debt is based on data from the BIS. Data include HIPC and MDRI debt relief.
Senegal	Short-term debt before 2009 is based on data from the BIS.
Serbia	Beginning 2006, the data for Serbia exclude Montenegro. Short-term debt before 2014 is World Bank staff estimates based on Central Bank data.
Sierra Leone	Short-term debt before 2016 is based on data from the BIS.
Somalia	Long-term public and publicly guaranteed before 2018 are World Bank staff estimates based on the original terms of the loans. Beginning in 2018, the data reflect the outstanding debt stock and principal and interest arrears and include late interest/penalties amounts following the reconciliation exercise by the Government of Somalia with respective creditors.
St. Lucia	Short-term debt before 2012 is based on data from the BIS.
St. Vincent and the Grenadines	Short-term debt data are excluded since BIS data include debt liabilities of offshore centers located in the country. BIS short-term debt data for 2015, 2016, 2017, 2018, and 2019 are $676 million, $806 million, $787 million, $532 million, and $363 million respectively.
Sudan	Long-term public and publicly guaranteed debt data exclude penalty interest. Short-term debt is based on data from the BIS.
Syrian Arab Republic	Long-term public and publicly guaranteed debt data are World Bank staff estimates. Short-term debt is based on data from the BIS.
Tajikistan	Data include MDRI debt relief.
Tanzania	Long-term public and publicly guaranteed debt data include debt liabilities of Zanzibar. Long-term public, publicly guaranteed and private nonguaranteed debt data from 2015 are World Bank staff estimates based on the original terms of the loans. Short-term debt is based on data from the BIS. Data include the effects of HIPC and MDRI debt relief.
Timor-Leste	Short-term debt is based on data from the BIS.
Togo	Short-term debt is based on data from the BIS. Data include the effects of Paris Club debt restructuring agreement and HIPC and MDRI debt relief.
Tunisia	Long-term private nonguaranteed debt data from 2008 are estimates based on reports provided by the country.
Turkey	Long-term public and publicly guaranteed debt data include nonresident deposits made under the Dresdner Bank scheme, amounting to $8.2 million at end-2019.
Turkmenistan	Long-term public and publicly guaranteed debt from 2010 are World Bank staff estimates. Long-term private nonguaranteed debt data (excluding bonds) only cover European Bank for Reconstruction and Development lending.
Uganda	Long-term private nonguaranteed debt data are World Bank staff estimates based on market data. Data include the effects of HIPC and MDRI debt relief.

Country	Country Notes
Uzbekistan	Short-term debt is based on data from the BIS.
Vanuatu	Long-term public and publicly guaranteed debt data for 2019 are World Bank staff estimates based on the original terms of the loans. Short-term debt is based on data from the BIS.
Venezuela, República Bolivariana de	Long-term public and publicly guaranteed debt are World Bank staff estimates based on creditors data and estimates on the 2016 debt stocks. Long-term private nonguaranteed debt data and short- term debt are World Bank staff estimates based on country reports.
Vietnam	Long-term public and publicly guaranteed debt data for 2019 are World Bank staff estimates based on the original terms of the loans. Short-term debt before 2016 is based on data from the BIS.
Yemen, Republic of	Long-term public and publicly guaranteed debt data for 2019 are World Bank staff estimates based on the original terms of the loans. Short-term debt is based on data from the BIS.
Zambia	Long-term private nonguaranteed data before 2016 are World Bank staff estimates based on reports provided by the country. Short-term debt is based on data from the BIS. Data include the effects of HIPC and MDRI debt relief.
Zimbabwe	Long-term private nonguaranteed debt data in 2017 are World Bank staff estimates based on reports provided by the country. Data from 2001 include late interest fee owed to Paris Club and Commercial Creditors. Short-term debt is based on data from the BIS.

Sources of the Macroeconomic Indicators

The macroeconomic data are prepared by The World Bank from a variety of sources. Data on Personal Transfers and Compensation of Employees are prepared by World Bank staff based on IMF balance of payments statistics. Data on foreign direct investments and current account balance are prepared by World Bank staff based on IMF balance of payments statistics and UNCTAD publication. Other macroeconomic data are from IMF balance of payments statistics.

Data on exports of goods, services, and primary income are based on countries' balance of payments statistics for the following countries:

Algeria (2018)
Botswana (2019)
Comoros, Union of the (2019)
Djibouti (2019)
Ethiopia (2019)
Gambia, The (2019)
Ghana (2019)
Guyana (2019)
Haiti (2019)
Iran, Islamic Rep. of (2001–2019)
Jamaica (2019)
Jordan (2019)
Lao People's Dem. Rep. (2019)
Liberia (2019)
Madagascar, Rep of. (2019)
Papua New Guinea (2019)
Peru (2019)
Rwanda (2019)
Samoa (2019)
Sudan (2019)
Tanzania, United Rep. of (2019)
Vanuatu (2019)
Zimbabwe (2018)

Data on imports of goods, services, and primary income are based on countries' balance of payments statistics for the following countries:

Algeria (2018)
Botswana (2019)
Comoros, Union of the (2019)
Djibouti (2019)
Ethiopia (2019)
Gambia, The (2019)
Ghana (2019)
Guyana (2019)
Haiti (2019)
Iran, Islamic Rep. of (2001–2019)
Jamaica (2019)
Jordan (2019)
Lao People's Dem. Rep. (2019)
Liberia (2019)
Madagascar, Rep. of (2019)
Papua New Guinea (2019)
Peru (2019)
Rwanda (2019)
Samoa (2019)
Sudan (2019)
Tanzania, United Rep. of (2019)
Vanuatu (2019)
Zimbabwe (2018)

Data on current account balance are based on countries' balance of payments statistics for the following countries:

Algeria (2018)	Grenada (2019)	Papua New Guinea (2019)
Benin (2019)	Guinea-Bissau (2019)	Peru (2019)
Botswana (2019)	Guyana (2019)	Rwanda (2019)
Burkina Faso (2019)	Haiti (2019)	Samoa (2019)
Burundi (2019)	Iran, Islamic Rep. of (2001–2019)	Senegal (2019)
Comoros, Union of the (2019)	Jamaica (2019)	St. Lucia (2019)
Côte d'Ivoire (2019)	Jordan (2019)	St. Vincent and the Grenadines (2019)
Djibouti (2019)	Lao People's Dem. Rep. (2019)	Sudan (2019)
Dominica (2019)	Liberia (2019)	Tanzania, United Rep. of (2019)
Ethiopia (2019)	Madagascar, Rep. of (2019)	Togo (2019)
Gambia, The (2019)	Mali (2019)	Vanuatu (2019)
Ghana (2019)	Niger (2019)	Zimbabwe (2018)

Data on personal transfers and compensation of employees are based on countries' balance of payments statistics for the following countries:

Djibouti (2019)	Lao People's Dem. Rep. (2019)	Tanzania (2019)
Guyana (2019)	Peru (2019)	Zimbabwe (2018)
Jordan (2019)	Rwanda (2019)	

Data on primary income on foreign direct investment are based on countries' balance of payments statistics for the following countries:

Djibouti (2019)
Rwanda (2019)

Data on foreign direct investment are based on countries' balance of payments statistics for the following countries:

Botswana (2019)	Jordan (2019)	Peru (2019)
Jamaica (2012–2019)	Liberia (2019)	

Data on portfolio equity are based on countries' balance of payments statistics for the following countries:

Botswana (2019)	Jordan (2019)

Country Groups

Regional Groups

East Asia and Pacific

Cambodia (A)
China (P)
Fiji (A)
Indonesia (A)
Lao PDR (E)
Mongolia (A)
Myanmar (A)
Papua New Guinea (A)
Philippines (A)
Samoa (A)
Solomon Islands (A)
Thailand (A)
Timon-Leste (A)
Tonga (A)
Vanuatu (E)
Vietnam (E)

Europe and Central Asia

Albania (A)
Armenia (A)
Azerbaijan (A)
Belarus (A)
Bosnia and Herzegovina[a] (A)
Bulgaria (A)
Georgia (A)
Kazakhstan (A)
Kosovo (A)
Kyrgyz Republic (A)
Moldova (A)
Montenegro (A)
North Macedonia (A)
Russian Federation (P)
Serbia[a,b] (A)

Tajikistan (A)
Turkey (A)
Turkmenistan (E)
Ukraine (A)
Uzbekistan (A)

Latin America and the Caribbean

Argentina (A)
Belize (A)
Bolivia (A)
Brazil (A)
Colombia (A)
Costa Rica (A)
Dominica (A)
Dominican Republic (E)
Ecuador (A)
El Salvador (A)
Grenada (A)
Guatemala (A)
Guyana (A)
Haiti (A)
Honduras (A)
Jamaica (A)
Mexico (A)
Nicaragua (A)
Paraguay (A)
Peru (A)
St. Lucia (A)
St. Vincent and the Grenadines (A)
Venezuela, RB (E)

Middle East and North Africa

Algeria (A)
Djibouti (A)

Egypt, Arab Rep. (A)
Iran, Islamic Rep. (A)
Jordan (A)
Lebanon (A)
Morocco (A)
Syrian Arab Republic (E)
Tunisia (A)
Yemen, Rep. (E)

South Asia

Afghanistan (A)
Bangladesh (A)
Bhutan (A)
India (A)
Maldives (A)
Nepal (A)
Pakistan (A)
Sri Lanka (A)

Sub-Saharan Africa

Angola (A)
Benin (A)
Botswana (A)
Burkina Faso (A)
Burundi (E)
Cabo Verde (A)
Cameroon (A)
Central African Republic (A)
Chad (A)
Comoros (A)
Congo, Dem. Rep. (A)
Congo, Rep. (A)
Côte d'Ivoire (A)
Eritrea (E)

Eswatini (A)
Ethiopia (A)
Gabon (A)
Gambia, The (A)
Ghana (E)
Guinea (A)
Guinea-Bissau (E)
Kenya (A)
Lesotho (A)
Liberia (A)
Madagascar (A)
Malawi (A)
Mali (A)
Mauritania (A)
Mozambique (A)
Niger (A)
Nigeria (A)
Rwanda (A)
São Tomé and Príncipe (A)
Senegal (A)
Sierra Leone (A)
Somalia (A)
South Africa (A)
Sudan (P)
Tanzania (E)
Togo (A)
Uganda (A)
Zambia (A)
Zimbabwe (A)

Note: Letters in parenthesis indicate DRS reporters' status: (A) as reported, (P) preliminary, and (E) estimated. The status "as reported" indicates that the country was fully current in its reporting under the DRS and that World Bank staff are satisfied that the reported data give an adequate and fair representation of the country's total public debt. "Preliminary" data are based on reported or collected information, but because of incompleteness or other reasons, an element of staff estimation is included. "Estimated" data indicate that countries are not current in their reporting and that a significant element of staff estimation has been necessary in producing the data tables.
a. For Bosnia and Herzegovina, total debt before 1999, excluding IBRD and IMF obligations and short-term debt, is included under Serbia.
b. Data prior to 2006 include Montenegro.

Income Groups

Low-income countries	*Middle-income countries*		
Afghanistan	Albania	Eswatini	Nigeria
Burkina Faso	Algeria	Fiji	North Macedonia
Burundi	Angola	Gabon	Pakistan
Central African Republic	Argentina	Georgia	Papua New Guinea
Chad	Armenia	Ghana	Paraguay
Congo, Dem. Rep.	Azerbaijan	Grenada	Peru
Eritrea	Bangladesh	Guatemala	Philippines
Ethiopia	Belarus	Guyana	Russian Federation
Gambia, The	Belize	Honduras	Samoa
Guinea	Benin	India	São Tomé and Príncipe
Guinea-Bissau	Bhutan	Indonesia	Senegal
Haiti	Bolivia	Iran, Islamic Rep.	Serbia
Liberia	Bosnia and Herzegovina	Jamaica	Solomon Islands
Madagascar	Botswana	Jordan	South Africa
Malawi	Brazil	Kazakhstan	Sri Lanka
Mali	Bulgaria	Kenya	St. Lucia
Mozambique	Cabo Verde	Kosovo	St. Vincent and the Grenadines
Niger	Cambodia	Kyrgyz Republic	Tanzania
Rwanda	Cameroon	Lao PDR	Thailand
Sierra Leone	China	Lebanon	Timor-Leste
Somalia	Colombia	Lesotho	Tonga
Sudan	Comoros	Maldives	Tunisia
Syrian Arab Republic	Congo, Rep.	Mauritania	Turkey
Tajikistan	Costa Rica	Mexico	Turkmenistan
Togo	Côte d'Ivoire	Moldova	Ukraine
Uganda	Djibouti	Mongolia	Uzbekistan
Yemen, Rep.	Dominica	Montenegro	Vanuatu
	Dominican Republic	Morocco	Venezuela, RB
	Ecuador	Myanmar	Vietnam
	Egypt, Arab Rep.	Nepal	Zambia
	El Salvador	Nicaragua	Zimbabwe

Note: Low-income countries are those with a GNI per capita of $1,035 or less in 2019. Middle-income countries are those with a GNI per capita of more than $1,036 but less than $12,535. Italicized countries are IDA-only countries as of July 1, 2020; IDA-only excludes blend and IBRD countries.

Glossary

Debtor Reporting System (DRS)

Bilateral official creditors are official agencies that make loans on behalf of one government to another government or to public (and, in some cases, private) borrowers in another country.

Bonds are debt instruments issued by public and publicly guaranteed or private debtors with durations of one year or longer. Bonds usually give the holder the unconditional right to fixed money income or contractually determined, variable money income.

Commitments of public and publicly guaranteed debt constitute the total amount of new long-term loans to public sector borrowers or borrowers with a public sector guarantee extended by official and private lenders and for which contracts were signed in the year specified.

Concessional debt conveys information about the borrower's receipt of aid from official lenders at concessional terms as defined by the World Bank, that is, loans with an original grant element of 35 percent or more. Loans from major regional development banks—African Development Bank, Asian Development Bank, and the Inter-American Development Bank—are classified as concessional according the World Bank classification.

Contractual obligations on outstanding long-term external debt are the anticipated debt service payments on long-term external debt contracted up to December 31 of the reporting year.

Debt buyback is the repurchase by a debtor of its own debt, either at a discount price or at par value. In the event of a buyback of long-term debt, the face value of the debt bought back will be recorded as a decline in stock outstanding of long-term debt, and the cash amount received by creditors will be recorded as a principal repayment. For example, if a country buys back long-term external debt of face value B at a price P, then long-term external debt will decline by B, and principal repayment will increase by P. The difference between the price at which the debt was bought back and the face value is recorded as a debt stock write-off (the related transactions are not separately identified in the International Debt Statistics [IDS] publication but are available in the online database).

Debt forgiveness grants include both debts canceled by agreement between debtor and creditor and reductions in the net present value of official nonconcessional loans resulting from concessional rescheduling or refinancing. Data are recorded on a disbursement basis and include debt forgiveness from bilateral and multilateral creditors.

Debt outstanding and disbursed is the value at year's end of long-term external debt owed by public and publicly guaranteed debtors and private nonguaranteed debtors.

Debt restructurings are revisions to debt service obligations agreed on by creditors and debtors. Such agreements change the amount and timing of future principal and interest payments.

Debt service to exports is the ratio of the sum of principal repayments and interest paid on total long-term debt (public and publicly guaranteed debt and private nonguaranteed debt) to the value of exports of goods and services and receipts of primary income from abroad.

Debt stock-flow reconciliation shows the indicators that affect the change in debt stocks from one period to the next.

Disbursements are drawings during the year specified on loan commitments contracted by the borrower.

Exports of goods, services, and primary income constitute the total value of exports of goods and services, and primary income.

External debt flows are debt-related transactions during the year specified. They include disbursements, principal repayments, and interest payments.

External debt stocks comprise public and publicly guaranteed long-term external debt, private nonguaranteed long-term external debt, use of IMF credit, and short-term external debt, including interest arrears on long-term debt.

External debt stocks to exports is the ratio of outstanding external debt to the value of exports of goods and services and receipts of primary income from abroad.

External debt stocks to GNI is the ratio of outstanding external debt to gross national income.

Foreign direct investment refers to direct investment equity flows in the reporting economy. It is the sum of equity capital, reinvestment earnings, and other capital. Direct investment is a category of cross-border investment associated with a resident in one economy having control or a significant degree of influence on the management of an enterprise that is resident in another economy. Ownership of 10 percent or more of the ordinary shares or voting stock is the criterion for determining the existence of a direct investment relationship.

Government sector debt consists of all external debt obligations of all levels of the departments, branches, agencies, foundations, institutes, nonmarket and non-profit institutions controlled by the government, and other publicly controlled organizations engaging in non-market activities.

Grace period is the time between the date on which a loan is committed and the date on which the first principal payment is due. The information presented in International Debt Statistics is the average grace period on all public and publicly guaranteed debt committed during the specified period.

Grants are legally binding commitments that obligate a specific value of funds available for disbursement for which there is no payment requirement. They include debt forgiveness grants and grants from bilateral and multilateral agencies (such as the International Development Association).

Gross national income (GNI) is the sum of value added by all resident producers, plus any product taxes (less subsidies) not included in the valuation of output, plus net receipts of primary income compensation of employees and property income from abroad. Yearly average exchange rates are used to convert GNI from local currency to U.S. dollars.

Heavily Indebted Poor Country (HIPC) Initiative is a program of the World Bank and the International Monetary Fund (IMF) to provide debt relief to qualifying countries with unsustainable debt burdens.

Imports of goods, services, and primary income constitute the total value of goods and services imported and income payable to nonresidents. Interest arrears on long-term debt are interest payments due but not paid, shown on a cumulative basis.

Interest arrears are due and payable immediately and are therefore regarded as short-term obligations. Thus, an increase in interest arrears on long-term debt will be recorded as an increase in short-term debt. Interest in arrears on the use of IMF credit is also considered to be part of short-term external debt.

Interest payments are the amounts of interest paid in foreign currency, goods, or services in the year specified.

Interest rate is the interest rate applicable to a loan commitment as specified in the loan contract. The information presented in International Debt Statistics is the average interest on all public and publicly guaranteed debt committed during the specified period.

IMF charges are the amounts of interest paid in foreign currency in the year specified for transactions with the IMF.

IMF purchases are the total drawings on the general resources account of the IMF during the year specified, excluding drawings in the reserve tranche.

IMF repurchases are the amounts of principal (amortization) paid in foreign currency in the year specified for transactions with the IMF.

International reserves constitute the sum of a country's monetary authority's holdings of special drawing rights, its reserve position in the IMF, its holdings of foreign exchange, and its holdings of gold (valued at year-end London prices).

Long-term external debt is debt that has an original or extended maturity of more than one year and that is owed to nonresidents by residents of an economy and is repayable in foreign currency, goods, or services.

Maturity is the date on which the final principal repayment on a loan is due. It is the sum of the grace and repayment periods. The information presented in International Debt Statistics is the average maturity on all public and publicly guaranteed debt committed during the specified period.

Multilateral Debt Relief Initiative (MDRI) is a program of the World Bank, the IMF, the Inter-American Development Bank, and the African Development Bank that provides additional debt relief to countries that have completed the HIPC process.

Multilateral official creditors are official agencies owned or governed by more than one country that provide loan financing. They include international financial institutions such as the World Bank, regional development banks, and other intergovernmental agencies.

Multilateral to external debt stocks is the ratio of the stock of debt owed to multilateral creditors to total external debt.

Net flows on external debt are disbursements on long-term external debt and IMF purchases minus principal repayments on long-term external debt and IMF repurchases. Up to 1984, this calculation included only long-term external debt and IMF flows. Since 1985, the calculation includes the change in stock of short-term debt (excluding interest arrears on long-term external debt).

Official creditors are governments or other bilateral public entities, such as export-import agencies, development agencies, and multilateral financial institutions, such as the World Bank and regional development banks.

Personal transfers and compensation of employees is the sum of personal transfers and compensation of employees. Personal transfers consist of all current transfers in cash or in kind made or received by resident households to or from nonresident households. Personal transfers thus include all current transfers between resident and nonresident individuals. Compensation of employees refers to the income of border, seasonal, and other short-term workers who are employed in an economy where they are not resident and of residents employed by nonresident entities.

Portfolio equity is the category of international investment that covers investment in equity securities. Equity securities include shares, stocks, participation, or similar documents (such as American Depositary Receipts) that usually denote ownership of equity.

Present value of debt outstanding is the nominal value of all future debt service obligations on existing debt discounted at prevailing market rates of interest. The interest rates used in this calculation are the Commercial Interest Reference Rates (CIRR) for each relevant currency compiled and published by the Organisation for Economic Co-operation and Development.

Primary income on FDI are payments of direct investment income (debit side), which consist of income on equity (dividends, branch profits, and reinvested earnings) and income on the intercompany debt (interest).

Principal arrears on long-term debt are principal repayments due but not paid on long-term external debt, shown on a cumulative basis.

Principal repayments are the amounts of principal (amortization) paid in foreign currency, goods, or services in the year specified with respect to long-term external debt.

Private creditors are bondholders, commercial banks, and other trade-related lenders.

Private nonguaranteed debt is debt owed by private sector borrowers to external creditors on loans that do not benefit from a public sector guarantee by the debtor country.

Public and publicly guaranteed debt outstanding and disbursed is the value of debt at year's end of public sector borrowers, or borrowers with a public sector guarantee, owed to official and private lenders.

Public and publicly guaranteed external debt comprises public debt (an external obligation of a public debtor, such as the national government or agency, a political subdivision or agency, or an autonomous public body) and publicly guaranteed external debt (an external obligation of a private debtor that is guaranteed for repayment by a public entity).

Public debt is an external obligation of a public debtor, including all levels of government, state-owned enterprises, public corporations, development banks, and any other autonomous public bodies of government.

Publicly guaranteed debt is an external obligation of a private debtor that is guaranteed for repayment by a public entity.

Reserves to external debt stocks is the ratio of international reserves to outstanding external debt.

Reserves to imports (months) is the ratio of international reserves to the value of imports of goods, services, and primary income in the year shown and is expressed in months:

$$\frac{\text{Reserves}}{\text{Imports}/12}$$

Short-term external debt has an original maturity of one year or less. Available data permit no distinction among public, publicly guaranteed, and private nonguaranteed short-term external debt.

Short-term to external debt stock ratio is the ratio of short-term external debt to total outstanding external debt.

Special Drawing Rights (SDRs) refer to an international reserve asset that was created by the IMF in 1969 to supplement its member countries' official reserves. The value of SDRs is based on a basket of four key international currencies: the U.S. dollar, the pound sterling, the Japanese yen, and the euro. In addition to playing a role as a supplementary reserve asset, SDRs serve as the unit of account for the IMF and some other international organizations.

Technical cooperation grants include (a) free-standing technical cooperation grants, which are intended to finance the transfer of technical and managerial skills or of technology for the purpose of building up general national capacity without reference to any specific investment projects, and (b) investment-related technical cooperation grants, which are aimed at strengthening the capacity to execute specific investment projects.

Total amount forgiven is the total amount of principal and interest due, principal and interest in arrears, and debt stock forgiven in the year specified.

Total amount rescheduled is the total amount of external debt rescheduled, including principal and interest due, principal and interest in arrears, charges, penalties, and debt stock in the year specified.

Total change in external debt stocks is the difference in the external debt stock between two consecutive years.

Use of IMF credit denotes members' drawings on the IMF other than amounts drawn against the country's reserve tranche position. Use of IMF credit includes purchases and drawings under Stand-By, Extended, Structural Adjustment, Enhanced Structural Adjustment, and Systemic Transformation Facility Arrangements as well as trust fund loans. SDR allocations are also included in this category.